For five shillings a day

For five shillings a day

Experiencing war, 1939-45

Edited by
Richard Campbell Begg
and
Peter H. Liddle

Dedicated to those who served but did not live to tell the tale

HarperCollinsPublishers
77-85 Fulham Palace Road
Hammersmith
London W6 8JB

First published in Great Britain by HarperCollinsPublishers 2000
This paperback edition published 2002

1 3 5 7 9 10 9 6 4 2

Copyright © R. C. Begg and P. H. Liddle 2000

The editors assert the moral right to be identified as the authors of this work

ISBN 0 00 713720 6

British Library Cataloguing in Publication Data:
A catalogue record for this book is available from the British Library.

Printed in Great Britain by Clays Ltd, St Ives plc

Contents

Foreword

by
Vincent Orange BA, PhD, MRAeS
Reader in History, University of Canterbury
Christchurch, New Zealand

*H*ow often have we heard someone say, 'Oh, how I wish Uncle Bob was still alive. He used to tell us kids such tales of his life and when he was in the war, but I can't remember details now, and, to be honest, in those days I wasn't really interested about *his* life – I was more interested in my *own*!' As for Bob's letters and papers: 'Well, they used to be in an old cardboard box in the garage roof, but after he died the house was sold, we had a grand clear-out and I'm afraid they went to the dump.'

Fortunately, Peter Liddle has devoted the best part of his life to catching the numerous Uncle Bobs in many parts of the world while they are still with us. He and his associates have recorded their memories and collected their various letters and memorabilia, which are now stored in the Liddle Collection at Leeds University and at the Second World War Experience Centre, also in Leeds. There they are available as a permanent and lasting record of personal service and experience in both world wars for the benefit of this and future generations.

The impressions of those at the 'sharp end' of great events are an essential part of history, just as salt and pepper are to a boiled egg. How pleased we would be if, for example, one of Peter's ancestors had acquired for us an account of all the hassles involved in getting Hannibal's elephants over the Alps, or if a later ancestor had left us an interview with one of Henry V's archers at Agincourt. Peter, of course, set his sights on *all* those who survived the crucible of world war experience: on all services, all ranks, civilian and pacifist experience, and indeed on those who served in opposing forces or endured enemy occupation. Until now his books have had the First World War as their focus. This book marks an advance into what is for him, in published work, new terrain.

Like his namesake, Peter is a fisherman and has thrown out many lines during the last umpteen years. In Richard Campbell Begg he caught a whopper! Richard is a New Zealand-born doctor, now retired, who also had a lively time of it in the Royal Navy during the Second World War, as you will read within. In 1993 Richard visited Peter Liddle in Leeds and, being most impressed with what he was doing, presented him with his memoirs, letters, etc, and was duly taped. Then, quite forgetting the immortal words known to all servicemen in all ages – 'never volunteer' – Richard did just that and, inevitably, found himself hard at work. Peter asked him to tape Commander Hickley. One interview led to another and Richard ended up with well over 50 personal accounts of experiences of war on land, at sea and in the air. Enough for a book – as Harper Collins readily agreed.

But this book is not merely a written record of what appears on the tapes. It is a history of the Second World War from the beginning to the end, covering many theatres of conflict and seen from the personal perspective of individuals who took part, using the relevant extracts from their accounts. Its 18 chapters are supported by illustrations of the contributors and the events described, and in each there is a short introduction by the editors giving background details of that particular campaign or operation. Biographical notes on the contributors appear in the Appendix. The language, grammar and idiom used by the contributors in talking of their experiences are largely reproduced in the written account in the book. All this tends to give the reader the feeling of being right alongside the raconteur as he or she relives the experiences of long ago.

For the general reader with an interest in the Second World War, I can think of no better starting point from which to grasp the huge scale of the conflict and yet its dimension in terms of the individual. For the specialist reader there are countless personal insights into what will, of course, be a more familiar story.

Sadly, at least five of the contributors will never read this book: they are gone. But thanks to the endeavours of Peter and Richard their experiences will not be forgotten. I am sure that all the contributors would say, 'What I did was nothing special. Better men than I did much more. Some were killed before anyone could record what they did and others did not get my opportunities to make a mark.' On the other hand, each one of these survivors can be seen as representing dozens of their less fortunate comrades.

As for me, and countless men and women of my generation, we will ever be in their debt. At 64 I have never heard a shot fired in anger, never seen anyone killed or grievously wounded, never been frightened by anything more lethal than a cricket ball, hardly ever been in any physical distress, and my only real worries have been over such unavoidable subjects as women, money and promotion. The contributors to this book have been far more fundamentally tested. I am deeply grateful to them for helping to spare me their experiences.

The wonderful words inscribed on a memorial stone near the entrance to the Commonwealth War Graves Commission War Cemetery at Kohima, Assam, India, can never be quoted too often:

> 'When you go home
> Tell them of us and say,
> For their tomorrow
> We gave our today.'

Acknowledgements

*T*he authors of this book are really the contributors, and we thank them for their approval to use extracts from their tapes and, in the case of Kenneth Frater, from his excellent manuscript.

We are grateful for the invaluable contribution and support given by Margaret Begg, which included transcribing the contents of the tapes on to the computer. No easy task. We also acknowledge with gratitude the advice, enthusiasm and support of Ian Drury of HarperCollins, London with whom it has been a pleasure to associate.

Finally, we thank the donors of the illustrations and photographs. The occasional print, by reason of age and obscure origin, can only be acknowledged in a general way. Those where the copyright has been determined receive specific mention.

Introduction

*I*t is the sheer scale of the Second World War that most of us, however keen to grasp its course in outline and the interrelation of its geographically and sometimes time-separated parts, find daunting. In terms of its time-span, its land masses and oceans that were the scene of prolonged conflict, its nations, races and peoples committed to or drawn into the conflict, its human and material cost, the statistics of the Second World War challenge the capacity to comprehend.

At one and the same time, the link between the Eastern Front and its Stalingrad, North Africa and its El Alamein, the Arctic, Atlantic and Mediterranean with their sea-lines, the aerial bombing offensives, Home Front war materials production and civilian morale, is clear, and yet it is only retained in a collective sense by the most self-disciplined mind. As we write this we can almost hear the protests of readers, 'Have they not heard of the Pacific War too?' To which we make response that indeed we have, and this book will certainly not fail by under-representation in that respect.

While the editors of this book have no grand ambition to succeed where few have attempted and success is rare – achievement in conveying a world-wide vista of warfare – they believe that in reducing the unmanageable scale to one of individual participants recalling the part they played in key events, general or special circumstances, major campaigns or battles, they bring the reader as near as he may wish to be to living through the challenge of World War from September 1939 to August 1945.

This book had its roots in the first meeting of the editors in Leeds in 1993. The rescue of the evidence of wartime experience was the main subject on the agenda. Retired New Zealand doctor and public health specialist Richard Campbell Begg, a naval officer in the Second World War, had responded to a New Zealand newspaper appeal by British historian Peter Liddle, keen to draw attention to his work in rescuing the evidence of wartime experience. At that stage Peter was the Keeper of the Liddle Collection, a world-renowned archive of personal experience in the First World War, based at Leeds University. Over some years he has been turning his attention to the Second World War, and has already achieved a substantial collection of material of personal involvement in that war, so much so that since the original meeting with Richard it has been necessary to set up a separate collection, which is also housed in the city of Leeds as a Second World War Experience Centre with charitable status and its own Trustees, staff, Patrons and Association of Friends. Peter has left the University and feels highly privileged to have been appointed the Director of the Centre, which continues to grow and flourish.

The New Zealand doctor had travelled to Leeds, his recollections had been recorded on tape by interview and, with personal accord quickly established, the possibility of association in the rescue work was discussed. It was not long before Richard, in his responsibilities growing younger by the day, was recording men and women resident in New Zealand. The friendship between Richard and Peter developed, with the doctor travelling not only through much of New Zealand in the work but returning to Leeds on three further occasions fuelled by an increasing awareness of the importance, urgency and fascination of the work. He had found that there were few areas of British and New Zealand service experience in the war not covered by one or more of the people he was meeting. So graphic were many of the tapes, and so wide their representation of air, sea and land service, that it was clear the material invited being shared with a wider audience than that of researchers in an archive.

This book grew as a result of a decision to draw together, as appropriate, the most striking of the testimony. It contains extended recall of the experiences of 53 men and one woman. Most theatres of war are represented from beginning to end of the conflict. This is the story of the war by those who were in it, given spontaneously without rehearsal 53 or so years after the event. For most, it was the first time anyone had asked them to relate their experience and had then been prepared to sit and listen, sometimes for hours on end. With remarkable lucidity and recall, with humour, sometimes with emotion, even distress, thoughts and descriptions of events long ago were vividly expressed.

With most theatres of war covered, and with the three Services and the Merchant Navy represented in many ranks, from those quite senior to those very junior, it has been possible to present a chronological story but also one from differing perspectives. In the book, as the war progresses, we sometimes meet for a second time those whose story in a different theatre and from a more junior rank has already been presented, and this may bring the reader to a still closer identification with the memories of some of those whose story is told here.

Each chapter has a contextual introduction so that the wider scene from which the particular vignette is chosen is properly made clear. The book is largely the written expression of oral testimony. As such there has been a little editing to clear away ambiguity, any lack of clarity through imprecision in the words as spoken. In the main, grammar has been left as expressed.

In the first chapter, what the 'Phoney War' was like for the ordinary soldier is made clear, and just as clear, the drama, confusion and swirling events from the German attack that would leave him evacuated from Dunkirk or St Nazaire or captured. Naval operations in the North Sea, including the first battle between battlecruisers, when HMS *Renown* engaged the German ships *Scharnhorst* and *Gneisenau* are next in line for recall. For the Battle of Britain and related developments there is graphic record; vivid descriptions of London burning, Coventry blitzed, aerial dogfights, crash landings and parachute descents, and a wealth of detail including men recalling their treatment after serious burns.

The story now moves to North Africa and the great campaigns fought there. There are two chapters devoted to this, separated by those dealing with the operations in Greece and Crete, both ending in defeat and evacuation. The parachute and aerial landings in Crete, in which the Germans suffered heavy losses, are dramatically recalled. We then move to the Italian campaign, with the first successful Allied landings on the Continent, at Sicily, documented by many men who were present on land, at sea and in the air, then the dearly bought and narrowly achieved landings at Salerno and Anzio and the battles around Cassino, the hard slog to the north and eventual victory. Events in the Mediterranean, including the epic convoy 'Operation Pedestal', are covered, as are other naval engagements, bombardments and action by British forces operating from the island of Vis in support of Marshal Tito's partisans and, not least, the valiant defence of Malta and air and sea operations from that island.

With Japan entering the war, there is experience of the military defeats in Malaya to relate, the surrender at Singapore and, not least, a vivid account by a destroyer officer of the sinking of the battleship *Prince of Wales* and battlecruiser *Repulse* by Japanese air attack. That officer's ship was sunk shortly afterwards at the second battle of the Java Sea. There follows a remarkable account of the brave determination of a nurse escaping from Singapore as the Japanese entered the city. She experienced the bombing, then the sinking of her ship. She swam to an island, caring for wounded there, then, one step ahead of the Japanese, she travelled all the way across Sumatra, where the Japanese finally caught up with her. There is coverage of subsequent events in South East Asia at sea and in the air, and eventually the recapture of Burma, including a graphic account of Chindit operations in that country.

Meanwhile, in the Arctic, there were the Russian convoys, including the disastrous PQ17, with which three of the contributors were involved, and later the sinking of the German battlecruiser *Scharnhorst*. There is material on naval events in the English Channel and the Atlantic and the increasing air attacks on German-occupied Europe. D-Day itself, then the advance through Northern France into Belgium, Holland and across the Rhine into Germany, have many contributions from all three services.

Returning to the war in Asia, where the tide was running against the Japanese and the British Pacific fleet was in action, there are accounts of this and what it was like having a kamikaze aircraft attack and crash on your flight deck. The New Zealand Air Force was now in action in force in the South Pacific and there is an interesting story to tell here.

Finally the prisoners of war, both in the Japanese theatre and in Europe, tell of their experiences in captivity, hardships and lighter moments. The sinking by an American submarine of a Japanese freighter with 800 prisoners under the hatches, and the frightful 'death march' back into Germany from Poland, provide sombre reading. Those in Japanese hands were perhaps saved from imminent execution by the dropping of the atom bombs. The comment of one of these men, 'forgive but never forget', provides a fitting finale to this chapter and a book written with respect for all the men and the woman mentioned, and the generation which they represent.

Richard Campbell Begg
Nelson, New Zealand

Peter H. Liddle
The Second World War Experience Centre,
Leeds, UK

CHAPTER 1

The 'Phoney War' in France and its aftermath

Britain had pledged support for Poland in the event of a German invasion, and when this occurred on 1 September 1939, Britain and France were soon at war with Germany. By prior agreement with Germany, Russian troops entered Poland on 17 September, and by 5 October Polish resistance was largely at an end. Hitler, his peace overtures to the West spurned, wished to make an early attack on France, but the weather, the hesitancy of his Generals and finally the loss to the Allies of the initial plans for the attack, resulted in delays.

William Seeney, an apprentice printer from Ealing, London, was quite convinced a war was coming, so, in 1937 at the age of 17, he joined the Territorial Army:

'I became a member of the 158 Battery of the 53rd Brigade, Royal Artillery. We were at training camp in Devon somewhere in 1939, must have been the beginning of September, when war was declared. As Territorials we were now fully involved. We didn't get home, we went direct from training camp to a place, Abbeyfield outside of Reading, where we were inoculated, etc. It was evident that the authorities had decided to get people overseas as quickly as they possibly could, so we were among the first to go.

On the morning parade, it must have been maybe one day, two days, after war had been declared, those who could drive a car were told to declare themselves. Not too many people drove in those days, but a dozen or so did and we ended up by driving a whole lot of rather antiquated and requisitioned vehicles, with the members of the Battery on board, to Southampton, where we eventually boarded a transport which took us to Cherbourg.

We arrived in Cherbourg and there was a lot of confusion – we were hungry but no food had been laid on. The officers in charge were told to

William Lewis Seeney

march us out of town and they obviously had a destination – we knew that eventually – and as it so happens it was a farm and we marched for about 8 to 10 miles, still nothing to eat – we'd had nothing to eat since the night before and this was well into the following day.

We eventually arrived at the farm and they'd obviously just kicked out the pigs and the sheep and the cows and tossed in a few bales of hay, and we were told to make ourselves comfortable, but still no food. We were told to organise ourselves into small units and half a dozen blokes would get together and that was their mess. Well, we had money – after all, we'd still been working, or had been a couple of days ago – and we did just as we were asked to do, and we chipped in, in these little groups, and we made a list of the things we'd like people to buy for us for food – then the truck took off for Cherbourg. So we had a sort of meal eventually and it was the same the next day until they got things organised. One thing that tickled me, on our march to our farm – we passed some blackberry bushes and the British Army broke ranks and picked blackberries.

However, the time arrived to leave. We were only there for a couple of nights, which was just as well, because the rats, you see, they'd never been so happy in their lives with all these bits and pieces around and we were quite happy to get out of the place. We marched down to the siding by a railway and there we got on to a train, and the train – you may not believe it – they'd obviously got these carriages out from the sheds, had them parked away from the last world war and they were still marked with 40 men and 8 horses – it was marked on the side of the bally trucks. They just had sliding doors and they tossed on a couple of bales of hay and we were told to get on board and the train took off.

Eventually, after many delays because we were being constantly shunted off the main line to let regular trains through, we arrived at Epernay, which is about 30 or 40 kilometres west of Rheims. There we disembarked. We had no weapons at that time but we camped alongside the station, just for the night – not so much camped as bivouacked – we just had to get our heads down. Then another train came along and there, lo and behold, were our guns and our transport.

We had difficulty in getting them off the trains but time passed, and eventually we got everything off the train and we moved off once again going east towards the Ardennes. Eventually we were to the right of the British Expeditionary Force [BEF] and up against the French on our right in the Ardennes The nearest village was Aguilcourt, and there was another village called Guinecourt, and there we were told to prepare. You've got to remember we were there for battle and there we were running around in circles, digging in, waiting for things to happen, and there was infantry floating around and nothing happened.

Of course in the Battery itself, things had to happen. First of all we had no cooks, so it was a case of saying, "You, you and you, you're the cooks." It's hard to believe this, isn't it, and we're supposed to be at war! The interesting thing about all this really is, we'd been trained to fire a gun. Now, basically, that's a very simple operation, but the important job – and I learned this and it took a long time to learn it – we'd never been taught to be soldiers. This was very important. Well, obviously to be a soldier you've got to be trained to be a soldier, not just to fire a gun. In my view that's the simplest thing in the world, and all the things that go to make a soldier we just didn't have – we'd never been trained to do it. We'd never been trained to kill people. I mean just think, we were soldiers – we'd never heard of a killing ground, and as for being killed yourself, blimey, that was the last thing you thought about.

Time passed, nothing happened. We'd been under canvas all this time, and just before winter began to break we got a number of Nissen huts and life became a bit more comfortable. Christmas came and the usual festivities and nothing happened apart from the "recce" aircraft overhead. They were there all day and every day – German, French, British, they were always there.'

Another 17-year-old who joined the Territorial Army in 1937 was William John Campion, a railway clerk from Liverpool. His introduction into France was rather more leisurely and comfortable:

'During 1938 and '39 there was always talk of war, so later in 1939 – and war was obviously imminent – I wasn't surprised to receive notice that my regiment, the 59th Medium Regiment, Royal Artillery, had been mobilised and I was required to report with full kit on a certain date, 1 September. I went along there as ordered, and met all the other crowd who were being bussed out to Tarporley in Cheshire, where we spent the next month receiving new equipment, new uniforms, and, as far as time permitted, continuing our training both as a regiment and as individuals. We were there for a whole month and then, about 1 October, we took train to Southampton and then across to Cherbourg. We arrived there early in the morning after a dreadful crossing.

Then, later that evening, we were on the train travelling south or south-east. Anyway the train took us as far as Laval, fortunately a proper train, not the sort the French soldiers travelled in, with was it 40 men or 8 horses? The train took us to Laval, and at Laval we met our own vehicles which took us on to the small village of St Jean sur Mayenne – Mayenne is a tributary of the Loire. It was a beautiful spot. It was at that little village that I had my first experience of champagne and Camembert cheese – one I liked and the other I couldn't eat. We stayed there only one night and we then set off on a three-day journey up north where we eventually arrived at a little village of Chaemy in the Pas de Calais in the old First World War battlegrounds.

Once we'd settled into billets – it was a small village, we were scattered in all sorts of places, small cottages, and men were even billeted in the morgue – our first job after that was to dig gun pits on the Belgium frontier, a small place called Ask. So that was 5am reveille, our task digging gun pits and Command Post, back at 7 and next morning up again at 5.30. Our guns were 6-inch howitzers, which are pretty big things and take big holes, so it was some time before we got that job finished. When it had finished, we were in the middle of a very cold winter and life was a bit hard, but not to be compared with trenches in the First World War.

William John Campion

Our little cottage had an outside pump where the ice had to be broken off every morning, and also two cesspits, but our time in Chaemy, again, was made up with training. We had one special day when we were taken to see the Vimy Ridge Battlefield and Memorial. I don't know whether this was to give us an idea of what to expect particularly; we found it most interesting, but we were young and had plenty of optimism, so it really didn't teach us much about war.

The nearest town to Chaemy was Lille, a big industrial town. We were only allowed there once a fortnight, and in Lille there was very little in the way of entertainment for troops. I can't remember seeing a canteen – we used the estaminets and cafes for a meal – but there was one other place which always struck me as being very interesting. For one thing being so unlike the English people's conception of such a place. France, as everyone knows, had what, I think, were called "maisons de tolerance". They were illegal really, but the French Government just turned a blind eye. These were the brothels, and the ones I'm thinking of weren't "mucky" places. They were big houses, and when you went in there was a big room. There would be a bar and a small band, a three-piece band. The girls there would dance with any man who wanted her, and if the men didn't want anything else that was fine, but it would help to occupy an hour quite well, and Madame, who ran the place, was a disciplinarian who insisted on the highest standard of conduct, so you see we didn't always misbehave ourselves. We stayed in Chaemy until February, then we moved up to a suburb of Lille and were billeted in a girls' school and we just kept on the everlasting training.'

Meanwhile Lance Bombardier Seeney tells of a shooting accident that resulted in what must have been one of the first British casualties of the war.

'On this particular evening, it was New Year's Eve as a matter of fact, there was a party going on. The boys were drinking in one of the huts and one of the men left the hut, obviously to go and relieve himself, and the guard, he just pointed his rifle at this chap and pressed the trigger. The silly so and so had a round there, pressed the trigger and shot this poor chap straight through the head – killed him stone dead immediately.

The following day after this tragedy I had to go with one of the drivers into Epernay to collect a coffin. In Epernay we picked up this coffin and a Union Jack and then we were told to go to a convent which had been turned into a hospital for when the casualties would be coming into that area. Anyway, this other fellow and myself, we wandered to a shed, which we'd decided must be the mortuary, and by this time the Battery MO turned up. We dragged the coffin in and we just stood by. This poor chap was lying on a table, dead with his boots still on, and the doctor told us to get him into the box, and this was the first time that I had handled a dead body. This other chap and myself, we picked up this poor fellow and put him in the box, and of course the box was too small, and if you can imagine in this eerie light – no electricity, just an oil lamp – pushing this poor chap, just as well as we could, into this box and then getting the lid on and screwing it down, and the following day the poor chap was buried. And I might add he was buried where we were. It's understandable why the French, in that area anyhow, were very anti-war – it was just one huge cemetery after another from the First World War, thousands of crosses in all directions, and this began the new cemetery with this Number One, with this poor chap who had been killed in such tragic circumstances.

The "Phoney War" continued and, like all soldiers, we settled down to making the best of what was available. The way of living became quite easy; the spring came along, the weather became pleasant and we settled down to a nice easy war; we also had a few days leave back in the UK and the war generally was almost forgotten. But all the time those people in their recce planes above were busy day in, day out.'

The assault, when it came on 10 May 1940, involved simultaneous and overwhelming attacks from the air, with German forces advancing through Holland and Belgium. British and French forces deployed into Belgium but were soon forced to withdraw. In the meantime a major and unexpected attack by German armoured panzer divisions, advancing through the Ardennes, overcame troops guarding that sector, disgorged into France and soon reached the Channel coast behind the British lines. This, and the surrender of the Belgians on 27 May, resulted in the evacuation of the bulk of the British army from Dunkirk, completed by 4 June. France signed an armistice, on German terms, effective as from 25 June.

Lance Bombardier Seeney awoke to the fact that the war was on:

'...and we were getting an awful drubbing. It was fairly evident that the Germans were very much aware of where we were, and that's not surprising – I mentioned the recce planes – and we were very severely damaged at that time. There were quite a few casualties, but that was the way it was – it was war, and also, what was so astonishing, almost immediately the roads were chock-a-block with farmers and people coming in from the war areas and retreating towards Rheims, Epernay and the south. It was the audacity of these German aeroplanes – there was little opposition, and also remember that at that time a gaggle of 50 bombers seemed enormous. I know it was nothing like the enormous numbers towards the end of the war, but 50 bombers on the way to bomb... And you must remember that, as far as I was concerned, they were coming to me, little Willie. Obviously they were covering an area and they seemed to move towards the south-east, towards Rheims, and there was bombing all the way round there. And then they would come back and they would do this hedge-hopping, coming very low, and the rear gunners on these bombers having a grand old time just shooting up everything in sight. Once again it included me, and I wasn't a very good soldier – I was quite happy to keep my head down.

Unfortunately, because of the easy way we'd been living, we'd been a bit careless and one of the bombs destroyed all our GTVs – that's Gun Towing

Vehicles – all in one swipe. We had no way of moving our guns. Also, an interesting part about this question of transport was, because of the very heavy winter that we'd passed through – and remember we weren't accustomed to such things as freeze-ups in big motor vehicles – many were damaged with iced-up engine blocks and so on. They'd been sent back to the Service Corps people for repairs so that at that time there was a huge shortage of vehicles available to move people and things about – they were still being repaired – and I was told that this was a general situation throughout the BEF. In our case we were just one troop of four guns, and we lost their mobility in one swipe. Once again it was panic stations; nobody knew just exactly what was happening. We had certain targets at which we fired, but it was all a bit half-hearted; I suppose it was just a show of strength. After two or three days of this odd situation, news came around that we were going to retreat, we were going to retreat south of the River Aisne, which was in our area. That was fair enough; we seemed to think that would be a good idea, soldiers being what we were – we weren't all that good. But, unfortunately, we couldn't take our guns with us, so we just took the blocks and ammunition that was available, we blew that and off we went. We left fairly early in the day, crossed the river and continued till the evening, and there we stopped and there we were, a half battery of the Royal Artillery with no guns. We were a bit stupid.

This is rather an interesting one. They issued us with Boys rifles, and whenever I mention Boys rifles people just simply don't know there was such a thing, but these things were called Boys rifles. I don't mean "boys and girls" – it was just the initials of this particular rifle and it fired a .5 bullet. In other words it wasn't like an ordinary rifle and the recoil was pretty severe, so it was necessary to get on your stomach and use it in that way. These Boys rifles were considered to be anti-tank and, when you think about it, the whole thing was once again, at that particular time of the war, pretty pathetic.

We were given a silhouette of these various German tanks and there were crosses marked on them to tell us that was the place to fire at to put them out of action. There was no question of destroying them, but we could stop them – but you needed to be a brave man. Well I know that the very thought of just waiting around for a tank to turn up so you could get a shot at it didn't appeal to us very much. We were split up into small groups and we were told to lie around and destroy these tanks when they arrived, which they didn't, which was just as well.

As I mentioned early on, in the first stage of retreat, we stopped and bivouacked and got ourselves comfortable and then somebody suggested – the other half of the Battery were in the area – we should borrow their GTVs and get back and retrieve these guns. Well, of course, that seemed to be a very good, bright, very dashing thing to do, and then of course the question was volunteers – "You, you and you", the usual drill – and I found myself one of the people on the way back to where we'd just come from.

By this time, when we re-crossed the Aisne towards Guinecourt, the French had moved in with anti-tank weapons on the south side of the Aisne and were waiting for the Germans, who were close by, to arrive at the river. So our Officer decided we couldn't hope to pick up the guns, so we backtracked and eventually rejoined our unit.'

For John Campion, manning the guns outside Lille, events following the abrupt ending of the 'Phoney War' were equally memorable:

'Then on 10 May the Germans invaded the Low Countries and all was feverish activity. Infantry, light tanks were ordered up immediately to beyond the frontier. We didn't move until three days later when we were ordered up to a place overlooking Louvain. It was intended to be part of the defensive line of the River Dyle. We got the guns into position but immediately we were ordered back; we kept going backwards with various stops until we reached the town of Templeuve, just outside Lille, so we were practically back in our old country.

There was one little incident which interested me when we were moving back from Louvain to Templeuve. We were passing through Brussels and saw a most unlikely sight: there were cavalrymen, like our own Horse Guards, but with blue cloaks, blue uniforms, plumed helmets and with beautiful black horses, and not a flicker of emotion on their faces. I couldn't decide whether they were waiting to surrender to the Germans or just waiting to see what would happen, but anyway we carried on and eventually reached our next gun position in Templeuve. It was there we had our first casualties, not very severe, but it reminded us that this was a war. We had our Command Post in what should have been a wonderful place – it was a winery with a well-stocked cellar with all of the shelves filled with all kinds of drinks, but, not being much of a drinker, I wasn't able to take much advantage of it.

During our three days in Templeuve, I think we managed to at least frighten the Germans. From the LP [look-out post] Germans were seen digging what appeared to be gun pits. Because of the situation, ammunition was rationed and we had to get permission to fire on the Germans, but when we did we couldn't tell whether we killed or injured any, but we do know we sent them flying.

We stayed only a few days and then we had to start moving again. This time we moved to Flers, which, again, was only a short distance from Lille. After leaving Flers we started meeting the refugees. We also benefited from two factories which had been completely abandoned and full of cigarettes and chocolate, which we didn't feel too guilty about taking. It was on this move that the refugees and the Army were hopelessly mixed, and a British ambulance driver stopped us to find out if we could tell him where the nearest aid post was because he had a load of wounded. We couldn't, so he just had to drive on.

We pressed on and eventually went into "harbour" [rest and recuperation] for a day, and then later that day our CO was given orders to destroy the guns and vehicles and send the men down to the beach. He was a Territorial Army Officer and not a Regular, so he had no hesitation in refusing. So he took himself off to Headquarters, probably Corps Headquarters, and said, "I've got a good regiment, well trained and good morale – give me something to do." So he was ordered to take a position on the defensive line around Dunkirk, so we were ordered back to Dunkirk and eventually arrived. There again it was complete pandemonium – soldiers, some officers, French and Belgian, who had no further interest in the war, looting our vehicles; one of them stole my trousers, which had my personal diary in the pocket.

Eventually we got our orders and dug our guns in, did the necessary survey, set up the Command Post and then we just had to sit and wait, but the few days that were left had a certain interest. A French colonial cavalry troop had decided to abandon their horses in a field next to our guns. They took all their bridles, etc, unsaddled them and went off on foot. Soon as our chaps saw this, as many as could grabbed a horse, re-saddled them and rode up and down the village going to collect their meals, etc. However, I couldn't get a horse so I got someone to teach me to ride an abandoned motorcycle. We'd been living on preserved rations until then, then our cooks found some pigs on a farm, with no farmer around, so the next two or three days we were living on pork, which was done with fresh vegetables.

There were four light tanks which had been abandoned by the French Army, so we looked inside and found that from their ammunition racks only one shell was missing; it was hard to believe it had been fired. Our position was on the rearguard, which we expected would result in our being taken prisoner, because Churchill, at the time, had said that it wouldn't be possible to get everybody out. In many ways we were better off than the men who had been rushed down to the beach and to the port to be taken off as best they could. The road past the guns was one of the main routes down to the coast, and as time went by the troops leaving that way thinned out until they were just mostly British infantry marching down in proper military order. We also used them to give us an idea where the Germans were so that we could pick our targets.

In fact, life became quite quiet for a little while, but then the Germans found our gun position. We'd seen a plane flying overhead and after a while it went away, and then the shells started coming. It was getting a bit hot, in the dangerous sense, so we surveyed an alternative position about 300 yards away, moved the guns and started firing again. When we fired, the Germans fired back on our old position. When they did that we stopped firing and, fortunately, we were able to keep them fooled until we actually left that place. In our alternative position we found a concrete pillbox, and that housed our Command Post. We had taken in a young mother with her baby, who was in a state of hysteria every time a shell exploded, but fortunately her father was there who kept an eye on her. Her cottage had been hit by a shell, and the three of them had got away safely, but our concrete pillbox was really the only safe place for them, for which they were extremely grateful.

This went on till 1 June when orders were given from BEF Headquarters for the whole BEF to cease fire and move off down to the beach to be taken off. The orders were, artillery would cease fire at 10pm, infantry at 11pm, and between 11 and 12 there would be a small mobile force just keeping a watch. So we destroyed our guns by smashing the breech blocks with heavy hammers. That was the best we could manage, but they would have been useless after that.

Then we started making our way down to the beach carrying the guns' dial sights – that was the other essential, not to let a dial sight from the guns fall into the Germans' hands. As we marched down, all gunners – we were more like staggering – we heard infantry marching, marching to a light infantry pace, and it was the Guards, probably a platoon of Guards. One passed us like a shot out of a gun. As I told myself at the time, they had the energy but they hadn't been throwing around 100-pound shells for a few days.

We got down to the beach and the sailors started coming in with lifeboats. I had to go into the water almost up to my shoulders, and I suddenly found somebody holding on to my hand. It was our signal sergeant; he was rather short and if he'd tried to stand on the seabed he would most certainly have gone right under. He couldn't reach high enough to get hold of the gunwale of the boat, but he had some strong sailors there to lift him in. I was half in and half out when an officer decided to play the hero and ordered everybody out simply because he'd heard a big cry of "Take shelter!" from the opposite side of the boat. Actually the sailors were very rude to him and continued hauling people in on my side. That is just by the way. We got out with very little interference, shells occasionally falling on the beach, but otherwise there was little danger.

We got away on I think it must have been a minesweeper, an old ferry boat which used to operate between South Wales and Dorset; it was called the *Glendower*, the name of a Welsh patriot way back. The sailors hauled us aboard and put us in a room. I was in with half a dozen other men, just in what looked like an alcove with a curtain across it. Bread was handed out to everybody and then, a few minutes later, a bottle of rum was passed round. So we got away and without any unpleasant incidents, and then we landed in Harwich. The wounded were taken off first and then we were all given a good feed on the dockside.'

Meanwhile Lance Bombardier Seeney had been hopelessly cut off from the main British Expeditionary Force. He recalled that:

'We had no idea really what was going on and we got on our trucks and wandered off towards St Nazaire and, after a few days, we eventually arrived there.

What we weren't aware of at that time, Dunkirk had happened and it was all over and the French had already asked for an Armistice, and for two days we'd been wandering around in France, the northern parts of which the Germans really had control, but the French themselves were in such a muddle, they weren't in a position to stop us. We continued on – where we got the petrol from I'll never know – but we did and we eventually arrived at St Nazaire, and that had been heavily bombed early on in the piece. Much to our surprise, there was a boat pulled up in the harbour by the quay and it turned out to be the *Phillip N*, God bless it, a collier which was actually on its way, of all places, to Gibraltar. However, it had been stopped and turned back and asked to go into St Nazaire to pick up the remains of some British troops.

Well, I suppose there were about 100 to 150 of us. There were men from the Air Force, Army, you name it, there we were on the deck of the *Phillip N*, a collier, and we took off. Fortunately the weather was beautiful and, of course, once again I remember the full moon and thought, gosh, all these U-boats hanging around and there'd be the odd bomber... But, for some reason or another, which is so difficult to explain, this one little boat with all these men on board, with no real self-defence – except we did have some Bren guns with us and we tied them to the railings – and we did this, that and the other thing to give ourselves some sort of cover, which might have helped, but I doubt if it would have been a lot of good. However, it gave us something to do.

There was the problem of food, and somebody had the sense to toss in crates of tinned food, but mostly it was apricots; we had stewed apricots for a day or two but the biggest problem was water. One must remember it was only a small boat, probably with a crew of five or six, and it really became a problem. By the time we arrived into the Bristol Channel, they were aware that we were in trouble with the lack of water and the barrier was opened, the anti-submarine barrier, and it was opened and allowed us to continue up the Channel and we eventually arrived at Swansea late one evening. It must have been three days later – goodness knows, it was a long time.'

Pilot Officer James Hayter saw it all from the air. He remembered:

'When the Blitz started we were doing low-level flying, low-level bombing on mainly the bridges of the River Meuse and convoys. We had big losses, we lost most of our aircraft. At the end of the collapse in France several of us were told to go to various airfields where our armament boys were, pick up our bombs and they'd re-arm us. We were told by the Adjutant, because

James Chilton Francis Hayter

all our senior officers had gone back to England, we were told to pick our own targets, which we did. We finished up at Nantes and I'd lost all my tail part except for the steering elevators and the rudder, which were damaged, and we asked for petrol from the French, which they refused to give us, so we took off and, as my engine cut out, we landed at Manston. We were tired and hungry and I remember saying that we thought our senior officers had let us down, and I received a ticking-off, which I felt ill-deserved.'

Bernard Brown was another Royal Air Force pilot involved in operations over France during those fateful days:

'During the evacuation of Dunkirk I was a Pilot Officer and I was detailed, on one occasion, to go out to Ghent in Belgium to try and find the British Army because they didn't know where they were. So I knew about the British Army, how extremely dangerous they were, and it was necessary always to fly at least 3,000 feet above the Army, because they would like as not give one a pannier of 303 and you'd see the shells coming up and curling down behind the aeroplane – they were very bad shots. But anyway, I did find the British Army and I found the Germans too, and they were busy riding along quite happily in their trucks and they didn't fire a shot. So that was that little episode.

Then while the Dunkirk operation was progressing, they discovered that there was a German artillery unit in a chalk pit in Calais firing at the British Army, so they decided that we should go along and drop some bombs on them. So the Squadron – I think there were about nine of us – we left from Manston in things called Hectors, that they used to use on the North West Frontier of India to keep the people there in order. Anyway we had two bombs loaded underneath the wings and on the way over across the sea I thought I'd better try the guns, which fired through the prop. I did all the necessary bits and pressed the button and there was a mighty bang, and the next moment there was petrol in my face. I had actually ruptured the main fuel tank. I released the bombs and turned what I thought was back to England – I could barely see because the petrol was burning my face. Fortunately I had my goggles on and I flew in a general westerly direction.

Eventually I saw land, and by this time the engine was nearly sort of stopping, but I switched over then to the gravity tank and as the petrol sort of drained away from the aeroplane, no more petrol was in my face and I saw this land and I saw the Herne Bay Golf Course. I was pretty good at landing an aeroplane in those days, so I popped it on to the golf course, then got the map out and found out where I was. So I turned round and away I went, took off again and landed back at Manston, which was just up the road. At a subsequent investigation, when I got back to base, they

Bernard Walter Brown

discovered that the split pin on the front of the machine-gun, which operated a gas-operated thing, had not been fitted and the piece had blown off and gone right through the side of the aeroplane and into the petrol tank, a great big hole 3 or 4 inches across. The other Hectors were all right and had come back. They thought I had been shot down.'

CHAPTER 2

The Battle of Britain and the Blitz

'Never in the field of human conflict was so much owed
by so many to so few.'
Winston Churchill

On 1 August 1940, Hitler, finally accepting that no compromise peace was possible with Britain, ordered the destruction of the Royal Air Force as a prerequisite to the invasion of Britain. So the great air offensive started in earnest on 13 August, commencing with attacks on fighter airfields and radar installations on the South Coast. By the end of August many aerodromes had been badly damaged and the heavy loss in fighter planes had become almost unsustainable. Pilots were very tired and morale was slipping. Goering then decided to switch his main effort to day attacks on London, which gave Fighter Command the respite needed to revitalise its effort in fulfilling and expanding its defensive and offensive capabilities. From the end of October 1940 the aerial Battle for Britain could be said to have finished in Britain's favour. Hitler's aim of destroying the RAF had become completely unattainable. Heavy German bombing of cities, with considerable damage and disruption, continued until 16 May 1941, then the air armadas were withdrawn to the East, where Hitler had another role awaiting them. The invasion of Britain was quietly shelved.

One of those who fought in the Battle of Britain was Alan Gawith, a New Zealander, who was accepted for a short service commission with the Royal Air Force and commenced training in the United Kingdom in June 1938:

'I managed to complete my training and was posted to a Blenheim Night Fighter Squadron when all I really wanted was to get into a Hurricane or

Alan Gawith

Spitfire Squadron. It was No 23 Squadron based at Wittering Airfield, not far from Peterborough. In many ways it was a pretty leisurely and enjoyable life, but I wasn't what I would call the least bit well trained by the time the war started. Those months of September/October 1939 were busy months for me. I was a Pilot Officer, busy all during the day for long hours on the adjutant's job and trying to get a bit of flying in, and I had become engaged to my New Zealand girlfriend a few weeks before the war started and we decided to get married because she was caught in England and couldn't get home again. That meant getting the Station Commander's permission, which was quite an experience, but he granted us permission and even went through and shouted [treated] us immediately after the wedding, on 4 October 1939. My wife had got herself a job as a landgirl on a farm not far away and she carried on with that and I carried on with my work.

My work as adjutant terminated at the end of October and the flying went on, mainly searchlight co-operation at night and training, practising, getting some hours in, getting experience during the daylight. Life was pretty busy, particularly because we had to keep crews on standby every night in case of enemy activity, which didn't start up for many, many months. We were busy expanding, forming more squadrons and, with shortage of crews and aircraft, we were doing stretches of perhaps seven, eight and nine nights consecutively on standby in the hangar or flying. Not a great deal of spare time during the day after one had caught up with a bit of sleep, eaten and so on, and I didn't see a great deal of my wife during that time, but as the winter wore on and the weather was getting colder I felt that I couldn't leave her struggling with milking cows twice a day in those sort of conditions, so we got digs in the village of Wansford. I was living out from then on, which meant that I missed out on the mess life, which is half of the fun of the war really, and I had the extra responsibilities. However, we got by.

Nothing much happened until, oh, we got radar, airborne radar in June 1940, which was pretty useless but still we had to practise to try and make it work. It was in June 1940, I think, that we had our first combat as a Squadron, when both Flight Commanders, Spike O'Brien and Duke Willy, had combats and managed to shoot at two enemy aircraft, not using radar but by visual sightings. Unfortunately O'Brien's aircraft got into a spin and he tried to get his air gunner out of the aircraft with difficulty and eventually got himself free, but the gunner had met the prop on the way out and was killed. I think we lost two aircraft that night, but I think we got two enemy aircraft so we were all square. It wasn't a very satisfactory start to the Squadron's war.

The Battle of Britain then came on and, of course, the Day Squadrons were thoroughly occupied. We were in No 12 Group, which was the back-up group for Sir Keith Park's 11 Group, which really fought the battle in the south. Our job then became care of the convoys around the coast of Norfolk. The Day Squadrons had been doing those patrols and the enemy were raiding the convoys quite regularly, sinking ships. We used to start before dawn and I can remember many occasions when we took off in the dark and flew up into the dawn, long before it was daylight on the ground. In some convoys we would often find a ship or two sinking but no enemy in sight. We patrolled for month after month. It wasn't dangerous, simply because we never seemed to be there when the enemy was there and we couldn't quite understand that, but there wouldn't have been much point in patrolling at night.

On 13 August my son was born. I'd just got my wife established back at home from the hospital with our infant, and on 11 September I got a call to say that I was to report back to the Squadron immediately. The Squadron had been posted to Forde airfield, which we'd taken over from the Royal Naval Air Service just south of Arundel on the coast of Sussex. So I had to desert my new family, leave them in the tender care of the landlord and landlady, and disappear down to the South Coast where we landed on a very small airstrip about 800 yards long with our Blenheims, which were used to longer fields.

We hadn't been established there very long before the attacks came in from the coast. The enemy would swoop in about dusk and machine-gun the camp. We lived in wooden huts whilst there, and we'd guard our aircraft. Two or three times we had those attacks and, of course, nothing much we could do about it. We were in the front line at last; there were one or two casualties and we had one or two aircraft destroyed, and we found what it was like to be under fire. You get machine-gun fire when you're in the mess and you sort of burrow under the carpet – it's as simple as that. Bullets whistling through these wooden walls made one duck. However, we survived those all right.

We saw the battle going on, the day battle up above, and we knew what the base squadrons were tackling. We didn't know a great deal more than the civilian population; we could see what was going on, and we heard from pilots who came in and our pilots who visited base squadrons nearby, Tangmere Airfield and others. We knew, as the time went on, how grim things were; Fighter Command was strained to the limit. Sir Keith Park – he wasn't Sir Keith then – was not getting the support he needed from his friend Leigh-Mallory to the north, who insisted on holding his squadrons back until he'd got them mounted into wings of three or five squadrons. The Hun doesn't wait for that sort of nonsense. Park's theory was to attack every time; even if he only had three aircraft, they would get out and do their best. It's amazing how much a single attack by a small number of aircraft diving down through a lumbering flotilla of bombers, shooting down two or three of them on the way through, is effective in diverting the attack or splitting it up, and Park never missed the opportunity. He'd get aircraft from somewhere and make sure that the Hun got some sort of reception.

Of course, we were aware that everybody's nerves were getting frayed when the attack on the airfields was at its height. We weren't getting the same plastering as they were getting at the sectional airfields where the Day Squadrons were. Biggin Hill, Tangmere, Manston and others were getting it all the time. It was not the actual bombing so much as the constant day and night attacks, and nobody was getting any sleep. It was the exhaustion that was wearing out the aircrew, the ground crew, the controllers, the WAAF staff, everybody. Had that gone on for another week I don't think Fighter Command would have survived, and there was nothing to stop the enemy coming across except Fighter Command's air supremacy. However, it's doubtful to me whether we had air supremacy, but at least with the help of radar and the system that had been set up by Dowding in the few years before the war, and the systems like the short service commissions getting in young fellows from around the Empire, then the British, mainly British, getting them trained just before the war, that was the only reason that Britain survived, I think, the Battle of Britain. It wouldn't have survived if Hitler hadn't made the mistake of switching the attack away from the airfields and concentrating on London; it gave the airfields a breathing space and the aircrews, everybody, time to get a little bit of sleep and catch up and get operational again.

Then I think it was just after that, when the Huns thought they had Fighter Command finished, that late in their raid a big wing from 12 Group arrived. When the German pilots saw this, their morale suffered accordingly. By this time the enemy had started night raids on London, and there was much more enemy night activity for the night fighter squadrons, and we were often out every night patrolling, more or less, across the track of the bombers, because radar hadn't reached the stage where it was making too many interceptions and there was more chance of combat by visual sightings. There was one night, when we were patrolling at about 20,000 feet across Southampton or that area, and there was a huge blaze in the sky, it seemed like at least 100 miles to the north, and it was a good night, and what I was watching from that distance was the blitz on Coventry – we read about it next day.

Because of that, it was decided that the Squadron should mount layer patrols from 20,000 feet down to about 12,000 feet at intervals – four aircraft at intervals of about 3,000 feet. The first pilot off was the Sergeant Pilot, I was Number Two, the Squadron Commander, who was then Squadron Leader Haycock, was Number Three, and I forget who was Number Four, but it doesn't matter because he didn't take off. The weather started to close in and Sergeant Dann was first and I was listening to his report about how he was in cloud at 5,000 feet, 7,000 feet, and the controller kept asking him and he kept saying he was still in cloud, and he got up to about 10,000 feet. Sergeant Dann obviously wasn't happy, so the controller called him back to base and asked me where I was. I said I was at

10,000 feet by then and still in dense cloud; he kept me going up and reporting periodically while he tried to get Sergeant Dann down.

Meantime the Squadron Leader had taken off. He listened to the radio, and kept under the cloud, which was about 3,000 feet when we started and was down to about 1,500 feet; then the Squadron Leader decided the sensible thing was to get back on terra firma, so he landed. Then the controller was fully occupied trying to get Sergeant Dann down, but as there were hills in the region of several hundred feet not far from base, the controller couldn't get him to come below the cloud to land. I had plenty of time to think, well, I've still got to land, and when I got to 17,000 feet and reported that I was still in dense cloud, no sign of the moon, he called me in also. I acknowledged and, as we were flying over the South Coast, I just pointed my nose to France and kept going until I got below the cloud.

By that time the cloud was about 600 feet, so I just kept coming in to the north. I kept a bit to the right of the airfield because I thought, well, if I get very far right I will see the White Cliffs of Dover, even on a cloudy night – in moonlight you'd see those cliffs and have time to do something about it. When the controller asked me where I was, I told him I'd made landfall to the east of base. He was still trying to get Sergeant Dann down; by this time I think he'd got him below the cloud base, so I kept heading for the base and if the weather was descending fairly rapidly I thought, well, I'm not going to muck about with the circuits when I get there – I'm going in to land. As luck would have it, Sergeant Dann got there just ahead of me, and when he was landing I was sort of coming over the eastern boundary of the airfield and Dann called out, reporting that he had landed. I didn't wait for any acknowledgement from the controller or anything else, I said, "Get off the bloody runway because I'm right on your tail," and I landed within half a minute probably of Dann landing. He'd moved off all right – we didn't collide on the ground. The weather was such that one did not feel like staying up there any longer than was absolutely necessary.

Well, the patrols carried on until December 1940, when No 23 Squadron was selected to do Intruder Patrols.'

Robert Hugh Barber was serving in the Metropolitan Police Force when, in 1939, he joined the Royal Air Force:

'Having completed my training I was sent as a Pilot Officer to Hawarden where I learned to fly Spitfires and Hurricanes and was posted to 46 Squadron at Digby; 46 Squadron was in 12 Group, and we were there till towards the end or middle of August 1940, when we moved from Digby down to the North Weald's Wing to an airfield, one of the satellite airfields. We operated from there and, on 4 September 1940, the CO told me to be the Weaver, who watches the rear of the squadron. We set off on a flight and I could hear a lot going on on the RT, and as I went down the sun I could see it was clear, but I was suspicious, so I turned very quickly, and as I turned I saw a 109 approaching me. Before I could take much action there was a bang on the side of the plane and the plane was hit and my right leg slightly. I immediately dived and was covered with glycol, because he'd hit the glycol tank and it came out and it was all over me, hot and sticking. I lost considerable height and finally managed to sort of wipe the screen a little and see exactly where he was. I didn't see any more of him but I'd lost a lot of height, so I decided that the only thing I could do was to bring it down with wheels up in a field somewhere.

So I looked around for a field, finally saw a field and landed the plane successfully with wheels up. Unfortunately, with no engine, the impact was very considerable and I was laid out. I don't remember anything of that particular moment, but the next thing I remember I was getting out of the plane and a man was walking across the field towards me. This gentleman took hold of my parachute and carried it for me, and he led me over to his car and I was taken into Maldon in Essex to a lady doctor's. She had a look at me and rested me up, but she had to leave and left me alone and, in the meantime, I phoned up North Weald and spoke to them, and they said, "Will you be all right for tomorrow?"

I said, "Well, I'm a bit shaken up but I should be OK."

They said, "OK, we will send for you."

So they sent an open-flap wagon down to pick me up and I bounced in this with my parachute all the way back to North Weald and was immediately taken to the MO. The MO looked at me and said, "I don't like the look of you – I'm taking you down to St Margaret's Hospital, Epping, right away," and he took me to St Margaret's, where I was immediately taken in hand. Exactly what they did I don't quite know, but they eventually told me I had fractured three cervical vertebrae in my neck and I had broken my jaw in three places.

At hospital I was eventually picked up and taken to Halton, the RAF Hospital, and after a spell there was sent down to Torquay where the RAF Convalescent Hospital was. It was the old Palace Hotel taken over by the RAF. I had a long time to reflect in the hospital and was there with one of our most famous fighter pilots who won the VC, Nicholson – it was announced whilst we were in hospital. In my thoughts, after my being shot down, I'd wondered if I was the only flat-footed policeman who'd been walking the streets in 1938 in London in the Metropolitan Police and was, two years later, a Flying Officer in the RAF, flying aeroplanes 20,000 feet above that fair city.

After getting out of hospital eventually, I was posted to 10 Group

Headquarters as an Assistant Controller. I quite enjoyed this job, seeing the fair ladies pushing discs all over the table down below, but my main purpose in life had been to join the Air Force to fly aeroplanes, so I was very keen to get back on flying. Although my medical category had been considerably lowered and I was off flying, I couldn't wait till I could have another medical and finally get back on it again. I succeeded, but not on operations.'

Back from the 'Phoney War' in France, Flying Officer James Hayter had some difficulty locating his Squadron:

'Eventually, after landing at about three aerodromes, we located our unit. We were then given an opportunity of either going on to Wellingtons or into Fighter Command, and seeing as I'd been shot down the odd time in the Fairey Battle, I thought this was a bit of a dead loss. I volunteered to go into Fighter Command.

I joined 615 Squadron and they gave us about five or six hours conversion on to a Hurricane, and then I went to 605 Squadron which was stationed at Croydon – that was towards the end of the Battle of Britain. Things were fairly hectic – we'd do sometimes two, three, four trips a day. I was shot down again over Kent and landed in Major Cazalet's place – who I understood was England's champion squash player and an MP – when he was having a cocktail party. I was slightly wounded and went back to my unit, and I was flying again in another three or four days.

When they had the big formations at night, Heinkels and 88s coming in, we were still flying formations of a number of fighters which the Germans had showed us not to use. Invariably, if you got into a dogfight or if you were attacking a formation, everybody got split up, so actually that formation was the most stupid thing we ever used. The Germans had showed us how to fly and attack but we didn't learn. We had some big formations of 300 or 400 aircraft coming in, and we'd attack a formation and it would be a shambles. The formation that we were flying in was completely useless as everybody would break up into their own little thing.

At that stage I remember going to our Intelligence Officer and saying, well, look the claims were absolutely outrageous. There were some very, very good pilots in the aeroplanes – but I think it's history now, and I suppose it was to keep the morale up, maybe, but we had a whole lot of glamour boys who over-claimed and this is proven now. I think the thing that impressed me most was that, while there were some individuals who were most likely the genuine scorers, there was a whole lot of people there that weren't.

I think that what impressed me quite a lot in England was that when we arrived we'd come from all sorts of walks of life and were pretty rough, I suppose, socially, and a lot of these so-called English gentlemen looked pretty anaemic, weak physically; but when it came down to the real nitty-gritty, the anaemic-looking Pom was most likely the bravest of the lot. Of course they had something to fight for, it was their country, but what did impress was that these very, very nice chaps were tough.

We went through until we finished the Battle of Britain. We went to Scotland for a spell and then I joined 611 Squadron at Hornchurch where I did another tour on Spitfires, and then we were sent for a spell to Prestwick where Peter Townsend was the Wing Commander, Flying. He had a rose garden, and one night I had a nice little sports car and I tried to drive through the front doors of the Officers' Mess and couldn't make it, and backed out, but unfortunately I backed into Peter's rose garden. Then I got my immediate posting to the Middle East.'

Another New Zealander, John Gard'ner, was accepted for a short service commission in the RAF and was under training in Britain when the war started:

'On getting my wings I was posted as a Pilot Officer to 141 Squadron at Grangemouth, where I trained on and operated Blenheims. Our job in the Blenheims was to patrol in the Firth of Forth area, and as I recall the Germans were coming across from Norway or somewhere in that direction and I believe their target was the Forth Bridge and, of course, going on down to the Glasgow area. After a few weeks of flying the Blenheims – rather unsuccessfully as far as any action with Germans were concerned, and during this time we lost a number of aircraft, just plane crashes at night-time – we were told we were going to be re-equipped with the new Boulton Paul Defiant aircraft. Now those of us who had been on the Blenheims had to be now converted on to single-engine-type aircraft, and they brought in an old Fairey Battle. It was on this Fairey Battle that all of us pilots, who had been flying the Blenheims, were converted from twin-engined on to single-engined aircraft. Again, just circuits and bumps, and because the old Battle took so long to have its flaps come up and its wheels come up, we flew them just round the airfield wheels and flaps down until it was considered that we were well enough flying on single-engine ones to get into the first Defiants.

In the meantime we'd heard that No 264 Squadron, which was down south, they'd had their Defiants for some time before us and in the first few days they were doing extraordinarily well. The Germans didn't know what they were and were being shot down rather rapidly by 264 Squadron. When the time came for 141 Squadron to get into the action, No 264

John Rushton Gard'ner (left)

Squadron had been "sorted out" and the Germans actually had decimated it. We went down to take over from where 264 Squadron left off.

We were posted to the airfield which is now Gatwick – it was a little grass strip quite near to Biggin Hill I think – and again we were put on to day flying training out of this little grass airfield there. It was a one-squadron airfield as I remember it. Anyway, this was day flying – we were just doing day training – and as soon as we were considered to be experienced enough we were sent down to Hawkinge for the first of our operational sorties. We flew daily; we flew out from Gatwick each morning down there and went at night-time back to this airfield.

The first patrols of the Defiant in daylight were not successful in any way – no fighter actions occurred – but on the third patrol which I was involved in we were sent off – 12 aircraft were ordered off. Nine of us got airborne because three of them turned out, well, had trouble, either engine trouble or trouble before they got to the take-off point, and didn't get airborne. We took off and had got to some, I think it was, about 7,000 or 8,000 feet when we were jumped by 109s coming down out of the sun behind us. In those days we flew in formations of three, and I was tail-end Charlie in the third section.

I vividly recall what appeared to be white streaks of light going through my cockpit and out the front of the aeroplane and the smell of cordite and stuff, and, glancing to my left, I saw aeroplanes in flames and suddenly I realised that my engine was just stopping on me. I found that the rudder was loose, there was no control over the rudder, and I could wobble the joystick. Anyway, I thought I'm going to get out of here quick, so as far as I recall I sort of pulled the nose over and dived for the sea, which was down below me, thinking, "God, is that chap on my tail?"

Anyway, I just went down and down and I found I still had a measure of control. The engine had just stopped dead, and as far as I can remember the prop was dead in front of me. Anyway, I got down and I was able to level off and I could see a naval vessel way ahead and I thought, gosh, I don't know what the speed was then, but I seemed to be going at quite a fast speed, and I thought, well, I'm going to try and land beside that naval vessel. Anyway, I overshot it and I went on and on and on and my speed was dropping off and dropping off, and finally I got to the point where I felt that at any minute now I was going to have to make a landing. Now, why I did it I don't know, but I undid my straps, thinking I'm just going to plop on to the water and get out quickly. The result of that was, when the aeroplane finally stalled on to the water, the next thing I knew I was in Stygian blackness and I was in the water.

Anyway, I realised that I had to get up. I got out of the cockpit – I must have been knocked out just for a fraction – and I managed to struggle up to the surface which seemed a helluva long way up. Anyway, I came out of the surface and I realised that I'd been hit on the head; I felt a bit sore on the head, but otherwise I felt OK.

During this sortie, immediately after I knew I'd been hit by the enemy from behind, I had no response from my gunner – I'd heard no shooting from the gunner, my gunner sitting in the back there, and I presumed at the time that he must have been hit, because whilst I had armour plating behind my head, I knew that all he had to protect him was his own big gun turret. So when we went down and into the water, I did worry about him, but then he didn't appear. I'd landed beside another little naval vessel – I think it was just a little torpedo boat of some sort which came roaring over and picked me up – and I recall again seeing my parachute, which I'd been sitting on, floating on the water, and I'd kicked off my lovely big black leather flying boots and they appeared to me to be floating almost side by side on the water. I suggested to the chaps who were picking me up, please go and pick up my boots, but they ignored me.

At this time I realised that I'd had a gash on my forehead. I was wounded in the sense that blood was pouring down in front of my eyes and I kept seeing blood, then I can't recall much after that. I do know that the next thing I found myself in was a hospital in Dover, a small public hospital there, and there I came to again with stitches up the back of my head and stitches on my forehead and so forth, but otherwise unharmed. Thinking back on it, I realise, I think, that what got me on the back of the head was the fact that some bullets or something had hit that armour plating and had shattered something and had just torn the back of my head.

Anyway, I stayed in that hospital in Dover, and actually it was beautiful weather and I was lying in a bed and I could watch some of the battle going on and I was able to look out and see blue sky and the vapour trails of aircraft, whilst battles were going on just over that narrow part of the Channel where Dover is. I stayed in the hospital, I think it was about 10 days, and I was posted off on sick leave and I had the next two months on sick leave, where I was joined by another New Zealander who, unfortunately, was killed later on in the war, but he and I were on sick leave together. We had a marvellous time under the auspices of the Lady Frances Ryder Scheme. We went to Northern Ireland and even into Southern Ireland, and I stayed in some of the stately homes of Britain and it really was an interesting and exciting time of my life.

However, good things come to an end and I was posted back to 141 Squadron, by which time they had been converted on to night fighting. After my sick leave period I reported back to the Squadron at Gatwick. Now at Gatwick we were on to night fighting, but at some stage after that the Squadron was moved over to Gravesend. But I know most of my night fighter work, done on the Defiant, was out of Gatwick, and it was during this period that London was being heavily bombed and we in the Defiants were sent up over London night after night. I recall vividly that the night of the really big fire of London, I happened to be airborne that night and I was being controlled by some control unit from the ground, who was getting most frustrated, as I was, because he kept telling me I was right alongside enemy aircraft, and neither I nor my gunner could see any enemy aircraft there, and during this whole time when I was airborne and I had many, many operational flights out of Gravesend, but I personally never saw a thing.'

David Hunt left his studies at Birmingham University to take a short service commission in the RAF, and during his training the war started. He has recalled that:

'As the threat of invasion loomed closer, some of the single-engined pilots, having now acquired their wings, were posted direct to squadrons with no

David Hunt

time left for operational training courses. I was posted to Hendon and no one appeared to know our purpose, least of all ourselves. It was an interesting time during the fall of the Low Countries, with Sabena and KLM Dakotas flying into that historic Hendon airfield. Parked around the perimeter track were these venerable Imperial Airways biplanes, *Hengist* and *Horsa*. We spent our time watching these arrivals and inspecting the ancient aeroplanes with their cane and bamboo "pomp-forming" splendour, redolent of Empire.

Eventually planes started arriving, brought in by Air Transport Auxiliary pilots, including some lady pilots – a Magister, two Masters and numerous Spitfire Mark 2s. We sat in the cockpits of the Spitfires, which felt as small as Tiger Moths, and wondered if we should ever be able to fly these sleek, powerful machines. Later we found that they handled as easily as Tiger Moths, with a few additional complications like flaps and retractable undercarriages and massive instrument panels.

Our spell in wonderland had to end sometime, and after the fall of France and Dunkirk the war-torn remnants of the Allied Air Striking Force Squadrons returned from France. It wasn't long before we were flying, first the Magister, which is a light open-cockpit, club-style plane, then the Masters, real gentlemen's planes, and at last the great day, the first flight in a Spitfire. This had to be at Northolt with its single long runway. Everything went well and it called for celebration.

During June all the Spitfires were removed by the ATA pilots and replaced with Hurricanes, because Spitfires were in short supply, and we grew to like the Hurricanes. Another thing happened in my life at this time: I got married and we managed a honeymoon of a few days down at Midhurst, Sussex.

On 14 July we were posted to Northolt where our training went on apace, including formation flying and air-to-air firing at Sutton Bridge with a target towed by a Hawker Henley. Air-to-ground firing was at Dengie Flats in East Anglia. One amusing experience was RT practice – that's Radio Telephony. We were taken by coach to an Uxbridge football ground complete with stadium, where we pedalled around in low gear on El Dorado ice-cream tricycles which had been converted for blind flying with screens around and magnetic compasses and RT sets and headphones. We had to carry out the orders received over the RT to "fly" on various courses using the appropriate call signs and terms such as "Fly victor 120", "angels 20" and "yellow through", "pipsqueak in", "scramble", "pancake", "tallyho", "under bandits" – all that sort of thing.

In July 1940 operational flights were becoming an everyday occurrence with convoy patrols and interception of enemy sorties. The Squadron was operating from forward bases at Hawkinge near Dover and Tangmere near Portsmouth, as required, and intercepted small formations attacking the ports and radar installations. The Squadron was now at readiness from an hour before dawn until an hour after dusk for most of the time. The Squadron RT call sign was "Alert" and my section was Yellow section.

At this point I should say something about the Hurricane, powered by the Rolls Royce Merlin of a 1,030 brake horsepower. Its top speed at 15,000 feet was over 300 miles an hour, and the three-bladed propeller converted this power into thrust, and the aircraft ceiling was 30,000 feet. An optical gunsight projected an aiming ring and crosswires on to a glass screen behind the bullet-proof windscreen. She was armed with eight Browning 303 machine-guns with 2,660 rounds of ammunition, which could all be fired off in three or four short bursts of 4 seconds each. The pilot's face-mask was plugged into oxygen and RT connections. After bonding and earthing was carried out by a radio expert, the RT was as good as the ordinary telephone. The cine camera-gun recorded the action when the guns were fired.

In early August the Squadron had the honour of escorting the Prime Minister on a tour of the East Coast Defences. Next day the Squadron left Northolt for its forward base at Tangmere; three sections were scrambled with a big contact over St Catherine's Point. This was an attempt by the Jerries to put one radar station, our radar station, out of action. The raiders were driven off with losses to both sides; we lost our Flight Commander and two other pilots. The great German "Eagle" attack was due to start on 10 August, but was delayed by bad weather. This was aimed at destroying coastal fighter airfields and radar stations.

A few days later the Squadron returned to Tangmere, but before landing we were vectored to the Portsmouth area to repel a raid by 500 enemy aircraft. Our new Squadron Commander, Squadron Leader Harkness, led us straight in to drive off the big formations of Heinkel 111s, Dornier 17 Flying Pencils and a fighter cover of Messerschmitt 109s and 110s. The Squadron shot down several aircraft and we lost one pilot; another pilot lost a finger which had to be amputated.

We left Northolt for our new sector at Debden where the Station Commander, Wing Commander Fullergood, welcomed the Squadron and explained the characteristics of Sector F. After settling in at Debden the Squadron moved to its forward base at Martlesham Heath near Ipswich. Yellow section was scrambled early at 0622 hours on the southbound convoy escort patrol off the East Coast. It dawned a bright sunny day as usual that summer, and it wasn't long before we saw a Dornier Flying Pencil sneaking in for an attack. Cockram yelled over the RT, "Bandit tallyho!" and roared into the attack, and we struggled to keep up with him and had the satisfaction to see the Dornier limping away after the attack, quite out of control with its undercarriage obviously damaged. As we tailed the plume of smoke we resisted the temptation to chase him out to sea and stayed with the convoy.

In the late afternoon the Squadron was scrambled and we intercepted a raid of German bombers and fighter escort proceeding up the Thames Estuary in box formation, also accompanied by top cover fighters several thousand feet above the main formation. It was an awesome feeling to realise that there was nothing between this large formation and the City of London except our little squadron. However, we stalked them steadily for a minute or two, keeping well ahead, until the time came and we just had to attack. As we closed in to attack, the bombers started to move into the sun and split up into smaller formations, jettisoning their bombs all over Kent and Sussex. At that moment the top cover came screaming down out of the sun, hotly pursued by Spitfires. All hell let loose in a series of dogfights all over the sky. A formation of Stukas decided to make a break for it, having shed their load; I helped them on their way with the occasional squirt from my guns as they gradually came into range. I must have caused some damage as one dropped out of formation. I closed in for a good stern attack. Smoke started to stream as he dived down steeply, dropping a few bits as he went. I turned back towards the main scrap but by that time the day was done, the battle over and the sun dipping in the sky.

The next day the Squadron received orders to fly to the forward aerodrome at Martlesham Heath and to stay there for several days using 17 Squadron's ground staff. We carried out convoy patrols. Blue section intercepted an unidentified aircraft; after a few warning shots the aircraft, a friendly Blenheim, gave the correct identification signal for the day. More convoy patrols next day, and Green section flushed out a Dornier 17 which was stalking the convoy. He put up a spirited defence with his rear guns and did some damage to our lads. He disappeared into cloud trailing some smoke. On their next convoy patrol Green section had better luck and destroyed a Dornier 215.

Another day of intensive flying followed and we had the Squadron at readiness all day from dawn till dusk with continuous precautionary patrols and convoy duties. This state of affairs was to last until 26 August when Debden was bombed, killing three airmen of 257 Squadron and damaging hangars badly and many other buildings, including the Sergeants' Mess.

The whole Squadron was scrambled at 0830 hours at the end of the month on 31 August. In the Clacton area at 18,000 feet a formation of 50 Messerschmitt 110s was attacked and they went into defensive circles, each plane covering the next one's tail. I attacked one ring from the reverse direction in which they were turning, which must have put the fear of God up them, and me too. One of them dropped out of the formation, smoking from both engines, and made for the coast. I pursued him out to sea, past the Dengie Flats, filling him with some final bursts, and roared back to Martlesham in a power dive of 450 miles an hour plus. In these late stages of the battle there had been little contact with the rest of the Squadron. One of our pilots was killed and another one shot down in flames. At that stage the Jerries gave Debden another drubbing, but this time there weren't any casualties.

After two days of patrols, the Squadron was scrambled from Martlesham with orders to orbit Chelmsford. On that day my aircraft had been taken into the workshop for maintenance. I had an earlier mark Hurricane with fabric-covered wings and non-self-sealing tanks, and when the scramble came over the field telephone she wouldn't start. The whole Squadron took off and there I was still on the ground with a dead prop, but

I was determined and 5 minutes later we had her going and I took off to join the Squadron. I'd only just closed with the formation when there was a terrific concussion with coloured lights flashing all around me. In a moment the fuel tanks and the cockpit became an inferno, but I knew I had to get out quick and I reached up to open my hood but it had jammed tight. I struggled and, putting my feet up on the instrument panel, chopped it open with an air axe and ripped off my safety harness and helmet and jumped. I should say that my father's war effort was the production of this air axe and the ARP axe, and they were insulated to withstand a high voltage. One of them saved my life on that occasion.

I pulled the ripcord without delay and felt the satisfying jerk as the canopy opened. Everything went quiet, save for a gentle flutter from the parachute. The Squadron droned away into the distance. It took me about half an hour to come down. As I floated closer, I could hear cars, people shouting, "There he goes." I came down in a Brigadier Brazier Craig's garden in Stock near Chelmsford, narrowly missing a glasshouse of grapevines by bumping into a tree trunk on the way down. There I sat on the ground with sheets of skin hanging and flapping around me and all my sleeves and trouser legs burned off, just my rank stripes hanging limply from my wrists.

My plane had crashed into a railway embankment near Margaretting and was burning fiercely and ammunition was exploding. Onlookers held up my parachute to shield me from the bright sun – I couldn't find a comfortable position to be in. Under my instructions they managed to remove my parachute harness and my Mae West lifejacket with the Croix de Guerre painted on it.

I was told an ambulance was on its way. I said, well, I couldn't get under the anaesthetic quick enough. I must have had morphine. When the ambulance came they arrived in such a hurry that they knocked the gatepost down. By that time I was in the Brigadier's living room on the sofa, offered brandy and all I wanted was water. I remembered no more until I woke up in a hospital bed after a cleaning-up operation. I was covered from head to foot with a dye called Kelly's Blue. My arms were soaked for hours at a time in a saline solution to soften up the bandages. My wife, she spent almost all her time by my side, but I was pretty low and miserable.

After some weeks Archie McIndoe called in to see me and asked if I'd like a transfer to Queen Victoria Cottage Hospital. I placed myself in his hands and I was transferred and admitted to the Kindersley Ward under the care of Sister Hall. After a day or two I was moved out on to the balcony and joined by other charred pilots, Richard Hillary, Tony Tollemache, Geoff Page, Ian McPhail, Geoff Noble, Roy Lane and Smith Barry. We soon took over the ward, which had been geriatric.

Archie fitted me out with new nose and eyebrows, new eyelids, upper and lower, during which time I had plaster casts over my eyes and wandered about the ward on dead reckoning, reinforced by directions from all sides. I had Tiersch and pinch grafts and during the course of the operations it was also discovered that I had some cannon shell fragments in my right shoulder, which until then, when extracted, had not wanted to heal up. Archie's new saline bath treatment helped to heal the third degree burns on my arms and legs and by Christmas 1940 I was allowed out, after much pleading to go home on leave. I must have been in and out of Queen Victoria Cottage Hospital for six months between ops, but I was fortunate compared to many.

Archie came to see me before the ops and showed me photographs of myself before the burns and said, "How would you like it?"

I replied, "That's all right, but I might have the nose a bit bigger."

Archie would do his rounds of the wards accompanied by his team and as soon as he entered the ward it was rather like a visit by Royalty. The general tone went up straight away accompanied by smiles and laughter; indeed it was as good as a tonic.

The Guinea Pig Club was started almost as a joke when one of the patients was heard to observe that we were being treated like guinea pigs to improve Archie's technique. The reply came back smartly, "Good name for a club, old boy." This was the start of the club and Archie was the obvious choice for Chief Guinea Pig.'

The perspective of the air-gunner in fighter squadron aircraft in the battle is conveyed by James Walker, who joined the RNZAF and was seconded to the RAF. He arrived in Britain in May 1940 where he qualified as an air-gunner with the rank of Sergeant:

'I was posted to City of London Auxiliary Squadron 600, which was stationed at Manston. I arrived there in the middle of an air raid and I witnessed combat between a Spitfire and a Messerschmitt 109, which the Spitfire got the better of, and the Messerschmitt 109 crashed in front of our eyes as we were driving along to the Station, so that was our baptism of fire, as it were. Arriving at 600 Squadron I was met and introduced and I was the only New Zealander there, which was quite a novelty to them, and I was treated rather well and everybody was very friendly. I had my first flight in a Bristol Blenheim, a training flight, and I think the second day or the third day there we really experienced the might of the German Air Force. We were having lunch in the Sergeants' Mess when the bombing raid took place, which was so unexpected; we had no warning whatsoever, and I remember a concerted dive under the tables. The peacetime Warrant

James Ian Bradley Walker

Officers, who at that time had rather looked down on us as jumped-up sergeants without any experience, they were all levelled to the same grade under these tables and it was quite amusing to see these Warrant Officers and us jumped-up sergeants in the same situation.

So, after that more precautions were taken and the air raid sirens became more operational and we did get some warning in the future raids. The first raid they concentrated on the hangars and there was major damage. How many planes were lost I do not remember, but I know that there was quite substantial damage done. The runways were put out of action but were quickly re-instated, the holes being filled up. That was the first raid that Manston had experienced and was the start of many.

We at that time were a night fighter squadron and we were engaged in defensive operations mostly over Southern England, London especially, as

London then became the target, the main target for the German Air Force. The fires were burning, the docks were hit; the Germans needed no navigation, they just had to fly over the Channel and the fires identified their target for them. We had very little success, in fact no success in tracking the German bombers, although we had the earliest form of radar, which was operating quite well, but we found that because the German bombers were faster than we were, we had no chance of making contact because they were dropping their bombs and then hightailing it back to the Continent.

But then we received Beaufighters. Beaufighters had an improved radar on them and some success was achieved. I did not experience any success, although we made contact but we were unable to gain sufficient closeness of range to open fire at any time. From then on the raids increased on our own aerodrome. One air raid shelter was hit with great loss of life, including WAAFs, English girls; quite a number of them were killed and we spent quite a lot of time in the air raid shelters.

Then on one occasion I was dining, lunch I think it was, in the mess and we were called to immediate readiness and we had to travel quite a distance. I had by that time obtained a bicycle and I rode this bicycle across the aerodrome at the time when, I think it was three Messerschmitt 110s were dive-bombing the aerodrome. However, I managed to arrive at the readiness point but the aerodrome had been damaged so much that no one was able to take off. Fortunately one of the Messerschmitt 110s was brought down by ground fire and that was a rather horrific sight because it crashed in the vicinity of one of the hangars and the crew were all killed. That evening, when we were taking off for a patrol, as we were driving out to our aircraft the cranes were removing the 110 and the dead bodies were very apparent, and we at that time found that rather traumatic, seeing these bodies.

We took off on our patrol. We patrolled the London area with the fires so bad in London that it was hard to believe that the city could survive. We maintained these patrols night after night and also enduring the many air raids on Manston aerodrome, which eventually became so bad – the aerodrome was damaged so badly, the hangars, the runways were put out of action – that it was decided to evacuate Manston completely.

We moved then inland to Redhill, Hornchurch and various other stations, which we operated on for the remainder of the Battle of Britain.'

Norman Ramsay joined the RAF Volunteer Reserve and, when war broke out, qualified as a pilot and was posted to his first squadron as a Sergeant Pilot converting directly from Harvards to Spitfires:

'Here I was given a couple of rides in a Master in the back seat, which is about the same angle as the Spit coming in to land because the slower you get the higher the nose gets – you can't see forward, you've got to look out forward and to the side. I got the general idea and I was pushed in a Spitfire and took off. In those days we had to pump the undercarriage up, and the elevator controls were very, very sensitive, so you had to change hands, take your hand off the throttle to hold the joystick in your left hand and pump with your right hand. It was very difficult not to pump and equally weave up and down in the sky with the stick; as you were pumping forward you tended to move the stick forward at the same time. However, I eventually got it all together in the air and when I turned round and went back, it had

Norman Hugh Donald Ramsay

taken me so long I couldn't even see the airfield. So I flew back on a reciprocal and found it and after, I think, I made one approach and overshot and then came in and landed, that was it.

After that they took me for a bit of formation flying and that sort of thing, and then one day they said, "Well, we're thinking of going over to France this afternoon." By this time of course Dunkirk was over and we were isolated. "Pop over there, Ramsay, and go and see what the weather's like over there."

So I took off and I wasn't at all keen on it, I can tell you; it seemed rather a lonely affair going across the Channel on your own and not knowing what to expect when you got to the other side. Anyway, I crossed over to France and nobody shot at me; obviously I couldn't fly very high else I would have been shot at, but I was fairly low and I had a look around and I could see that it was fairly clear so I didn't go as far as I was supposed to go, but I just turned round and came back. Nipped back across. I was very pleased when I crossed over the coast again, being on my own, and of course I couldn't see England, just set a northerly heading and eventually it turned up and I recognised where I was and I got back to the Squadron.

So that afternoon I had my first sweep over France, which I was quite interested to see, you know, the fields and colours and all this sort of stuff. That was my introduction there and then, of course, that stopped very quickly, because then they started to come in over England and we were kept mainly confined to fighting over England and over the Channel. I remember once, when we climbed out over the Channel, it was a hazy day, lovely, it was sort of a marvellous summer that year – a lovely hazy sunny day, and there was a bit of cloud about and we were climbing up over the Channel and I looked behind. We flew in a section of three in those days, and looking back when we were out in battle formation, which is flying out and wider so you're not in close formation, I saw three aircraft and I thought, oh good, they must have scrambled another section.

The next time I looked behind there was a great big Iron Cross on a 109 and I knew instantly that I had one right behind me, so I rammed the stick hard fully forward and hard over to the left, and I just about started to move downwards when there was a huge bang and I'd been hit. The shell went into the engine and glycol streamed back and I was way out over the sea. I thought, my God if I catch fire, which mostly you did; fortunately I didn't, and I got into a huge spiral going down and eventually looked back and could see I wasn't being followed, so straightened up. I couldn't make out which coast I could see in the distance was England, so I thought, well, there's nothing for it, the next coast that comes round I'm going towards that – if it happens to be France, well, I'm a prisoner and that's it. As it so happened it turned out I was east of Dover – I recognised it and it was pure luck. The reason why I had to do this was because the compass was spinning and I couldn't see the sun to get a bearing of which way to fly, north or south. Anyway I was lucky, it was England, and I glided in and I realised I was east of Dover – we'd taken off from Hawkinge near Dover. I glided back and was going to do a wheels-up landing, but then I suddenly realised I had plenty of height and was quite all right, so selected wheels down and blew them down and locked them. I hadn't time to pump them down so used the emergency air bottle and landed and taxied in. I went down after I'd turned and taxied and just swung off the grass field – it was a grass field, had no runways – and climbed out of the aircraft and went to Air Traffic Control to go and report in, which I did. Walked back and then eventually I met the CO, who came up and said, "I've been looking for you, I've been searching for you down in the water. Number Three went down in flames."

That was that, so we went back and had a look at my aeroplane and he said, "Well, we'll have to wait here and I'll get somebody to come and pick you up and bring you back to Biggin Hill," which is where we were stationed then. Eventually a Blenheim came and I went off, had a look at my aircraft on the ground – which you'll probably be interested to know is AB910, which is flying today and is preserved by the Battle of Britain Memorial Society.

So we had interesting times there, scrambles and stuff like that, and the most scrambles – take-offs to go and meet incoming enemy – was seven in one day. Then you get a bit tired after a while, even if you are only 20. You didn't know anything else, there wasn't anything to compare it with, so it was a way of life, it was just accepted and that's all there was to it. There was no sort of bravery or stuff like this or stiff upper lip and that stuff – that was the way it was. It was a learning period and a fairly steep learning curve because if you didn't, you didn't live and that was quite simple. You didn't realise, of course, it was that sort of thing, because as I say, and I can't emphasise enough, if you'd never experienced anything like it before you just carry on. People come and go and that's it. My first Squadron, which was 610, we lost a lot of people in fairly quick time; they were all experienced flyers, they were Royal Auxiliary Air Force characters, having been flying in their spare time for some years.

When, at last, we were pulled out of that scene, and as the casualties came in, I went to join 222 at Hornchurch. I remember my introduction, my first day there. We went down to dispersal – I was a sergeant of course – and a chap said, "Oh, you see that burnt patch over there by the railway line?" This is I think at Romford, which was our forward base, so I looked over in that direction and could see a brown patch, so he said, "That's where Baxter went in – you're his replacement."

That was that. Baxter having been shot up and got back to the airfield, collapsed and obviously crashed coming into land, after being wounded, as I subsequently was told.

Eventually we went up to Coltishall, which is in Norfolk and near Norwich, where we used to do what we called Kipper Patrols, which was guarding the fishing-boats, because the Germans used to send the 88s and 110s over and bomb the fishing-ships or nip in and go and bomb the local ports, and that was our job to guard against such intruders. The next time I was shot up was night flying one night and a chap attacked me when I was coming in to land at night at Coltishall and I saw all this stuff going by. I didn't know I was being attacked, and pretty shortly afterwards I saw the tracer going by me and ducked and weaved and got the aircraft down and swung off the runway, which was grass and lit with grid lamps, and swung through those into the darkness, switched off, had no lights, turned everything off. Climbed out and got away from the aircraft in case I was going to be strafed, but in actual fact it didn't happen; he was driven off by a couple of friends of mine, one was Ray Marlen, and in the end we got back to dispersal. It took us ages walking about there trying to find the aircraft in the darkness again to bring it back to the Squadron.

On those fishing patrols I remember tackling the odd 88 and Heinkel 111 there. I don't know, but I think the Flight Commander and I definitely got an 88 between us because we fired every round we had into it and we weren't getting any return fire, but he was dropping down, in level flight; he just disappeared into the clouds and we never saw him crash, but I would say pretty certainly he didn't get back because I could see all my ammunition exploding and flashing all on the upper wings of the 88. As I say, there was no return fire, so I presume the gunner had been killed. They used to come over at night and try and bomb us. I told you, I got attacked by a chap who used to come round and find us; we used to call him Coltishall Karl because, you know, if anything's a bit on the light-hearted side, when things aren't going too well or you're getting a bit frightened or worried, so you just laugh it off. While I was on that Squadron I got commissioned; Ray Marlen and I were commissioned together. Ray was, unfortunately, killed in the desert later. So I stayed with the same Squadron, which was very unusual after being commissioned.'

Alan Bennison, another New Zealander, joined the RNZAF on the outbreak of war. He left for Great Britain in May 1940 and was duly promoted to the rank of Sergeant Air-gunner:

'We were posted to Aston Down No 5 OTU for further training in the power-operated turrets. We were there for virtually four weeks and we

Alan Bennison

were flying with Czech, Polish, Belgian and English pilots, and some of the foreigners were very aggressive in their method of flying and they used to throw the aircraft around like a single-seater, or try to. They had a pet hobby of flying under the Clifton Suspension Bridge, and the span of the bridge wasn't just quite wide enough to take them down going straight through, they had to side-slip through. This went on, until one day one of the Polish pilots, I think it was, he clipped the mud bank on the other side of the bridge with his wing tip and that was that – that put the end of that episode on flying under the bridge.

Then there was one day when we were quite surprised to hear shooting going on up in the air, and we rushed outside and looked up and here were some Hurricanes that had attacked a couple of German Junkers 88s. Both of the Junkers crashed fairly close to the aerodrome and we tore across the field, and although we weren't supposed to, we snaffled souvenirs and took illegal photographs and we got away with that anyway.

Well then, about the second week in September 1940 the party started to break up as we were posted to various RAF Squadrons. I was the only New Zealander posted to 25 Squadron, which was based at North Weald, near Epping Forest. There was another English lad, he was posted there with me, and we'd only been there about a couple of days when the Jerries came over one morning and an aircraft flew round the aerodrome and laid a smoke circle right round the aerodrome and all the bombers had to do was to drop their bombs inside the ring. We had a great number of bombs there in a matter of an hour and a quarter to an hour and a half, which did quite a lot of damage to the station. Fortunately we didn't lose any aircraft through it. That was our first introduction to active warfare.

The Blenheim carried a crew of three, a pilot, the air-gunner and radar operator. Now, radar was very much in its infancy at this stage – we were only operating on about a Mark 1, Mark 2 set – and the Blenheim wasn't always the best aircraft for the job because it was too slow. It was fast to what we'd been used to in New Zealand, but it still wasn't fast enough for the Germans, and we were employed mainly as night fighters, but during the daytime in the Battle of Britain we had to do area patrols over designated areas, as for aerodrome defence and also out on the coast. The Blenheim was a very cold aircraft because of the opening where the Vickers gun pointed out through the Perspex; it was an open "V" and the wind used to come in through there; it was sucked in, and even with all your flying clothing on you still used to freeze to death almost. A lot of our flying was up round 15-19,000 feet.

There were two other New Zealanders in the squadron at that time, and one was Stewart Lusk, who at that time was a Pilot Officer and had been a law student at Oxford University. About the second or third trip I did at night with Stewart Lusk some idiot vectored us into the London balloon barrage, and then the control came up and told us that we were to turn on to given courses on a countdown and to turn and to be accurate to within a degree. After some two hours they got us out of it and we landed back at base.

We were at North Weald until about the first week of November, I think it was, when we went to Debden. It was in September the Squadron had received its first Beaufighter and, of course, the pilots had to have ground instruction on it and do some daylight flying on their own to familiarise themselves with the aircraft. One or two of us went up and did some daylight flying with the pilots. The Beaufighter was a very much more sophisticated aircraft than the Blenheim; it was faster, it only carried a crew of two, and it had an armament of four 20-millimetre cannons firing through the nose and six machine-guns, four on the starboard and two on the port I think it was – they were Brownings.

We went to Debden in about the first week in November, as I said, and whilst there we took delivery of quite a number of Beaufighters, and the Blenheims were gradually phased out, but Debden wasn't a good aerodrome from the point of view of night flying – there was always a danger of fogs. We took off one night and we'd been away for about two and a half hours and when we came back they switched the floodlight on for us to touch down and it gave us a false ceiling – it showed up a blanket of fog, and we landed on top of a 20-foot fog. When the pilot cut the motors the machine just dropped straight to the ground and damaged the undercarriage. It was rather fortuitous for us because the Flight Commander had done exactly the same thing only a matter of about half an hour before us.

When Coventry was bombed we were about a straight line, about 40 miles from Coventry; we could see the blaze of the city and we were patrolling a given line, and although we patrolled for three hours we never even saw a sign of an aircraft. Now, there was always a danger at night that you could be directed on to a friendly aircraft, and one night we did actually line up on a Stirling and it took a minute or two before the pilot was able to get identification of the aircraft because it was one which was only just coming in to beam at that time and we didn't have a silhouette of him. Fortunately the ground control was able to identify it for us and so we didn't give it a reception.

Getting back to 1941 again, Stewart Lusk had to go off flying for a while, on account of indifferent health, and I had to fly with the CO of the Squadron. One day I hadn't had any leave for about three weeks – hadn't had a night off – and I asked him if I could go into town. I wanted to do some shopping, and that was all right. When I got back, the boys in the mess were quite surprised to see me and I asked them what was the matter.

"Well, we thought you were with the CO."

I said, "Why, what happened to him?"

They said, "He took off and instead of going down the runway, he took off at right angles to it and finished up and hit a tree." So I was lucky to be in the right place at the right time sometimes.

Anyway, he went into hospital and there was another pilot came on to the Squadron and he just looked like an English schoolkid and I flew with him a couple of times and I wasn't very happy. He didn't master the machine. The Beaufighter is like a frisky horse – you either mastered it or it would kill you. I flew with him for about a fortnight, I think it was, and then I went to the Flight Commander and told him that I'd like to be taken off and given another pilot because I didn't feel safe with him. He listened to my story and swapped me over to fly with an Australian pilot. It was only a matter of two or three nights after that, that this English lad was coming into land and he had to come across the Great North Road – it was on the boundary – and he had to come over that at night and he missed it and he was too low and his undercarriage hit the verge on the Great North Road and he crashed into the airfield and he broke his radio operator's legs at the knees and he had to have his legs amputated.'

Pilot Officer Bernard Brown, after his activities over and around Dunkirk, was to transfer to a more modern type of aircraft, but the introduction was stark:

'As they were losing lots of Hurricanes at that time they asked for volunteers to go to Fighter Command, so two or three of us went; we were sent to Hawarden, near Chester, and we learnt how to fly a Spitfire and it was very interesting because I'd never flown anything like that. You didn't have any dual or anything; they said there it is, sort it out. Well, I got it off the ground and got it back again.

After this training at Hawarden I was posted to Biggin Hill, and on arrival I was just in time to see that a number of Junkers 88s had plastered the airfield and there was a big cloud of smoke all over the place. I arrived at the entrance and, as I looked, there were people running round with little red flags, and I enquired what it was all about. They said, "Oh there's unexploded bombs down there." Then, when I got to the Mess, there was an orderly putting letters in the rack and taking a number of them out again; there was a big pile of them on the floor. I was quite surprised about this and I said, "What are you doing?"

"Oh," he said, "I've got a list in front of me," he said. "People's names that are on this list, they won't be collecting their mail; I'm taking it out and putting it on the floor."

I said, "Thank you very much, that's a very good introduction to Biggin Hill." They were losing quite a number of aeroplanes every day.

When not on duty, people would say, oh, let's have a party. On the particular day that I got shot down, it must have been about 2am, the Flight Commander came along to me and he said, "Oh, it's a pity it's your day off tomorrow, but you're on at 6." It didn't mean very much – I'd had quite a lot to drink, but I would be off duty at 9am. Anyway, at 8.55 the hooter goes – oh dear – and I was fast asleep, so it was straight into the aeroplane, everything on and away. At 20 minutes to 10 I was floating down in a parachute over Eastchurch.

We had been jumped from above and scattered, and I saw an aeroplane miles below me and I thought, oh, you can't shoot me, but he did; he must have pulled his nose up and let me have it. That next second there was a big bang in the cockpit and the throttle assembly underneath my left arm and leg just disappeared, gone. There was no control on the aeroplane whatsoever, the thing was roaring its life out and I couldn't steer it, I couldn't do anything with it, so I thought, "Right Brown, this is the time." Someone had said, "This is what you do when you jump out," and funnily enough, I remember the drill exactly. They said, "Take your helmet off, because your helmet is connected to the aeroplane and you'll probably get hung." So I took my helmet off and I remember hanging it on the hook in the cockpit. "Right, now undo the straps," because we always went into action with the hood open because if a bullet went by, one could not get the hood back, so the hood was already back, so I just undid the straps, said, "Right, here we go," and turned over. The next moment I knew I was out; I didn't remember going out, I could feel air coming past my face and then no air. Ah, I'm turning over and over – I'd better find that D ring, which is underneath my left arm, and I just gave it a quick pull and then all went dead quiet and I just sat and I went out at about 16,000 feet.

Everything was quite happy and I saw where I was going to land and I landed in the marsh just out from Eastchurch airfield. Of course, what I didn't know was that I had a hole in my left leg; I hadn't any pain, I hadn't noticed anything. When I landed I really did fold up, thinking I'd got two legs and I only had one, so that was that. Then I looked up and there was one of these Home Guard people coming along and he stopped before he got to me with his .303 rifle and loaded it, so I swore at him and I did everything I could to him, and he approached me with this .303 and I knew it was loaded and he just didn't say a word, just stood about 10 yards off me and kept me covered with his .303. Well, by this time I looked across and I could see the little van arrive from the RAF, people coming, and they came along and all was well and he just walked away.

Then I ended up in the hospital there and that was the end of my flying career as far as the Air Force was concerned because my left leg was there but I couldn't stand on it. There was a hole at the back of the knee and the tendons had gone. After they had fixed me up and I was out of hospital I badgered them to keep on flying and they said, "Well look, you can go into Training Command," so I said, "Yes, I'll go into Training Command," and so they gave me an instructor's course up at Montrose. I could fly a little aeroplane all right, but I had to be very careful, I had to keep the leg absolutely stiff, I couldn't put any pressure on it. I could bend the leg and walk on it, but I couldn't stand on it – a little moment and the knee would give way.'

Also flying Spitfires was Roy McGowan, who had joined the RAF Volunteer Reserve and, with war considered imminent, was undertaking six months' training and was posted to 66 Squadron as a Sergeant Pilot:

'In those early days the Spitfire still had a number of teething problems. The manufacturers, who were both the Supermarine, who built the air frame, and Rolls Royce, who were builders of the Merlin engine, were always with us and sorting out some of these problems. That first Spitfire 1 was very, very different from the later Marks. It had an enormous two-bladed wooden propeller, low revs on take-off and a long, long take-off run on the grass airfields, and a lot of rudder to offset the torsion of the engine and of the propeller. Immediately the aircraft got unstuck you had a big hand pump on the right-hand side at the top bit, which you used to pump up your

Roy Andrew McGowan

undercarriage because your left hand was on the throttle holding that wide open. What you saw, having opened up the throttle, was an aircraft taking off in a series of rises and falls because pumping this hard hydraulic pump meant that you had movements on your stick as well, so the aircraft was going up and down, quite an unusual sight but everybody did it.

We started building up hours with the Spit, a beautiful aeroplane, but in May of that year I was commissioned. In those days one couldn't remain with the same squadron if one moved up from Sergeant Pilot to Pilot Officer, so I was posted to 46 Squadron at Digby in Lincolnshire, where we flew Hurricanes, also, of course, another monoplane fighter. No difficulties in moving out of Spits into Hurricanes. It, too, was a very, very pleasant aeroplane.

I continued with them, and should have returned to civilian life in July, but by then it was very clear that war was a matter of weeks away. We went up to Yorkshire to do our liaison two-week operation with a bomber squadron – Whitley bombers. After one week we were recalled because in late August war was going to start any day, as it were. As soon as we got back to Digby we lived under canvas in Bell tents, alongside our aeroplanes, in what was known as a dispersal point. We started digging slit trenches and really doing 24 hours a day on the job.

We were somewhat relieved to hear on the morning of 3 September that war had been declared. As soon as that announcement had been made we got on to a wartime arrangement of one flight being released, another flight available, another flight at standby, so of course we had more time off immediately after war started than we had before.

Early days in Digby in wartime, our main commitment was convoy patrols. We used to fly out, and the operations room guided us out to a convoy moving either northwards or southwards on the North Sea off Norfolk and Suffolk. We would patrol seawards of them; they usually had an escort of a couple of destroyers or armed ships of some sort. We patrolled for probably an hour, three of us in a loose formation, and then we'd be relieved by another section, as they were called, and we'd go back and refuel and wait for our next turn. We were told by the Navy we mustn't come within, I think it was, 1,000 metres otherwise they would open fire and, yes indeed, they did from time to time. During clear air we didn't see any hostile aircraft. In poorer weather, with a lot of comparatively low cloud, yes, you would see that there was something going on, because the Navy opened up; we might get a sight of a hostile aircraft, but it would immediately disappear into cloud.'

Although Roy McGowan doesn't mention it in his tape, the Squadron was sent to Norway in late May 1940 and lost many of its men and planes when, during the evacuation shortly afterwards, the aircraft carrier HMS Glorious was sunk.

'Anyhow, later – I guess by mid-June – things started hotting up. We were very much outnumbered in those days. The Operations Room controller would scramble us and climb us to 15,000 feet or something like that. Initially in sections of three, and then a flight of six aircraft and eventually, because of the numbers of enemy aircraft, whole squadrons and later the whole wing. It took time to form up but of course you had to get some numerical strength.

I made many interceptions; I fired my guns on pretty well every time we took off. I didn't get any confirmed victories, but we were very involved. We would see aircraft smoking, we would see pieces coming off. The pattern was that we in the Hurricanes would attack the bombers whilst the Spitfires, with their ability to climb faster and higher, they would go higher and get involved with the escorting Luftwaffe fighters.

We were still operating from Digby in Lincolnshire and the Air OC of 12 Group, Leigh-Mallory, Air Vice-Marshal Leigh-Mallory, conceived this "big wing" theory. The problem was getting it formed up in some kind of order before we went south to make an engagement. It wasn't anything like as manoeuvrable as a smaller operation of 12 aircraft. We would go down and most days often go down to an 11 Group airfield in the immediate London area, land there and refuel, and do operations from there, and then we'd return to Digby in Lincolnshire.

However, in September some time we were posted to a little airfield called Stapleford Tawney, which was a satellite of North Weald, which was one of the well-known Sector Fighter Stations. Stapleford Tawney had this sloping grass airfield and I recall Hillman Airways, a pre-war small Civil Airline, they used to operate London-Paris out of Stapleford. With our Hurricanes it was a little bit of a problem; irrespective of wind direction you certainly couldn't land downhill, so often you had to make cross-wind landings and monoplane fighters weren't too happy with a strong cross-wind landing. However, we coped.

On one occasion, I guess it was the Sunday before 15 September, which was also a Sunday, I got shot up quite badly. I was losing glycol, the engine temperature was going up pretty rapidly, we were down somewhere in the Kent area, I had to get down quickly before the engine packed up, and I landed at Biggin Hill. Looking down at Biggin I saw all kinds of bomb holes; I selected a line between bomb holes, landed safely and I quickly taxied in, because by then the glycol was well over the permitted temperature, and switched off. Nobody came out to meet me, no attendants whatsoever near the tarmac. However, an airman ran out and said, "Quick, get down, we're being attacked!" So we got into a slit trench and, sure enough, Biggin on that day, Sunday, was being very, very heavily bombed. Their transport, I recall, their Transport Section, had a direct hit; quite a number of ground crews and airmen and WAAFs were injured and killed.

I then found I had an unserviceable aeroplane and I had no way of getting a ride by a vehicle, by a transport vehicle or anything else, and certainly not by an aeroplane, to get back to my own station, Stapleford Tawney, north of London. I was south of London. The end result was I hitch-hiked; I hitch-hiked up to the southern end of London, I took a tube across London. I called my own unit from the most northerly point and they came and picked me up. That was the way of life in those days. I guess I should mention that in this journey back to Stapleford I carried my own parachute on my back, not open of course, and so was ready to get into the air again.

Moving along, that following week we were very hard worked; we were doing three or sometimes four patrols a day or flights a day, up to two hours in length, often making an interception and having an engagement.

For me, 15 September was a day I certainly will never forget. I think I was on my third flight of that day. Around midday we joined up with another squadron, probably two squadrons, of 24 aircraft climbing up into an enormous raid which was coming over. We made an interception. The pattern was with these that when you came across these bombers with the Hurricanes you could get in perhaps two good attacks, by which time the bomber formation would break up, your own comrades would break up and you'd find yourself in a sky full of single-engined aircraft of both nationalities, German and British, and you'd have to try and make some re-forming if you had any ammunition left. During that act, on that day, I suddenly was shot at and in no time my aeroplane was on fire, burning merrily, and I got out very smartly. I recall that I was probably about 12,000 feet and I had in mind, right, I won't open my chute immediately – there was some scattered cloud – I'll wait until I get just about to the bottom of the cloud layer, which might be 5-6,000 feet, so I wouldn't be a target, I wouldn't be shot at, and this is what I did.

I opened my parachute around 5-6,000 feet. I looked around at myself – my trouser legs were in tatters from having been burned, I didn't have shoes any longer. Contrary to all advice – like most other pilots, because we were searching and you can't search with a pair of goggles on – I had not had my goggles over my eyes. I realised I had some burning in my face; the oxygen mask, of course, is round your nose, and as soon as the aircraft caught fire that oxygen burned up, so I was quite damaged with burns and so on. I saw I was coming down to land in the sea. I landed in the sea perhaps a mile, perhaps a little less, from the mouth, the southern mouth, of the Thames estuary, and I had a Mae West on and I just sat in the water and saw a small craft coming towards me, a power craft, and they pulled me aboard and they saw I wasn't in good shape. I, too, saw I wasn't in good shape. They got me ashore, they put me into a vehicle and took me to a First Aid Post in the Isle of Sheppey, north of Rochester, and called Rochester Hospital. They said, well, do nothing with this man, bring him here immediately. So in a private car I was taken to Rochester Hospital.

In Rochester Hospital I was immediately put in the theatre and given a full anaesthetic and had my burns worked on. The following day I learned that – I didn't ever see him – but I learned that a Luftwaffe pilot was also a customer at Rochester Hospital. I was extremely well looked after at Rochester Hospital. I was treated with something called gentian violet, which was a dark dye, and that was put all over my face and my hands and my legs. I had a few shrapnel injuries upon my legs.

Eventually, after several weeks, I guess, a civilian surgeon was going around South East England looking at RAF casualties and evaluating them. He decided that I should go up to RAF Halton, which was the hospital near Aylesbury. I and two or three other fellows were transported up there by ambulance. I recall we drove through the centre of London, saw all the damage that was being regularly inflicted, stopped at a local pub and had a glass of beer brought out to us in the ambulance and off we went again to Aylesbury and into the Halton Hospital.

From there, the New Zealand burns specialist, Archie McIndoe, decided that I should go to his hospital in East Grinstead for skin grafts. So I guess it was in November 1940 I went down to East Grinstead where a whole mass of mainly RAF people suffering burns, some away back to the early days of the war in France, were all being attended by Archie, as we all called him, and he did wonderful work. He recognised not only the necessity for surgical work, but also rehabilitation. He got on to all the families in the East Grinstead area – the solicitor belt as it was called – and said to them, look, you've got to make these fellows, who are badly disfigured, more conscious of everyday life and invite them to your homes, and so on. So he had great success in that aspect of his work as well.

I only had grafts on eyes – top and bottom eyelids were replaced. The pattern was, you had an op and then you went off from there to a Convalescent Hospital down in Torquay, the Palace Hotel, which had been taken over. Then you'd come back for your next op, so it was a long and slow business, but we were well looked after.

After several medical boards I was cleared for home service only and with limited non-operational flying. I was posted as a Flight Lieutenant to the post of Air-ground Control Officer running the watch office, now known as "flying operations", and this was at Martlesham Heath. They were interesting times. I had control of a dummy town, which was supposed to be Ipswich, and lights came on at night and made it look for all the world like an operating city, and it attracted some German bombs. Also a dummy airfield – we would switch on the flare path at night and aircraft movements showing on the ground, all disguised of course and artificial, but that too attracted bombs from time to time.'

A final vignette of the 1940 air war over Britain comes from Alan Burdekin, who had joined the RAF Volunteer Reserve in March 1939 as a wireless operator/air-gunner:

'We did get some flying; apart from the training in the town centre, we had camera-gun exercises flying. We were flying Fairey Battles and Audax mainly, open cockpits of course, strings and wires, biplanes, all very little different from the aircraft they finished up the Great War with. A monkey wire to stop you falling out and your scarf flying in the breeze, all real Biggles stuff, and for a young man interested in flying all very exciting. So then, of course, we were into the "Phoney War". We did war training, we did hangar guard, duties at the aerodrome and that sort of thing. I think it was 1 October 1939 I was posted away to join 266 Squadron at Sutton Bridge.

They had Fairey Battles, the odd one or two, that was all. Got no flying there until I went off to Penrhos in Wales for a gunnery course, where we were flying again almost last-war aircraft, the Westland Wallace for instance, which was a fair sort of antique, even then. However, I passed my Gunnery Course and back to Sutton Bridge, where the Squadron had then re-equipped with Spitfires, so there wasn't a job for me, and I transferred to 264. We went to Martlesham Heath and trained with our new Defiants, which had a good turret, a four-gun Boulton Paul turret – it really was magnificent.

Then I was detached on to a Parachute and Cable outfit; there was just one pilot, myself, a sergeant fitter and a couple of erks [ground crew]. The idea of this Parachute and Cable was that we would lower the bomb-bay of our Handley-Page Harrow, again strings and wires, biplane and canvas, and, when the enemy approached, we would steam across their bows but higher up, if we could get that far, and drop this load of 1,000 feet of piano wire with a parachute on one end and a bomb on the other. The enemy would obligingly fly into this, which would either wrap round the prop or soar back over the wing with the resistance of the parachute and either wreck the engine or blow the wing off. Well, it was a nice idea!

Then, on 10 May 1940 the Squadron was told to be at Knutsford that same afternoon and ready to go into battle, so I went across the road and

Alan George Burdekin

saw my Flight Commander and said, "What do I do, sir?" and he said, "Well, you're working on this experimental job – you'd better stay there. I'll speak to the CO."

Well, they went in a rush to Knutsford, went into battle that same afternoon, and the Flight Commander was shot down so he never did speak to the CO and it wasn't until the thick of that particular battle was over that somebody thought to ask where I was, and I was sent for to join them at Knutsford and found a very depleted lot of aircrew. There were 23 when they left Martlesham and there were seven when I walked into the crew room.

So then they decided virtually to disband the Squadron; they'd had a fair sort of beating because the Germans, once they found out that we couldn't fire downwards, they used to come up from underneath and that was it because the aircraft was underpowered. So I then did a conversion course on to Blenheims and went to join 600 City of London Squadron at Manston, and this was Battle of Britain time of course. Looking back on it, it was a very, very interesting time. We were night fighting. The Blenheims were undermanned as far as armour goes, of course. We didn't have a great deal of fire power. The aircraft was too slow and we chased around London – we were supposed to be defending London – we chased around being vectored by all the ground control, and they would say, "There's enemy aircraft ahead of you," and so forth. We never did catch one – at least, I never did – and our biggest danger was the anti-aircraft; they'd open up a quarter of a mile behind the enemy and under our nose, which wasn't a pleasant feeling. Then they'd cone you with the searchlights and that's an awful feeling when you're coned – you feel just like, well, as I imagine a moth on the end of a pin feels, you really feel pegged there.

I think our Squadron did get the odd one, but we did lose quite a number. They seemed to hang around – the enemy that is – they'd hang around and when we scrambled, somebody would come down and before you were really airborne you'd be shot down. I know one finished up in Dover Harbour or finished up round Ramsgate. It was a pity because we were, well, we were outdated, that's the basic thing I suppose, and the Germans weren't above using their brains. I was going to the Mess one night, going down the main road towards the Sergeants' Mess, and I heard these aircraft on the circuit and just looked up and saw them, six aircraft with their wheels down, and said, oh, she's right, as everybody else did, and suddenly up with their wheels and opened up with everything they'd got, and they were 109s. The next thing there was a mixed cannon shell and machine-gun fire coming right up the road behind me and I didn't wait very long. Barney and I dived behind the nearest hut, which, of course, were concrete block at Manston, and all in 10 minutes they dropped 110 bombs, apart from shooting everything up. There must have been others there because 109s didn't carry bombs, but they gave us a fair plastering and finally we had to leave Manston – it was wrecked.'

CHAPTER 3

The war at sea –
North Sea,
Channel and Arctic

*T*he Blitzkrieg in the Low Countries and France was preceded by dire
events in Denmark, Norway and the North Sea. The British Home
Fleet had sailed from Scapa Flow on 7 April 1940 to cover mine-laying
operations off Narvik in Norway and in response to the reported sailing of
German naval units from their bases. The Allies were preparing to land
troops in Norway but Hitler got in first, and, on 9 April, occupied the major
ports in Norway as far north as Narvik and the whole of Denmark. Then,
in the North Sea, the first naval battle involving capital ships in the Second
World War took place.

John Musters was a Sub Lieutenant RN when he was appointed to HMS
Renown as Captain's Secretary:

'The *Renown* was a battlecruiser of considerable antiquity; she was
finished in 1916, the sister ship of the *Repulse*. In 1939, when I joined her,
she was just finishing a three-year reconstruction, a total modernisation,
new engines and boilers, new superstructure, new gunnery control, new
armoured main deck. In fact, they really hollowed out the ship and started
again. We carried out sea trials in July 1939. There was a bit of urgency
about completing the ship then, because it looked as though we were going
to have a war fairly soon, and we finally commissioned for service in the
end of August. We arrived at Scapa Flow on 4 September and then started
working up in basic gunnery.

On 6 April 1940 *Renown* was sent out with her own destroyers and also
as the cover of a force of four other destroyers fitted for mine-laying. The
plan was to go and lay mines in Vestfjorden in Northern Norway, as a

John Vivian Auchmuty Musters

rather conservative measure, to interrupt the German iron-ore traffic which brought the iron-ore down from Narvik and which had been brought across from Sweden. This traffic would come down the west coast of Norway, down to Germany using neutral waters for this traffic, which was just legitimate, if somewhat borderline. Anyway, this operation had been overtaken, although we did not know it at the time, by the German plan to just go into Norway and take it over, and it practically coincided.

On 8 April our destroyers went into Vestfjorden, laid their mines, while we and our destroyer screen hovered off somewhere near the Lofoten Islands outside. Meanwhile the German invasion of Norway was going full swing and the ten big German destroyers, which took the German troops into Narvik at the head of Vestfjorden, passed our mine-laying destroyers, which had laid their mines and were on the way out. Neither side saw the other because of a snowstorm. There'd have been a considerable slaughter if they had sighted each other, and we would undoubtedly have come off worst.

Before that, on our way north, one of our destroyers, *Glowworm*, had lost a man overboard and she turned back with the permission of our Admiral, Admiral Whitworth in *Renown*, in order to try to find him. I don't think they had a hope of finding him alive in that very cold and very rough sea, but they did what they could and searched for him, and then they turned north again to rejoin *Renown*'s group, from which they were, by now, probably a couple of hundred miles astern. *Glowworm* fell in, at that point, with two German destroyers which were part of the German invasion group, which included the heavy cruiser *Hipper*, waiting to go into Trondheim, when the moment arrived for all the Germans to go into Norway at different places at the same time. *Glowworm* fought a gun battle with the German destroyers, which fell back on *Hipper*. *Glowworm* was overwhelmed and sunk by *Hipper*, after having rammed her and done a bit of damage. It didn't stop *Hipper* going into Trondheim and landing her 1,700-odd troops there.

Well, meanwhile we were up north with our own five screening destroyers plus the mine-laying destroyers, which had rejoined us. The weather now was quite appalling, a north-westerly gale and a very heavy sea indeed. Very early in the morning of 9 April we were patrolling somewhere south-west of the Lofoten Islands and news was coming through of German activities all the way up the Norwegian coast, and we'd been at action stations since the previous afternoon, which took us to about half past three in the morning of the 9th. By that time one of our anti-torpedo bulges on the port side for'ard had been damaged by very heavy weather, having quite an effect on our potential for full speed.

My job in the gunnery control team was range-spotting officer, which meant making the corrections to range up or down. I was stationed in the Gunnery Transmitting Station, a sort of calculation station. We had six 15-inch guns in three pairs, two pairs for'ard and one pair aft and, since the ship had been reconstructed, we had a gun range of about 32,000 yards, which was quite good for an old ship. The loading interval of a 15-inch gun is about 40 seconds, it takes anything up to 60 seconds for the shells to arrive at the other end. This meant a long pause before any alteration to bearing and range, based on observation of the splash made by the preceding salvo, could be made, and, in the meantime, the enemy could have altered course or speed. So what we did was fire one gun in each turret simultaneously, as the "A" salvo, and then, 10 seconds later, having made some arbitrary corrections to line or range, we'd fire the other three, which would be termed the "B" salvo. That gave you a better idea of how you were getting on than if you just had one great clump of shells landing at longer intervals.

Well anyway, we are now in the very early morning on 9 April somewhere south-west of the Lofoten Islands, steaming rather slowly north-east, keeping our speed down because the destroyers were astern and they couldn't really go very fast in that sort of sea. At about 3.50 in the morning, people on *Renown*'s bridge sighted one and then two warships to the eastward, quite a long way away in a clear patch between snow squalls. The eastern horizon was just then beginning to get light as dawn was breaking. At first it was thought that it might have been *Repulse*, our fellow battlecruiser on this operation, plus somebody else with her. We did not know quite where *Repulse* was, but we did know that she was at sea somewhere off the Norwegian coast. Anyway, we increased speed and turned to a parallel course while we tried to identify these vessels, and then a little later we made a positive identification that the leading ship was the German fast battlecruiser *Scharnhorst*, and we thought that the ship next astern, the second ship, was probably a 'Hipper' Class cruiser. All the German naval ships looked extraordinarily alike. Accordingly, we turned on to a parallel course, which was about north, and we were all at action stations already. What we did then was to bring the main armament to the ready, checking receivers, testing firing circuits, usual drill before a shoot, and then the order came through to load the main armament with 15-inch armour-piercing shells on full charges.

My memory of time is a little uncertain, but some 20 minutes after we sighted the ships we decided to engage. The Captain, Captain Simeon, at this point turned *Renown* slightly away from the enemy, in order to bring their return fire further aft on a relative bearing, because we only had 6 inches of side armour and that wouldn't stop an 11-inch armour-piercing shell, certainly not a German one. I should say here that we could not place the enemy's range by our optical range-finders because they were so full of salt water from heavy spray, so nothing could be seen through them. We had no radar. So the Gunnery Officer, who was up in the main director, estimated the range at 18,000 yards, which was not a bad guess at all; in fact, it was only 1,000 yards out. One of our first two salvos was reported spotted short and that was passed down to me and I then took over the range spotting. So for third and fourth salvos, the next pair, I ordered an up 400 ladder, up 400 for the first salvo, our number three, and then up another 400 for the next one, and then we waited for those to arrive. In retrospect, it is quite clear that, on such scanty information about the enemy's range, 400-yard steps was a bit too conservative. It would have been prudent to have gone up in two steps of 800. Well, we waited for those second pair of the up ladder to fall, and they were both short and this had me slightly worried. Anyway, I ordered another up 400 ladder, hoping to hell that this would cross the target and do the trick, because it is necessary to cross the target, to bracket the target, and the smaller the bracket the better, and then you can start filling in the gap. Well, at this point we got our first salvo away, which was number five of the shoot, and I was waiting to see the gunnery lamps come on for the second salvo, and that never happened for quite a while. Apparently they had quite some trouble in the turrets; the violent motion of the ship due to the heavy seas resulted in water coming down the spouts of the for'ard turrets. So I waited and then the first salvo fell, and to my relief it fell over, so then I was able to take off the last up 400 correction and come down 600 in order to push the middle of the bracket we had now achieved, so we got that one away and we waited for that one to arrive, and that, to everyone's astonishment, hit the leading ship, which happened to be the *Gneisenau*, not the *Scharnhorst*, and that was Admiral Lutjen's flagship. That was seen to produce an orange glow in her for'ard superstructure, which was a hit straight in their sort of tower mast which those ships had, just abaft the bridge. On top of that was their Main Armament Control Tower Director.

After that *Gneisenau*'s shooting was considered to have gone a bit ragged and uneven and erratic. Then we fired about half a dozen more salvos and we got two more hits on *Gneisenau*. One hit its for'ard turret and put that out of action, another hit arrived somewhere amidships – people up top saw a flash and clouds of smoke.

After this *Gneisenau* turned away to the north-eastward and her next astern, which we thought was *Hipper*, actually *Scharnhorst*, which was the other half of that dangerous pair, came across her stern and we shifted fire on to *Scharnhorst*. We never got a chance to sort of settle down for a shoot at her before she turned away, following *Gneisenau* away to the north-north-east. They went off at very high speed. We turned to follow and from time to time they were obscured by more snow squalls, but occasionally we had a good sight of them. We were only able to fire our two for'ard turrets at this stage, because we were more or less end on to the enemy and two gun salvos don't get you very far if you don't get a hit. Gradually they drew away and, after about 20 minutes of pursuit, obviously we weren't going to catch up with these people. Because of the damage due to bad weather, we could only make 26 knots and, for firing, we had to come down to about 23, because when we went into that sea an awful lot of water came down the spouts of the 15-inch guns, making loading quite difficult. So after about 20 minutes of ineffectual shooting by us and plenty of ineffective shooting by them, they finally disappeared into a snow squall. So after that we finally gave up the pursuit, came back, found our destroyers and in due course made our way back to Scapa.

We discovered afterwards that we'd been hit a couple of times; one shot went through the foremast and broke all the radio aerials, stopping our enemy reports in the middle. The Admiralty were reading them with a great deal of interest, saw our signals break off and feared the worst. We also got another one through the hull aft; it came in abaft of the main armoured belt and it came in under the quarter-deck, through the midshipmen's berth and then went down through the unarmoured bit of the main deck there, through a baggage store at F deck and out through the other side, below the water line, without exploding. If it had burst inside the ship it would have done considerably more damage. As it was, we didn't discover that until after the action, when the damage control parties opened up the watertight doors to see what was what, and when they got down there they were met with a wall of water, so they shut it fairly quickly. That was the end of the Norwegian campaign as far as we were concerned.'

After this the German battlecruisers Scharnhorst *and* Gneisenau *took refuge in Brest in March 1941, having spent two months in the Atlantic where they had destroyed over 80,000 tons of Allied shipping. They had been blockaded there for nearly a year when Hitler decided to bring them, together with the cruiser* Prinz Eugen, *back to Germany through the English Channel. On the night of 11 February 1942 they slipped out of Brest and, because of a series of circumstances unfortunate for the British, succeeded in reaching their bases in Germany by the morning of the 13th. However, both battlecruisers had been damaged by mines, which put the* Scharnhorst *out of action for six months and the* Gneisenau *for the remainder of the war. Their Channel dash had been threatened, but not seriously impeded from the air.*

Pilot Officer John Checketts, RNZAF, who went to Britain in September 1941 and was posted to a Hurricane Training Unit at Sutton Bridge, has memories of the brave but largely futile attacks made from the air:

'Halfway through the course we were hastened to finish the training and we did so in a matter of three weeks. We were posted at the completion of the training to various squadrons throughout England. My posting was to Royal Air Force Squadron 485, which was manned by New Zealanders operating from Kenley, south of London.

An interesting battle during this first period on operations was the escape in February 1942 of the German ships *Scharnhorst*, *Gneisenau* and *Prinz Eugen* from Brest through the English Channel to their home ports in Germany. The weather was extremely bad with snow, hail, rain, wind and fog. The Germans successfully evaded detection until they were seen by

John Milne Checketts

Group Captain Victor Beamish. They escaped detection until that time by virtue of a series of misadventures by the British intercepting people. The submarine which was to keep a guard on the Port of Brest had to go out to recharge its batteries in the evening, and the radar stations were successfully jammed by the Germans until quite late on the morning of the operation. Victor Beamish obeyed the rules and did not speak to warn the British organisations, but flew home and landed first, which let the Germans get up almost to Boulogne before any attempt was made to do anything about it.

The British coastal guns had so far fired on the vessels without success, and I cannot remember the exact times, but it was round midday. The cloud base was 300 feet, the Navy sent up six Swordfish armed with torpedoes out to attack these vessels, and they were all shot down by the Germans without success. Their leader, Lieutenant Commander Eugene Esmonde, was posthumously awarded the Victoria Cross.

We were sent out into the area where these vessels were and made contact with them off Ostend, but we could do very little against them. We destroyed some German aircraft and attacked E-boats – successfully, I might say – and were applauded for our action. However, it was of little consequence as far as the vessels themselves were concerned. I was impressed with their size and their speed; they were immense ships and the British were caught wrong-footed and had little that they could put against the ships. There were mess-ups with torpedoes and torpedo-carrying aircraft, and bomber aircraft had little chance to bomb from such low level. The only success against them were actions by aircraft which had laid mines ahead of the ships. *Scharnhorst* was mined and lay idle for nearly half an hour, but was not intercepted. The British destroyers were severely handled by the Germans and the torpedo-bombers were not effective; it was a convincing victory for the German Navy and a sad day for Britain.'

Following upon the German offensive against the Soviet Union in June 1941, the Arctic became the main route for the despatch of supplies to Russia, Britain's new ally. The first convoy sailed in September 1941. By May 1942, with almost perpetual daylight and the rapid build-up of German naval and air strength in northern Norway, the convoy route had become very hazardous indeed. Not least was the risk from major units of the German Navy, including the battleship Tirpitz, *attacking the convoys at a time when British capital ships could not be exposed to the overwhelming German air superiority in the region.*

Lieutenant Commander Roger Hill, RN, in command of the 'Hunt' Class destroyer HMS *Ledbury*, was involved in some of the Russian convoys:

'Our first Russian convoy was PQ 15, which sailed from Iceland on 24 April 1942, and our job on this was to screen the tanker – I can't remember the name – and we went and lay in a position called "Y", so if there was a Fleet action and the destroyers needed fuel they would come there and fuel from the tanker, or the ones going to Russia would come and the ones coming back from Russia also. So we made a rectangle which was labelled "AUNTY", and we just steamed round this to keep the tanker moving all the time, as it would be very easy for the Germans just to send a U-boat to

Roger Hill, Commanding Officer of HMS Ledbury, *on his bridge.*

pick her off. The whole Home Fleet came by – the battleships, aircraft carriers, cruisers and destroyers – a most tremendous sight. We had a system of identification where you had to signal certain letters. The battleship *Duke of York* signalled the wrong letter and later on in Scapa I was sent for by the Commander-in-Chief. The Captain of this huge ship, which seemed absolutely colossal to me, with its great big guns and enormous quarter-deck, said, "Oh we had a bit of a mix-up over the recognition, didn't we?"

I said, "That's all right, sir, I knew you would know I wasn't going to open fire," and I thought he was going to choke, going to have apoplexy.

Then we went on another one, PQ 16, and then we came to 17, when for the first time we were in the close escort of the convoy. By this time (we know now) the enemy main code had been broken and the Admiralty would intercept the German signal when they ordered the *Tirpitz* to sail, if she was going to attack the convoy. She was lying in the fjords in the north of Norway and we never got this signal. However, Admiral Dudley Pound, who was the Head of the Navy, he got this fixed idea that the *Tirpitz* was coming out to attack us.

We had a mother and a father of an air attack; about 50 or 60 torpedo-bombers came scarcely over the top of the sea right over the top of the convoy. We shot one down, which was great, and I thought that they had made a brave attack, lots of ships firing at them, so I picked up the chaps we had shot down, despite the pom-pom's crew saying, "Come on, sir, one short burst, one short burst."

I said, "You can't do that – you'd be had up for war crimes."

Anyway, we picked them up and they were quite nice chaps and after this I know we were all very cheerful – only one ship had been torpedoed – and suddenly the Yeoman of Signals said to me, "My God, sir, the signalman in the Commodore's ship has made a balls."

I said, "Why?"

He said, "They've got the signal up to scatter!"

So I said, "Oh Christ," and it wasn't the signalman. They had got the signal from the Admiralty: "You are about to be attacked by a vastly superior surface force – your duty is to avoid destruction and pick up survivors." I've never known the Navy to have had such a bloody awful signal as that, and then this order to scatter was made.

We all formed up behind the *Kepple* with Captain [D.] Jackie Broom ready to do a torpedo attack. I hadn't any torpedoes, so my idea was to ram something, and everybody was just looking for the *Tirpitz* to come over the horizon, which was the effect of the Admiralty signal. Then nothing happened and all the merchant ships went off in different directions, and they said, "Cruisers are to retire at high speed to the west." We had two English cruisers and two American cruisers, the *London*, *Norfolk*, *Wichita* and *Tuscaloosa*, and the Admiral, Admiral Hamilton, signalled us by lamp to join him and form a screen. We asked whether we could go back and we were refused, and then we went into thick fog and he made to me [signalled]

"Try to keep up but don't rupture yourself." I remember because we only went 23 knots or 26 knots, whichever it was, which was the speed they were going, and I thought should I just slow down quietly and go back, but then, you see, from the moment you join the Navy you are taught obedience and it is very, very difficult to disobey. I did after that, but not then. And so we went on, and we came up out of the fog and eventually got back to Scapa.

There were 23 ships sunk in that PQ 17, 190 seamen killed, 400-500 aircraft were lost, about 300 tanks and 100,000 tons of war material. That's what resulted from that Admiralty signal. It was really terrible – even now I have never got over it, because for the Navy to leave the Merchant Navy like that was simply terrible. And the *Tirpitz* was not within 300 or 400 miles of the convoy. She came out eventually, but not that day, the next day I think, or the following day. She was sighted by a submarine which made a signal, the Germans intercepted that signal and called her straight back to harbour. All these poor merchant ships – one merchant ship signalled, "I can see seven submarines approaching me on the surface," and there was continual air attack. It was simply awful. Anyway, that was PQ 17.'

The 'County' Class cruiser HMS *Norfolk* took part in many of these convoys. Arthur Denby, a Signalman on board that ship, recalls that:

'The first convoy I was in, there were four cruisers, there was *Norfolk*, *Cumberland*, *London* and I can't remember the next one – it might have been *Suffolk*. We steamed around the convoy firing off everything that we could find at all these aircraft, and we got quite a few of them, but they made most of the attacks on the merchant ships. There was an oil tanker with a sort of catapult from which they fired off this Hurricane, and that certainly settled a few of the Germans, but the Hurricane could only land in the sea and the pilot had to be picked up quickly because you didn't get very long to live in that kind of water there.

PQ 17, that was a real fiasco if ever there was. I don't know where they got the information from, but they said there was either *Tirpitz* or one of these big ships coming out and we left all the convoy, the whole lot – the escorts and the cruisers and everything left at speed and the U-boats and the aircraft had a field day with all the merchant ships.'

Also in the *Norfolk* was Midshipman Richard Begg. It was his first ship and events were noted in his journal at the time:

'Then we went on my first operation and it was the well-known and rather infamous Russian convoy labelled PQ 17. We went up to Iceland with three

Arthur Godfrey Denby

other 8-inch cruisers. They were HMS *London*, which was Admiral Hamilton's flagship, ourselves and the American cruisers *Tuscaloosa* and *Wichita*. We had three destroyers as an anti-submarine screen. We fuelled at Seydisfiord in Iceland and next day went to sea as the cruiser-covering force to provide protection to the convoy against enemy surface ships. We didn't travel with the convoy, we sort of hovered on the edges. At times we could see the convoy and at other times we were a bit too far away to see it.

About the second or third day out we were joined by a German reconnaissance plane, a Blohm und Voss, which kept us company for most of the time. They would come out and they would circle round the Squadron, and then about four hours later their relief would come out from

Richard Campbell Begg on the quarter-deck of HMS Norfolk *at sea.*

Norway and so they kept up their reconnaissance on us and the Germans knew exactly where we were all the time, and this applied to the convoy as well because, in those days, we didn't have aircraft carriers accompanying the convoy and so we had no air cover. Of course, the Germans were very close in Norway, not far away. We couldn't do much about these planes except to try and lodge the odd 8-inch shell in their vicinity on occasions, and there was the occasional exchange of signals; one, for which I cannot now vouch, was to the effect, "Squadron to Blohm und Voss – you are making us giddy, could you please fly in the opposite direction?" which brought an acknowledgement from the plane which obligingly turned and went in the opposite direction!

In the meantime, the German bombing and torpedo attacks had been going on against the convoy and, on about the fourth day, we were fairly close up to the convoy and we could see an air attack in progress; one plane was brought down and three ships hit, one exploded, an ammunition ship. Then, late in the afternoon, there was a hive of activity about the ship and the rumour went out that *Tirpitz*, the German battleship, had been reported just over the horizon and we were about to engage her and other ships of the German Fleet. Flags were flying from the masthead as we

Left and above HMS Norfolk *refuelling destroyers on convoy PQ 17. (Begg)*

turned away at high speed, forming single line ahead whilst the destroyers from the convoy formed up in line on our starboard quarter. While this was going on, the merchant ships were to be seen breaking away from the convoy and moving off in all directions. It was an awesome moment.

It was only later that we heard that the Admiralty had signalled that German heavy units were at sea and attack was considered imminent. The ships in the convoy were to scatter and find their own way into Russian ports whilst the Cruiser Force was to retire to the west at high speed. Anyway, it soon spread about the ship that we were withdrawing and leaving the ships of the convoy. It was a dreadful moment really; this was a thing the Royal Navy was not accustomed to do. So over the next few days we continued steaming at speed towards the west. Incidentally, our Walrus aircraft seaplane had been up in the air at the time all this activity was going on, and our Captain requested permission from the Admiral to stop to pick up the aircraft because, of course, she had to land on the sea and we would cruise alongside it and pick it up with our crane, but permission was refused. So we had to leave our poor old Walrus aircraft up in the air as we went off. Incidentally, the pilot kept in the air as long as he could and then landed behind one of the merchant ships and got a tow into Murmansk, very fortunate because he chose a ship that got in.

During the days following our leaving the convoy, we kept receiving wireless messages from individual ships of the convoy, "Am being bombed, torpedoed, etc", and requesting assistance, and, of course, there was no assistance available. Out of the 34 ships that sailed from Iceland, only 11

Catapulting the Walrus aircraft from HMS Norfolk.

made it – 23 ships were sunk. This was my first operation, not easily forgotten.

So over the next few months we spent our time either in Hvalfjord in Iceland or at Scapa Flow or carrying out gunnery exercises and so forth until the next convoy, PQ 18, which had been delayed because of the disaster occurring with PQ 17, was ready to sail. So it wasn't until September that we went off again as part of the cruiser escort, but this time we also covered ships which were landing supplies for the Norwegian meteorological group, which was stationed in Spitzbergen and had, the previous week or so, been bombarded by the battleship *Tirpitz*, which had inflicted a lot of damage. PQ 18 was considered to be a fairly successful convoy, losing only 13 out of the 40 ships which set out, and these were lost by both submarine and torpedo-bomber attack. We hovered around the vicinity of Bear Island and picked up the returning convoy, the remnants of PQ 17 now labelled QP 14. It was this convoy where the 'Tribal' Class destroyer HMS *Somali* was torpedoed and later sank with the loss of 45 men.

Then there are those recollections which have little to do with enemy action. The weather and seas in the wintry north was one of them. I remember watching the great battleship, *King George V*, struggling to gain the summit of a roller as broad as the ship was long, and then crashing down into the trough beyond. Then that Russian convoy when, in the destroyer HMS *Orwell*, we were close escort to a motley collection of small naval craft, mainly ex-Italian, being donated to and manned by the Russian Navy, and how we were hove to for days with mountainous seas and, with the spume and winter darkness, not able to see or communicate with any of them. They all survived. Then those mad dashes from aft to the open bridge of *Orwell*, trying to avoid seas breaking over the deck en route. The cold, with the inner bulkheads coated with ice and one's breath freezing on to one's balaclava, and the decks, guns and stanchions all iced up. The awful occasion when we lost Ordinary Seaman Kelly overboard from *Orwell* while we were exercising in the tempestuous Pentland Firth, and the hours of fruitless search that followed.

On the other hand, there were those occasions when, at sea in the far wintry north, we were graced with the magnificence of the aurora borealis with its sheets of blue light moving across the sky and reflecting into the oily sea below, giving the impression of the ship being suspended in space. Then those lovely vistas of snow-covered mountains in Spitzbergen and Iceland, the almost holiday atmosphere when we left the frozen north for a spell to escort the massive troop convoys to the Torch landings in North Africa, escorting Mr Churchill to and from Canada, the camaraderie and good humour of the ships' companies – all helped to compensate for the discomforts. And all this for 5 shillings a day – board and lodge included!'

With the approach of winter and the almost perpetual night in the Arctic, it was decided to sail merchant ships independently at intervals and without escort to Russia.

Reginald Urwin experienced that Arctic route in a lone freighter and was fortunate to survive and tell the tale:

'I was 16 at the time and did the usual induction courses and so forth at a training establishment at Tyne Dock, where we learnt how to use Bofors, Oerlikons and machine-guns. I did a fairly uneventful trip across the Atlantic and was then on a collier in the Channel and had a scare or two with E-boats and things, and then it was back to the Tyne where we heard about PQ 17, and we'd also heard about PQ 18, convoys that went to Russia, from some of the survivors who got back, and that was interesting. About the middle of September 1942, I think it was, I was sent to a ship at Tyne Dock and she was loading at the time. She was loading tanks and dismantled planes and engine parts, medical stores and general equipment, everything to do with warfare, and the last thing that they did before we left was that they welded brackets on the afterdeck, three a side, and these were gun mounts for Vickers machine-guns, and that didn't look very good. We

Ralph (Reginald) Urwin

had a Bofors on board, we had four sets of twin Oerlikons, everything abaft of the bridge. This was the *Empire Gilbert*, and we had an ancient 4-inch on the stern, which the gunners weren't very happy with because, I think, the date on it was something like 1916 or something, but it worked, it went OK.

Then we sailed north. We thought, well, we're going up to pick up a convoy, and we went off up to Iceland. Arrived in Reykjavik and we sat around there waiting for other ships to arrive; some were coming from America and other places and I think there were, in total, 13 vessels. Anyway, just prior to our departure there was a conference ashore and all the skippers were called to this conference, and when our skipper came back he got us all in the messroom and explained to us what was about to happen; it seemed that the idea was that the ships were to sail from Reykjavik at staggered times and try and get to Russia on their own, without escort or anything.

So we went out, we set off from there about the latter part of October and it was pretty rugged; the only ships we saw actually on the way were Icelandic fishing boats, and they were immune because the Germans didn't bother them. I think it was about three days out from there that we were torpedoed – this was 2 November 1942. The idea had been, of course, to get to the most northern part and get straight on to the main route to Murmansk, but this didn't happen – as I say, we got torpedoed.

My station was the port-side Oerlikon, and when we were hit I finished up at the foot of the starboard lifeboat davit and I didn't know very much about how I got there or anything, but the explosion must have been quite severe because it must have thrown me right over the top, over the bridge. I got to my feet and tried to cut the lifeboat free, but the ship was going so fast that I was awash before I could do anything and the ship just went down – it completely disappeared within a very, very short space of time. It couldn't have been any more than 3 minutes, well 2 minutes, and there was nothing to be seen. I don't know how long I'd been out at the foot of the davit, of course, but it was just so sudden and then, after it was all over, it was a most weird, weird feeling, because suddenly about me there was nothing there, and you were just on your own with people all around just sort of hollering out at each other and trying to make contact.

It didn't seem very long after that that I spotted this shape and it was the submarine that had sunk us, coming towards us, and we were screaming out for help and doing what we thought, you know, was the best thing, and they steamed up alongside us and I felt myself being dragged over the side on to the submarine, and after that I just didn't remember very much more. I can remember going to the conning tower, but I just collapsed and the next thing I knew was that I was being sort of revived. I think it was the Medical Officer and the Mate or the Chief Officer who were working on me, and I'd been stripped and they were rubbing cognac and everything into me in order to get the blood flowing again. I afterwards found out that there had been two other people picked up and they were from the Mercantile Regiment, and these guys were responsible for the Bofors, the anti-aircraft guns aft, but I didn't know these people because they had been put on board just before we sailed.

Other than that, we finished the patrol on the submarine. We were fairly well treated; I think the Navy looks after the Navy, the Army looks after the Army, and so on. Well, we weren't treated too bad. We were fed the same sort of food as they were fed and we had pretty well within reason what you could expect; we had free rein of the submarine. If there was any action or anything like that we were told in no uncertain terms what to do and where to go and we just had to stay put at that. There was a couple of flurries but I didn't find out too much about them, but there was some hectic activity there on two or three occasions actually. We finished the patrol on the submarine and we went then to Narvik. We were about two weeks on the submarine.

While I was in the submarine there was the usual questions; they asked about what cargo, what tonnage, where we were from and other activity. At that time I think the Air Force was fairly busy in Reykjavik; they were particularly anxious to know if there was any air activity in Iceland at the time. They weren't too sure whether we had aircraft there or not and of course we couldn't tell them anything because we didn't know. We told them that we didn't know. We had seen aircraft but they didn't get too much information. They knew that we were carrying arms because of the explosions on the ship and all that sort of thing, but that was a dead give-away.

When we got to Narvik they put us into a holding camp, which was very close to a big Russian camp they had there; they had a lot of Russians there, and these fellows they treated like subhumans there. It was really, really bad, and of course it was a different calibre of German too that we got in with there. When we got to this holding place they actually strip-searched us and we thought that was rather funny, because we'd only come off a German submarine straight to the camp, and why they had done this I don't know, but there didn't seem to be a lot of trust between the services anyway. They took all our clothes away and deloused us, had our clothes done and they all came back pressed and cleaned, ironed, brought by two Russians, and we were told by the Germans that we were to make full use of the Russians and use them as our servants, because they were to prepare our meals, which was fish, consisting of nothing but fish and potatoes. They were to do anything – get the firewood in, do the washing and do anything that we required of them, which we didn't do anyway of course. We did our own thing but, to all intents and purposes, these Russians were just earmarked to do precisely what we wanted them to do.

It wasn't long before the rest of the Russians found out that we were there, and we could see these Russians, when we took our exercise we could see these Russians who were being made to pull sledges loaded with firewood and all this sort of thing, and they were very brutally treated, and it didn't augur very well for us. I thought, well, if this is captivity under the Germans I wonder how it will go when we get to wherever we're going in Germany. We were there, I think, about eight or ten days, and then one of the Germans came in, and in effect said pack up all your gear, you're now going to Germany.

We were then taken down by truck to this little ship, about 2,000 tons, called the *Danferspray Bremen*, and she was an iron-ore carrier and she was going down to, well she was to drop us off at Wilhelmshaven. We dodged all the way down the Norwegian coast; we went to Stavanger and Kristiansand, which was just before we made a rush across the Skagerrak to get to Kiel, and the thing was only capable of about 7 knots. Of course, our first thoughts then were that if this thing ever got hit... When we got on board this *Danferspray Bremen* we were put into cabins and we were locked in these cabins all the time we were on board this thing, and the crew would bring us food to the cabin and that was it; we weren't allowed out at all, not until we were leaving Kristiansand. Then the Captain, with another man in uniform, came down and he had a gun and he told us that this was going to be a bit of a dicey run: "Your cabin doors will be left open, here are life-jackets – should anything happen, then it will probably be every man for himself. If you get in the way or if you interfere with the running of the ship you will be shot."

So we set off then across the Skagerrak and we made about 7 knots all the way, and we thought probably it would be a bit tough if we were going to be knocked down by one of our guys, say one of our MTBs or one of the RAF or something like that – that would have been just too stiff to take, but we got through luckily. Then we were taken ashore and put into a holding camp in Wilhelmshaven, and they held us there for a few days and they interrogated us and they wanted to know a lot of things. We didn't know very much about what was going on, and we were being quite honest about that; there were a few things that we knew about, of course, but shush, they got no information from us. We were cajoled and treated to English cigarettes if we told stories and so on, but didn't tell them anything much.

They gave us two meals a day there; we got one at 6 o'clock in the morning, another at 6 o'clock in the evening, which consisted of a couple of potatoes, a bowl of watery soup and a cup of coffee if you wanted it. There was black bread and jam or either margarine or butter or whatever it was. It didn't taste nice anyway, but I thought, well, if these guys are eating this sort of stuff they must be in a pretty bad way, so that made me feel perhaps a little bit better because we were feeding much better in England. I mean these were the troops and we were civilians at that time and living on a damn sight better stuff than they were.

It wasn't long after that that I think they might have given us up as a bad job; they made preparations for us to leave and go to where we were to finish out the war in a regular prison camp. In between Bremen and

Hamburg there was one big compound; virtually it had been split into two and one side consisted of the Navy, of which I think it held something like about 800 ratings, and the other side the Merchant Service, with about 3,400 people.'

To continue the saga of the Russian convoys, it must be recorded that in September 1943 the battleship Tirpitz *was disabled when attacked by British midget submarines, then, in December of that year, when the battlecruiser* Scharnhorst *ventured to sea on Christmas Day to attack a convoy, she was sunk with heavy loss of life by ships of the Home Fleet.*

Signalman Arthur Godfrey Denby in HMS *Norfolk* remembers the occasion well:

'We were covering this convoy when we got this information that this *Scharnhorst* was coming out with three destroyers. This was on Christmas Day 1943. It would probably be about 9 o'clock next morning when we spotted *Scharnhorst*; it was quite near because it was very dark at that time of year, you know you get 24 hours of darkness at Christmas-time in those latitudes. At that time I was up on the bridge at action stations and, about 9.30 it would have been, we fired on *Scharnhorst* and I think one of the shells did hit it, but I'm not sure because it was so difficult to see, but they turned away. [One shell hit the foretop, wrecking her forward radar, and another landed on the fo'c'sle.]

Well, the next time, we'd changed action stations. I'd gone back into the after action station where everything is fitted up so that if anything happens at one end, the ship can be conned from the other, and Commander Lichfield Spiers was in the after control. X and Y turrets were just behind us. At that time *Norfolk*, *Sheffield* and *Belfast* were in line and, as we were steaming along, *Scharnhorst* came up the port side and we fired again, but they fired too and, at that time, we were turning to starboard so the shell came through the X turret – went straight through the X turret – out through the upper deck, out through the side into the sea. The other one came in through into the office flat and blew the whole lot to pieces except for the wireless telegraphy office, which was properly armoured, and then went up through the torpedo deck; I think three of the fellows there were killed. We never saw anybody left in the office flat at all – they'd just been blown to pieces.

The battleship *Duke of York* was coming up with the destroyers and they attacked *Scharnhorst*, but the destroyers didn't get much joy because the *Scharnhorst*'s secondary armament was a bit too fierce for them. Anyway, by that time *Duke of York* came up and we had to fire star shells up to illuminate or to backlight the *Scharnhorst*, and then when *Duke of York* opened fire, at about 4 o'clock in the afternoon, it was just like a flock of white lights going up into the sky, the fire from her 14-inch guns. You could see these things going higher and higher and then they'd just drop nice and gently down and eventually they put paid to *Scharnhorst*.

Now that the German heavy ships were no longer a problem, and with improved air support due to the use of escort carriers, the route to Russia became much safer, and enormous amounts of military and other supplies were sent by that route.

CHAPTER 4

North Africa to the eve of El Alamein

Italy entered the war on 10 June 1940, and on 13 September its troops advanced from Libya into Egypt, establishing fortified positions around Sidi Barrani. The British, under General Wavell, outnumbered by the Italians, attacked the Italian positions on 7 December, and by 8 February 1941 they were on the borders of Tripolitania, having soundly defeated the Italians and taken many prisoners. Then, as a result of operations in Greece and Crete, a greatly reduced British force was left to guard Cyrenaica and Egypt. Rommel, now in North Africa with his Afrika Corps, went on the offensive in late March, and by 11 April the British were back in Egypt, leaving a force in Tobruk, which came under siege. Rommel's subsequent attacks to take Tobruk and British attempts to relieve the town were inconclusive and resulted in heavy losses to both sides.

Finally, towards the end of December, after a month of bitter fighting, Tobruk was relieved and the Germans were back on the western border of Cyrenaica. On 21 January 1942 Rommel went on the offensive, and by 30 June was in Egypt some hundred miles west of Alexandria. After heavy fighting he was forced on to the defensive south-west of El Alamein, while the Eighth Army, now under General Montgomery, prepared itself for what was to prove the decisive offensive in October, which will be the subject of a later chapter.

Rex Thompson was one of the New Zealanders who arrived in the Middle East at an early stage when the Italians were without German support:

'Early in 1940, as a driver in the NZ Army Service Corps, 2nd Expeditionary Force, I left New Zealand on the *Sobiesky*, a Polish ship which was very modern, and in it got to Egypt. I went to Maadi camp, had more training there and, being a driver, I had a job at one stage testing tyres

Rex Montgomery Crowther Thompson

on the trucks in the desert sand and reporting on their performance, etc. Early on I was attached to the 4th Indian Division, and that was quite an experience. They were tremendously adept at camouflage in the desert. Twenty minutes after camping for the night you'd never know there was a vehicle or a person on the desert.

As a Division, we moved to Mersa Matruh and I was attached to the Regimental Transport Office there. We used to take the troops up from the train to the border; they'd been on leave or were going on leave. And that's where we struck our first taste of bombing by the Italians. They used to come over at 4 o'clock every afternoon when the train arrived. And we had slit trenches along the road by the station and we made the mistake of getting into them very early to start with, and all the natives would pile in after us. They'd wait till we got in and pile in on top of us so we had to reverse that. And it was quite an event to be waiting and watch the bombs leave the planes. And from then on we were providing transport over the various parts of the desert, and we soon found out the safest place with the Italian bombing – they were doing over a petrol dump or an ammunition dump – was to get on the dump because it was usually safer than scattering round it.

After a period carting supplies, petrol, etc, to various dumps over the desert area we started taking Italian prisoners of war back to Egypt. We had a little bit of fun with them; they appeared to be so pleased to become prisoners, you couldn't very well lose them, and when you backed up to the compound they were in, instead of getting about 25 you got about 50 of them. And so we'd leave room for as many as could get in. One day we were stopped for a spell – we used to stop every hour, while they had a comfort stop – and the prisoners would all scatter over the desert, all over the place, and you'd only have to start the vehicle up, they'd be there. This particular day we were stopped and a British staff car came along and one of the officers said, "What are all those chaps doing out in the desert? You're supposed to be looking after them and taking them into Alexandria." So we just jumped into the vehicle and started the motor, and they all just piled in and away.'

Another to experience the war in the Western Desert was Leo Hannah, a New Zealand doctor about to undertake post-graduate studies in London. When the war broke out he joined the Royal Army Medical Corps:

'I arrived in Cairo in February 1941 when the British forces had just succeeded in routing the Italian Army in Libya, and the bulk of those British forces had come back to Cairo to refit, and the front line was being held by fresh troops from England. I was posted as Medical Officer with the rank of Captain to a regiment, the First Battalion The King's Royal Rifle Corps. They had been fighting the Italians and had actually been training in the desert before the war and were thoroughly conversant with the Western Desert.

At that time the New Zealand and Australian Divisions and British troops had gone to Greece and it was expected that the bulk of the troops in the Middle East would go to Greece and that the war would be fought in the Balkans. However, we suddenly were told that our battalion was to go back into the Western Desert right up to Benghazi, which was just behind the front line, to guard Italian prisoners of war, of whom there were many thousands. This was rather unexpected and mysterious, and we had to be hurriedly refitted with trucks, etc, and we made our way back through the Western Desert. When we got to Tobruk we were told that there were German troops in Libya, that they were driving back the British troops in

Leo Gordon Hannah

the front line without any difficulty and that we would be fighting a battle in the next two or three days. This took us by surprise because nobody had mentioned the presence of German troops in Libya until then.

We continued westwards and got just short of Benghazi and found ourselves attached to the 9th Australian Division, who were on the coast road whilst the British troops were further south. We were then posted to be rearguard to the 9th Australian Division and withdrew behind them back to Tobruk with our Rifle Companies fighting various rearguard actions with the advancing Germans. It was decided that Tobruk should be held at any cost, and we thought that we would be shut up in Tobruk, but somebody decided that as we were the only mobile infantry regiment with our own transport, we should not be shut up in Tobruk so we went out into the desert and the Germans came in between us and Tobruk, in which we had left the 9th Australian Division and various other British troops.

We went back to the Egyptian frontier and stayed there for some weeks. As reinforcements gradually came up from Cairo, the Germans occupied themselves with surrounding Tobruk and we kept them under observation from the outside and fought various minor actions with them. There were two attempts made to relieve the Tobruk garrison when forces of tanks and artillery came up from Cairo, but these were unsuccessful and our life was mainly one of patrolling and observation, and at times we were the only troops in close proximity to the Germans.

The medical set-up was very primitive. At first we didn't have an ambulance; we got an ambulance later on, otherwise everything was just done with trucks – we had 15cwt trucks. Each section of infantrymen had one – I had one and the stretcher bearers had two – and we just put what casualties there were on these trucks as comfortably as possible, and the distances were very great. There was a field ambulance behind us, but it could be anything from 10 to 40 miles behind us, and the unfortunate casualties just had to put up with bumpy trips as there was no air evacuation in those times. One could only give morphia for pain and splint broken legs and bandage wounds; the situation wasn't suitable for suturing wounds, and these had to wait until the trucks got back to the field ambulance, which, as I say, was a variable distance back.

The usual type of action would be when we were approached by marauding columns of German tanks and armoured cars, in which case we would usually make a quick retreat but come under fire from the tanks until we had got out of range, as at that time there were no British tanks anywhere near us. We were also liable to be strafed from the air by German fighter planes and occasionally bombed by Stukas, but the casualties were not heavy at those times.

Finally, a determined effort was made by what had become known as the Eighth Army, and in late October 1941 an attack was made on the Germans who were still around Tobruk, and there were several days with heavy fighting between the Egyptian frontier and Tobruk. The casualties then were very heavy and the situation was always extremely fluid in that in tank warfare in the desert there was no front line and one could be attacked from front or rear or either side unexpectedly by mobile columns of tanks and armoured cars. The fighting was very complicated and at times one side appeared to be winning and at other times the other side. Casualties were better looked after at this stage because the Field Ambulance was up in the midst of this fighting and were able to do a reasonable amount of surgery when they were not actually under shellfire.

Eventually the Eighth Army seemed to get on top, largely owing to the actions of the New Zealand Division, who fought very, very well at that time. A link-up was made with the Tobruk garrison, which by this time was entirely composed of British troops because the Australians had been evacuated a few months previously at the express demand of the Australian Government. The evacuation had been done by British destroyers at night coming up from Mersa Matruh to Tobruk and going back again before daylight came, when they would be vigorously bombed.

Our battalion had heavy casualties in this fighting, which is known as the Battle of Sidi Rezegh, and we were taken back to Cairo to get reinforcements and generally refit. It was very sad to see the number of men and officers who were killed. I remember vividly dressing the wound of the Brigadier to which my Battalion was attached, who won the VC in the fighting at Sidi Rezegh because of his outstanding leadership and heroism. He was Brigadier Jock Campbell and he drove in and out of a section of the fighting in an 8cwt truck directing tanks and the fire of artillery in the most heroic manner. I was circling an area of heavy fighting in my truck looking for casualties one afternoon and a British tank came driving out of the thick of the fighting towards my truck, which had a Red Cross flag on it, and as it drew near I saw that the body of the Brigadier was lying across the front of this tank and he appeared to be unconscious. However, by the time the tank got up to my truck, he was on his feet again and the tank commander said that he had seen the Brigadier struck by some object and he had fallen off his truck unconscious. The tank commander had jumped out and picked him up and put him across the front of his tank and brought him over to me.

By this time Jock Campbell was on his feet and wanting to get back into things, but I insisted on examining him and he had deep graze on the side of his chest, but it was not a really dangerous wound so I began to put a dressing on, and I had to order him to stand still while I put it on. And he said, "Well, hurry up, hurry up – I must go and rally those bloody tanks." And so as soon as I got the dressing on he was away again, his truck having come up in the meantime. I might mention that one of the riflemen of the 1KRRC also won the VC when the battalion had to attack a heavily held German position and he unfortunately lost his life in doing this.

We were in Cairo for several weeks and then up to the Desert again and took over much the same role as we had been at before until May 1942, when the Germans, who had been refitting also back in Tunisia, attacked and in much greater strength than before. There was again a period of several days' vigorous fighting in the same fixed set-up analogous to a naval battle, with troops being attacked from all directions, on all sides. The Germans got the advantage in this because they had much better tanks and much heavier artillery, and the Eighth Army had to withdraw.

My Battalion had to withdraw past Tobruk in the middle of the night, and about 3 o'clock that morning my truck was blown up by a mine which fortunately was just in front of the truck and just blew the front off it, and my driver and I received only minor injuries, but sufficiently severe for us to be evacuated to hospital. So that was the end of my association with the 1KRRC.'

Another New Zealander, this time a gunner, Lance Bombardier Bruce McKay Smith, was recalled with his unit from Syria because of the deteriorating situation in the Western Desert:

'We packed up very quickly and took off in a mad dash back to Egypt. I've forgotten just how long we were, but it was a record time with all the gear we had. We got just to the outskirts of Cairo, then to Alexandria, and then straight up the desert road as far as Baggush, where we camped for two or three days and then went on up to Mersa Matruh, where we were put into vacated gun positions. The whole place hadn't been used for a wee while and was infested with fleas, so we got out of that very quickly, out on to the open ground, but the Jerry used to bomb us fairly repeatedly. By this time we had an anti-aircraft unit of Bofors guns, which helped quite a bit.

After three days, I think, in Mersa Matruh, General Freyberg decided it wasn't the place for us to be, and we headed out into the desert to a place called Minqar Qaim, and we didn't realise at the time, but the Jerries were only a matter of miles behind us as we moved out. We came to this Minqar Qaim, which consisted of a very flat area of desert with an escarpment of about a hundred odd feet rising up out of it, and the guns were put in position below the escarpment and the infantry in front of them again, and we knew the Germans were coming because we could see these great clouds of dust heading towards us. The second night we were there I happened to be amongst a group setting out on a reconnaissance towards the German positions. We had two 25-pounder guns, two Vickers machine-guns, a platoon of infantry and some wireless vans. We were out in the dark and we stayed there all night and, at first light, we could hear the German tanks and apparently we got orders over the radio to get back quick, which we did, and I'm very thankful about that, but we got back and as we arrived back the Germans started shelling and our guns started replying.

For the whole of the day it was an artillery duel. Every now and again the German infantry would approach in vehicles and head towards our positions where our infantry would be waiting for them, and our own guns, of course, managed to repulse them most of the day. But up on the escarpment behind us – actually just straight above where I was – General Freyberg was in a bivouac arrangement directing things, when he got

Bruce McKay Smith

wounded by, I think, a mortar shell, and he was out of action because of that. I don't know how they got him out, but he was got out anyway. Our guns kept firing and then they started to get low on ammunition and as dark approached the Germans cooled off their attack a wee bit, but we knew that they'd got round on both our flanks so we had a very narrow alleyway behind us.

As it got dark all the guns that were serviceable were lined up behind their quads to pull them, and all personnel were allocated space in a vehicle of some kind to get out. Then – I'm not sure what time of night it was – but we set off going south. Now the Maori infantry put in an attack towards the Germans and all hell was let loose. The Germans, apparently, hadn't expected us to move at night; they weren't prepared, so they were firing blindly at anything. The vehicle I was in, we had quite a few machine-gun bullets through the canopy, but nobody got hurt. There was just utter confusion – flares, gun shots, machine-gun fire, mortars, anything that could make a noise seemed to be going. We got through the main line of German defences, or whatever they were – they were pretty scattered and ineffectual – and carried on in the vehicles. There were always some vehicles knocked out and some casualties, but not a great many.

We got out and by daylight were clear of the whole area. The vehicle I was in was a 3-ton truck with a fairly high canopy, and we became separated somehow or another from the main body and all we could do was follow the wheel marks of the vehicles that had gone ahead of us. We got strafed once by a German fighter plane, but he didn't do any good; I think he must have had tracer bullets, which set fire to the camouflage net, and that was the only trouble we had. Fortunately, all the vehicles had plenty of petrol and we kept going for all that day and I think most of the next night. It was moonlight, of course, and we were able to see the tyre tracks; we daren't show a light of any kind. Eventually we finished up back at Baggush again where the rest of the regiment had gradually made their way. How we all found our way there I still don't know, but we did.

Then the regiment reformed and we were divided into our individual batteries again with what gear we had. Eventually we got reinforcements to build our numbers up and then we were set to work to build defensive positions about the Alamein area. We went to the south until we got in amongst the sand dunes where it was pretty well impossible to travel with vehicles and guns and things. We dug positions there and we seemed to occupy positions for a day or so and then move off on to somewhere else. Then we were told we were to be in what they call Jock columns, which was a mixture of, perhaps, a troop of artillery and a platoon of machine-guns and a platoon of infantry, plus an ack-ack gun too, and we were told to virtually wander round the desert to see if we could see any Germans. It was a pretty ridiculous idea really because as soon as the Germans saw us they would open fire and we'd fire back and they had superior numbers so we'd clear out again, and it carried on like this for several days.

Then the Division gradually came together and then the big battles started, Sidi Rezegh and so forth; one of them was where Charles Upham won his VC. We carried on with this mobile column, reconnaissance it was really, and then gradually the whole Division moved back to the Alamein line after quite a number of minor actions. We were put into virtually fixed gun positions on fairly stony ground, rocky ground – took a lot of hard work. Meantime the German bombers knew where we were and they gave us a bit of hurry up every now and again. But we had more anti-aircraft defence than we'd had prior to this, and on one occasion a German aircraft was shot down in our lines and the pilot said that they knew where all our different divisions were.

We spent quite a considerable amount of time there. Now and again the Germans would attack, particularly on our left flank, which we nearly always repulsed fairly well, but there were quite a number of tank battles. In the meantime some of us were individually given leave to go to Cairo for a few days, which was much appreciated. And also I took part in building dummy gun positions out of scrim and timber, dummy vehicles, all sorts of dummy stuff to try and fool the Germans. It was a wee bit away from our lines and the Germans did bomb occasionally, but I am not sure how effective they were. This all went on until the fateful day of 23 October 1942 when the big battle of Alamein started.'

James Hayter, DFC, now in the Middle East, continues his narrative:

'I was sent to the Western Desert in early 1942 where I joined 33 Squadron as a Supernumerary Flight Commander, and I came back on the last retreat. I was shot down by a Macchi 202 and that was annoying, because I don't know how long we had a dogfight for, but we got lower and lower and lower until my ailerons were jamming, and I thought, well, I'll force land. It was an Italian boy – he overshot me, and as he overshot me I thought, God damn it, I might be able to get a shot at him, and I managed to hit him and he crash-landed up in front, landed up in front of me and I landed on top of the Australian lines. This was OK – we went to have a drink afterwards and the Australians were all for shooting him, and I wouldn't let them do that and I took him back as my personal prisoner. We had a tent and I was drinking with this chap and he could speak perfect English, and the Military Police arrived and they were most annoyed with me for talking to this guy. I got a ticking off from Air Marshal Saul for consorting with the enemy.

We now started to do some low-level stuff, and eventually we were told that we were not to come lower than 7,000 feet; we were Hurricane bombers and, you know, one bomb, dropping it from 7,000 feet, you'd never hit anything. You were very lucky if you did. If you went down and strafed anything you got a rap on the knuckles – it was so bloody stupid. I went to "Mary" Coningham [Air Vice-Marshal] and I said, "You know, this is absolutely bloody ridiculous, sir, we're not being effective." You know, low-level strafing on the desert, there was miles and miles of transport you could shoot at. Sure, you have casualties, but it was worth it and we did it from D-Day onwards. We did a lot of it – all our stuff was low-level. Even if you didn't set a vehicle on fire you frightened the hell out of them, which was pretty demoralising, you know. If you get 12 aircraft line astern and they're shooting up a convoy, it causes a hell of a panic.'

Keith Newth, a Corporal of Regimental Signals in the NZ 20th Battalion of Infantry, moved up to the desert in the latter stages of 1941 and went into his first action there. But before long his unit was sent to Greece:

'Back in Alexandria from Crete, we were entrained back to Cairo. The next day, I'll never forget arriving back in the Cairo station – there was Lady Killern to meet her New Zealand boys. We were taken up to King Farouk's castle or whatever it was and given a wonderful dinner. The Egyptians seemed to absolutely fall in love with the Kiwis. They were wonderful to us, and yet they would rob their own mothers. I had a little boy come to me, "Kiwi, cigarette Kiwi", so I handed him a packet of cigarettes. It had only one cigarette in it – he said, "It's your last cigarette," and he wouldn't take it.

And I'm certain no soldier ever dreamed of the idea of being a prisoner of war. Anyway, I was wounded and captured at Sidi Rezegh by the Germans. And the next thing I knew was, a German officer said to me, as he leaned out of his tank, "For you the war is over." I had my left arm broken and he got a splint and put my arm in this splint, stopped an Italian truck, kicked the co-driver out of it, stuck me in and told the driver to take me to the hospital at Derna. And the next morning I remember Rommel coming along and looking at everybody with his stern look. First words he said were, "Why so many prisoners?" which made you shake a bit. The next thing he said was, "You will attend to the worst cases here, be they British, German, Italian or what," and that was the type of man he was.

So then I was taken back to hospital in Derna and they took me to the German Hospital. It was full, so they took me to the Italian Hospital. It had 20 beds in the ward and they were full except for one for me and these Italians – I thought they were all Italians – and I was a bit unpopular, as you can understand. They said, 'Your RAF, boom, boom, boom."

I said, "Oh yes, I know what you mean."

By gosh, they knew what they were talking about, because that night, in the middle of the night, the RAF came over and they bombed all right, because the hospital had ack-ack guns all around it. And all these Italian orderlies at the hospital had taken off – they didn't worry about us. And the bombs blew all the glass out of the windows and so forth and my bed

Keith Lewis Newth

collapsed with the top end of the bed down on the floor and my broken arm had nothing done to it – it was broken in two places. I had to get myself up off the floor and get myself out of that.

And that was on the Monday night, and on the following Friday they decided to do something about my broken arm and the doctor – they had no anaesthetic, nothing at all – he just got one chap to hang on to the elbow and another to pull on the hand and he bound it up. But he bound it up with the bones in the wrong direction – instead of butting to each other they were crossed – so it was a dead loss and eventually they had to be broken again and reset. That's another thought that will never leave me, what I went through there. There was in the operating room five beds. I was in the first one, luckily. They did my arm, no anaesthetic, and if I started to faint the chap behind slapped you across the face because they did not want you to go out on them. But next to me they took a chap's leg off, and you could hear them scraping the bone, and another one, they did work on his kneecap and another one's arm was taken off, and all were done without anaesthetics. The chaps who had the amputations said for a start there was very sharp pain, but then once they hit the bone it sort of went dead. But, oh hell, you could almost hear chaps scream back in New Zealand.

I was lucky, in fact, because I was taken across to Italy in a hospital ship, *Cecilia*, but the ship our boys, the 20th Battalion boys, were being taken across to Italy on was torpedoed by our own people and, while not all of them were drowned, I don't think many of them were saved because they were battened down anyhow, so they couldn't get out. More of the horrors of war of course.'

New Zealander Kenneth Frater, a driver in the 2nd NZ Supply Column, part of the 5th Brigade, was also caught up in the fighting around Sidi Rezegh:

'When daylight came we were near a New Zealand Field Dressing Station at Sidi Rezegh. Our escort went off apparently to join in the battle, which seemed to be in progress on all sides. We were asked to move as we were making a target of the Dressing Station. There was constant tank and artillery fire, and wherever we moved we were told to get the hell out of it as we were spoiling a line of fire or making an unnecessary target. An Artillery Major told us we were interfering with a perfectly good battle. Eventually we moved to a comparatively quiet area near Divisional HQ behind our troops, who were attacking the enemy forces besieging Tobruk. Here we unloaded our loads of rations. At last somebody was glad to see us. The forces at Sidi Rezegh had not received rations for 48 hours. Tich Cotterell, in charge of our unit, was awarded the Military Cross for bringing soft transport through three enemy armoured columns and getting urgently needed supplies to our fighting troops. Sergeant Stan Grubb had also been a tower of strength, but he received no recognition.

Through the day other transport trucks and personnel trickled into the area and we were becoming a large target and limiting movement of fighting weapons. The General decided we had to be got rid of, so as soon as it was dark we lined up nose-to-tail and the infantry punched a hole in the German line to allow us to move through behind the Tobruk defences. The engineers moved behind the infantry and swept a clear track through the minefield, which was about a mile deep. The only indication was a tape left to show the way. It was a stop-start trip with shells flying around. At times during a stop someone would go to sleep and the vehicles in front would be out of sight. Then someone would have to walk with the tape in hand to find the way. By daylight most were safely through.'

Kenneth Carrol Frater

Kenneth Frater's Supply Column joined the rest of the NZ Division in Syria, but in June 1942 was in the rush to get back to Egypt because of Rommel's rapid advance. Working from a supply dump at Mersa Matruh, his unit just made it back to the Alamein Defence Line ahead of the Germans. However, his troubles were by no means over:

'We dispersed our trucks singly at about 75-yard intervals. The cook started up the burner to cook a meal. There were four planes stooging slowly round with wing lights on, so we naturally assumed they were ours. People were drifting towards the radio truck to listen to the 9pm news. The driver from next to us arrived at our truck and my No 2 and I were just starting off with him to hear the news when bombs started screaming down. We saw the radio truck hit and threw ourselves to the ground. The last bomb in the string exploded alongside us, luckily in soft sand. The other driver took most of the damage as he was nearest to the bomb with me alongside him and my No 2 further away. I was deaf in my right ear and couldn't hear much out of the other, my neck hurt, and when I stood up I was lame, but couldn't find anything wrong. I later discovered the heel had been sliced off my right boot. I guess it took a minute or two to recover our senses, then we discovered the bloke nearest the bomb had taken the full impact and was quite badly wounded. We carried him to the HQ truck and found quite a number of wounded already there. Ambulances started to arrive so we got out of the way. We learnt that there had been about 20 men at the radio truck when it sustained a direct hit, killing 12 and wounding the rest.

Several trucks were on fire, so the area was well lit up. Most of the drivers elected to move further away from the burning trucks, but when we got back to our truck we found that a lump of shrapnel had flattened one tyre, so decided to stay put until daylight. That same night, those with the Division at Minqar Qaim had a worse time. The infantry cut their way through the German lines with bayonets, with the transport vehicles following behind. Two of my friends who were carting explosives for the engineers received a direct hit and were literally blown to kingdom come.

After several days we were all sorted out and back with our own units. I still couldn't hear with my right ear and my neck was pretty sore. I reported sick and was sent to Field Hospital. There I was told I had a burst eardrum and a whiplash. I was told that my problems would heal themselves and was sent back to my unit. My ear has never healed properly.'

Apart from the dangers of battle, there were other real problems in the desert. Kenneth Frater again:

'From my point of view, my worst enemy was the Egyptian fly. With German and British troops combined there were 3-400,000 troops in an area 50 miles long and probably 8 miles wide. On the battlefield dead bodies often lay unburied for days. The only hygiene was to be like a cat. Scratch a hole in the sand and cover it up. The flies during the heat of summer moved in dense swarms. Having a meal was a real conjuring trick. You had to keep your food covered and then try and get a spoonful in your mouth with as few flies as possible. I contracted dysentery. I was taken to Field Hospital, but I continued to get worse. There was talk of evacuating me to Base Hospital. I didn't want that, as when you returned from Base, you were liable to be drafted into the infantry. Fortunately an orderly, an angel in disguise, brought me a tin of Highlander condensed milk and said, "Get that into you – it'll stop anything." Within 4 hours my contractions had stopped and I was thinking perhaps I could manage some food. I had a couple of days on mashed potatoes and gravy and was then sent back to my unit. Our Medical Officer apparently didn't like the look of me so recommended that I have convalescent leave. I had five days in Cairo. I wondered who the strange guy was when I saw myself in a full-length mirror. I had lost just on 3 stone.'

New Zealand Gunner Officer and Battery Commander, Leonard Thornton, had clear memories of the alarm caused by Rommel's advance towards Alexandria:

'The NZ Division was in Syria when Rommel began his push in the Western Desert again, and Tobruk fell and we were hurtled back into the battle. And we made what was really, for a division, a lightning move. It took us only about, I suppose, five or six days, to move all those hundreds and hundreds of kilometres back into the Western Desert. And as we went up into the desert from Alexandria and went up that narrow and well-known desert road towards the west, the Eighth Army and the Air Force were coming pell-mell back down the road and it was, shall we say, not exactly riotous, but it was certainly a very disorganised retreat. And morale had fallen to pieces, so it was quite a challenge. The Kiwis rather liked the idea that they were going to save the situation, so we went in the most orderly way we could. Up alongside the road, mostly against the stream of traffic coming back from the disordered battles that had occurred further to the west. And we were ordered to take up a fixed position as they prepared defensive positions at Matruh. General Freyberg, who was our redoubtable commander, made one of the best decisions of his life when he said, "I command a mobile division and I am not going to have them shut up in old-fashioned silted-up defences protected by rusty and not very effective wire. I must fight the battle in a mobile way." And because of his insistence we were allowed to get out on a flank and fight the battle at a place called Minqar Qaim.

Freyberg was an unusual man and he was in a unique position really, because he was the overall force commander as well as being a fighting commander, and as the Divisional Commander, so he had wide responsibilities, wider than an ordinary major-general commanding an ordinary old infantry division. However, secondly he was directly responsible to the New Zealand Government for the safety and, indeed, the employment of the New Zealand Force. The New Zealand Force was a

Leonard Whitmore Thornton

pretty large and mobile force. We had, at that stage, three infantry brigades and the usual bits and pieces, so if really necessary, if he thought it was necessary, he could at any time refer to the New Zealand Government to say, I have been asked to do, perform such and such a task here, and I think it's either appropriate or I think it's not appropriate, and I'd like you to say whether I am to conform. I don't think that, in this case, he found it necessary to refer the matter back, although after the debacle in Greece to which New Zealand troops had been committed, he was a little wary. We then fought the battle at Minqar Qaim and, of course, in the nature of things, as the battle flowed towards us and then round us, the Division was surrounded. You had to accept that as a normal situation in a mobile operation, but it's not a very comfortable one.

I had, in the meantime, been detached from my regiment, which was, as you might say, in the bag at Minqar Qaim, because I had been sent off with an infantry battalion, the 21st Battalion. I was now commanding a field battery to defend another small outpost area to the south of the main divisional position. We were quite detached so we fought our own operation down in this lonely part of the desert while the Division defended itself in its locality at Minqar Qaim. The Division, having defended itself through something like two days and nights of defensive fighting, realised that the situation was rather threatening and they would have to break out. And at that critical moment General Freyberg, making a reconnaissance of the front-line areas towards Cairo, that's to say on the eastern side, was wounded by some stray shelling and quite badly wounded in the neck, so that was just the wrong moment to lose your commander.

However, the reserve commander took over and that night the whole Division did an extraordinary operation, just charging through the night, a silent attack, and broke through the German lines and the entire force escaped with very, very low casualties really. An extraordinary operation – my own regiment came out on the Saturday and broke their way out separately and they all moved off towards a defensive position, which had been prepared further towards the east. In the meantime, of course, I didn't know what had happened; communications in those days were very chancy indeed. You seemed to think that in the field everyone would be in touch; we had no idea really what had happened to the Division. And so I had a rather uncomfortable day being pursued by a few tanks and armoured cars and that sort of thing and trying to support the battalion. The battalion itself got scattered and, anyway, the long and short of it was that after a very uncomfortable night in the middle of the desert and not knowing quite what was happening, we moved off back and got the buzz, really from a chance encounter with an engineer officer, a lone figure travelling across the desert. We then fell back on to the main position.

So we reorganised ourselves back on what was eventually to become the Alamein Line. And there was fought a series of battles, and these were very untidy battles indeed with very poor co-ordination. I look back on it now, I realise how poor the co-ordination was between the arms. We had lost a large number as prisoners at that time, which is always a sign of poor control and c-ordination. There was a total lack of understanding between the British armour and the infantry – I don't mean only ourselves, but the armour and infantry generally were not working well together. We had no armour at that time, no tanks in other words at that time, apart from some light tanks. So it was a very, very unhappy period and our losses were very high, including, I can't remember the figure now, but we must have lost something over 2-3,000, probably prisoners. So we were in a very depleted state when that phase of the battle came to an end. It came to an end really because Rommel had outrun his supplies and couldn't maintain the attack, the offensive any longer. And we fought a particularly painful final operation with two borrowed British infantry brigades because our brigades were now so fought out, and eventually the line settled down.

In the meantime the brigade in which I had served as a brigade major had been severely mauled and the entire brigade headquarters had been lost, had been taken prisoner, including the brigadier, and some of course were killed. And so I was then called back from my enjoyable role as a battery commander. It's much nicer being a line officer; of course, you don't have to work nearly so hard and it's more interesting; you have better contact with the men and so forth. Anyway, I was pulled away from that job as battery commander and I was pulled in to go back and reconstitute the brigade headquarters and retrain a new brigade headquarters in the middle of this rather desultory period.

The battalions were right down in strength, the weather was extraordinarily hot, we were afflicted with mosquitoes and flies and dreadful things called desert sores because the diet and living conditions were very poor. There was not enough water for washing and that kind of thing. People became afflicted; any kind of scratch would become a suppurating sore and people would be covered with these terrible sores. I don't know how I managed to escape them – it was just good luck I guess. So it was a very difficult period – something like 11 weeks we were in the line under these very unpleasant conditions. There wasn't a great deal of enemy action. On our side we felt we had to dominate the battlefield, so we did a lot of patrolling and raids went on. Again it was very hard to sustain the troops' morale, which I thought was getting a bit low. I actually ran a daily newspaper for a long time because I realised the chaps were getting rather depressed, so I ran a sort of paper to try and give them some information about what was happening, and before long it was pretty widely circulated among the British units as well as our own, I might say. I think that was probably because an enterprising editor, who was my sergeant clerk, managed to dream up rather an unwholesome joke, which he added to the end of every issue, so that was much sought after.'

CHAPTER 5

Greece

The Italians had invaded Greece from their bases in Albania on 28 October 1940, but were soon being repulsed, and by the end of the year had been driven back into Albania along the whole front. On 6 April 1941 the Germans, in great strength, invaded Greece and Yugoslavia from their bases in Bulgaria. Britain had started landing troops in Greece in early March and had established a line along the Aliakmon River in the north. Yugoslavia surrendered on 17 April, then, with the disintegration of the few Greek divisions on its right, both flanks of the British Army were exposed to the enemy. There was no alternative but to withdraw. Greece surrendered on 24 April and the bulk of the British forces were evacuated on the nights of 24, 25 and 26 April in a variety of naval and merchant ships, which took them to Crete and North Africa.

Major Leonard Thornton had been very much involved in these events. He recalled:

'The decision was taken, rather reluctantly by the New Zealand Government, to agree to our Division forming part of a small so-called Imperial Force, which was sent to Greece to help the situation. When we look back at it now historically, it was a forlorn hope. There was ourselves, a British and Australian Division, which was to be supplemented with another division, and a British Brigade with rather worn-out tanks. That was the total force, and we were a little concerned to discover, while we were in the process of embarkation, that a planning committee had already been set up in Cairo to work out plans for our evacuation if possible – not a very encouraging sign!

Anyway, we moved up into Greece, Northern Greece, and got ourselves established in a defensive position up there. By this time I had left my role as adjutant in my previous regiment rather to my relief (it was a staff job), and I was now commander of an artillery battery. And so the battle began and it really hardly lasted at all because an overwhelming force of 12

German divisions came in; we fought as well as we could in the Olympic passes on Mount Olympus, and that was where I had my first experience of being under fire in a battle on the Aliakmon River. It was a foregone conclusion; we fell back as rapidly as we could and the battle on the Aliakmon River was really a delaying action, in order to enable the main force to get past us and down to the road back towards Athens. And we fought another battle near Thermopylae where a famous battle had been fought long ago. So round about Hitler's birthday, which is almost ANZAC Day as far as I can recall, the decision was taken that we should have to evacuate. Jumbo Wilson was the force commander and he, an Englishman who had served with the New Zealanders in the First War, took the decision and it was the right one to take, although it was pretty hard on the Navy. We then made off towards the south as fast as we could, and in three or four days the embarkation was completed.

We had lost, of course, most of our equipment in that evacuation; nothing could be moved in the way of hardware, and it was a very unpleasant campaign to be in because of the fact it was under a totally adverse air situation. We were continuously bombed, strafed from the air throughout the hours of daylight. Mercifully the German Air Force couldn't do much at night, which meant, at least, that you could get a bit of sleep if you weren't on the move, but it was very demoralising for the troops not being able to hit back. And I think a lot of men became a little bit jumpy about the business of having to move, having to be out on the roads and so forth. We got ourselves off the beaches; I actually got left behind briefly because I went back to try and souvenir some or get some radio equipment which I thought it was a pity to leave behind, although we had been ordered to do so by the embarkation officer.

However, back on to the beaches, my regiment had already left, which turned out to be a strange stroke of fortune, because most of my regiment, which was now the Fourth Regiment, went on for the defence of Crete, and because I went in a different ship I was moved directly back to Egypt, so I missed the Crete campaign, which was very expensive from a New Zealand point of view.'

Sergeant Richard Kean, Battery NCO of Signals, NZ Artillery, saw it all from a slightly different perspective:

'We arrived at Piraeus, the port of Athens, disembarked and through Athens to somewhere outside Athens where we stayed under the trees. We stayed there for a while and then moved up through Greece, finally settling in the south of the Olympus Pass, moved on again over the top of the Olympus down the other side, and got in a village just outside Kuphos and

Richard James Kean

camped there. And we dug a fairly good deep hole to house our living quarters and the telephone exchange. Did a bit of scrounging and found stuff, you know, derelict Anderson shelter tops to put over the top of our hut. However, it sufficed when covered with earth, and we got a Greek farmer to plough over the top of it and it couldn't even be seen.

We then moved further on and for some reason, known only to himself, my major decided that he wanted a forward listening post and that was me. Why I don't know, and when I arrived I could see constant movement, places being bombed and burned, and there was I sitting in the middle of nowhere, just me and the telephone. Then I heard crinkling, crankling rustles coming from the undergrowth. My armament was a .45 revolver, so I drew it and in the prescribed manner, toes and elbows rigid, listening, listening, followed the rustling – and I finally found it, and it was two turtles mating. One of the biggest scares I've had in my life!

We were moved up and down all over the place, and finally my battery was detached and sent to the 17th Australian Brigade over on the other coast. I was left on the end of the telephone and wasn't allowed to close down, although the battery was gone. And I was very worried because the bombers were coming over and there was great holes in the ground there where our guns had been but, finally I got the message to close down. It was dark as hell and all I had was a telephone and a motorbike, and I got back to our HQ and the colonel said, "Oh, sorry, Sergeant, I forgot all about you – your battery went over the hill and if you can find that number three post on the other side they'll tell you which way they went." I finally caught up with them and went up through Larisa and up almost to the Albanian border, and there we camped – took me 36 hours on the bike. On the way up we were watching the planes come over and could see tracers and, my God, they're not going up, they're coming down. We hit the dirt pretty smartly at the side of the road. However, we got used to that.

And we got into position there and stayed there for a while, and in the evening I got off my bike, about 4 o'clock, and lay down beside it and went to sleep, and shortly after there was cheers and I looked up and saw about 30 planes in the air; Spitfires had arrived, or Hurricanes, and it turned out they were Messerschmitts, and they were coming down not going up. There was an airfield just behind where we were, equipped with Gladiators and Lysanders, and a Lysander got up and two of the Gladiators got up; they managed to bring down two of the Messerschmitts, but later on the German planes came back again and cleaned up the whole of the outfit.

We got down eventually to a fishing place called Volos, quite a good spot actually, because we were in a trench about 10 feet deep, pretty wide and we could move around quite a bit. We dug the exchange into the side of the bank and ran the appropriate lines and were quite happy there for quite a while. The fields behind us had peas and stuff and they were getting near ripe and we kept popping up and picking a few peas and back down into the village when the planes came over – at least we'd got green peas. It got a bit hectic after a while, and the lines were getting shot up.

Then we got word that the Greeks had packed it in and we were evacuated. I smashed my good BSA motorbike up with an axe and pulled the bank down over it. We had to leave our guns; we couldn't spike them and destroy them because that would have given the enemy a clue that we were perhaps moving. All we had to do was take the breech blocks, and we took as much of the equipment as we could. I closed the exchange and got on the truck and drove down. We finally got down to the water's edge and after loading put the telephone exchange into the drink. Our packs, our main packs, all went into the drink; it meant that through the three packs we'd discarded, another man could get on the ship. We didn't have too much: I had binoculars, gas-mask, revolver, compass, technical haversack, a small haversack on my back, greatcoat, and we had to dump our blankets, mess tin, water bottle.

We made it out to whalers that came in, and every time I tried to get on board I missed out. I'd two cartons of cigarettes, tucked in behind my gas-mask, and after several attempts to board, a big Navy hand came and grabbed me by the back of the belt of my greatcoat and hauled me in head over heels, and I never saw the cigarettes again. We got out and climbed up the net on to the side of the destroyer, the *Kandahar*, and I got assigned to the Petty Officers' Mess. The entrance into the Petty Officers' Mess was through a hole in the deck, and I got stuck half way down the hole – it was all the stuff that I had on me – and the next thing I know is a big Navy foot on top of my tin hat, gives me a push and I went through pretty quickly. Things soaking wet, everything was wet having to wade out, and the Navy boys there took all my clothes down to the engine room, gave me Navy pants and a skivvy, and they dried all my uniform out down in their engine room and brought it back. It was great to get a good feed with fresh vegetables, which we hadn't seen for some considerable time.

We were bombed a bit on the way and I was lying on my bunk resting and saw the side of the ship being pushed in and thought that this is no place to be. I tried to climb up the ladder to get through, but the manhole was closed and the Chicago piano – what they call a "Chicago piano" was a pom-pom – kept them busy firing up on the top, so I had to stay down there wondering whether I'd get out of that. However, we finally made it and landed at Suda Bay in Crete.'

George Brown was a Lieutenant in the 20th NZ Infantry Battalion, and recalls his initial enthusiasm for Greece:

'We landed in Greece at Piraeus Harbour and marched to our bivouac, which was lovely after the heat of the desert. We explored Athens, learnt a little bit more about its history, drank their lovely wine, ate their lovely steaks and eventually entrained to Katerini. After a few days there we went by truck, I think, to Ryakia; from Ryakia at night you could see the lights of Salonika.

We dug in there, and found the people very hospitable. We officers of our company were billeted in a house and the Greeks would bring us some of their food and bring their babies in to see us. Our battalion pioneers put in a pump in the well in the town. The padre had received a few dozen bars of chocolate – well, a few dozen bars of chocolate weren't much good to a thousand odd men, so the colonel and the padre went down to the local school and I believe the delight that the children showed when given a cake of chocolate was well worth their effort. We took up various defensive

George Arthur Brown (left)

positions round Ryakia. Yugoslavia was expected to fall to the Germans and we were to defend Greece.

Late one night we were all called out and we marched and marched to the front line overlooking the Aliakmon River. It was snowing, and we had no shelter; we settled down for the night, cold, unfed and miserable. Eventually we dug in there, did various patrols and had a communion service. During the service, conducted by a Padre Dawson, the Jerries came over in their planes and took pot shots at us, but nobody was hurt. We then went forward as a battalion for a short time, didn't really have any skirmishes with the German infantry, and eventually we were withdrawn. During the withdrawal the German Air Force had dominance of the skies and we were severely bombed; there were a few casualties and I think we went back as far as Larisa.

One morning we were told that our company were to take up a position on a very high hill – it must have been about 3,000 feet high. We climbed up that hill – there were no paths, it was really beautiful through the bush, squirrels everywhere. We stopped for lunch and Colonel Kippenberger arrived and sat by me, and whilst we were having lunch a runner came up and delivered him a message. He read it and passed it to me. He said,

"George, don't tell the troops until I am well on my way – we are withdrawing." After having climbed thousands of feet, we went down. We were then told to destroy everything. My friend Jack Baines, who was tenting with me, he and I had an 'His Master's Voice' gramophone, and we each shouldered a pick and broke it up with all the records. It was devastating.

So then the withdrawal started; we were still being bombed and we got through Athens when the German advance party were actually there. This was fairly late at night; we got on to trucks that were directed to a certain area and we were told to destroy everything except our arms. So we set to and pierced the tyres of the trucks and ran the oil out and started the motors. Then the order came that we were to stop that, because we were going on further, still retreating. We went through a village and there B Company of our Battalion had the most casualties from machine-gunning and bombing from the air. I don't think our company had anything, although we did fire a few shots. The Germans didn't seem to be taking any action at night-time, so we marched down to the beach. I don't know how many miles it was, but it was interminable.

We had got to the beach and dropped down to rest when one of my men came round and said, "Sir, give me your water bottle – we've found a dump of rum," and he brought my water bottle full of rum, which I eventually drank. The caiques appeared to take us out to the Navy ships and I got on the caique and the next thing I heard was a voice from this Navy ship, the destroyer *Kimberley*: "Hurry up there or you'll get left behind!" I had fallen asleep.'

Rex Thompson, a driver with the NZ Army Service Corps, related that:

'We supplied the base at Larisa, which was about half way up Greece. The dump there was a big dump and the Germans, being keen on routine, used to bomb every lunch-time, and the personnel on the dump there would bail out as soon as the sirens went and, being inquisitive Kiwis, we used to take a look around. The rum was very popular and that helped out a lot.

Eventually we started the retreat out of Greece and on the south side of the Larisa there was a tremendous convoy and the road was raised, must have been about 12 or 14 foot above the land – it was all flat. And here we were parked almost nose-to-tail and the Germans were bombing and strafing, bombing with anti-personnel bombs and strafing. And once again we decided it was safer just to get under the truck because they were bombing each side of the road for personnel and we realised later that they didn't want to actually blow the bridges or clean up the transport. While we were waiting here – we were just held up in this particular place – there was a Dornier, I'm pretty sure it was a Dornier, and the top of the telephone poles were just a wee bit higher than the road, and this particular plane ambles along just above the telephone lines. And we were just looking at it – we weren't allowed to fire at them because this would bring the whole lot of them on us – and this gunner pulls his turret back half way along the plane there and tosses out a couple of rolls of toilet paper for us – that's the fun they were having. It wasn't well received verbally, however, at the time, but it was quite humorous afterwards. And we found out later that a couple of Australians were having breakfast further down the road there and that's what held the convoy up – they weren't very popular. But all the way down through Greece we were blowing the approaches to the bridges and on again, and the villages where the road went through, and there was only one road, they bombed them. And that went on most of the whole of the way; we continued the withdrawal until eventually we were set for embarkation.

And we went to a beach south of this area of Greece and this particular night we managed to get on a barge to go out to the destroyer. However, they diverted us to Kea Island and we arrived there in the morning. It got too late for us to embark on the destroyer and they put us on this island for the day. We had to cross the island and there must have been about 100 of us, and it was a very bare island and quite hilly and we had to go to the opposite side to be picked up the following night. And it was quite nerve-racking at times with German planes flying over it regularly, and we were all stretched out on virtually bare land and we went to ground every time we saw one. However, apparently the Germans are inclined to be single-minded and so set on a certain job, well, that was all they worried about. So we put the day in hugging the ground and walking and eventually made the other side of the island where we were picked up that night and put on the *Kandahar*, and we thought we were heading for Egypt, but apparently during the trip they decided they had to make another trip and put us off on Crete for a couple of days.

We had 13 raids on the way over and we got a couple of holes through the back of the destroyer – they were borderline, fortunately – but without doubt the skipper was very, very adept. He used to wait nonchalantly for the plane and he'd hard to port or starboard and the water would come right up over the decks as he turned. But we missed any direct hits. One or two of the convoy got badly hit.'

Bruce McKay Smith, Gunner, 25th NZ Artillery Battery, was there too:

'Then we moved to the outskirts of a place called Trikala, which, I understand, had been hit by an earthquake some reasonably short time beforehand, but we were put into olive groves and various scrub and stuff and camouflaged ourselves in. And the next morning, at daylight, the Germans mounted a ferocious attack on Trikala itself; they bombed all day, but how or why we'll never know; they never saw us. I don't think anybody breathed for the whole of that day, and that night we moved out. The war was getting fairly intense then. The roads were choked with not only refugees but various units, Australian, British Army and New Zealand – surplus vehicles going one way and us trying to go another way – but eventually, through a lot of manoeuvring and toing and froing, we got into defensive positions again and carried on moving every now and again to more secure positions. The guns were firing a vast amount of ammunition because ammunition was plentiful for some reason, which was most unusual, all the guns getting almost red hot with their continuous rate of fire.

From there the whole show started to deteriorate, and then we were told that the place was getting untenable and we'd probably have to evacuate. So this started a bit of kerfuffle and we had to travel on very exposed roads, mostly being bombed and strafed most of the time, but with little effect, by the German planes, but very scary all the same. We still had all our equipment intact at that stage, but then we were told we'd have to put our defensive positions up if we found a position that was suitable and we'd go into action against German tanks and infantry. Their Alpine troops were a pest – they seemed to be able to go anywhere. The tanks were not as big a problem as we thought they would be – our gunners became very good at knocking them out, especially when they were trying to do river crossings.

From there on we carried on going south; the whole thing was getting chaotic by then. Nobody quite knew what was going on. Actually we got to the outskirts – I'm not quite sure how far out from Athens – and were told that we had to destroy our guns and vehicles and hopefully disperse and await transport by sea. The guns were destroyed as best we could, most of the optical equipment taken off them. The vehicles had a pickaxe put through the sump and the engine started up and raced until the engine seized up.

After destroying the vehicles, we went to a position whose name I can't recall, with a lot of scrub and stunted trees and olives and one thing and another, not far from the sea. We were told to hide in this undergrowth and, hopefully, we'd be picked up that night by a ship. We spent all day in this scrubby area. The German planes came over continuously, but somehow or another they couldn't have seen us because we had a trouble-free day. As it approached dark, runners were sent round to various groups to tell them to be prepared at anytime to move and to dump any surplus equipment such as rifles and gas-masks and stuff like that. However, very few of our chaps dumped their rifles – they hung on to them.

About the very early hours of the morning, possibly 3 or 4 o'clock, we were told to form up and make our way down to the seaside, and there the Royal Navy had arrived with their lifeboats and we were bundled aboard these lifeboats; any gear the sailors manning the lifeboats considered excess, they'd chuck overboard. We were ferried out to, in our case, HMS *Carlisle*. We eventually got aboard her and we finished up in the Stokers' Mess where the off-duty stokers couldn't do enough for us, making copious mugs of cocoa and bread and buns and whatever they could find to feed us, for we'd had no food during the day. Then we set off, as we found out later, of course, for Crete. However, we were bombed several times, but the *Carlisle*, being an ack-ack cruiser, put up a terrific display of anti-aircraft fire and we only had about three or four near misses, which was pretty good. Eventually we arrived in Suda Bay just before dusk, I think it was.'

On the retirement and under bombing, the practical common sense of the 20th NZ Infantry Battalion's Padre was well-remembered by Keith Newth, then a Corporal of Signals:

'We had slit trenches, dug in we were, and the bombers, German bombers, came over and I can always hear Padre Spence saying, "Well, boys, it's all very well to believe in the Lord, but it's better to take action or get down into our holes when this sort of thing is going on," which we did.'

Sapper Alexander Rodgers, NZ 7th Field Company, recalled the voyage to Greece only too well:

'We'd only been gone a few hours when the whole convoy turned round and headed back towards Alex. The Italian Fleet were waiting for this convoy to put out, but the British were one jump ahead. We retreated and the whole of the Mediterranean Fleet, the British, took up their positions and they blew every one of the Italian ships out of the water. Fantastic – you could hear the noise in the far distance there, and the next day they told us what had happened. [This must have been the Battle of Matapan when, on 28 March 1941, the Mediterranean Fleet sank three Italian cruisers, two destroyers and damaged at least one battleship, all for the loss of one aircraft.]

Our job was to put through a secondary road to meet up with the Maori Battalion in the Olympus. We would start at daylight and work to dark every day, sleeping underneath the trucks, no tents or anything, only bully beef and hard biscuits, and after a couple of weeks we eventually got the road open. Bridges were built and the bridges and the road mined in case

Alexander Rodgers

those Jerries came down. That was the officer's job – they mined them all right, but they didn't put the leads in the mines and the first ones across the roads and the bridges were the Germans. They came round the Maori Battalion and cut them off and they were the first to use our road.

It was chaos from there, all the way down through Larisa, all these other places, machine-gunned, bombed all the time. Eventually we embarked on lighters that took us out to catch up with Navy boats that were there. There were destroyers, cruisers, a few big troopships, and we loaded our gear, our rifles and that, thinking, well, we'll need them. We were going out to the ack-ack light cruiser there on a Greek boat and I was carrying this machine-gun, it was a Lewis Gun, and a sailor on the boat says, "Where're you going with that?" and I said, "Going on the boat – we might need it," and he says, "Well, it's either you or that." He said, "Give us it." I gave it to him and he threw it overboard. He said, "There's no room for that, mate."

Well we went there and we took off. There must have been a dozen ships and a big troopship in the convoy, and we were halfway to Crete and you could see these planes there, way in the distance. We were on deck, there must have been 200 or 300 of us there, and we said, "By God, we don't like the look of that." We'd seen too many of them. Someone said that those were British ones come as our escort. We said, "Like hell they are!" They had big black crosses on them, so we opened up on them. Well, they didn't hit us but they ripped a hole about 50 foot long alongside just about the water line with a bomb. We made it all right, but there was a troopship there, she got a direct hit and went down, and one or two other ships were hit too.'

Before the Germans struck in Greece, one New Zealander, Kenneth Frater, driver in the NZ Army Service Corps, had an unexpected encounter:

'Goods were coming from Piraeus by the narrow-gauge railway which ran through Katerini and on to Bulgaria. I was loading stuff at a station near Katerini and I went to the corrugated iron urinal to relieve myself. I heard a train stop at the station and a bloke in a striped suit and a homburg hat rushed in and stood alongside me.

He said, "You are a New Zealander?"

I said, "Yes."

He extended his hand and said, "Eden."

I changed hands and said, "Frater," and that is how and where I took a leak with the British Foreign Minister and a future Prime Minister. He'd been in Bulgaria meeting the Bulgarian Government and said he expected to fly back to the UK the next day.'

Kenneth Frater was one of a small number of drivers who volunteered to drive back north to pick up troops holding Thermopylae Pass for evacuation back towards Athens and the coast:

'Around 9.30pm on 24 April we drove north to the foot of the mountain pass road. I thought I was fairly cunning by being last out of the forest. I'd presumed that each truck would have to turn round and then I'd be first away. Alas, the best-laid plans! I wasn't to know that there was a place to turn and I would stay on the end of the column. A bit after 10pm there was the sound of feet tramping on the road, and shortly after the first truck left. At about 11pm, when there was only one truck left in front of me, some more troops came along and boarded the other truck. A sergeant came to me and said, "You're to wait – Lieutenant Wesney will be here shortly." Ages later – at least 15 minutes – when I'd been sitting by myself in the middle of nowhere on a dark night and feeling extremely lonely, I felt a movement at the back of the truck. The passenger door opened and a voice said, "Stay where you are – the men are getting in the back. My name is Arthur Wesney." There was a slap on the cab roof and he said, "Right, get going."

I said, "Are you the All Black?"

He replied, "Yes, I am. Now I'd like to get some sleep."

Driving without lights is a tiring business. You can't see through the windscreen and have to hang your head out the window, which gets very tiring. Some of the other drivers had knocked their windscreens out, but this meant that all of you was cold instead of just your head. Either way, top speed was never more than 10 miles per hour, which caused the engine to overheat. By daylight we'd travelled about 60 miles and had just gone through a cutting on top of a low hill a few miles south of Marathon. When we were down on the flat again I was told to pull into an area of trees and scrub well off the road.

Lieutenant Wesney and his men climbed the hill and spent some time observing the road north for any sign of the enemy. I thought it would be a good time to change my socks and have a feed. When I climbed into the back of the truck I found my tucker box was empty, and they'd also flogged my clean socks and underwear. Of all the ungrateful sods! After about one and a half hours the squad of 20 returned.

I said, "You're an ungrateful lot of bastards, pinching my food and clothes, and it would have served you right if I'd driven off and left you."

Arthur Wesney said to them, "Who is responsible – has anyone anything to say?"

Nobody said a word. He said, "Right, let's get going then."

When we moved off he said how sorry he was that I'd been treated like that, but they'd been without food for 24 hours. I was very hostile towards the blokes in the back for the four more days I was to have them for passengers.

We drove round a bay with two destroyers standing at anchor. I wondered if we were to be taken off by them, but we kept going and crossed the Corinth just after 10am on 25 April. After finding our way through the town we had just reached the open road when we were stopped by a despatch rider. Parachutists were dropping on the Canal area and we were ordered to go back. Turning round, we headed back to Corinth. Back in the town I was told to pull into a narrow street and wait. My passengers went off and I was left on my own to guard my truck. I got out my rifle and tried to make myself as small as possible. Another truck driven by a chap pulled in behind me, and his passengers went off. It was good to have company. He'd apparently been about 10 miles south of Corinth when he was turned back. The aerial activity was intense and pretty scary. We couldn't see what was going on but saw plenty of planes passing overhead.

Around midday things quietened down, and shortly after our passengers returned. I then realised that the officer in the other truck was Colonel Rusty Paige (another All Black), CO of the 26th Battalion. We gave the other truck a few minutes' start and started off again. On two different occasions I saw a plane diving towards us and the road ahead being chipped by bullets. Each time I went to stop to bail out, but Arthur Wesney made me keep going. On both occasions the plane had to pull out of its dive before the bullets reached us. I was beginning to really dislike the Luftwaffe.

Any time we passed over a rise or hill we would stop and the blokes would go out on a recce. At long last the penny dropped. We were "tail-end Charlie". During one stop, which was in a village, I heard a hen cackle. I hopped over a mud wall and found a nest with three eggs in it. As I hadn't eaten for nearly 48 hours, I decided to suck the contents, and boy, did they taste good! Moving over the Argos Pass we stopped at sunrise and pulled off the road down a tree-lined track. My passengers did their usual disappearing trick and I was left on my own again. It was a nice sunny morning and, holding my rifle, I went to sleep by the front wheel of my truck. I awoke about midday and filled my water bottle at a small stream nearby, filled the tank with the rest of my reserve petrol and then thought I would do something really rash and have a shave at the stream. When I went to get my small haversack from where I carried it under the driver's seat, I found somebody had flogged it while I was asleep. Now all I possessed was the truck, which belonged to the Army anyway, my rifle, the clothes I stood up in and the contents of my pockets.

Early afternoon the troops returned and we resumed our journey, travelling over a mountainous area. There were lots of abandoned and burnt-out trucks, but we had a safe journey and went on to take up positions near Tripolis. Whilst I was playing my usual waiting game, I was parked near an aerodrome which had well and truly been done over by enemy planes. Nearby I found an abandoned pick-up in a ditch. I made a search of the vehicle and found a large tin of green peas. I couldn't believe my luck. Food! I opened the tin with my pocket-knife, drank the liquid and shovelled the peas down my throat. What a marvellous, delicious taste! Fifteen minutes later I had my trousers round my ankles with a stream of green water running from my bowels. It wasn't nice.

Next morning we moved through Sparta and my passengers went into a holding position until early on the morning of 29 April. We pulled out just after daybreak. The old Bedford was now only firing on five cylinders. My original load had overnight grown from 20 to over 40. Over 4 tons on a 3-ton truck. She still went good downhill, but I was in low gear going uphill. However, this didn't last for long and we started a steep descent of about 10 miles toward the sea at Momenvasia. I think, for my passengers, this was probably the most hairy part of the entire trip. Being well overloaded, even in third gear it was hard to keep under 50 miles an hour. I must admit I was anxious to get off the road before the strafing started, so perhaps took some unnecessary risks.

The road flattened out and about a mile from the sea I was directed into an olive grove. Arthur Wesney thanked me for a job well done, the rest said nothing. I was still pretty terse with them for pinching my food and gear. I guess if they had known I would be responsible for carrying them safely for over 400 miles and five nights and days to the evacuation beach, they may have acted differently. I hope the act of them leaving without a word was an act of shame.

Parking under an olive tree I looked around the dozen or so trucks dispersed and hidden through the olive grove. This was all that were left of the 30 that started. One of our officers had caught up with us during the day. At sunset we drove our trucks to a cliff edge. There we drained the oil and ran the engines until they seized up, then pushed them over the cliff. When it was fully dark we marched down to the beach and for hours sat there wondering if and when something was going to happen. Finally, about midnight a few row-boats appeared and were quickly loaded. It was about 2am before it was our turn. We got into a row-boat and pushed off, and after a few minutes drew up alongside an old Greek fishing-boat. There were probably over a hundred aboard when the one-cylinder engine was started. I thought, "My God, if we're going in this old thing we'll be dead at daylight."

However, after puffing round for about 10 minutes, there, at anchor, were two beautiful destroyers, HMS *Isis* and the *Hotspur*. We were put aboard the *Hotspur* where a mug of cocoa was put in my hand and, grasping my rifle, my only possession, I went to sleep on the steel deck under a stairwell. This was the last of the organised official evacuation, although I understand the *Ajax* picked the General up at 4am.

Around mid-morning on 30 April I was awakened by the tannoy telling us to assemble on deck. We were in a bay which someone thought was Canea in Crete. We were just tying up alongside an old freighter called the *Thurland Castle* and were quickly transhipped to her. There were a number of sunken ships. There was an air raid and bombs dropped near several ships, but we were left alone although the *Thurland Castle* showed marks of previous strafing. It was suggested by the ASC Officer that we would be returned to our units who were now on Crete. However, Colonel Paige said that we were going to stay under his command until he had orders to the contrary. Hooray for Rusty Paige!

We sailed about midday. There were three troopships with survivors of the 6th Brigade and odds and sods like us aboard. The 6th Brigade had been placed in reserve. The troopships were in line ahead and on either side was a row of warships, probably most of what remained of the Mediterranean Fleet. They stayed with us until we were out of range of the Luftwaffe, and then we were left with only one destroyer for escort. During that 24 hours, though, they were continually attacked by German planes. Fortunately they were after the warships and left us alone. The day we arrived in Port Said was 2 May, exactly one year since sailing from New Zealand. Happy anniversary!'

CHAPTER 6

Crete

A *nd so, towards the end of April 1941, the war-weary troops evacuated from Greece, minus equipment and often rifles, began to arrive in Crete. They settled in and waited for the anticipated German invasion.*

Lieutenant George Arthur Brown, 20th Battalion NZ Infantry, who was evacuated from Greece in the destroyer HMS *Kimberley*, arrived at Suda Bay to see:

'…the masts and funnel of the cruiser *York* that had been sunk in Suda Bay by the Germans. The Colonel was on the wharf with his Adjutant and RSM. We officers gathered together and had breakfast. The men were told to report to a certain area – there was only one road. "Take your time," said the Colonel, so take your time meant that the boys visited the bars. I set off for my area, which was a lovely area, trees and a stream; I stripped off, washed my clothes as best I could, laid them out to dry and put them on. No tools for digging, but we relieved a battalion of the Welsh Regiment, who had been on the island for about six months and had not completed their trenches.

We dug and we dug with what we could find – we only had M&V, that is meat and vegetables, to eat, all tinned. I got a couple of blokes one day and I said, "We'll go to Canea and see if we can get some food." So we went to Canea and we bought what we could, and one of the chaps said to me, "Sir, do you mind going back on your own?'

I said, "Why?" and they said, "Well, the battle will be starting before very long and we want to go to the brothel. We'd hate to be killed without having been to the brothel." So I let them go to the brothel and one of them was killed.

We were at Division when the real aerial bombing started. The island had a couple of Hurricane fighters, which had been shooting down the odd German plane, but they didn't last long so we were completely at their mercy. The Germans were concentrating on the port of Suda Bay, which was the only port which our supplies came through. The sky was black with heavy oil smoke.'

One of those who endured that wait for the German onslaught was Rex Thompson, a driver in the NZ Army Service Corps:

'There were a few vehicles on Crete, not many, but we had virtually nothing else. It was just a matter of supplying Maleme aerodrome on Crete and the battalions who were dug in round the place. And the Germans, to start with, used to come over and bomb occasionally, bomb Canea, that was the main town there. It must have been about 14 or15 May they really set in and bombed virtually most of the day off and on. They bombed the town, they also bombed the harbour, but despite all that and the noise and the dust our casualties were not that heavy.'

Bruce Smith, Gunner in the 25th NZ Artillery Battery, recollected that:

'Suda Bay had a lot of shipping in it, which was being bombed fairly frequently and ineffectually, actually. And we eventually disembarked and were told to make our way some distance out of Suda Bay where there was a reception area, where we got some basic food, bully beef and biscuits, and told to find somewhere to sleep for the night. We had no baggage, just what we stood up in. Some of us had greatcoats, others didn't, and fortunately the weather wasn't over cold.

In the morning we were lined up and those of us that had rifles were put into groups of eight to 12 and usually with six rifles assigned to each group. We had a bombardier in charge of us; we were told to carry on, I think, in a southerly direction and keep going until we were caught up with by a guide or a runner to take us to a particular area which we were supposed to defend. We kept going all day and part of the night and then came to a little gully, not far off the sea, and told to make ourselves comfortable in this little gully. Four to five gunners were to stand on duty with their rifles at all times, taking shifts – I think four hours on and four off. We were supposed to look for any sea invasion or aircraft invasion, and that went on for two or three days. Not a lot of activity except somebody came out on an old broken-down vehicle and gave us a bit more food and water, which was pretty frugal.'

When Richard Kean, Sergeant, NZ Artillery, arrived at Suda Bay:

'We were told to march along the road, but every time we stopped and said, "How far have we got to go?" we were told, "Oh, its only another couple of miles." We were finally told that our camp was 10 miles away. So we walked 10 miles and settled in. It was pretty cold but I managed to scrounge a blanket from somewhere and another bloke had a ground sheet. We dug a slit trench with a bayonet and we got into that, put the groundsheet on the ground and covered ourselves with the blanket and we slept. Well, this went on for a while and things improved; we got a bit more food and got sorted out and we finished up with the armed personnel staying on the island – that was the fellows that had rifles – but I, unfortunately, was armed with a .45 so I was classed as armed personnel.

We were turned into infantry and I became the CSM with four sections under me. The section was comprised of infantry guys, drivers and gunners who had rifles and ASC men, and we moved backwards and forwards, laid wire in the area in sporadic attempts to make ourselves useful. I got friendly with an innkeeper in the village of Galatos. So we would "stand to" about 5 o'clock in the morning, keeping ourselves warm by having the odd liqueur.'

Alexander Rodgers, Sapper, NZ Engineers, remembered everything being a proper shambles:

'We had no ammunition, no guns, no nothing. Eventually we managed to pick up the odd rifle and the odd rounds of ammunition; some had a machine-gun. The artillery was not far away from us. We were at Maleme aerodrome.'

From Canea, after a fair route march, Keith Newth, Corporal of Signals, had joined the encamped NZ 20th Battalion:

'I picked my signal station and dug holes and put ourselves in. And then every morning we would "stand to", I think it was just at daylight and until about an hour after daybreak, expecting the paratroopers which we knew were coming at any time, and then we would stand down. Colonel Kippenberger sent back to Egypt for entertainment for the troops, such things as cards, you know, and that type of thing. Cairo sent the New Zealand Band over. Well, those boys were giving a Sunday afternoon concert and all of a sudden this sweep of planes was coming across – "Oh, here's our boys" – but it wasn't and the next minute they started to scream down. It was a squadron of Stukas. As you can imagine, band instruments, they went one way, the men the other.

That was our first real taste of what it was going to be like to be the actual targets for these Stuka bombers with their screamers on them. And that was a terrible noise to hear. Then we went to our main camp at Galatas; that was quite a big village, and I set up my signal station there and "Kippy" had the biggest house in the village. It was a big white house, so that was to be his Battalion Headquarters. And I remember in the basement of this place there were 20 or 30 huge wine casks – they would hold 600 or 700 litres at least, probably more. Well some of the boys got a little bit troublesome on wine, so Kippy had every one of them staked and they were smashed to let the stuff pour out, which was sacrilege as far as we were concerned, but it had to be done of course.'

On 20 May 1941, after very heavy bombing, the Germans, who had complete mastery of the air, proceeded to land parachute and glider-borne troops in their thousands, on and around the airfields in Crete. In so doing they suffered severe losses.

Captain George Brown recalled:

'The morning of the invasion we had just finished breakfast, I think I was about to shave, when the first bombing planes came over. We had a few casualties. We took up positions but no parachutists landed in our area; they were really concentrating on Maleme aerodrome. There were three aerodromes on the island. The Australians further to the east were looking after two of them, and it was our job, New Zealand's job mostly, to deny Maleme to the Germans. It was our 5th Brigade that was centred around Maleme aerodrome, and we must remember that we did not have the full three brigades, we only had two – the rest had gone direct from Greece to Egypt. The General had formed composite battalions of Cretans, Greeks, odds and sods. We lost our company commander and our second in command. The company commander went to a composite Greek Battalion – he was killed later – and the second in command went to another company of our battalion.

Eventually we were told that we were to counter-attack Maleme aerodrome. There was a piece of land, a river valley, west of the aerodrome, that was practically undefended, and the Germans had landed there by troop carriers and parachutists almost ad lib. The slaughter of the Germans was terrible, so I believe. We were to be relieved from Division Reserve by a battalion of Australians; they, however, arrived late, and it was General Freyberg's instructions that we were not to move until we were relieved. Out at sea we could see flashes of guns and searchlights and we knew that the Navy was dealing with the seaborne troops that the Germans were sending over and that General Freyberg was concerned would arrive and attack Division, hence our staying there.

Of the Australian battalion, I spoke to the colonel later in prisoner of war camp and he alleged that they were being bombed en route – the Germans didn't bomb at night-time – and when they got to Canea they, the Australians, lost their way. I forget the starting time of the arrival of the relief, but they were hours late. Our colonel, Jim Burrows, disregarded Freyberg's instructions and sent two companies of the battalion up to the starting line. There was only one road; it was chock-a-block with civilians, miscellaneous people, wounded coming back. We had three officers in our company; Denver Fountain had a platoon (he was acting Company Commander), I had a platoon (I was acting Second in Command), and Charlie Upham had the 3rd platoon. Denver Fountain went in to Brigadier Hargest of the 5th Brigade Headquarters, I waited outside, and when Denver came out I said to him, "What's the story?" and he said, "George, you know as much about it as I do."

So we took up position on the starting line. The Germans must have known we were there – we were being machine-gunned very heavily – but with a cry we rushed forward, made a lot of ground, wiped out their machine-gun post. By this time it was light, German bombers were overhead, the fighters were overhead giving us hell. I believe we got to the edge of the aerodrome and I was wounded, so I was out of it. There was muck flying everywhere and I lay on the ground, and I think I put my field dressing on my knee, and Charlie Upham and his driver Patterson came along and I told them to get the hell out of it, frightened that they'd get hit, but they went and pulled the door off an old derelict building, placed me on it, and some others came along and carried me out of danger and I landed in the 23rd Battalion Regimental Aid Post [RAP]. It was being attended by Padre Griffiths and Doctor (Captain) Ron Stewart.

They had some German wounded there, walking wounded. I and another chap were put in the RAP, which was in a dry creek bed about 10 or 12 foot deep, and the medical people had scooped alcoves out of the bank and I was put in there with another chap of B Company who had a chest wound. And some time in the morning somebody came along and spoke to him, and he gets up and I said, "What's happening?" and he said, "I'm not allowed to tell you." So the Padre came along and I said, "What's happening, Padre?" and he said, "Well, the evacuation is on, the withdrawal is on, and walking wounded are to make their way back." So I said, "Give me a stick I'll go too," and then I fell back. So then, after the troops were withdrawn and we were being mortared by the Germans, the German walking wounded that we had with us climbed up the bank and waved white flags and the mortaring stopped and we were taken prisoner. I was still on the door, taken out into the sunshine, and I don't think we had anything to drink or eat. We were moved from place to place until eventually we were taken down to an RAP that had been set up on the edge of the 'drome. The RAP consisted of a farm building with a first floor and a couple of rooms outside. I think I was taken into the dressing room or the theatre a couple of times and put on a hard wooden table; my dressings were taken off and put on again, and I was taken back, still on my door.

We had an Aussie who was quite fit and he said he didn't want to work for the Germans in clearing the aerodrome, but he'd work for us. So he used to scrummage round and on one occasion he got a couple of fowls and he had them cooked and the medical people had the meat and we were given a bit of the soup, which was very refreshing. But this Aussie had found that underneath us was a cellar in which there were a lot of carafes of red wine, and he gave me and, I suppose, he gave others a couple of tins. One was to drink wine out of and one was to urinate in, and I'd drink wine, fall asleep, wake up, hope I used the other tin, drink wine again, and fall asleep. The Medical Officer, Ron Stewart, said, "I wouldn't drink too much of that wine, George, it's not good for you," and I said, "Well it's given me some relief from pain and it's making me sleep."

I don't know how many days we spent there – it seemed to be interminable. Then the word came that some were going down to the airport to be taken to Athens, so I said, "Well, leave me and take the others." So they agreed and a couple of Blenheim bombers came over whilst our wounded were lying on the aerodrome, and plastered the aerodrome. A day or so later it came my turn and the others that had stayed behind. I was still on the door, laid on the aerodrome fringe in the heat, and a German officer came along and saw my rank, gave me a cigarette, and lit it. I half finished it when he ordered up a plane and put two of us on board and we flew across to Athens.'

Keith Newth recalled the battle for Crete:

'We were there, standing by every morning until the morning that the Junkers 52 transport planes came with their paratroopers, with a lot of them dragging one and two gliders behind them. We were up on the side of a hill and watching, and a lot of the German boys were shot as they were floating down. There were gliders crashing into olive groves, a lot of men killed, but a heck of a lot got away. And eventually they took the bottom of the valley where they were landing. In this valley there was a prison, and the first thing they did was throw the doors to the prison open and let the prisoners out. We tried our best to hold the Germans back, but their numbers were what actually beat us in Galatas, and we were eventually forced back out of the village.

And then we went back to Canea, an event I'll never forget. We got amongst Maori Battalion boys – Captain Love was in charge. The Jerries were in a long line with machine-gunners standing beyond this fence, and these Maori men just went through in a bayonet charge with their war cries, caught them there and killed them on the spot. And when the boys went through behind them, we came across this one Maori boy, his chest was blown wide open, his lungs were just beating away and his mates wouldn't leave him; he had no chance of living, but they wouldn't leave him till he had gone.'

Lieutenant Stanley Jervis, RNVR, was serving in the escort vessel HMS *Syvern* operating from Suda Bay in Crete, and had a grandstand view from the sea:

'We were on patrol just off Canea and at daylight we watched the whole invasion on Maleme and Canea, rather a remarkable sight because it was a very still morning and the whole of the sky seemed to be filled with coloured balloons which were parachutes, paratroops. They coloured all their parachutes for different purposes, different colours meaning the different types of ammunition, food, whatever. And it was an amazing sight to see the whole of the sky filled with these paratroops. We went to action stations because there was a report of aircraft approaching. I was handling the ship and I said to a sailor, "How many aircraft?" and he looked over his shoulder and said, "There's four," and we turned towards the aircraft to open fire and they turned away. And so then it became apparent that something else was going on and they were not interested in us. Then the signalman came up to me and he said, "Well, sir, I've lost count, I can only go up to 261." Then we went back on to patrol.'

Ashore, in Crete, after more bombing, Rex Thompson recalled the unnerving sight of the German gliders:

'They were being towed, quite a number to each plane. And they just coasted quite quietly and would land, but they were dealt with fairly smartly unless they were very adept or landed in a remote area. And then the paratroops came in; they were in Junkers 52s, about 30 odd in a plane, and they were dropping them off at very, very low levels, oh, perhaps 100, 150 feet. And there were quite a few of them caught up in the tail fins of their planes, just hanging there and the rest; they were fully exposed, equipped with automatic rifles, etc, but they were absolute sitting shots during that 10 or 12 seconds they were in the air.

At Maleme airport, the airstrip, our chaps had Bofors and artillery with

Stanley Godfrey Jervis

open sights on the airport and they created havoc with the planes. And in the end the Germans just beached their planes along the beach there, crash-landed, and those that could get out got out, and eventually they got established at the cost of about 200 planes. Then one thing led to another and it just got tougher and tougher, and we had to do the withdrawal and that was bad, after six days fighting. And remember, we were a non-combatant unit and, while the fighting was on, trying to get supplies through, but these were virtually non-existent. We were sent on a bayonet trek up the valley just between the aerodrome and Canea – there were about 60 of us, and I think we had two bayonets. Fortunately we didn't meet anybody, so that was it.'

When the first paratroops descended, Gunner Bruce Smith was off duty:

'I was unarmed, so five or six of us without weapons or guns were told to make our way back to where we came from, which we did. It took us a couple of days, I think. What with lack of food, we were fairly weak – we didn't have a great lot of stamina. Anyway, we got back to Suda Bay. We swanned round there for, I think, two days being bombed and strafed and all that carry-on, and then they told us, late one afternoon, to be prepared to embark on a vessel which would be pulled in to one of the wharves. It did eventually happen. We piled aboard this ship, which was a Norwegian lumber ship, as I remember, called the *Belray*. We were all on deck – there were no cabins or any accommodation, just a seething mass of soldiers sprawled out all over the deck. We moved out into the stream and then moved over to, I think probably, a western area of Suda Bay, and it was good to stay there. All this time there were ships being attacked, bombed and strafed, but nobody came near us – we could never work that out. At dark, they said, the air attack would probably finish – the Germans were not very keen on night work. So at dark the ship weighed anchor and we took off for Alexandria.'

Unnerving it may well have been, but endeavour was made to neutralise the German parachutists, as was recounted by Battery NCO Sergeant Richard Kean:

'In the morning the parachutists had landed. It was a great sight but very scaring; it reminded me of the duck-shooting season to see all these fellows coming down. We managed to pick off a few of them as they were coming down, but there was quite a lot of them. Then we split up into two sections and Lieutenant John Dill, who was a nephew of General Sir John Dill, a nice fellow, he took one section and I took the other and we patrolled through the gullies, around the olive trees, to see if we could find any of the parachutists that had landed.

Later on I had a section across the road, the prison road leading from the prison in the valley up to the village of Galatas. On one side of the road were a lot of beehives, and down in the front of this was a machine-gun that kept firing over and disturbing the bees, and part of my section over there weren't very happy about this. However, John Dill came along one evening and he said, "We'll get him – I've got an anti-tank rifle," and he lay down. We knew the general direction, and he said, "Stand up and light a cigarette." I said, "You've got to be joking, mate." However, I stood up, lit a cigarette and hit the deck pretty smartly. By the time I was on the deck the tracers were coming over. John said, "I think I've got him – do it again," so it was a repeat performance, and he said, "Right, I've got him," and he put five rounds in and we never heard any more.

Then things were getting a bit hectic and there was a machine-gun down in front that was a bit annoying, so I got out of the trench and crouched behind an olive tree, and by this time I had a rifle and bayonet and two bandoleers of ammunition. There were plenty of rifles lying around. I could pick up the shadow of a German soldier standing, and I put five rounds into him there and he dropped. And then I worked out as to where the gunner would be crouched behind his machine-gun and I put five rounds in there. Instead of hopping back into the slit trench, I stayed crouched behind a tree, waiting for somebody else to come up and take over the machine-gun. But unfortunately they'd picked up my position as well, so they mortared it, and John Dill's overcoat had been lying on the ground and a mortar landed on that, at my feet. I got fairly spattered with the mortar; one fellow got wounded and he panicked, so I sent him out to the dressing station with the other chap, and then I realised that I was there on my own. I began to realise then that I'd been wounded when my boots squelched as I stood, and I looked down at a fair-sized hole in my leg.

I had a lot of home-made bombs containing anything from four to 16 sticks of jelly and a 7-second fuse and a big cigar, and my job was, when the German tanks started coming up the road, to light the cigar, smoke it and use the cigar to light the fuses and chuck them at the tanks. But I was more worried about the bombs being hit by the shrapnel and exploding around me than I was about anything else.

However, I realised that I had been hit and went back, as there had been a dressing station behind me. It had gone but I found John Dill lying in the yard; he'd been shot by an explosive bullet. I was pretty mad by this time; the effects of the mortar blowing me up hadn't worn off and it was just as if I was fighting drunk. However, I remembered that in our position there was an old gun that was supposed to be manned; it was one that was broken and it was propped up, but there was no sign of a gun crew. However, I poked around and saw a pair of feet sticking out of a hollow olive tree, so I poked my rifle in and said, "Come out of there." It was a gunner, an English gunner, who was in a pretty bad way, drunk. There was an officer who was a pretty good bloke, but these others were all hiding and not making any attempt to take part, so I rounded them up, found the Sergeant and I said to him, "There's an officer lying there, in the yard back there – tear a door or something off the building and get him down to the RAP and make sure you get him there. If you don't I'll be looking for you for the rest of your lives." I found out later that they'd had a pretty rough time of it, but that's no excuse for their lack of duty and inability to hold themselves together.

Then I finally arrived at the dressing station and met a fellow out of the machine-gunners who I'd known in civvy street, and he'd got hit by a mortar too. He could walk fairly well. The medical orderly came out and gave us a cup of tea and said, "It's pretty busy here – there's another dressing station about 4 miles down the road if you like to go down there." So Jim and I had another cup of tea, had a smoke and so off we went. That 4 miles turned out to be 11; anyway we got there, and an hour after we left that dressing station, the Germans took it over and the blokes that were there were taken prisoner.

So I finished up in an Australian Dressing Station under the olive trees. They took my rifle, tin hat and that, revolver and ammunition away from me and I felt naked. The officer that I had sent out was there, and he was operated on there but he died; he had an explosive bullet through the buttock. A good bloke, but I was pleased that at least he had got to a dressing station and they could try and do something for him.'

Also involved in the attempt to render the German airborne invasion ineffective was Alexander Rodgers, Sapper, NZ Engineers:

'Some we shot down straightaway; we would manage to confiscate their weapons and use them. Their machine-guns were very good – they were light, like Sten guns – but it was a stinking business. Luckily the Navy was there and they attacked a convoy of German boats in the early hours one morning and that just lit the sky. The Navy got in there and they sunk the lot of them – a good job, too.

So the Jerries, after a while, they captured Maleme Aerodrome and the planes were still coming in. Quite a few were being shot down; they were travelling very low and there was strafing and bombing, and they had screamers on. Anyhow, we made a counter-attack on Maleme and it was just a muck-up. Of course, there was no way of communicating in those days, none at all, and we were kicked out of there after a while. Then the next thing, we were chased back to a village called San Marino up in the hills, and from there to Galatas, where there was some heavy fighting, and when we took over we saw the atrocities that had been committed there, and these were shocking. I've seen it with my own eyes – some of these women and children had had their throats cut.

So then we were kicked out of there and took up a position off the beach. Opposite was the 6th General Hospital, but the Germans had overrun that and they put up the flags, the Red Cross flags, there and mounted their machine-guns on the roof. We had an old place there, a little old farmhouse down on the flat, which was our first aid station, Red Crosses all around us to say it was a Dressing Station, and at the back, about 12 or 15 foot high, was this bit of a hill there. Bare as could be, no cover, and we're on the side of this hill and nothing to dig in with and the Germans are only about 200 or 300 yards away, and they had their machine-guns set up behind a Red Cross flag. We weren't allowed to fire where the hospital grounds were, and I got smacked with an explosive bullet and it shattered across through all the muscles and everything, and we got slaughtered with machine-guns, mortars, etc, and we lost a lot of men there. So that's where I ended my fighting days. They got me into this dressing station down below, but all of a sudden mortars are landing all round and then the Jerries came in and then shot two or three of our orderlies. A couple of days later the rest of us injured ones were taken down to the Maleme Aerodrome by the Germans and flown over to Athens.'

Stanley Jervis in HMS *Syvern* recalled:

'We took up our normal patrols again and at that time we were patrolling from just south of the bottom end of Crete, up past Canea and up to the other side of Heraklion, which is a little port about half way up the northern coast of Crete. And one afternoon, off Suda Bay, we were attacked by a German aircraft, one only, because it was the tail-end of an air raid attack, a large air raid attack on Suda Bay, which they did just about every day in those times. This fellow obviously diverted himself to kind of "beat us up", which he did very effectively. We tried to dodge him. My Captain was aft, I was on watch, and we tried to stop him machine-gunning along the full length of the ship by giving him the starboard side so he could get over us quickly and without too much damage, we hoped. However, eventually he caught me head on and he raked us very severely with machine-gun fire the full length of the ship, and he'd already done that on broadside. We had a 3-inch gun forward and we hit him because he blew up and disintegrated right over our bridge, and on the way to that he took our foremast with him.

The unfortunate part of that was my Captain, who was aft, he got badly wounded, and we had the machine-gun operator, who was rather a wonderful chap from South Africa, and he was standing alongside me on the bridge and he suddenly flopped down on to the deck. And I thought, well, that's a good idea, I don't know why I didn't do that, so I flopped down too. But anyway, I got up and when I went to give him a hand up I took his tin helmet off as it was in the way a bit, took that off, and to my dismay half his head came off with the tin helmet. And we'd quite a lot of our chaps been wounded aft, nine of them I think; and one of our good chaps, he was using an Oerlikon gun to great effect and the Huns got him and explosive bullets hit him on both feet and he lost both his feet. We gave him a rum, brandy or something until we could get him patched up. I can still remember this – I lit a cigarette and gave it to him and held it for him while he had a couple of puffs, and I really have never seen ever before such a change in a man's face. Everything went out of it except for a look of peace and comfort, so I'm a great believer in smoking and cigarettes.

Anyway, they were all put ashore and we went in to Suda Bay and all these chaps were shipped out pretty swiftly to Alexandria because all sorts of shipping was coming in at night-time, and going out again bringing ammunition and goodness knows what and troops. In Suda Bay we tried to refuel, but we were only able to get a certain amount because we had another air raid and we had to slip, but we had enough for the time being and off we went. By that time I got something like a commanding officer's assignment, by attrition – because we'd already lost two captains and I was the only one in sight – they gave it to me, temp. Then we were back on patrol and had to take four small landing craft up to Heraklion because the Army had run out of digging gear, picks and shovels, ammunition and all that sort of thing. Heraklion was on fire, so we weren't allowed to go into the harbour because they didn't want us to get sunk inside and block the fairway. So we left the landing craft at the entrance and pushed on back to Suda Bay, leaving the landing craft to find their own way back.

We went into Suda Bay to go to a berth, just after daylight, and we tied up to the jetty. There was a lot of movement going on and we didn't take terribly much notice of it until a Sergeant of Royal Marines came out of the end building. We were just putting the last rope on the jetty and to get this on we had to be terribly careful because there was an unexploded 500-pound bomb sticking up at the end of the jetty, and we had to put our ropes round that bit, and he came along and said, "What the hell are you doing here?" And we said that this was where we usually tie up, and he said, "Those so and so's up there are Germans," and they were just at the end of the jetty and we couldn't believe him.

We carefully and hurriedly retrieved our line from shore, and he said, "Can I come with you?" We said yes, so we were off and no one took any notice of us. I think the Germans must have thought we were one of their own ships; they'd hardly expect one of our Navy ships would come in and tie up to what was now their jetty. However, that's how we got away with it, I suppose. We went out of Suda Bay and went under the great cliffs of Cape Dhrapanon, which is right on the end of the nor'eastern entrance to Suda Bay, a little cove where we anchored. We were in the shadow of the cliffs and decided then the only thing we could do; we had 70 tons of fuel, just about enough to get us into Alexandria. We decided we'd have to beat it for Alexandria, but we couldn't move in daylight because it seemed the whole of the German Air Force were flying round, so we anchored there and made the ship look as deserted as we possibly could, rope falls hanging down the side, etc. We were close in shore and most of the crew were on the beach ashore, and we told them to get under cover. The engineer and I and some others went out to the ship every few hours and topped up the boiler, topped up the steam, and that was all right. We used to lie on the beach and watch the aircraft flying past and they used to fly so low looking at the ship, and we rather hoped they'd think it was an abandoned ship.

And that worked quite well until about 7 o'clock in the evening. We'd been out, topped up the fuel, topped up the steam and waiting for dusk to board the ship and be on our way, and they sent 13 Ju 88 aircraft and they bombed us, you've no idea, one after the other. We were waiting to get on to the ship – we'd got everything ready so that everybody could get on the ship and off. One after the other – and they all missed. And then they came round again and they all missed again, except the last Ju 88 – we just watched this. He hit her right on the stern, right astern on what we call the quarter-deck, and one bomb, it didn't seem to be a very big one from what I can remember, but any rate it exploded and the ship caught fire immediately aft. Well, we knew that couldn't go on terribly long because just under that part of the ship aft we had 90 depth charges, and I don't know how long it took, I can't remember, before they exploded and they blew the whole ship to pieces.

There was a track from Suda Bay going up to a village and we got on it. We had this Sergeant of Marines with us and he took us up to the village because he'd been up there. He'd been a Royal Marine on the *York*, which had been bombed and sunk at the end of Suda Bay. And they unloaded some of their 6-inch anti-aircraft guns and they took them over to Cape Dhrapanon as an anti-aircraft battery, so he knew the place very well, knew everybody in it, because he was in charge of this gun battery.

They were marvellous, absolutely wonderful to us. They sat us down and they brought buckets of water for us to drink because we hadn't had water in Suda Bay, and hard-boiled eggs, painted red, which is part of their kind of Easter celebrations, so I believe. So we sat down there until dark, and then a Greek policeman, who was in the village, took off his uniform, got himself into plain clothes and led us over tracks out of the village and down on to a rough sort of road, which finished up at Sphakia. This was the main and only road and was filled with retreating Army. So the policeman, good chap, said, there you are, I have to get back down, out of this, I don't want to be caught sort of thing, so he just put us on the road, shook us all by the hand and gave each of us a hug and just disappeared into the scrub.

The worst part of that was in the village. We had 19 rifles only, Canadian rifles, 303s, and I had dished them out to chaps who knew how to handle a rifle. I had a .45 revolver and a couple of packets of ammunition and about nine Mills bombs shoved in my shirt. From the top of the ridge, coming along the coast to the village of Rethymnon, a large car suddenly appeared. It had its lights on and we thought, with these lights on, it could only belong to the Germans. Anyway, we were on a little roadway with a stone wall, which was the road into and out of a village. So we stacked these fellows with the rifles round about the place and I went to the front a little and the whole idea was to let them get closer, and if they didn't take their lights off they were probably armoured cars or something belonging to the Germans. And the whole idea was, I would fire three shots, the first one a signal to stop, and if they didn't, fire two more, and the idea was to aim at the headlights; by so doing you are bound to hit the engine of the car itself, as well as putting out the lights. And after the third shot they didn't stop.

There was nothing else we could do, so the men with the guns opened fire. This was the worst thing that really happened to me. Anyway, the car was a very large vehicle, which could probably carry about 20 people in it, and it was full of refugees from Rethymnon. They were leaving Rethymnon heading for this village to get out of the way of the Germans, I suppose, and we shot them up, which was dreadful. And the car hit a cottage, I think first, and then it charged the brick wall, turned over on its side and we all rushed to try and do something about it. The policeman came up and he said, "Come on, get out of this, get on the road before the Germans find you because the villagers will look after these people," and it's the last we ever saw or heard of them.'

With the Germans succeeding in attaining and maintaining a hold on Maleme airfield, they were able to build up their forces rapidly. The withdrawal and evacuation of British forces became inevitable. The main point of embarkation was the beach at Sphakia on the south coast of Crete. The only access was a poor road going through and over the mountains from the northern parts of Crete where the action had been taking place.

Sergeant Richard Kean took part in this withdrawal:

'And then word came out that anybody that could walk 16 miles, I think it was, should join in the withdrawal and I went down to the side of the road and the Aussie doctor said, "You can't walk that far, Kiwi, you'd better stay – you'll only be taken prisoner. I'm staying, a lot of the boys are staying and we'll look after you."

I said, "No, I'm getting out if I have to crawl," and I started hiking. I hiked with Meadow and another mate of mine and, thank goodness, we had a packet of biscuits and a tin of bully. And we walked at night and hid up during the day, and we stopped in a stone hut – it had been a shepherd's hut – and slept there, and two men from the Welsh Regiment joined us, and certainly I don't like the Welsh. They shared our meal with us that night and bedded down, and when we woke up in the morning we found they'd eaten the rest of our rations and were pulling their rifles to pieces and throwing them away when we could have used them. However, we pushed on and pushed on and finally got to Sphakia.

We got on to lighters, rowing-boats, whalers, and rowed out and climbed up the side of the ship, *Glengyle*. She was one of the invasion ships. Drank about a gallon of hot cocoa which the Navy made up – it was good stuff too. The other ship that was in the convoy, they bombed that on the way; it was the same as the ship that I was in and they bombed it down her funnel and it exploded down there. She was a mess. Eventually we got to Alex.'

Keith Newth made his way along the same road to Sphakia:

'And we were then formed up and started the retreat march right across Crete, and we must have been about three days on that. And we got through down to Sphakia Bay and we were down the bottom of a ravine hiding there because of the Stukas and that coming over trying to find us, and who should turn up there but Freyberg.

From there we were taken by rowing boats to HMAS *Napier*, a destroyer, which was to take us back to Egypt. And on the first day out Jerry caught up with us, the Dorniers, and at the time we were handling 4.5 shells – they were coming up on a lift from in the bowels of the ship – and we were pushing these through to the gunners out on the deck and the skipper was lying on his back watching the bombs coming down and dodging them. One went through between the deck and the rail on the side of the ship and blew the port propeller clean off.

There was an awful crash and a bang. I remember one of the chaps, just inside the door, saying, "It's all right, boys, we're still going," and we went on for quite a while. And then, all of a sudden, the engine room pipes burst and the engineers were driven out by the steam and we sat still, just straddling the ocean with the other two destroyers going round us, and luckily the Dorniers never came back. After about an hour and a half the engine room got cool enough for them to get to work again and get engines going. In that way we limped back to Alexandria, and when we got there they put a signal up to say we were out of control, and the other ships went on into Port Alexandria and they sent a tug out which attached itself to HMAS *Napier* and we were taken in. And I'll never forget, we went past the aircraft carrier, the *Illustrious*, with the whole of the bow blown off it; all the sailors, who were in the bow, went down with it and she was laid up there. There were quite a number of warships there and they invariably were smacked about. I remember the *Orion*; she had her 6-inch guns bent up in the front just as if they were putty from the blast of the bombs as they came down.

That was a wonderful experience in a lot of ways, but something you would never want to go through again, but I wouldn't have liked to have missed it either. It was a wonderful experience to realise what a ghastly thing war was and how it made men act as heroes and some as animals.'

As has been narrated by Lieutenant Stanley Jervis, RNVR, the crew of HMS *Syvern* had joined the general exodus on the road to Sphakia. He continues:

'We joined the Army down on the road, which was a metalled road. It had been a track and mostly the Army had straightened it up a bit and put metal on it. Nothing else in sight anywhere, just huge boulders, so we had to walk on both sides of the road because Germans were strafing and, of course, you had to keep off the middle of the road or keep off the road itself so we could get under cover with boulders and so on. At any rate, we didn't do that for very long because we didn't walk during the daylight, only at night-time, because there was too much strafing going on. So we rested up during the day behind rocks and so forth and the Army were all round us, with us. There was no water and no food.

Anyway, eventually we got on to a clearing, a small village which was inshore from Sphakia, I think it was somewhere about 7 miles. That's where the Army was concentrated, holed up, and you couldn't move during the daytime because of the German aircraft. And not only that – it was announced that the Germans were paratrooping snipers into the area and the snipers were dressed in British uniforms. So no movement at all until dark, and that's when they put the calculated number of survivors, if you like, on the road to be taken off by ship, rescued by the Navy. So that's where we gathered all our chaps plus a whole lot of merchant seamen.

There were Asians and Chinese, all sorts of fellows – anyway, we got them all together. And we got them into a cave, one of these huge caves which you find all over Crete, and we parked them under cover in there. There was plenty of water, which was marvellous, and I can still remember sitting at the mouth of this cave with a 2-gallon can of water with me, and I couldn't drink it because you can't drink too much water if you haven't had any for a long time.

Anyway, the Army knew nothing at all about us; we'd been sunk and we'd walked across Crete and the Army had no idea what to do with us. We were mixed up with their men and they had no orders for us, so I saw the Commanding Officer, who was a Colonel, a nice chap, and he got a bit fed up with me after a while because he didn't know what to do with us. The Navy didn't know that we had been sunk, they didn't know where we were, so I said, "Why don't you get someone to tell the Navy that we're here?" and he said, "We can't because communication between here and Sphakia is down – we're not in touch, can't do anything about it."

So I got a Petty Officer chap, a really nice fellow, and we toured this vast number of abandoned vehicles, trucks and cars and motorbikes, and he was a motorcyclist, this chap. He found a good motorbike – we didn't have any petrol or anything, so we got to a truck which had plenty of petrol, we siphoned fuel out of the truck into the motorbike tank, got it all set up and I went back to the Commanding Officer and told him what I had done and said that we'd get word to the Navy. And he said, "You can't, this is no man's land. You can't have anybody moving in daylight; you'll have to wait until darkness." Eventually he said, "All right, you give me a note to say that I will not be responsible if you get killed," and we set out on this jolly motorbike.

It took us 4 hours to cover the distance. We got on with it – we were getting on pretty well, and reckoned we'd not too far to go – and coming down a bit of a slope there were two Army fellows who shot out of the side of the road with rifles and bayonets, so we got off the motorbike and one chap said, "Put your hands up and stand still – now don't bloody well move," so we did this. One chap walked up to me and he said, "Jervis, you bastard, what are you doing here? If I hadn't been able to recognise you, I would have bloody well shot you as a so and so German," and that's how we got through. They showed us the way to get down to the end of the road, which was covered with cars and buses and goodness knows what. There was only a steep track from the top of the escarpment down the cliff face to the bottom where all the people were. The Navy, the Army, people involved in the evacuation, were all down there, and just across from the escarpment was the beach, Sphakia beach, the rescue beach.

So I found a naval Captain and told him what had happened. Anyway, he told us that the telephone line was being restored: "You stay here and we'll do something about you and your men up in the catchment – we'll get them out and away."

A bit later a Commander came along and he said he was the Beach Master. He said, "There's a whole lot of seamen of all sorts and we've got them all together." He said, "I'm going to take you down to the beach, and we're going to put them all down there; you've got to look after them and see that they get on board ship." And on the way to the beach there was a little village, only a few houses, fishermen's houses, and alongside it an enormous round stone, almost round, almost split in half, standing on the top of the small track that went from there, down straight on to the beach. Only about one person at a time could go down it.

And on the way we found a New Zealand soldier, if you please, lying in the scrub and he'd broken his leg. He'd been out with the rescue party, whatever it was, survival party, the night before, he'd fallen over and broke his leg, and no one knew anything about it. He shouted to us, so we picked him up; he put his arms around our shoulders and we carried him, dragged him almost, to the top of the village. And just at this time the enemy started to do the place over again, and I can't remember how many enemy aircraft there were, but they bombed over and over again, all over that area. I suppose the whole idea would be to put the fear of God in anybody who wanted to go there. They literally did because there was no one in sight, we were all under cover, but we got into the middle of this rock, the only cover there was. We got in where it had split and we dragged this wounded soldier, one on each side, into this cave, the Beach Commander and myself, and we had to stand up and go through this bombing. We couldn't sit down – we could just lean on this rock. You've no idea – we were holding up this wounded chap – by this time he was unconscious anyway, he was out to it – and we had to hold him up. I don't think I've felt anything heavier in all my life than having to hold this chap up, the weight of him, until the bombing was over. And then we were able to get out of the rock and get him down on to the beach where there was a party of Australian Army people down there, and they took him over.

So things went on, and round about dusk they put me on a part of the beach. "These are your men and no one should move away – if they do, they're lost." Then the Beach Master said to me, "Have you had anything to eat?" and I said, "No, not for three days," and he said, "Give me two or three hands and I'll see what I can do for you," and he took them along to a warehouse way along the beach and they came back with three cases, open cases, containing tins of baked beans and vegetables. So I dished all this out and I could smell this lovely smell of baked beans and meat and vegetables, you know, and came to the last case, just a small tin left, no label on it, and I opened it up and there was a pound tin of plum jam. So I sat and ate the best part of half a tin of plum jam, and I don't think I've ever eaten plum jam since.

And then after midnight I got the word to take these fellows down to the beach on to a landing craft, and they delivered us to the *Perth*, an Australian cruiser, and the *Perth* took us to Alexandria. And she was tail-end Charlie, if you like, in a big convoy with cruisers and destroyers and I don't know how many merchant ships, an enormous convoy, anyway – must have been 40 ships. And the *Perth* got a 500-pound bomb in A boiler room. It killed about 40 people – it went straight in front of the bridge, just missed the mast and went through the for'ard galley and there it killed everybody in that area. Concussion killed most of them, because all these lifeless corpses hadn't a mark on them. Any rate, we buried them that afternoon and fortunately *Perth* was still able to steam at 16 knots, so they pushed her up a bit into the middle of the convoy and carried on. That reduced the whole of the speed of the convoy to 16 knots until we got out of the danger area from enemy aircraft. Anyway, we got in at 16 knots and we buried those chaps in sewed-up canvas with a weight at the bottom, over the side one after the other. The poor old Padre kept on reading the burial service, going over and over and over again, until we got rid of the whole lot of them. So there you are, we finished up back in Alexandria.'

Driver Rex Thompson, on the same road to Sphakia, was not so fortunate:

'We started the withdrawal and went over at night a very, very mountainous track to Sphakia; that was the southern port area of embarking. We got there on the second night and the road only went half way down the mountain, which rose almost directly from the beach, Sphakia beach. At this stage we were just walking; the trucks we had were for wounded and disabled chaps. The road only went half way down the mountainside and we just had to scramble down, and a few of us that were together, we holed up in a cave just off Sphakia and we ran out of ships. The Navy must have lost about six there in the last days of the withdrawal. And so we were left there and eventually the word came round, 1 June I think it was, that the island had capitulated and we were virtually prisoners of war. A little sad note there: one of the battalions was on a spur and they got the word we'd capitulated, so they walked out into the open and stacked their rifles. They hadn't told the planes and they got strafed.

We stopped in the cave; we said, no, they can come and get us, and eventually they clambered down this very steep slope, clambered down, and in German, which I'm now quite conversant with, shouted, "Kraus darmint!" and it didn't mean much to us, but we decided they wanted us out. So we got out and they marched us back to Canea, where we'd come from, and it took two days. We'd had three days in this cave with nothing – there was six of us – nothing but a packet of Bournville cocoa, which we had with water, and the Germans gave us virtually nothing on the way over.'

The Royal Navy managed to evacuate over half of the Allied forces from Crete on the nights of 28 to 31 May, but suffered heavy losses in men and ships.

CHAPTER 7

Malta and the war in the Mediterranean

With the fall of France and the entry of Italy into the war in June 1940, the British position in the Mediterranean became increasingly difficult. Operating from airfields in Sardinia, Sicily and North Africa, the Axis powers had superiority in the air over the Central Mediterranean. The Mediterranean Fleet had withdrawn to its base at Alexandria and the smaller Force 'H' was established at Gibraltar. The Central Mediterranean became hazardous in the extreme to shipping, and convoys to and from the Middle East had to be routed via the Cape of Good Hope. Malta, under the constant threat of invasion, became the target of heavy and sustained bombing attacks, and it became more and more difficult to keep her supplied with materials of war, oil and food. The Italian Navy also posed a continual, if potential, threat. On the other hand, the passage of Axis shipping to North Africa was facilitated, although some limited damage continued to be caused by British submarines and aircraft. Such was the situation in the Central Mediterranean until 1943, when the position was reversed due to an expansion of Allied air power in the region together with their victories in North Africa.

Serving with Force 'H' was Lieutenant John Musters RN in the battlecruiser HMS *Renown*:

'In July 1940 *Renown* was sent off to Gibraltar to become the flagship of Admiral Somerville who commanded Force H, which was the Western Mediterranean Force. We had in company the aircraft carrier *Ark Royal* and the *Sheffield*, which was a modern 6-inch cruiser, one old 6-inch cruiser, *Emerald* or *Enterprise*, I'm afraid I can't remember which, and most of the Sixth Destroyer Flotilla, the F Class destroyers. We had the job of being the resident Naval force based on Gibraltar for operations into the Western Mediterranean or where necessary into the Central Atlantic.

We did a series of Malta convoy covering operations into the Central Mediterranean and they followed much the same pattern. We would slip out of Gibraltar during the night and hope that we wouldn't be seen – I think we always were because, of course, the Spaniards were all around us across the Bay in Algeciras and various points of vantage along the coast. The Italian and German consuls or other agents kept a pretty close eye on what was going on. Anyway, we used to slip out of Gibraltar, occasionally lay a false trail by steaming westward into the Atlantic and then double back in the dark into the Mediterranean, but that never seemed to work because they always knew exactly where we were going. We would make our way eastward through the Central Mediterranean. The first day would be peaceful, about half way through the second day you'd expect to see the Italian reconnaissance flying-boats, which occasionally *Ark Royal*'s fighters would be able to succeed in knocking down, and on the third day we would be well into the Central Mediterranean and we would expect to get air attacks from Southern Sardinia or Sicily.

These followed much the same pattern. There would be a succession of torpedo-bombing attacks, very occasionally a level bombing attack. We never had any dive-bombing, which was a German speciality and for which, I think, we were probably very lucky. We had one torpedo-bombing attack which very nearly put a torpedo into *Renown*. We had a group of them coming in on our port bow and they were seen to drop their torpedoes, and the Captain altered course towards the approaching tracks in order to comb them and steam in between them. There was one torpedo – we saw its track in the fairly calm water coming towards our bow – and we were swinging on full helm to port and it looked almost inevitable that the torpedo would get us. Its track disappeared under the flare of the fo'c'sle and then nothing happened – we were all standing on the balls of our feet and ankles slightly bent so we wouldn't get so much damage if we were thrown up in the air. It looked as though the thing had reached the end of its run; if so, it was a jolly lucky coincidence.

One of our Malta convoys resulted in an action with Italian surface forces. This was on 27 November 1940 when we had a long, complicated operation of covering an eastbound convoy through from the Gibraltar Straits to Malta, at the same time passing through a few cruisers to join the Eastern Mediterranean Fleet and meeting and taking back some ships out of the Eastern Mediterranean, back into the Western Mediterranean and so home. This reshuffle was probably the result of the successful torpedo-bombing attack on the Italian Battle Fleet in Taranto a little bit earlier. We followed the usual procedure of taking this convoy into the Central Mediterranean, having a few air attacks, and then on the morning of 27 November, when everybody was converging into the Central Mediterranean about the longitude of Tunisia, one of the *Ark Royal*'s search aircraft reported Italian forces, four heavy cruisers and, further to the north-east, two battleships with destroyer escort. *Renown* and *Ramillies* and all the cruisers we had in company set off to the north or north-west in order to meet this lot and of course keep them away from the convoy, which was pursuing its way eastwards towards the Tunisian Narrows.

Round about lunch-time our cruisers, which were ahead of us, sighted and opened fire on some Italian cruisers, and a little bit later we also sighted them to the north of us. Visibility was now very good; the sea was calm so there were no problems of frightful weather or spray in our range-finders. We still had no radar and we opened fire on one of the cruisers at an optically measured range of 29,000 yards, and that fell over, that went into the sea – we could see quite clearly what was happening. We came down, as far as I remember, in a couple of either 1,000 or 800-yard steps. We crossed the target and started putting salvos short, so then the next pair of salvos was fired at a spread about the middle of the 1,000-yard bracket and, lo and behold, one of them hit it and I think we got a hit aft. Whereupon the cruisers altered course away. The damaged one, I think, made for Southern Sardinia; the others may have turned round to the north-east to rejoin their Battle Fleet.

Shortly after this we sighted the Italian battleships coming in at high speed from the north-east at very long range – visibility was extreme. The Gunnery Officer, John Holmes, knew that they were almost certainly still out of our range, but he still wanted to say that we had engaged the enemy Battle Fleet and he gave orders for fire to be opened on the nearer battleship, which I think was the *Vittorio Venito*. So we fired a couple of salvos at 32,000 yards, which was our limit, and they fell short. The Italian battleships turned away – they could have slaughtered us, no doubt, but I am also pretty sure that they were apprehensive of a torpedo attack from *Ark Royal*. They knew that *Ark Royal* was present on previous air operations, but of course they had reason to fear torpedo-bombing attacks so soon after Taranto.

In fact, a little later on, in the afternoon, *Ark Royal* launched a torpedo strike against the battleships; lamentably, they all missed. This demonstrated, I think, the lack of opportunity for intensive weapon training by everybody, particularly the air strike crews, because they never got an opportunity. We were on the go carrying out operations, not normally involving torpedo strikes against enemy surface ships, so there was never the opportunity for the training needed. So that was that – we turned back to rejoin the convoy.

In the evening another Italian torpedo attack came, again resulting in no hits. We did down one or two Italian torpedo-bombers; I remember seeing the wreck of one as we steamed past it with the crew still on a floating bit of wreckage, waving, whether in applause or "Do you mind sending a boat?" I don't know, but we had to leave them. I think a destroyer may have picked them up – I hope so.

There was a nasty accident in *Renown* at that point, because firing at very low elevation at these torpedo-bombers, which were flying and coming in low, one of our port 4.5-inch mountings put a round into the mounting immediately ahead of it. The safety gear which should have prevented that happening had failed, and there were some nasty casualties in the 4.5 mounting which had received the hit. That was tragic. Those were the only casualties we had in that ship throughout those operations.

We did one rather alarming sortie into the Gulf of Genoa in order to bombard the docks and the Ansaldo Armament Works, and with a little bit of luck we might have caught an Italian battleship which was supposed to be sitting in a floating dock – I think it was the *Andrea Doria* – according to our intelligence. For this we had done a lot of practice on maps, charts and so on. The map of Genoa Port on a large scale was divided up into lettered and numbered squares and the spotting aircraft launched from *Ark Royal*, which was with us, also had copies of the same map with the same lettering and they were able to radio back to us where our salvos went. For this thing we steamed off into the Gulf of Genoa; we had with us *Malaya*, which was a "Queen Elizabeth" Class battleship, unmodernised and not very fast. She could only do 22 knots and she hadn't got the same gun range as we had, but enough for that operation.

In the dark, just as day was beginning to break, we turned on to a westerly course which took us past Genoa and, entirely by navigational fixes and by map, opened fire on the Port of Genoa. Our first salvo was deliberately put short to fall into the harbour in order to give the aircraft something nice and visible to spot and to say, well, that one was short and so and so. This also was by way of getting rid of the armour-piercing shell which we had had in the gun loading cages during our run in during the night, in case we had to engage enemy warships at very short notice in the night. Those had to be got out of the way and the only way to get rid of them was to fire them out of the guns, and then the bombardment proper was carried out with high-explosive shells which you don't use against ships but you do use against shore targets.

After we had finished the bombardment and we headed back to Gibraltar as fast as we could, which was governed by *Malaya*'s 22 knots, an Italian Fast Battle Group came out from Naples, not unnaturally, and came through the Straits of Bonifacio, which is between Corsica and

Sardinia, in order to bring us to action. They had a force of 8-inch cruisers, each with its own aircraft, and they had two fast battleships. When they were through the Straits of Bonifacio they launched the cruisers' seaplanes from the decks on catapults, and each had a sector to search. The one that had the sector which would have sighted us had a defect and couldn't fly – it failed to launch. This was jolly lucky for us because, I think, they would have sighted us and they would have known exactly where to go. As it was, the Italians were confused with other aircraft sightings which turned out to be French merchant convoys going to and fro between Algeria and France, and they wasted valuable time investigating those.

Meanwhile, we got away. We did have an air attack by low-level bombers a little later that day, and as usual *Ark Royal* was surrounded with these flashes and smoke but she didn't get hit and that was it, we got away with it. (Interestingly, my older son, who is in the Navy, was in Italy during a course in the Italian Naval Staff College at Livorno, and he visited Genoa and, at one of the sights he went into, the Cathedral, was shown a 15-inch shell with a little plaque on it: "This was fired by Force H on 9 February 1941". He didn't let on that his father had probably had some slight hand in putting it there. It arrived in the Cathedral but didn't explode.)'

William Bryson, a New Zealander, commenced his naval training in Britain in January 1941 and went to sea as an Ordinary Seaman:

'My first ship was the fast mine-laying cruiser *Manxman*, and it turned out to be one of the fastest ships that the Royal Navy had at the time. The experience I had during my three months in that ship was out of this world. We did Malta convoys and we had more action going through to Malta than we expected to have in the whole of the war. We were bombed, we had torpedoes thrown at us, and the skipper of *Manxman* knew how to handle it so well that we survived it. *Manxman* and her sister-ship HMS *Welshman* were so fast they were used to run through to Malta from both ends of the Mediterranean with petrol and gear for the Air Force at night.

The experience in *Manxman* was pretty exciting, because when we were stationed up in the Kyle of Lochalsh, one night as soon as it got dark 300 ratings from Portsmouth landed on the ship; they painted it entirely, and put a false funnel on it with spark guards which most British ships don't have. They put a big lump of wood like a bowsprit on the bow and they falsified the bow shape; they put another great big sort of top side on the after end to make it look like a "Leopard" Class cruiser belonging to the French Navy. The idea was that we were to go through and lay mines off Leghorn, which was a jumping-off place for big ships taking war supplies to Rommel. Anyway, before it got light the ship had entirely changed. We

William Urquhart Bryson

were told to put red pom-poms on our caps, which were given to us; the ship's supply officer gave us some paint and we painted blue stripes across our dickies so that we'd look like French sailors.

We took off for Leghorn and into the Gulf of Genoa where we laid our mines, and each mine was dropped at a certain period of time because they had to make sure that the mines were not too close together, otherwise, if one went up, it would set off the whole field. We learnt quite a bit of what mine-laying was all about, and I was in the wheelhouse on the revolution counter and I heard one bright spark say, "Each time that mine splashes into the water that's the price of a brand new car." We laid our 150 mines and off we went. All the fake stuff fell apart and we returned to England.'

The effectiveness of naval operations was of course heavily dependent on support from the air. Albert Friend, a Londoner, was a Flight Sergeant air-gunner/radio operator in Blenheims:

'Back at base in Watton in Norfolk, I heard we were to be posted to Malta, and the general feeling amongst the ground crew was that it was a one-way operation; we would be going out but none of us would be coming back. This was in December 1941, before the Americans came into the war. Eventually, on about 27 December, we took off to fly to Gibraltar. We were flying on dead reckoning; we had no appropriate aerials, we had no astral navigation and we had no other means of navigating. We flew at 9,000 feet. There was cloud above us and cloud below, so we didn't see anything across the Bay of Biscay, and then we had a very brief sighting of Spain from a good way off and we continued between layers of cloud down the coast of Portugal, and then we descended through the cloud.

When we came down through the bottom cloud at 3,000 feet there was no land in sight anywhere, and we turned on to a 100 degrees course which, on dead-reckoning, should have pushed us into the gap between Europe and Africa, but instead the first land we saw was North Africa. We had an argument whether it was low cloud or land, but we decided it was land, not low cloud, and the navigator asked me to give him a course to steer, and, after a great deal of trouble, I managed to pick up Gibraltar and was given a rough course to steer to reach Gibraltar, which turned out to be spot on.

The runway at Gibraltar was short. It started on top of the sea wall, which was about 2 metres above the sea, and we flew in, flaps, undercarriage down, with the batman to the left of us giving us instructions whether we were too high, too low or about right. About 50 yards from the wall I looked over the side and there was a wing-tip under the water; obviously someone had gone in too slow and stalled before touching down. It was only 50 yards off the coast, but it was all under water.

We touched down and we stopped before we got to the Spanish road, which was only 600 yards down the runway. Beyond the Spanish road there was about another 150 yards before you went into the Bay of Algeciras. We managed to land the Blenheim all right, but with the Wellingtons it was touch and go whether they got in or not; some of them overshot, some of them undershot, as that one we saw.

At Gibraltar we had to wait for weather clearance and then we took off to fly to Malta. Another long trip. We saw very little as we were flying in and out of cloud. We saw very little of Algeria because the clouds were getting thicker, and we were flying for about seven hours and eventually we saw the coast of Tunisia and Pantelleria, which was an Italian fighter base where they had CR42s. We flew between Pantelleria and Tripani, which

Albert Bernard Friend

was the western part of Sicily, towards Malta, and eventually Malta came up and we touched down on to the main runway at Leuchar.

We were billeted in a wooden hut in the north-east corner of the aerodrome, but the air raids were so thick and frequent and there was a near miss on the hut which shattered it, so we were then billeted in the Poor House, very close to the Trotting Grounds, half way to Valetta. On the Trotting Grounds was a Battery of 4.7s, which kept us awake all night because the Italians came over in their Savoia Marchettis, one at a time, every night. The battery kept us awake so we complained that we couldn't sleep, and the Poor House was badly shattered by previous bombing, so we got posted to a hotel on the north coast, a small hotel very close to the harbour where the submarines were based.

One day, when I was lying in my bed, after my room-mate had been shot down, I heard Bofors pounding away, hard and heavy, so I got out of my bed, went across the landing to a bedroom on the other side, through that bedroom on to a flat roof to look up at four Ju 88s coming in at about 3,000 feet in a shallow dive. The first Ju 88's bomb was already on its way and it was coming straight for me, so I reversed my decision and I shot back across the landing, down the stairs, and I never touched a single step – I jumped the whole flight – and then turned the corner and jumped the next flight, and somebody came out of the bath and asked me a question, but I was going too fast to answer it. I then jumped the whole flight to the next landing with a big stained-glass window, a leaded stained-glass window, which bulged in about 9 inches. When it went out again I leapt, and it came back in again behind me when the bomb exploded. I couldn't understand it but I never heard anything, and I went ahead of the blast and I shot across the floor at the bottom, where we had our dining room, to the far wall, and I was uninjured, and the flying glass, the glass was completely shattered – there was no window left. When I got my senses back, I went upstairs to my room and I found the floor was too unsafe to walk on, so I had to crawl across the floor to get my kit out, and then I looked in the next room and there wasn't even a floor. The bomb had gone through the next room to mine and I could look down into the shop below. So we went back into the Poor House.

We had been on several raids – one was anti-shipping and another one was a flight to the North Coast of Africa – and we were on a mission, a seek-and-destroy mission, going along the roads shooting up trucks and, if we found something we could bomb, we'd bomb it. On the way into the coast I got a call from the No 1 aircraft – there were only two of us and I was flying in No 2 position – and he called up "12 110s." I thought, gosh, 12 of those, that's a death sentence, and I looked around and they weren't 110s, they were Caproni 311s, which was a completely different kettle of fish. There weren't 12, there were 11, and they were about 3,000 feet and they were heading west; we were heading south, but turned north to fly back to Malta. I can't imagine that they didn't see us, but they continued flying towards the west so we then turned south again and re-crossed the coast, and when we got to the road we turned west and went down the road shooting up all the trucks we could see.

It was all right from the navigator's point of view – he had a good view at the front and he could fire at the trucks as they came along – but I couldn't fire forward with the Bristol turret as my line of fire was restricted by the wing, the fuselage and the tailplane, and I didn't have a chance to get a frame on them, let alone fire on them. By the time I got my sights on them they were too far away. So I thought, this is no good; we were still flying in a No 2 position, we still hadn't dropped any bombs, and I looked over the top towards the front and I could see an SM82 on to Suwara airfield, a wooden, a big wooden transport plane, and I thought that's mine, but as we approached there was flak from Suwara and the lead aircraft got hit, so we turned north to fly back to Malta, and I never got close enough to the SM82 to fire at it. It was, as far as I was concerned, a waste of time my being there, because I hadn't had a chance to fire at anything really.

We also did reconnaissance searching for an Italian Battle Fleet, which was suspected of moving down into or out of the Bay of Taranto. At the same time the CO flew reconnaissance to find the British Task Force of destroyers and cruisers which were coming from Alexandria. Passing Sicily the weather was fine, but as soon as we got into the Bay of Taranto the weather closed in; there was a heck of a lot of low cloud. I had to get out of my turret to urinate in the bottle, and then on the intercom I heard the pilot say, "There's a float-plane down below," and I said, "Keep your eye on him, keep your eye on him." He said, "Oh, it's disappeared in the cloud," so I got back in the turret. A disappointment that we'd missed this float-plane, which was in and out of cloud. That was a sure sign that the float-plane was on anti-submarine patrol over the Italian ships, but we missed seeing them, the cloud was too thick.

On our way back down the coast of Sicily, which we could see to the west, the skies cleared again, beautiful clear sky, and the navigator asked me for a bearing on Malta, so I lowered the seat, switched my transmitter on, got my log-book out, and started calling up Malta. I poked my head out to find if there was anything around, and there was a Ju 88, and he was coming out of Catania or Syracuse, climbing and flying eastward, while we were flying to the south, and he'd passed our tail at the same height. I just said on the intercom, "Ju 88 – open fire!" and the pilot put the aircraft into a dive and he pushed the throttles open and poured in a 9-pound boost – you could only use a 9-pound boost for 5 minutes because you'd blow the cylinder head off. By the time I'd got my turret around – the Blenheim turret was so slow – and got a bead on the Ju 88, he said, "We're out of range," so another disappointment for me. They didn't attack us, and they must have seen us, but they probably thought we were a Caproni 311 because we were so much like a Caproni 311. They'd probably come across so many Italian aircraft that they didn't expect to see a British aircraft. Anyhow, they continued going out to the east to look for the British Battle Fleet, which the CO had sighted and reported in self-evident code. The CO was under the impression he was looking for the Italians, and reported them as such, and, of course, the Task Force then did a 180 and went back to Alexandria.

We'd lost several aeroplanes. Four Blenheims were coming back from North Africa from a raid, and four Me 109Es intercepted them, just south of the island, and shot the four of them down in less than 4 minutes. We had lost the CO on another raid and all we had was a flight lieutenant and a pilot officer; they were the only two officers left. On the raid where we lost the CO we were to attack an ammunition ship in Palermo Harbour, and I didn't like this because we were using 11-second delay bombs and we were number six, or tail-ender, and unless we got over the target pretty quickly we were likely to have it blow up in our faces. I preferred to attack it from the inland side because it was on the inside of a high outer mole and it was only a 3,000-tonner with only the superstructure visible from the side from which we were actually attacking.

However, there was a navigational error. The Island of Ustica in the Mediterranean Sea was our turning point. You were supposed to put that island just about abeam, port beam, and then turn, but we turned a minute too early and instead of going into Palermo Harbour we were on the other side of the headland to the west and all I could see was some rotting, rusty trucks on a railway siding, but no harbour, and we were down to 10 feet. The CO got too low and hit the sea, and his port prop hit first, and then he hit again and the aircraft broke up as it cartwheeled across the tops of the waves. There was my room-mate, he was the radio operator in the CO's aircraft, going down into the water and he was Canadian, French Canadian, a Jewish Canadian from Montreal, and I packed his things up. I didn't trust the stuff to get through the official channels – I thought I'd send them back after the war.

With the loss of the CO the squadron seemed to break up; nobody seemed to lead from there on. Although the forecast was for clear skies, it was overcast over Sicily and there was cloud up to about 4,000 feet base. We flew up and dropped our bombs on a masonry bridge. They both overshot and they exploded. We entered cloud, and because the navigator said the highest peak is 7,000 feet, got her up to 7,000 feet. We climbed up through the cloud and I had a brief glimpse of a crag swishing by underneath, and I thought to myself, gosh, we're closer to the ground than I thought. We climbed out to the top of the cloud – beautiful sunshine – and we were on our own and we flew across the south coast closer to Tirreno, and at the Gulf of Tirreno there were two Squadrons of Italian pilots there, based there, and none of them came up to challenge us, and we then turned on to a south-easterly course to get back to Malta, where we landed.

It was always a worry landing in Malta because quite often our planes were followed in by 109s, and I saw a Maryland shot down in this way. The navigator bailed out into a minefield just to the north of Valetta Harbour, and the aircraft then turned and crashed into the sea. Nobody seemed to bother about the navigator – nobody seemed to go out. The air-sea rescue aircraft had been shot up and they weren't going out when there were 109s around. When we'd lost the four Blenheims they wouldn't go out there because the 109s were out – they weren't going to be shot at – so all this nonsense about what a marvellous job the air-sea rescue did, didn't apply to Malta because there was far too many enemy aircraft around.

Where the Hurricanes were I never knew, but every time I saw a Hurricane it was being shot down. I watched a Hurricane try to get in; he'd lost glycol and his engine was blipping, and eventually his engine cut out dead and he tried to get back into Takali, which was a separate aerodrome to the rest of us, and the 109s were going in to finish him off, and another Hurricane came in behind the 109 and shot the wing off the 109. That was a rare sighting of Hurricanes. We never got a Hurricane escort in the entire time I was in Malta. The Whitley Squadron was down to one Wimpy; the 69 Squadron, with the Marylands, had no aeroplanes after the last one was shot down. There were two squadrons of Fleet Air Arm, there was a squadron of Albacores and a squadron of Swordfish, but they only had one Albacore left and only four Swordfish.

On another raid we took two reinforcement crews that had flown in reinforcement aircraft – the first time we had ever led another aircraft. We were No 1, we were still all sergeants, and we took them to south of Pantelleria, where there was a destroyer escorting a merchant ship. The merchant ship was about a 4,000-tonner so, one destroyer for one merchant ship, the merchant ship must have had very important supplies. The three of us, we tried to get the merchant ship between us and the destroyer, but a CR42 attacked our No 3 aircraft, which was lagging behind – he wasn't in formation, he was at least 100 yards astern – and when the CR42 attacked the No 3 aircraft I took my sights on the CR42, but the wing of the Blenheim was also in the sights so I couldn't fire. I thought to myself, well, I'll have to wait until he's shot down before I can attack the CR42, and I told the skipper that the gunner was probably killed because the guns went up in the air – when you got out of the turret you lowered the seat and the guns went up in the air – so I thought the gunner was either killed or wounded. So we broke off the engagement and flew back to Malta. He hadn't been killed. What had happened was that the bullet hit the small piece of armour plating around the gun sight and the flash had knocked him out, so he reckoned. He wasn't injured; he was all right.

Then we were given this task looking for the Italian Battle Fleet again. The Germans gave themselves away; whenever there was a convoy going past, going to Tripoli, they kept up a standing patrol around Malta to keep us on the ground, so we let this standing patrol go towards Gozo. We took off to the south-east and went straight down to the sea, 10 feet off the sea, and streaked out towards the south-east, with one of our planes going west, so as soon as we got far enough away we started our flying to 6,000 feet.

We were heading towards Benghazi. After about 40 minutes we started our sweeping search. It was very cloudy, three to four eighths cumulus, and the cumulus had a base of about 4,000 feet. The first thing we saw was a float-plane down below 1,000 feet, and that was a sure sign the float-plane was looking for our submarines ahead of the Battle Fleet. Then the pilot said, "There's a Ju 88 up ahead," and I looked around and it was flying west to east and we were flying south-west to north-east, so we were flying on his stern quarter. Then I heard the navigator say, "Gosh look at this!" and I looked out of the side and there were destroyers, cruisers, merchant ships, battleships and a liner, and I thought, gosh, that must be the *Conti de Cavour*, its screws astern, twin funnel, a really large thing, and I thought, well, that battleship looks like the *Littorio* and the cruisers looked like heavy cruisers. As the merchant ships were carrying tanks and guns on their decks they would be between 4,000-tonners to 12,000-tonners – there were three of them.

The navigator passed me the sighting signal to send to Alexandria and I started calling up Alexandria and as soon as I did my transmission was jammed, but I sent the message regardless and I got no reply and there was this transmission "blah blah" knocking my head off. I thought, well, I'll have to change frequency, and eventually I got a reply. I sent my signal and I got the acknowledgement and all of the time I was bobbing up and looking for this Ju 88, but our skipper was on the ball. He was dodging from cloud to cloud. This Ju 88 was trying to find us, but we were playing cat and mouse.

Anyhow, as soon as we had sent the message, we headed back to Malta. We were pleased with ourselves; we thought we'd done a good job because they'd listened to my signals both in Malta and in Gibraltar, and in Malta they'd stood to the Blenheims to attack this lot. There weren't many Blenheims left – I think we still had five Blenheims – and they were worried because we still had these 109s going round the island, standing patrols, to pass. As we got near the island I looked for these four dots – they had a special formation, the Germans, because they could watch each other's tails and you can't jump Germans without being spotted – and that swarm, they call it a swarm for 109s, were flying west bound towards Gozo. They were only tiny dots, so we continued on at about 50 feet and, I think, the cliffs there were about 100 feet, and we went into a steep climb over the Hal Far area, where the Fleet Air Arm were, and put our wheels down and went into the usual turn to land on the main runway. We taxied in and there was nobody around because there was a raid on. An emergency gharry came out and took us to the briefing room where the Blenheim crews were looking very, very disconsolate and worried. Bruno, the navigator, came in with a broad grin on his face, because he was so proud of the fact of what we'd achieved, and they said, "It's all right for you – we've got to attack that lot."

Anyhow, the AOC, Air Vice-Marshal Lloyd, decided the Blenheims weren't suitable to attack that lot, and he "stood to" the Swordfish and the Albacore, because that convoy was still within their range. It was pretty obvious they were heading for Tripoli. So they "stood to" the Swordfish, and put torpedoes on them, and this sole Wimpy, which was supposed to be bombing that ammunition ship in Palermo harbour. Even so they re-routed the Wimpy to the convoy to drop flares. Anyway, they sank the liner which was carrying the Afrika Corps. Apparently only 150 casualties came from that because there were plenty of destroyers to pick up the people who took to the boats.

Anyhow, the ammunition ship was still in Palermo Harbour and there were only three aircrews left and one of them was the flight lieutenant, the other was the pilot officer and we were all sergeants, so they gave us the job of sinking the ammunition ship. I still didn't agree with the way they were going to attack from the seaward side, because you could only see the superstructure; our bombs would hit the sea wall – they wouldn't do the damage. Coming from the other direction, the landward side, we'd have to fly over the town and very low, you could see the whole ship, so the chances of hitting the ship from the land side was far greater than from the seaward side, but nobody could see my point of view and we were told to do the same thing as before.

We were on our own and there were no less than 150 fighters capable of attacking us, besides the flak, and I thought, gosh, this is shocking. We couldn't start the port engine on the battery, so the ground engineer had to start with the crank, and I handed him the crank and he started the port engine and he handed me back the crank and I said, "Keep it as a souvenir – we're not coming back from this one," and he looked at me dumbly and he kept the crank handle. I couldn't see us possibly surviving this raid.

It was late afternoon and we were to bomb at last light, and coming in from the north-west with the light behind us. We should have come in from the other side, with the dark side behind us, but I was only a sergeant and nobody would take any notice of me. We were flying westbound and the "artificial horizon" wasn't working. We'd already air-tested the aircraft that afternoon, but the skipper had said, "The artificial horizon isn't working but it isn't absolutely necessary," but on our way he said, "I'm not happy about it, flying in the night in the dark without an artificial horizon." So between them, the navigator and the pilot, they decided that they weren't going to carry on with no artificial horizon, so we turned back and went back into Malta. However, we were put on standby – we had to do the raid 24 hours later, same one. I thought, we're not off the hook by a long shot.

Anyhow, next day we were told to fly aeroplanes to the Middle East and hand them over to the Middle East Command, so I had lived another day.'

By mid-August 1942 the people of Malta were on the brink of starvation, and the possibility of surrender was real. The shortage of fuel and ammunition and the loss of so many of the few available fighter aircraft resulted in serious difficulties in defending the island from the constant Axis air attacks and possible invasion. Convoys had been sent from the east and west under heavy naval escort, but few ships had got through. Almost as a last resort, the convoy code-named 'Operation Pedestal', using the few merchant ships available, capable of achieving 15 knots and with an overwhelming naval escort of aircraft carriers, battleships, cruisers, destroyers and submarines, set sail from Gibraltar for Malta in August 1942. Five of the 14 merchant ships, scarred and battered, made it to Malta after days on end of submarine torpedo attack, continual air assaults by dive-bombers, torpedo-bombers, high-level bombers, low-level bombers and then mass attacks by E-boats. The naval escort suffered heavy losses. Nevertheless, this, together with an added influx of Spitfire fighters flown in from the carrier Furious, *saved the day. Malta did not have to surrender and Axis was denied access to Egypt and beyond.*

Brian Prendergast from Manchester experienced Operation Pedestal as an Ordinary Seaman in the cruiser HMS *Kenya*:

'We sailed through the Straits of Gibraltar on 9 August, which was a Sunday. My cruising station was on the bridge, as bridge messenger, and on the Monday I could see a huge convoy extending outwards in all directions, with ships as far as the eye could see sailing in formation. This present state of affairs continued for another 24 hours until, very suddenly, the aircraft carrier *Eagle* took on a list and began to sink. She'd been hit by four torpedoes and she sank in 8 minutes.

Kenya went at once to action stations and I went to my station in A shell room in the foremost 6-inch gun turret. My job was to lift the 6-inch shells from the rotating ring and place them on a lift, which hoisted them up to the gun house where a seaman loaded them into the breech of one of the guns. I remained at this station for two days. We had very little information as to how the battle was going. We could hear the guns firing almost continually.

Some time on the Wednesday night there was a tremendous bang and the bow of the ship lifted and then fell before resuming equilibrium in a bow-down position, with the decks sloping downwards a few degrees, so it was still possible to move about without much difficulty. After a few minutes

Brian Prendergast

the Captain broadcast that we had been torpedoed for'ard, but would continue to Malta at reduced speed. We carried on loading shells and during the night we were given a tablet which we were told was a "keep awake" tablet, which must have been an amphetamine.

The next day we left the convoy to return to Gibraltar. The air attacks continued and a bomb exploded close to the ship's side and caused some damage in the engine room. On Friday the air attacks gradually ceased and we were able to stop loading shells. When we reached Gibraltar we could not anchor because of the damage, and tied up alongside another ship. We had time off watch to sleep, but I was still wide awake from the amphetamines and it was only gradually, over a day or two, that I managed to return to a normal sleep pattern.

We went into dock at Gibraltar for some temporary repairs to the bows. The anchors, cable lockers and stores compartments had been completely blown away. Fortunately they were unoccupied during action stations and there were no casualties. When we got into the Bay of Biscay, most of the repairs were carried away and the foremost bulkheads of the seamen's and stokers' mess decks had to be shored up.'

Lieutenant Commander Roger Hill, Commanding Officer of the 'Hunt' Class destroyer HMS *Ledbury*, was one of the escorts for Pedestal:

'Well, we went off to take a troop convoy through as far as Gibraltar, then we were going to go with the big convoy through to Malta, and we had this big convoy of troopships full of soldiers, thousands of soldiers, and they all put their machines-guns up on the upper deck. After a few days out, we were past the Bay of Biscay I know, we got in a fog and a Sunderland did a very foolish thing – he came down in the fog over the convoy. Of course, every soldier with a machine-gun opened fire at the Sunderland and I was on the port wing of the convoy and the Sunderland came over the top of me with one engine on fire and obviously was going to crash. So I followed him out and it crashed and then they were all sitting on the wing of the plane waving to us, and I got as near as I could. I knew I was about the best swimmer in the ship – this sounds very conceited, but I used to play a lot of water polo – so I tore off my clothes, gave my signet ring to an astonished stoker on the upper deck, dived into the sea and went out to the furthermost chap, who was actually the pilot of the Sunderland. Well, I got to him and a sailor swam up to me and said, "I've got a rope here, if you wish to use it." So I took the rope and tied it round me and then caught hold of this chap, who looked pretty sick to me, and waved to the ship. They had taken the rope to a snatch block and lined this along the upper deck, and about six sailors strapped on the end of this. I suddenly felt a jerk and went up about 3 foot in the water, and went tearing through the water, clinging on to this pilot, and then hit the side of the ship with my head and, you know how in the comic strips you always see stars, well I saw stars.

Anyhow, we got him on board and he was dead. They were all dead except one chap who couldn't swim, and the little float at the end of the wing had broken off and he had pushed himself over this float. What had happened was that they had two depth charges in the Sunderland and they hadn't jettisoned them when they were going to crash. They really were stupid, those chaps, and of course when the depth charges got to 50 feet, they went off and this killed all the chaps in the water because, by then, the Sunderland had sunk. It was a very sad thing. We had our Yeoman of Signals, a leading signalman, rather plucky, he had on a pair of thick

Roger Hill

trousers, which he had acquired in Norway at the beginning of the war somehow, and he went over the side, but he went down like a stone. In fact the whole signal department had to dive over the side to bring him up again. Anyhow, a lot of people went over the side but we got them all back, and I mention this because it had a good effect later on in the convoy. I started to make a signal to the Commodore to say what was happening, and he started to say that he was so sorry we had opened fire on the Sunderland, and I said, like hell we did – it was one of the troopships. Then we oiled at sea from a cruiser, which was very difficult as there was a big swell running.

Then we went into Gibraltar, where we went to a briefing with Admiral Burrough, whose flagship was the cruiser HMS *Nigeria*. A very dramatic

163

evening because he told us about the convoy and where we were going, because we hadn't really known about it up to then. And then everyone had a cup of tea or coffee and I asked for a whisky and soda and everybody was a bit horrified, and I had my whisky and soda. The next evening we sailed and by then the convoy had arrived, 13 merchant ships and the tanker *Ohio*, and we went through the Strait of Gibraltar at night. There was a spy on the African side of the Strait who reported the convoy, but they would have known about it anyhow, I expect, and the next morning a French civilian aeroplane flew over the convoy and reported it in plain language – the composition of the convoy, its course and speed and who the escort was – so the Germans and the Italians knew exactly where we were and what was coming. It was very friendly of our late allies, the French!

The second evening, I think it was, we got quite a big bombing attack, somewhere off Algiers, and the fighter pilots went up from the three aircraft carriers we had with us – *Eagle* by then had been sunk, but I will come back to that in a minute. It was amazing to see these pilots. They were chasing those bombers and saying, my fuel is showing nought, I must land, and so on, and they were landing and some of the carriers switched on their lights on the upper deck, which, of course, was very dangerous, and got their pilots back, or most of them. Occasionally we saw a plane catch on fire as it crashed on the deck, having run out of petrol, and they just threw the damaged planes over the side. Anyway, that was the last attack that night. The next morning the enemy reconnaissance planes picked us up at once, of course; the fighters from the carriers were shooting them down and then they started bombing us and, by God, we had some bombing that day. They came in high level, low level, torpedo-bombers and, as we got nearer to Sardinia and Sicily, we started to get dive-bombers. They near-missed one ship, the *Deucalion*, and she had to pull away. The destroyer *Bramham* went with her, and then the *Deucalion* was sunk by a bomb which went right through her, and that was the first loss we had.

Eagle, I should have said, was torpedoed the day before by a submarine; she had four hits. She was going full speed, landing on planes, and she just turned over on her side and went down. A terrible sight. The extraordinary thing was that about 800 or 900 men got out of her, but how an earth they got out of that aircraft carrier I can't think. The fate of the whole convoy was made at that time because we had one tug with us, which was a 15-knot tug, a big tug, and she wasn't told that the only thing she had to do was to tow damaged ships into Malta, and she, somewhat naturally, went and picked up a lot of the survivors of *Eagle* and took them back to Gibraltar, and that was the end of the 15-knot tug – and, by God, we could have used her later on. It was a very bad mistake – she should have been told.

Well, at last we had some lovely shooting because we had those high-level

Italian bombers coming over on an absolutely steady course and we were plonking away at them, and my station with the convoy was alongside the starboard-hand column and I was quite close to the third merchant ship in that column. He made me a signal, "If my owners could see me now, they would all have kittens!" The fire going up from the convoy was terrific and, of course, the fighters were up there and one of the interesting things was that I saw the bombs going by. I saw a cluster of bombs going past the bridge, and when you see the planes up there you think the bombs are coming straight down, but they are not, they are coming at a very sharp angle, coming at about 40 degrees, and the bombs went past the bridge, landing in the sea alongside our stern and going off, which is very interesting.

Well, that evening we were approaching the Narrows. We were only a few miles from Sicily and we had to go from four to two columns and go down the swept channel off Cape Bon. We were round about there and there was a submarine waiting for us there, naturally, and she fired a salvo of torpedoes and this was really deadly. One hit the *Ohio* in the pump room – that is where the machinery is for pumping out the oil – another hit *Nigeria*, which was Admiral Burrough's cruiser and flagship, and the next one hit the stern of *Cairo* – blew her stern off – so *Cairo* was a total loss, had the crew taken off by a destroyer and had to be sunk. *Nigeria* and *Cairo* were the two ships which had the control of the aircraft in the sky; we had no control after that, which was a great pity because we couldn't tell the Spitfires, which we got eventually, where the enemy was and when they were coming and so on, and that was bad luck.

Nigeria was listing about 15 degrees, and then the Admiral and his staff got into the destroyer *Ashanti* and rejoined the convoy, and *Nigeria* turned round and went back accompanied, in my opinion, by far too many ships, because the object was to get the merchant ships through to Malta, and if one of the cruisers was damaged, then, to hell with it, let her try to get back, but we were so short of ships after that. About that time the big ships, the carriers and the battleships – we had to have the battleships in case the Italian Fleet came out of port – they all turned round and went back to Gibraltar. The aircraft carrier HMS *Indomitable* was very badly bombed; the dive-bombers really took to her and she had three bad hits. She had one of the gun turrets hit and everybody killed, and a lot of people killed on the bridge. There were a lot of casualties and, anyhow, she turned round and got back to Gibraltar.

From then on we had no carrier and no fighter aircraft, but we did get a few long-range reconnaissance planes from Gibraltar. It had got dark by then, and just at dusk the Germans did an extraordinarily good attack. They came in with 88s and torpedo planes sort of combined, and I went through the merchant ships to the head of the column for a better place to shoot at these planes, and it was really, really hot, because the bombs were falling round me and planes all over the place, and the pom-poms said they got one of them. I didn't see it crash, but the pom-poms were sure they had. Well, then the convoy was in some confusion and, in fact, some of them were going back to Gib, and I went after them and got on the loud-hailer and said they were going the wrong way, and they turned round. To one of the Americans, I said, "Well, all the English ships are going on to Malta," so he turned round and came back. But I think one of those Americans ships, the *Almeria Lykes* probably, left the convoy and went off on her own that night and got sunk.

Well, I came up to the *Ohio*, which had stopped, went alongside and talked to Captain Mason, and the naval lieutenant called Barton and he said, "Well, we can steer from aft but we can't steer from the conning tower, but we can send messages to get the steering going," and he said, "I think we can steam." So I said, "That's fine – I'll put a blue light on my stern and you follow me." So I went ahead of him and went slowly and then, as he caught me up, I increased speed until eventually he was going at about 16 knots, which was marvellous, and, of course, he started weaving from side to side with his steering, but then he got that in hand and I took him right into the coast, right inside the international line or whatever it was. Anyhow, we went down the coast and all through the night ahead of us were these terrific battles where the E-boats, which were attacking the convoy, or what was left of it, and merchant ships were being hit and going up in terrific pylons of flame, which I was worried would reveal the tanker to the E-boats, but we were just far enough astern to miss these E-boat attacks. We just saw them ahead, a lot of gunfire, flashes, ships blowing up and so on; about every three-quarters of an hour there was another ship sunk. One of the ships hit by the E-boats was the cruiser *Manchester*, though she didn't sink – she was just torpedoed. We just got a signal saying, have been torpedoed or something, but we didn't know whether she had gone down or not.

Anyhow, in the morning I could see the convoy not far away, so I led the tanker into a column of the convoy. The Admiral made me a very nice signal from the *Ashanti* and I thought I would go and look for the *Manchester*. If I could find the *Manchester* I could get some fuel and there may be some survivors to be picked up, or they may have drifted to the shore and the French have taken them. So we went off to look for the *Manchester* and we steamed down the Gulf of Hammamet – lovely flat calm, blue sky, no wind, beautiful – looking on shore and looking at the sea, seeing if we could find her. There was no sign of her anywhere, so I said, "I must really have a few minutes sleep – I haven't slept for goodness knows how long." So I went down to my sea cabin and had hardly got there when I got called: "Captain, sir, Captain, sir, two aircraft coming!" So I rushed up on the bridge and there were two Italian torpedo-bombers coming straight at us, so I told the big guns, the 4-inch guns, to stay fore and aft and the guns' crews to stay in the shields, and I got the pom-pom and the Oerlikon to stand by. The pom-pom crew were a marvellous lot of villains – they always used to wear pyjamas, I don't know why, and caps, very large caps – and I had the loudspeaker in my hand and I said, "Wait, we will take the right-hand one first, stand by, stand by," then, when I thought it near enough, I said, "Fire!" and off the pom-pom went and the Oerlikon, and you could see the little shells hitting the front of the plane and all the way along, and then plonk, the plane just went straight down into the sea, on fire and very light brown smoke went up. Then I had them shift target to take the left-hand one, and we shot her down too.

Everybody was cheering and shouting and laughing, and I forgot that she had had time to drop a torpedo, and suddenly everyone shouted, "There's a torpedo!" and there was a torpedo coming straight for us. So I went hard a-port and the torpedo missed our stern by, well, it looked about 6 inches, but it could have been a foot, and I thought I would like to pick these people up because they will be picked up by an Italian submarine and taken back to Italy, but then I thought the submarine risk was so strong that I had better leave them. There was no sign of life in the first one. In the second one you could see them climbing over the side and getting into a dinghy. The pom-pom's crew were very bloodthirsty and, as they had been up in the Arctic, "Come on, sir, just one short burst," but I said, "No, you can't kill a beaten enemy – we would be up for war crimes if we did."

Well, we steamed on down the Gulf of Hammamet and the next thing that happened was a French signal station came up and challenged. I knew that they were working with the enemy, so I put up – oh, just before that I thought we would "splice the main brace" for shooting those planes down, and I didn't think we would be left alone for much longer, so I spliced the main brace; "stand fast the Hun" – that was the German we had picked up – and everyone had a tot of rum. And just to regularise the situation, we had a three-flag signal up the yard arm which denoted "splice the main brace". So when the French signal station challenged us, we put a flag on top of those three and twisted them all about so they couldn't read them, and hoisted an Italian ensign at the stern. The doctor came up on the bridge and said that he didn't want to join the Italian Navy, and I said, "I'm sorry, you've got to." He said, "What are you doing?" and I said, "It's a permitted 'ruse de guerre'," and the French station sort of acknowledged us and we hoped we were reported as an Italian destroyer.

Anyhow, we went on a bit more and then we decided that *Manchester* had disappeared and there was nobody about, so we turned round to rejoin the convoy, and we went streaking back to the convoy, getting very worried about fuel; and the dear old Chief Engineer, who always smoked a corncob pipe, kept coming up to the bridge handing me slips of paper which said how far we could go at so many knots. It was getting less and less, but we weren't far from Malta now, and we got back to the convoy. Soon after we got back there was a mother and father of an attack by Ju 88s, and they came from the stern of the *Waimarama*, which was a big merchant ship, and they just dropped a stick of bombs right on her and she just blew up. You never saw anything like it. The flames were hundreds of feet in the air, black smoke – it was a terrible sight and she went down in about 5 minutes. All its petrol was in drums on the upper deck and, of course, they all went off and then the heat exploded all the rest of it and the whole sea was covered in flames as far as you could see. It really was an inferno, and I said to the lads that as long as there was a merchant ship afloat, we were going to stay with it – we weren't going to have any PQ 17 stuff on this convoy, and I reckoned that by going into the flames I was sort of redeeming myself for the terrible leaving of the merchant ships in PQ 17.

So we dived into the flames. It was an extraordinary experience, for the whole sea was on fire. What struck me so much was the heat – it was terrific. I was leaning over the side looking for survivors and I was holding on to my beard because I was frightened it would catch on fire. So we went in and started picking up survivors, and the boys were absolutely marvellous They put a rope around themselves and over the side they went. This is why I said that picking up those airmen from the Sunderland was a good thing, because it gave the lads the idea of jumping into the sea and picking people up, and we got, I think, about 65 out of those flames – it was amazing.

The *Melbourne Star* had been astern of the *Waimarama* and the people on the stern of the *Melbourne Star* looked forward and it looked as though the whole ship was on fire because they steamed right through where the *Waimarama* had been. So we also picked up, rather to our surprise, some chaps from the *Melbourne Star*. The Gunner, Mr Musham, was away in the whaler, which was a wooden boat, picking up survivors from the edge of the flames, and we were sort of right in the middle of them. All I can say is that it was a very exciting time.

The Italian aircraft were coming round and dropping something on a parachute, which, we thought, must be mines. What I found out, I don't know when, was that they were not mines, they were *torpede circulare*, they were circling torpedoes. They dropped them into the sea and they went round in ever-increasing circles until they hit something or ran out of fuel and sank. So we were having these dropped, but fortunately we didn't know and we never saw them, so that was that. Well, when we got out everybody we could possibly see, I went out astern from the flames, and, just as I was about to go astern, the cook, the famous Walker, came out from his galley, which was aft, and he saw a man in the sea, so he kicked off his boots and over the side he went, and I was just about to go astern and it really was getting a bit hot, so I got on the loud-hailer and I shouted, "Catch hold of the net, Cookie, and hold on for Christ's sake, hold on!" and I turned to the others and I said, "That's the end of our good cook," because when I went astern there was a terrific wash at the stern. Anyhow, when we got out, there was the cook, still there, with the man he had gone over to save, and he was awarded the George Cross, that chap – jolly good. So, I thought, right, we would finally join up with the convoy, and the coxswain, who was steering the ship one deck below me, he had a porthole in front and he said, "There's a man over there in the flames, sir."

I said, "Coxswain, all I can see are flames and smoke." I didn't want to go back again.

He said, "No, I saw him move his arm, sir."

"All right, we'll go and get him."

It was John Jackson, who was the radio officer of the *Waimarama* and was the only officer survivor of that ship. He couldn't swim and he was on a sort of large bit of wood, so I put the ship right alongside him and he came up the netting.

So when we were really clear of it, off we went to rejoin the convoy, and we found the convoy had gone on and there was the *Ohio*, stopped with the destroyers *Penn* and *Bramham* hanging around and being bombed all the time. We tried to take her in tow, but where she had been hit in the pump room she had a great bit of steel sticking out and it just turned her round in circles. She was very difficult to keep straight or to turn at all. Then, with *Penn* and *Bramham*, we stayed there all day with her and the dive-bombers came and they dropped one bomb one side and one the other and they would come streaking down but they never hit her. Then *Penn* and *Bramham* went alongside, one each side, and made fast to her and I steered her by pushing the bows or pushing the stern, whatever course we wanted, and off we went. We were about 48 miles from Malta and we made up to 2 knots, I think, and it took us a long time to get there.

We went on all through the night and every now and again the tanker would veer off near to the minefield and we would push her back, and so we went on, and in the morning we could see Malta, which was a wonderful sight, as you could imagine. And then, as we came along the side of the island, the artillery opened fire on us and we tried every way we could to get them to stop the firing, and eventually made the signal "For Christ's sake stop firing", and they did. I think they said they saw a submarine following us or something, but I don't know, the shots were coming really quite close. The great thing, of course, the last day was that the aircraft carrier HMS *Furious* had flown off Spitfires to Malta, as reinforcements. They arrived and they just had enough fuel on the island for them to refuel, and we were protected by Spitfires on the last day, which was great, wonderful, and all the lads were cheering, you know, to see the Spitfires. So we went on and the bombing really had almost died down at the end.

The entry into Malta was really amazing. We stopped just outside the entrance to the main harbour and went and pushed the *Ohio*'s bows – I pushed her right round 140 degrees and had her pointed for going into harbour. A tug came out from Malta and she went in and the whole of the battlements were black with people. There were bands playing everywhere, people cheering, children shouting, "We want food, not oil," and I think it was the most wonderful moment of my life was when we went into Malta and everybody cheering. We made fast between the buoys where we used to lie when I was in the cruiser *Penelope*, and I went to sleep. My golly, did I ever, and in the evening I went ashore and went up to the Operations Room and the Admiral said, "We've got a ship coming from Italy – are you ready to go to sea and sink her?" I said, "Yes, certainly, but I think we will be a little more efficient if we had a night's sleep," and then, of course, the ship turned round, apparently, and went back, so we didn't have to go after all.

Penn was damaged by a tug which had come out from Malta and bumped into her quite hard. We were all right and we put most of our food ashore and all our stores we could spare and so on. The next day I went ashore and had lunch with Lord Gort, who said they were going to surrender on 9 September if we hadn't got in. He said you could make soldiers eat their belts but you can't make 500,000 civilians eat their belts, and he went off on his bicycle after a bloody awful lunch of vegetable omelette made of powdered egg. Everybody in Malta kept saying, had I heard about the destroyer that went into the flames, and I just said, well, it sounds like a bloody silly thing to do, and that rather shot them down.

Well, we stayed in Malta two or three days and then off we went to steam to Gibraltar, and I must say I had a big reaction as we steamed out of Malta. I literally had my knees knocking and I was holding on to the front of the screen of the bridge, I was so frightened going out again into all that bombing. What we felt was that the enemy would have some ships waiting for us. We were only three destroyers and, at daylight next morning, as it got light, we were sweeping the horizon with our binoculars and there was nothing there at all. We went on. We had some reconnaissance planes which came down to have a look at us, and I opened fire on them, and the worst thing that you could think of happened. One of the shells went off prematurely, just outside the muzzle, and killed one of my men. I was so upset, so upset about that, after getting them through all that battle to Malta, to lose one like that. But, there it was, it happened. I remember standing with my arm round the Captain of the gun's crew – tears were running down his face, he was so upset. Anyhow, that was the only person we lost on the whole of that trip. We eventually arrived at Gibraltar and fuel was short – we just had enough fuel to get into Gibraltar – refuelled and off we went again, and they ordered me to Londonderry.'

Desmond Dickens, apprentice in the merchant ship *Dorset*, took part in that convoy:

'It was a very sad thing that *Dorset* did not get through inasmuch as we had only 75 miles to go to Malta, but that was the way of the world at that time.

Desmond Antony George Dickens, a survivor, Malta 1942.

We were most lucky, in point of fact, in not losing any of our personnel, whereas other ships lost up to 70 or 80. Attacks, as such, had not stopped from the Tuesday until late on the Thursday. This involved all kinds of nautical sort of weaponry, and most especially bombing, and we were, of course, quite close to Sardinia, from which Mussolini sent out his Savoias, which were no doubt very effective. We went on till the Thursday, and then we were sunk after being bombed mercilessly all morning, and it became evident that it was quite impossible to save *Dorset* because she was, by 12 o'clock, literally full of water, up to the engine room tops. Her final end was at about 7 o'clock in the evening. It was one of the saddest things I have ever seen at sea when that great ship put her bow way out of the water and her stern sank, and at about 7.30pm she went down very, very slowly. It was something which left a very, very vivid impression on one's mind. We, of course, were not then in the ship, having been picked up by the destroyer *Bramham*.'

A wholly different perspective on events in the Mediterranean and Near East was experienced by Squadron Leader James Hayter, DFC, who had left the Western Desert and found himself on a rather different mission:

'I was in hospital for a while and then they sent me to the Special Duties Branch in Turkey. When I arrived in Turkey, they sent us to an Egyptian tailor and they told us to get a pin-stripe suit and we arrived in Ankara, and I soon discovered it was very much of a social scene with all the different consulates and embassies and all the rest in one street. One of the first cocktail parties I went to, there were Germans and Italians, the British and Americans, all the nationalities were there and we were all drinking together and everybody seemed very friendly, and I went to the Air Attaché and I said, "Look, we're supposed to be fighting these people, what's on?" I'd just come out of the Western Desert where I had been trying to be pretty unChristian towards the Italians and Germans, and here we were drinking cocktails with them, and he said, "As long as you don't say anything that you shouldn't, you know we've got to get on with these people." I didn't like this, and at the time I thought that things were pretty slack, and when I got back to the Middle East I put a report in. I reckoned that the British Embassy were letting us down. I remember I got into trouble over this and I got pulled up before an Air Marshal, and he told me that I'd let the side down, and I lost some seniority because of this.

As regards my work training Turkish pilots, I found that the serviceability of the aircraft was terrible, the ground crews were very rough and, invariably, when we took off there'd always be some instrument that was not working or the engine would be rough. I know I had one stop on me, but they had plenty of engine failures. Most of those pilots had been trained by the Luftwaffe and so a big percentage of the Turkish pilots were pro-German, and it was bit difficult working with them. I had an interpreter – some of them could speak a bit of English, but not many. They had Tomahawks, Kittyhawks and Hurricanes mainly, but the maintenance was shocking. It was no sinecure. You had no speedo and there'd always be something, the aileron cable wouldn't work, there'd always be something wrong. Night flying, I used to hate it. The interpreter was very good, but it was a bit of a job trying to get your story across, get your instruction across through an interpreter, because you couldn't do it while you were in the air.

British construction companies had been sent in to build airfields, and I picked some of the sites. The airfields were being made with the thought that we would go through the Balkans and so it was fairly well prepared. We were also helping people, in conjunction with the British Council, and we were helping escaped prisoners going through what we called the pipeline from Smyrna down the coast of Turkey, and we put them on trucks with a little bit of money and a bit of tucker.'

In the Aegean British Troops were landed on the Dodecanese Islands of Leros and Samos, and in early September 1943 a detachment of six Spitfires was sent to the Island of Kos, which had an airfield. With the Italian surrender imminent, this was considered an opportune moment. However, the Allied air bases were too distant and the Germans quickly built up their air and naval predominance in the region and the islands were soon back in their hands.

Flight Sergeant Alan Bennison, Air-gunner/Observer/Navigator, tells of his involvement in this operation:

'After Africa we were in Cyprus, and then the Army flew some paratroopers into Cyprus and we had to act as escorts to them to the Island of Kos, which at that time the British thought was a key point. We got them out there all right, but they were only out there a very short time, and the Hun, he attacked the island and he retook it and the detachment had to supply aircraft to go out and had to attack the incoming Germans. That wasn't very pleasant; however, we still survived.

Whilst in Cyprus we also had to carry out a few intruder raids on the Island of Rhodes, and to do this we had to carry four 250-pound bombs under the wings. We used to go in, and they were more nuisance raids than anything; the cannons and machine-guns would do as much damage as the bombs almost, and we were able to damage a few aircraft on the ground and that, and we were doing this at night. One of the boys didn't fly high enough and hit the mountain there.'

James Hayter piloted one of those Spitfires:

'From Turkey we went to the Persian Gulf and I had a flight, I got 74 Squadron then, and it was a Spitfire Squadron. Well, the flight was sent in from Cyprus into Kos. When we flew in we were attacked by 109s, just off Rhodes and Turkey, and we lost one chap there. We landed on the strip at Andimakhia on the Island of Kos but the Germans bombed that, so we couldn't land on it any more and we got four aircraft off and landed on the salt pan. When we took off the 109s were patrolling us, circling us, and we got the Bofors gunners to fire straight behind our tails to keep the 109s off them, and then it was all go. We lost most of our aircraft there, and then they got parachute troops on us one morning, and we were two aircraft left and we had a field telephone; some parachute troops had landed and one chap fired at me, and the bullet must just have flicked the handpiece and it shattered alongside me.

Then I took off into the hills and we got away, and we lived in the hills for a few days and found the odd sheep and killed that until we met up with the Special Boat Service. We tried getting away on a raft and that broke up, and then we eventually got a fishing-boat and we got to the coast of Turkey, where we got a better one and sailed and motored down to Cyprus. There were Italians, who had given up the ghost, and they wanted to come with us, so we let them come with us. We weren't sure how friendly they'd be, so we put them in the fish hold until we got to Cyprus. I think I was about 8 stone by the time we arrived in Cyprus because we were pretty hungry.'

CHAPTER 8

North Africa from El Alamein to Tunisia and overall victory

O n 23 October 1942 the Battle of El Alamein commenced. Victory for the British, Commonwealth and Allied troops led to German withdrawal. Under continual pressure Libya, then Tripolitania were cleared of Axis forces until the Mareth Line in Tunisia was reached. Meanwhile, following the 'Torch' Landings on the coast of French North Africa on 8 November, the Anglo/American forces were advancing eastwards into Tunisia. Progress was slow and the Axis was able to build up a substantial force within that country. However, despite vigorous counter-attacks on both the Anglo/American forces and on the Eighth Army at Medenine, and a spirited defence, the German and Italian troops, trapped on a fast-diminishing enclave of Tunisian coastline, and bereft of further supplies, surrendered on 13 May 1943, leaving a considerable number of prisoners in Allied hands.

From El Alamein onward, Leonard Thornton remembered clearly the denouement of the North African Campaign:

'And so then the preparations began for the build-up to the great battle that was to turn the tide. And Monty, being Monty, was able to resist the pressure from Winston Churchill to be doing something, to get on to produce some successes. He hung on then until the whole thing was carefully planned and prepared. We had our share in that preparation because it was to be an attack by the four divisions, the Scottish, ourselves [New Zealanders], the South Africans and the Australians, and we were now given, on our insistence, for the first time, a brigade of our own to be our own armour. You understand that, up till that time, you only had a sort of call on the armour if they felt that they wanted to join the battle; it wasn't a successful situation. Now we had the 9th British Armoured Brigade under our command and they were part, as it were, of our Division, and they were able to apply their activities according to orders received from us, the New Zealand Division. They were a marvellous brigade under a terrific chap called Currie, who was killed later on in France, and so I now was able to escape my staff job and I went happily back as a second in command, now of a Field Regiment – the old regiment that I'd gone to Greece with, actually.

We prepared the great battle under a tremendous barrage that was to herald the attack and protect the infantry as they went in to this night attack on 23 October. And my regiment was actually in support of the 9th Armoured Brigade and the plan was that the infantry would do their night attack on this huge four-division front with a barrage that hadn't been fired like this since, I suppose, the First War. And then they would move forward and consolidate on a line out in the desert on a ridge, literally a ridge, and then the armour would come through the empty lines through narrow gaps. Of course there were minefields everywhere; the armour would come out through cleared gaps in the mines to deploy out in front. We would move out with them and we would then be in a position to withstand the counter-attacks we knew would come against the position.

Well, like all battles it was pretty confused, but it was less confused than any battle we had taken part in up till that time. We did in fact move out; we found that the division on our left, which was the South African Division, had been held up and they were not really in position where we had hoped they would be. But anyway, we got out into the forward area with little trouble and got ourselves established and were supporting the armour. They were under attack but the situation was controlled and settled down over a period of a few days, and really that repeat grinding sort of battle went on for several days with no decision on either side – Rommel trying to react and get a counter-attack in that would be effective, ourselves trying to move our position and break out into the desert and beyond. And it really looked, at one stage, as though it might turn into a stalemate, and so that must have been a very anxious time for Montgomery, and he talked several times to my General, Freyberg, about what might be done. And the Australians had fought a marvellous action on the northern end of the line, right alongside the coast, but they were pretty well done in as a result of that battle, and they gained a lot of ground and lost a lot of chaps.

Anyway, at that point Montgomery, after consulting Freyberg, decided to shift his front, shift the direction of attack. By this time our infantry were pretty well worn out too, and we had been reduced to two brigades because one of the brigades was so knocked about that they had been pulled out and they were now converting themselves into an armoured brigade, so we'd have our armour permanently. So we only had two brigades. Monty wanted a good solid infantry attack, so we borrowed two British brigades, infantry brigades, and Freyberg and our headquarters were actually in command of the attack, which was called "Supercharge". And that infantry attack went in, the armour again were to break through, come through behind, and the 9th Brigade did, and they charged out and challenged the German armour, and they got very heavily knocked about. That was an extraordinarily courageous operation, marvellous really that the chaps could do it and would do it. They broke out and lost virtually all their tanks and a lot of chaps, of course, in the process.

But anyway, a line was cut and so we were now in a position to debouch out into Rommel's position and try and break up his formations from the rear, as it were. So that operation, the actual breaking out operation, was a very difficult one too, but, just as this operation was being prepared, I was suddenly called in to take over the appointment of what we would call the GSO2, the second grade staff officer on the Divisional headquarters.

Well that was all right – it was a bit sudden. The chap who had been doing the job, I don't know what had happened, but anyway, whether he was wounded or whether he fell by the wayside, I'm not quite sure, but anyway, there I was suddenly plonked into the divisional level as what you might call a second level executive officer of the Division. Fine, except that at that critical moment the principal staff officer, G1 as we called him, he fell sick of this thing called sandfly fever, which is a debilitating disease, and he had to be removed, evacuated. So there I was. I must have been 26, I suppose; I suddenly found myself as the GSO1, a full colonel responsible for the executive function in the Division, and I found that a little bit daunting.

But Freyberg was a remarkable man and we did our break-out in the most dreadful conditions because it was a night break-out and the dust kicked up by the battle was such that it was like operating in fog – you couldn't see anything. And anyway, I gave out his orders, how we were going to do this operation. We all moved out through the gap and somewhere about 2 or 3 o'clock in the morning I realised that I did not know where any of my brigades were. I could talk to them on the radio – I was talking to them on the radio – but that's not the same as knowing where the hell they are in the middle of open desert. So I must try and locate them and I couldn't find out exactly where they were in relation to us. In the meantime we'd had some people shooting at us, because there were a lot of loose bits and pieces moving about in the confusion of battle, so we were getting shot up a bit. Anyway, in the middle of all this General Freyberg turned up; I was in what we called the armoured command vehicle, a big sort of a pantechnicon, and I was sitting in there wondering, thinking this is the end of my professional career, and General Freyberg came in and he said in his peculiar high-pitched voice, "It's no good worrying about things that you can't help, my friend." So I thought, well, if he's not worrying about it this is all right for me, so I never, I really never looked back. And, of course, when the daylight came, we sorted ourselves out and we then started the great march, drive, thrust that eventually took us across to Tunisia and the end of the campaign.

It was a very interesting period from my point of view, because when, after a few days, my G1, principal staff officer, recovered and he came back to the Division, I reverted to my proper role of being the G2, the number two chap in operations in the Division. And General Freyberg was a chap who liked to know what was going on all the time – he liked to be in touch with the battle and he liked to be well forward. So he had constituted a thing called the tactical headquarters, which in effect was three protected tanks, light tanks, very light tanks, one of which had had the gun removed to make room for a staff officer; the staff officer was me. So we had the driver and we had the signaller – of course you had to have communications – we had me as the staff officer, and General Freyberg, and we travelled in that light tank. We travelled in that tank really right across North Africa, an entertaining experience and, of course, I was very close to Freyberg all that time.

I should say a little bit about Freyberg. He was a most remarkable man. He wasn't born in New Zealand, but he came out here as a child in 1890, as a child of two, and he had his schooling in New Zealand. Then, just when the First War broke out, he went off, not with the New Zealand forces, but because he happened to be in Mexico at the time, he went to the UK and assisted in Winston Churchill's famous Division, the Royal Naval Division, and then served throughout that war, winning the Victoria Cross and I think two DSOs, and being wounded eight times or something. So his total experience of war really was with the British Army, and then he continued as a Regular in the British Army right through until he was retired. So we were very lucky that he recommended himself to the New Zealand Prime Minister as a suitable chap to command the New Zealand Expeditionary Force, and it was a stroke of enormous good fortune that he was available and wanted to come to the New Zealanders and stay with us, resisting any offer of promotion so that he could stay with the New Zealand Division right throughout the war. So relationships with your senior commanders are always important to you, and I will only say that Freyberg's position was absolutely unchallenged throughout the war.

He was a very kind-hearted man and strangely diffident in many ways, although brave as a lion; I mean, he was an extraordinary chap and very dangerous to be with. He was, of course, a little bit aloof. A commander in the field has to make the difficult decisions himself when the lives of his men depend on his decisions. Freyberg was always conscious of that, and he made every effort to conserve the lives of his troops. At the same time he, more than anybody else I ever knew, was determined actually to take the battle to the enemy. He was going to do his bit to destroy this evil thing that was the Hitler machine. It was a personal thing with him, related I suppose to his experiences in World War I. Here they were doing it again, and he was going to do his level best to frustrate and to stop their successes, and so it was a personal battle with him. At the same time he had to think about the effect on New Zealand of the losses we were going to be suffering – we were a small country and so our contribution was disproportionately large – and I admired the way he therefore conducted himself. He had to keep some line of distinction between himself and his subordinate commanders and, I suppose it's fair to say, that he liked getting shot at himself. As a result I found that he was always happiest if there was a little bit of shelling going on or something like that. He was then exposed in the way that he was really ordering his men to be exposed time after time during every battle, so it was a personal thing. Anyway, it would be wrong to imply that I was in any way close to Freyberg. I mean, he knew I was a Regular officer and so the relationship was more like that in the British Staff where there were certain clear lines of distinction between association and your work in a professional sense. I found him a very good chap to work with; he would talk over the operations and discuss what might be possible and so forth, but he kept himself to himself in a personal sense.

And so that was an interesting professional time in which to be involved as we fought a number of battles and we went across on that great long march. There was an interim stage. We got to Tripoli and Churchill came out to visit us. He arrived under a false name – everybody knew it was going to be Churchill – and we had a tremendous ceremonial parade, the whole Division on parade led by the General. And Churchill appeared saying, "My old friend Bernard Freyberg..." etc, etc, so we thought this was tremendous; this is when he referred to him in his speech to us in such glowing terms, and we found that really very, very moving. He used to say privately – Freyberg used to say privately – that he'd been in all three of Winston's worst decisions, involved in all three of them. That was the First War when they, the Division, went to Antwerp, which was a mistake. Then he, Freyberg, had been at Gallipoli, which again was a very poor decision, and then he talked about Greece and Crete, especially Greece, as being another decision which had affected him personally. So we had that moving occasion at Tripoli, and Winston Churchill made a speech that really, I said to myself, this man's a politician I'm not going to be influenced by what he's got to say. However, as soon as he started to speak, there's no doubt it gave you a great surge, and I was really hanging on to his every word. This marvellous chap, and wonderful with the troops, and a tear occasionally would appear when he was talking to them, the brave defenders of Empire, and all that.

Anyway, we battled on – that's typical of the General. During the course of that advance on one day we were hurtling across the desert – we always had a protective screen out in front of light armour of our divisional cavalry, this was their job. And then we would be in my little headquarters, that's the tank, and my General and perhaps the commander of the artillery, a man called Steve Weir, we would be in a little cluster following on behind them. He liked being where he could decide what to do next, and on one particular day the cavalry squadron, in the advanced guard, got off on the wrong line and I had to be responsible to know where we were all the time, rather like naval plotting, and I realised that we were on the wrong line, and so I said to the General, "Look, the cavalry are taking us in the wrong direction so you'd better call up another squadron and we can get them to replace them and they can go through us here and take on the right line. "Oh no," he said, "we'll press on." That was his favourite expression: "Let's press on."

So we became literally the leading vehicle in the entire Division, very inappropriate thing to do, and we hurtled across the desert and sure enough we went over a little rise, and there in the bottom, in the wadi, as we called it, in a little bit of valley, there were three Italian tanks. Fortunately they were Italian tanks and the gentlemen who had been occupying them were more or less standing outside ready to surrender. They had, I think one of them had, run out of petrol and the others had run out of spirit, and so we stopped alongside these tanks, and we had three little light armoured tanks with us as a form of protection. So he, the General, stuck his head out – he used to ride on the glassy part, the plate in front of the tank – and he shouted out to the troops, "Frisk 'em, frisk 'em." So the troops started to – this was the only chance to loot these chaps had had I suppose for months – so they'd no sooner started to frisk 'em when the General became impatient. "We'll have to press on," he said. "Boys, press on," so we all jumped back into our vehicles and left all the Italians behind. No doubt they were to be frisked by the people who came behind us. Anyway, that was the end of that enterprise.

Well, we then went steadily ahead and fought a number of battles. We fought a battle out of Takrouna – well, the Takrouna Gap – which was again a critical battle. We were now approaching Tunis, you see; by this time the First Army had landed on the other coast, the western coast, and they were doing their operations in towards Tunis, so we were really applying a sort of nutcracker operation on Rommel and his troops. But that wasn't to say that we still didn't have some difficult battles to fight, and then towards the end Rommel moved some of his people across on to the other front, on to the First Army front, and gave them a very bad knock which took them some time to recover from. But inevitably the Allies closed in and squeezed the Axis supply lines, and after another couple of fights finally the moment came and something like 230,000 German and Italian prisoners were taken as that campaign caved in.

Then Freyberg was appointed as the Corps Commander of the British Corps, the 3rd Corps, on a temporary basis, and so it was he to whom the Germans made surrender. We thought that was very appropriate when the Italian Commander, Army Commander and his principal German supporter – who were once our old enemies in 90th Light and 164, they were the two divisions we had fought against most – came in to offer their surrender. So there was General Freyberg receiving the surrender from the Italian senior officer and the German Major General. So the Italian came forward, saluted and shook hands with the General, and then the German saluted and offered to shake hands, and Freyberg wouldn't shake his hand. He said, "He's an arrogant man and I will not shake hands with him." Anyway, that was the end of that campaign.

Well, that was also the end of my period as General Staff Officer Grade 2 to General Freyberg. The whole Division now moved back to Egypt – an enormous march back across Africa to resume our lives at the New Zealand Base Camp at Maadi and Helwan and get ourselves re-organised, because two things had now happened. One was that the New Zealand Government was under pressure at home to bring home the men who by now had all been away for three years. So there was political pressure for the New Zealanders to be brought home. This had already occurred after the Battle of Alamein when the Japanese threat to New Zealand became apparent and the Australians had all been pulled out. That Division left after the Battle of Alamein, and I must admit there was pressure then for us to do likewise and go back to New Zealand. Wisely, in my view, the New Zealand Government decided under pressure from Churchill to leave the Division there. We felt that we could make a better contribution there, and Freyberg felt that too. Churchill used the argument that he couldn't provide the shipping, and I think that was probably a fair argument – he would have found it very difficult to provide the shipping to get all of us plus the Australians back to our part of the world. So the decision was taken that we would stay in the Middle East Theatre, in the European Theatre in fact, and it was absolutely the right choice.'

Of the westward pursuit following El Alamein, Captain Roy Blair, Commanding Officer 4th Company, NZ Machine-Gun Battalion, recalled that:

'From the break-out at Alamein on 2 November 1942 it was in hot pursuit, but unfortunately two days out from Alamein it rained – one of the very few times I've known it rain in the desert – so hard that we were bogged down for 24 hours, or it might have been longer than that. Anyway, we dried out and those were exciting times in the North African Campaign – the fast movement across the open desert in formations, contact being maintained just by flags of various types, very little radio contact, although we did have some sets. We were fortunate in the Machine-Gun Battalion that we were all fully motorised – four guns to a platoon and each gun had its own truck and its own crew, and they were able to be independent throughout all the days, weeks and months. They were able to brew up and look after themselves foodwise. The infantry troops were carried in trucks and weren't so independent as the machine- gunners.

After leaving the Alamein position we stopped for a period of time at Bardia and then we moved on from there to El Agheila, where the Axis forces had prepared a defensive position. It was in this area where we commenced our first "left hook" around from there, around the Agheila position, and ended up at Wadi Matruh, up past "Marble Arch". We managed to get back and cut off retreating Rommel formations, but not completely – they carried on retreating. From there we went to a place called Nofilia, where we had our Christmas meal. We fought various little battles along the way, but the next important place we got to eventually was Tripoli. In Tripoli we settled down for some weeks there; the troops were mainly engaged in unloading supplies for the Eighth Army coming in through the Port of Tripoli, and New Zealand troops fed very well in this particular period.

However, we were told not long after to move off quickly to the west towards the Mareth Line, and the first action the New Zealand Division had there was at a place called Medenine. Medenine was a high-ground area, an Italian airport, and facing across a big plain on to the Matmata Hills in Tunisia, and at Medenine one of the classic battles was fought, it being considered a perfect defensive position. The 5th Brigade was under Kippenberger, and I had 4th Company Machine-Guns, and we had a tremendous view of this battle. The German attack came from the west-sou'west area of the Mareth Line. The Mareth Line was confronted by British troops mainly, and we were out on the flank, and we could see all the battle going on. The German panzer divisions and infantry coming down out of the Matmata Hills was an amazing sight, and it only lasted a

Roy Ian Blair

day, but they lost numerous tanks, troops and so on, and they retreated round about dusk of that day.

We went on from there through Wilder's Gap, it was called – the gap was found in the Ksour Mountains by Nick Wilder of the Long Range Desert Group – and we went round from there to what they call the Tebaga Gap. It was on 23 March when the New Zealand Division attacked the left flank of the Mareth Line positions through the Tebaga Gap. That's where Ngarimu won his VC, and once the Tebaga Gap had been breached, the armour poured through. It was the beginning of the end; it was only a matter of time. After that we went through to Gabes and on up towards Tunis.

On leaving Gabes we went on then to a place called Sfax, and then on to Sousse, where, about this stage, we passed the Eighth Army, and then, after that, passed the American forces coming from the west, and then the last and final action of Tunisia was at a place called Takrouna. Enfidaville was a little place on the coast, and Takrouna was a very big, high, rocky outcrop, and from the top of that one could see almost anywhere for miles around, and this feature became a problem that the 5th Brigade had to attack. Many people were lost there.

This attack on Enfidaville and Takrouna took place just around about ANZAC Day in 1943 and finished about the middle of May. At that time the Axis forces capitulated in Tunis and North Africa, and the New Zealand Division returned from there back to Maadi. The first furlough draft was relieved to go back to New Zealand from there, and I happened to be one of them, being a married man at the time and being in the First Echelon.'

The support of the Desert Air Force had been of major significance in the campaign. Pilot Officer Kenneth Dawick, RNZAF, having been an RAF Instructor at Aden, was posted to 238 Squadron as a Hurricane pilot:

'The Squadron was stationed just the other side of what they call the Bomb Line, that was in the desert. There was just a pile of tents around and a few aircraft and I'm the new one there. And they'd been up in the desert about 18 months, real Desert Rats I suppose from an Air Force point of view. Our main job was, just a few days before the battle of Alamein, escorting the bombers that came from down the Suez Canal and escorting them in at round about 10,000 or 12,000 feet; the top cover above us were the Spitfires. This went on for two or three days; we got some Stukas crashing through and got a little bit of ack-ack, and when you see this ack-ack coming up in a big puff and red hot stuff going by, it was quite alarming. I think the enemy broke early in November, and from then we gave them the "hurry up". Our wing Hurricanes, we did the strafing, nearly all low flying, and we kept them moving. We moved up to forward 'dromes, up through Derna, Mersa Matruh, Tobruk, and pushing the enemy in front. The bombers, they bombed them all along that coastal road – there's only about one road and it was just nose-to-tail for miles and miles and miles. And so in the camps we didn't get enough time to dig in, so it was more like a shuttle service, our squadron plus the other squadrons of the wing, and it was, well, a typical, horrible, ghastly wartime job.

As we got up towards the other side of Tobruk, I think we had a bit of a lull there and one very interesting thing happened. Our wing, four squadrons, got taken off and we went in from Fort Capuzzo along the wire

Kenneth Dawick

which was the border between Libya and Egypt. We went in there about 100 miles – didn't fly high, I suppose less than a 1,000 feet, because after all the enemy had RDF [radar] too – and we got into what they call the LG125, way behind enemy lines. And our four squadrons landed at this strip, and the Long Range Desert Group had prepared all this and we came in there and all the fuel was in there and everything had been coming by air. We refuelled and we had to fly 150 miles down the coast to Agedabia, all across the swampy marsh area, and do exactly as we did before, strafing, and just stopping the flow of enemy traffic from getting out. And next morning another squadron took over and we just more or less kept a shuttle service, strafing all down into that area. Tremendous damage.

We got out of it and got back to LG125, refuelled and flew back to El Adem near Tobruk. And as we heard later from the Long Range Desert troops, that night the enemy bombed that place; we got out in time after four days of intensive flying.'

Victories are far better than defeats, but they can still involve horrible experiences, as former Gunner Bruce McKay Smith recalled of El Alamein:

'My battery was given a barrage to fire, and then, when we'd completed our barrage, we were to go forward with the infantry as close support, through the minefields, and as far forward as we could go. This was a horrible experience, and we had several vehicles blown up on mines, and I happened to be in one vehicle which was blown up, but never got hurt. We finished up in the morning after the attack in a very confused state in the middle of a tank battle. We were in just a slight depression and reasonably safe until a German high-powered machine-gun opened fire on us, which created some havoc and a few casualties. The anti-aircraft Bofors gun which was with us suddenly found where this machine-gun was and fired about five rounds into it, and they surrendered very quickly after that lot. Amongst those who surrendered was an Austrian doctor who stayed with us for quite a few days. This Austrian doctor had been, literally, forced into the German Army much against his will, and we kept him for a few days. He attended to quite a few of our sick and ailing and wounded until the Field Security came along and took him off to be a prisoner of war. We were sorry to see him go.

But anyway, the war had to go on and although our units were kept in this forward gunnery position, it wasn't a very happy situation to be in, because we seemed to get involved in amongst tanks, and tanks and artillery don't go well together, as we found. However, after some days the Germans really began their retreat with our units following, and we'd go into action at various stages. Going through what had been the German front lines was quite an eye-opener. The artillery barrage had pock-marked the ground, and you'd think nobody could live through it, but the Germans seemed to have survived. We carried on two or three days, still chasing Germans, and eventually came to an area where the regiment was able to regroup and get re-organised again. Then it started to rain, and that put a complete stop to everything, the aerial activity, ground activity, the lot. A lot of our vehicles became bogged down. Our vehicles, most of them, were still equipped with mud-grip tyres. If we'd had the bull tyres which the Germans had for travelling on sand, we'd have done a lot better, although the wet weather didn't make much difference at that stage, but from then on we cursed having these mud-grip tyres on the sand.

But we then had a breather for some days. At that stage I was still a driver and they decided that I should go to a course on battery surveying in Cairo to the British Army Depot. Here I spent a fortnight, up to and including Christmas, learning the ways and means of trigonometry, which I'd forgotten, and various other mind-boggling things. Then coming back after that course I got promoted to a two-striper, which allowed me an extra shilling a day, I think.

My new duty was battery surveyor, establishing the position of the guns, bearings, etc. It also involved me in being the Battery Commander's assistant, so if he went forward to an observation post, I was to go with him, as his jack of all trades, which I did once or twice, which was fairly scary. Then suddenly the Regiment had the order to move again, and then began the long process of chasing up the desert, now and again stopping to have a skirmish at places for which we had no names, that I can remember.

The Germans were very determined till they came to the Mareth Line that they had established, and later we went into a pitched battle at a place called Enfidaville, and that was where the first lot of new anti-tank guns came into operation, used at this stage by one of the Guards regiments. We took our hats off to them for their cool, matter-of-fact way of conducting the war. They had their tents, the officers' mess was set up in as much shelter as they could find, and the officers used to dine. The infantry, as they were, wore all polished boots and spick and span until this battle broke out, and then they manned these guns, and I've forgotten how many tanks they were credited with knocking out.

Prior to this we went on one of General Freyberg's celebrated "left hooks", which meant moving in the dark and laying up during the day. The second or third day, I think it was, we woke up in the morning to find we were below a ridge on top of which was a German Tiger tank looking straight down at us, and I've never seen such a scatter in all my life. We didn't open fire because he was too high above us, and he couldn't depress his gun low enough to do any harm, and the 4th Field Regiment did one of its quickest moves in history, I think.

We carried on, supposedly still in secret, down to the south and then gradually easing west and then north again until we came to the Tebaga Gap, where a pitched battle was fought which destroyed a lot of the German equipment. It was at that time that the Hurricane aeroplanes, which had been converted to what they called Hurri-bombers, came into action as anti-tank weapons, and very effective they were too. At this time, of course, the RAF had virtual aerial supremacy, and that made life a lot better without having to worry about being bombed all the time.

We carried on after Tebaga and had several skirmishes, none of them very serious, until we came to our last position. The Germans were forced into quite a tight enclave and we were virtually surrounding them, but they still showed no signs of giving in and the shelling by the Germans was really very severe. Attached to us we had a battery of captured German 88-millimetre guns, which were the scourge of the German Army as far as we were concerned. They could be used as anti-tank, anti-aircraft, or for just ordinary shelling; they were very high velocity. But this battery of captured guns, manned by one of the British Army anti-aircraft units, came in for some colossal casualties with the Germans using their *nebelwerfers*, which were horrible six-barrelled mortars of about 6 inches or 8 inches bore, which revolved like the cylinder of a Colt revolver and squirted out these horrible projectiles, which were about a metre long, and I don't know what explosives they had, but they were shockers. They virtually wiped out this battery of captured 88s, much to our horror because they were doing a great job of plastering the Germans. But anyway, we had, as I said before, quite a good air cover there, and the Germans suddenly started to go completely crazy; they fired, I think, to destroy as much ammunition as they possibly could. They just fired anywhere and at everything. It was hardly safe to put your head above ground; we had shells flying around the place, a lot of which were duds.

Eventually the whole thing came to an end and General Freyberg took the surrender of the German Commander. The German 90th Light Infantry were given the military honour of carrying their weapons to a central point as they surrendered, as they had been a close adversary of the New Zealand Division right through the war, and that was one concession General Freyberg made. They were still full of cheek and very arrogant until they started putting them on lorries to cart them to prisoner of war camps, and that was the end of the war in North Africa as far as I was concerned.'

During the Axis withdrawal, Kenneth Frater had been part of the transport of a flying column that was supposed to cut off Rommel at Halfaya Pass:

'We moved through the minefields in the dark, and at daylight were out in open desert, when suddenly the skies opened and the rain fell down. The desert turned to mud and we were stuck to the axles. The German forces out on the sealed coastal road escaped back to El Agheila, leaving a delaying rearguard on the top of Halfaya Pass.

By the time we had extricated ourselves from the mud, Halfaya Pass had been taken in a surprise night attack by one of our battalions. We drove up the sealed road to where there was a bottleneck of traffic at Sidi Barrani, all waiting to go up the Pass. After a wait of 24 hours we went up the Pass, and a few miles later, opposite Bardia, to our surprise, we pulled off the road and were told that the Division would be stopping to rest and refit.

This was a good period. Inter-unit rugby matches were played. Bardia and Fort Capuzzo were explored. News of the First Army combined British and American landing in North West Africa came through. There was no enemy aerial activity. The general feeling was that we had faced the enemy all the time in Africa, and that we should be the ones to be in at the kill and not the latecomers in the First Army. Truth to tell, we were getting bored. I was persuaded by our captain that I should accept promotion to lance corporal. This meant I would only get ninepence per day extra instead of the shilling I got as a driver mechanic. However, within three months I was promoted to full corporal, so was 1 shilling and sixpence a day better off.

Montgomery left nothing to chance – no hurried attacks or getting ahead of supply, as previous desert generals had done. The New Zealand Rail Company pushed the railway to the wire. Tobruk Harbour was brought into operation after being destroyed by the enemy. A fleet of six-wheeler trucks carrying 20 tons operated on the sealed road. After about three weeks we moved to El Adem and went into Tobruk to load up with supplies. We then travelled overland to Msus, following the route which had become so familiar ten months previously. A trip into the re-opened harbour at Benghazi to collect supplies was a welcome diversion.

The El Agheila line extended from the sea about 10 miles to hills of very soft sand, and was impossible to take with a frontal attack. Around mid-December we were informed that the Division was going south, would then circle back and come in on Rommel's rear. Moving only at night, we made our southerly trek and then went north to cut the road. Despite having to defend two fronts, the enemy was stronger than expected. Our particular timetable took our soft transport into an artillery battle, and we retired rather hurriedly. Just when he was supposed to be trapped, once again Rommel slipped away.

The El Agheila line was clear and Rommel headed for Tripoli. The six-wheeler fleet was building a huge dump of supplies near "Marble Arch", a huge monument straddling the road and commemorating Mussolini's colonisation of North Africa. We started moving supplies to build dumps in the Wadi Zem Zem. This area wasn't just one wadi but a large expanse of hills and valleys of pure rock. We were stationed at Nofilia near a derelict fort left from Foreign Legion times. Here we had our 1942 Christmas dinner. General Freyberg had fresh meat and other goodies flown from Cairo for the occasion.

Once again the Division was elected to "left hook" and try to cut Rommel's retreat from Tripoli. We commenced our move into the Wadi Zem Zem. We swanned around for a few days, slowly moving forward. Eventually we reached soft sand again and heard the sound of combat ahead. Evidently Rommel wasn't leaving any loopholes for us to slip through. Driving along a bleak sandy landscape, suddenly below us, down a steep escarpment, was the beautiful oasis of Beni Ulid. This oasis had a population of 2-3,000 and covered an area of perhaps 50 hectares. It was about 20 metres lower than the surface of the surrounding country. We stocked up with water and climbed out on to the desert again.

Leaving Beni Ulid the sand was very soft. All around was the litter of war, burnt-out tanks, armoured cars and trucks. Souvenir hunters had a field day. My first attempt was my last. I went to have a look in a disabled armoured car. There were the bodies of two German soldiers in the front seat and the driver's head was lying in his lap. This effectively deterred me from future scavenging. However, some of the chaps collected a lot of souvenirs which they were later able to sell to the Americans for quite large sums of money. We came to signs of civilisation, fields divided by rows of trees and an occasional farmhouse, then more intense farm lands and olive groves.

Once again we went too far. Our advance forces had run into strong opposition. We hurriedly retired and spent the night a couple of miles back. Shortly after midnight the firing died down. In the morning, 24 January 1943, we drove into Tripoli. Once again Rommel had got away. Tripoli was a beautiful city with wide tree-lined avenues and magnificent buildings. Behind this showy facade were, of course, the usual Arab markets and jumble of cramped slum dwellings. Our quarters were in the Italian Barracks right in the city centre. The wharf and mole had been demolished by the enemy, but three days after our arrival our engineers had it open and ships were unloading cargo. The enemy was being pushed slowly back and we were carting supplies from the wharf to a forward dump at Ben Gardane. We had to take a load of ammunition forward and ran into a counter-attack by the Germans at Medenine. We also came under the last daylight aerial attack I was to experience. It was quite nasty while it lasted. Rommel retired to the Mareth Line. This was a narrow defile between huge sandhills running from the sea to a point over 100 miles south. To make the circular round trip back to the German rear was a trip of over 300 miles through some pretty rugged parts of the Sahara Desert.

General Freyberg was placed in command of a composite force to do another "left hook". We started building a secret dump around 80 miles south of Medenine. We would load up and as soon as it was dark leave Ben Gardane and, without lights or even cigarettes, do the 160-mile round trip and hopefully be back behind our lines before daybreak. Anyone who didn't make it had to camouflage and wait out the day. Fortunately the nights were still fairly long, as it was only the second week in March.

The Corps started its advance at dusk on 16 March. This time we had an Armoured Division for company. The tanks ground the sand track to fine dust, creating confusion. We travelled all night and holed up next day. The second night, when we expected to stop at dawn, we just kept on going. Freyberg evidently thought Rommel might have knowledge of our movement and so we kept going in the day. In the morning, despite the fact that every vehicle had a 6-foot red, white and blue Air Force roundel painted on its roof, we were attacked by American fighter planes from the First Army. The Americans were very unpopular – they were also rotten shots.

Freyberg's fears were justified and there was a fierce battle at Tebaga

Gap, which lasted from late afternoon until next morning. We went back to our dump for supplies and when we returned all the German forces except for a rearguard at Wadi Akrit had disappeared. The rearguard held our advance up for several days, then we were able finally to move forward again – through Gabes and Sfax, through miles of barley fields, past the amphitheatre of El Djom, past Sousse and on to Enfidaville below the heights of Takrouna, where the Germans occupied a very strong position.

Our forward troops were now in positions inaccessible to trucks. A Mule Company was formed to supply our troops in the hills. The Arab chiefs were asked to bring all available mules to the market at Sfax, and we went to Sfax to transport the mules to the Mule Company area in our trucks. Loading them was quite an hilarious experience. In the end the Mule Company never actually operated. However, they did put on a Mule Derby, which was attended by several thousand people the day prior to the German surrender.

Rommel had flown, leaving General Messe in charge. When he eventually surrendered it was to General Freyberg. The surrender took place on 13 May. We were informed that we would be leaving for Maadi Base on the 15th. With Tunis so close, it seemed a shame not to see it. On the 14th several of us made a quick illegal trip and had a drive around Tunis before hurrying back to prepare for our 2,000-mile journey commencing next day.

On the morning of 15 May we started our journey by making a detour through the town of Kairouan, a very holy place in Islamic religion. I wasn't really impressed. Travelling back through the places we'd striven to reach for so long and passing through these now peaceful places seemed very strange. With the weather now heating up, travelling at speed on sealed roads caused no end of tyre trouble, and engines full of sand were prone to overheating.

Back we went through Sfax, Gabes, the Mareth Line, Ben Gardane and on to Tripoli, where the New Zealand concert party put on a show for us. On through Homs, Misurata, under "Marble Arch" and through the El Agheila defences and into Benghazi, where the aerodrome was fairly bristling with Yankee Liberator bombers. Through the fertile Barce Valley and its pretty town, up again into the desert, and then down to the town of Derna for an overnight stop. Then through Timimi, Tobruk, Bardia, down Halfaya Pass to Sidi Barrani. Bypassing Mersa Matruh, then on to the familiar territory of Fuka and Alamein. Taking the bypass at Alexandria and down the desert road to Mena and the Pyramids, over Kas-er-nil Bridge, through Cairo, reaching Base at Maadi on 31 May 1943.'

The last months of the campaign left mixed memories for Private Arthur Gladstone of the NZ Machine-Gun Battalion:

'During the months of January and February we trained, becoming accustomed to desert conditions, becoming accustomed to having our boots full of sand, accustomed to having our eyes full of flies, just becoming accustomed to the desert. In March we moved to join the Division, and the machine-gun reinforcement actually reached the Battalion Headquarters on 8 March near the village of Medenine in front of the Mareth Line. We were then allocated to the various Companies of our Battalion, who in turn were dispersed throughout the Division because that was the nature of the Machine-Gun Battalion; one Platoon went with one Infantry Battalion. The Platoon to which I was allocated was No 10 Platoon in 4 Company, and we were attached to the 21st Battalion of the Infantry.

We moved into the Tebaga Gap and, in fact, were the first ones in operation in the Tebaga Gap, and the 21st Battalion had to secure the right flank of what was eventually to become the Division's start line for the Battle of Tebaga Gap in the Mareth Line. That took place on 26/27 March, and when the breakthrough was achieved, we moved on to Gabes and from Gabes to the next engagement at Wadi Akarit, where another breakthrough was achieved against combined German and Italian forces, and the New Zealand Division went through the opening.

We were then in a situation of mobility, passed Sfax, the magnificent Coliseum at El Gin – which just stood out in the midst of the desert, on its own, no indication of what had once been around it, a better-preserved Coliseum than the one in Rome – then Sousse, Sidi Bel Abbes and on to Enfidaville. The attacks against Enfidaville and Takrouna were particularly bloody. That was the virtual end of the war in North Africa in which I participated for two months as a very inexperienced soldier.

I really at that stage had not made my mind up about "affairs military", and I was not over-enthusiastic about some of the episodes that occurred during that short period of time, but there did not seem to be anything drastically wrong with what was being done. I can't say that I enjoyed the experience. I sat during the first day of action, as I said, on the right flank of the Division watching the Maori Battalion assail Hill 210, and Ngarimu earned his VC, but we sat there helpless. Even though we were virtually behind the German lines, there was no way that we could have helped in that situation; our fire would have been just as perilous for the Maoris as it was for those that they were attacking. So those types of episodes were frustrating. I had trained as a range-taker using a rangefinder, and that was my job with the Platoon – it gave me the first sight of our targets, and to me that was a responsibility.'

Also involved in the later stages of the campaign and with mixed memories was Lieutenant Edward Prebble, in command of an Anti-aircraft unit.

'When we arrived at the harbour, Bone, in Algeria, there was an air raid in progress and a ship in the harbour carrying petrol had been struck and the place was a blaze of light. Anyhow, we managed to get most of the stores

Edward Shard Prebble

193

off. Fortunately my guns came off very early, and so I was put into action immediately on the wharf. There were several sticks of bombs dropped but we had no casualties at all. The following day I was deployed round the harbour, which was much more sensible than being on the entry wharf itself. This was round about 18 December, shortly after the original "Torch" landings. We were in Bone for about three or four days, and then proceeded up to Souk a Arbra, which was in Tunisia. Shortly after arriving there my troop was detached and sent to join the French, who had also come over to our side, but they had no anti-aircraft or anti-tank protection. I was only with them quite a short time until equipment arrived for them.

On rejoining my regiment the Colonel asked me if I would become his adjutant. I was very flattered by this, as it meant immediate promotion to Captain. I did not know at the time that I wasn't his first choice.

He was a very difficult man, and I'll give you an instance. When we were in the Battle of Medjez, he and I were in a forward position just below the crest of the hill. We had two one-man tents, a batman and a signaller with us, and we were observing the enemy. On one occasion he said we would sleep in one tent and have the other one as a mess. On another occasion he crawled out of the mess tent and said, "I'm going to dress for dinner"; he then came back and he said, "Would you like to dress for dinner?" So I crawled out of the tent, waited a few minutes, then crawled back again, whereupon he said, "Good evening, Prebble, will you join me with a sherry?" And he was sitting there with his hip flask and a couple of jars and two sherries poured out, so we solemnly drank this sherry and he then said, "You can tell the batman he can serve dinner," and the batman came crawling on his stomach with two mess tins. Really the position was so ridiculous, and the stress sort of living with a man like that was more than I could bear, and I was hospitalised with very severe shingles.

I was sent down to the General Hospital at Constantine where I remained for some little time. While I was there I got a letter from the Second in Command who suggested that it would be to my advantage if I would return to the unit as soon as possible. I therefore got out of the hospital on the garbage truck and went to the nearest airfield, and I asked the air force if they could fly me to Tunis. When I reported to the Colonel, he said, "Oh, we've decided that you are going to be promoted to Battery Commander – you're taking command of No 347 Battery and with a promotion to Major." We spent a rest period at Sousse and then prepared for the invasion of Italy.'

CHAPTER 9

Italy: Sicily to Cassino

*V*ictory in North Africa predetermined that the Allies would attempt their first step into mainland Europe on Italian soil. With the seizure of the island of Pantelleria, Sicily was the next obstacle en route. The Allies launched aerial and sea assaults on southern Sicily on 10 July 1943 and, despite strong German resistance, on 17 August entered Messina. However, prior to this the bulk of the German forces had been able to make an orderly withdrawal to Italy. In early September the Eighth Army made almost unopposed landings on the toe of Italy in Calabria and then at Taranto, and began advancing up the Italian peninsula. While all this was happening, on 25 July, Mussolini was deposed and the new Italian Government began making secret overtures to the Allies, with the result that an Armistice was signed on 3 September, and broadcast on the 8th.

On 9 September the Fifth Army landed near Salerno, south of Naples, and suffered heavy casualties at the hands of determined German resistance, which was eventually overcome and, with the Eighth Army now on its flank, the Germans started their withdrawal to the north, the Allies entering Naples on 1 October. Thereafter it was a slow and arduous slog north for both the Fifth and the Eighth Armies (now reinforced by the 2nd New Zealand Division), with increasing resistance from the Germans, inclement weather and swollen rivers. By the end of the year the Gustav Line had been reached and breached in parts. However, a number of major assaults in the mountainous area around Monte Cassino were costly failures, while the landings at Anzio on 22 January 1944 were soon severely resisted by the Germans with heavy losses on both sides.

Among the troops landing in Sicily was Lieutenant George McMurtry, a New Zealander, serving in the Wiltshire Regiment:

'We soon captured the ports which Montgomery wanted and pushed on inland. At one stage the big German tanks, Tiger tanks, were getting at us, so we had to leave our anti-tank guns for a while and move around Mount

Etna, actually on a little goat track, just on our feet. I remember getting spotted by the Germans as we were doing this and they opened fire. We sort of lay down and a piece of shell came down, several inches long; sizzled, sizzled it did, along the ground, through between the man's heels in front of me, missing me by a head. I was glad I wasn't very tall. Anyway, we got round there and we got around the back of the Germans and then brought the guns up and went on to capture the eastern side of the island, while the Americans went around the west at Messina.

There was an occasion when we were sitting on the road and I had a gun by a corner, by a T-shaped corner, and four tanks came down the road very fast towards us. Some of my men had been wounded a few days before, so I was acting as No 2, which meant I was loading this jolly thing. We had a camouflage net over the top of it and I told them to wait until the tank was at a certain point and then take the net off, when we would open fire, which we did at about 60 yards. Well, 60 yards point blank range with a 6-pounder is quite deadly, and it went through the leading tank and killed everybody inside that, and the second tank came flying along behind and turned over, and that was the end of that one. The third one went up to the side road and it fell in the hands of a "Pheasant", which was a 17-pounder anti-tank gun belonging to an anti-tank unit. That left the fourth one, which was back up the road. The infantry were out in front of that and put some stick mines in front of it, stopped it, and they got prisoners out of that.

We had been hit a few days before that by an 88, and it took bits of skin off my arm and killed one of my men, wounded several others, and on that occasion we had the guns in Portee gun-carriers. So we came to a halt, of course, and we took the guns off, while this fellow was firing all over the place, and ran them into an orange grove, and there we got a line on him and he took off.

From there we hopped over to Italy on 3 September, which was just about four years exactly since the outbreak of war, and here I received my promotion to Captain. We landed on the toe of Italy. I went over in a thing called a "DUKW", a sort of amphibious vehicle affair with a crew and anti-tank gun on board, and we had some skirmishes there, but the Germans moved back fairly quickly. Within about, I'd say, less than an hour, maybe three-quarters of an hour or so, Montgomery was there in amongst my men dishing out cigarettes and chocolates and things. He didn't offer the officers any – he never did. He proceeded to push up that toe of Italy.

The Americans had landed about six days later at Salerno, and then they got into immediate strife, so Montgomery moved us quite fast up the toe of Italy. Calabria is very mountainous and the villages and bridges had been bombed by the Germans as they retreated, and we kept moving forward

Randal George Cannon McMurtry

and repairing the bridges and so on. Seventeen days it took us to do the 250 miles, and it would have been rather more than that, going around the villages and what have you, but in the midst of all this we'd gone so far that Monty had run out of supplies, and so he had to halt us for two days. He didn't give us two days' rest – he gave us two days' training.

So on we went, and I was a member of a Jock column, which was part of a reconnaissance corps, some carriers and my anti-tank guns. We went ahead, and the first person we met, before we got to Salerno, was an

Australian war correspondent in a jeep. Anyway, we relieved the Americans there, about the first of about half a dozen times we seemed to relieve them. Just as a sideline to that one, at Anzio, where they were in a tight corner, it was said they started saying, "Praise the Lord and send the Fifth Division."

Then we were switched across to the eastern side of Italy where there was heavy snow, and we were attached to the New Zealand Brigade as mountain troops. On one occasion, when I'd left the guns and was second in command of a company, I had to do a lot of patrol work. Anyway, one of the patrols was to find out what was going on with a castle. We were in a town with a castle, and so we approached this place and got up to the wooden picket gate and we were challenged, and fortunately we were challenged by Italians; they were partisans, so they took us inside. They'd got this place completely fortified and they had captured German weapons and they made a great fuss of us. They had women in the castle, too, and we had a sort of celebration dance. Then we went back and I made a report that the castle was in safe hands.

Anyway, we were switched again secretly across to the west and we had to cross the Garigliano River, which the Americans had failed to do and everybody else had failed to do. So we did that and we went – I think it was about 9 o'clock at night that we started – and we went across the river and were under fire from machine-guns on fixed lines, and a lot of these guns had tracer, so we could see where they were and we sort of headed across between them in little boats. The Garigliano was a big obstacle, but we managed to get across to the other side and we had several objectives. The first was to get up through trees to quite a thick little wood, to a little village on top of the ridge. I was second in command; I was supposed to be holding a central position between my two leading platoons and the one behind us. I realised that the British, and the Germans too, they were not particularly good in trees, but perhaps I was a bit more experienced from my days in the bush, and so I just kept on a line behind our shells as they exploded and arrived at the village. We went in there and there were some shell-shocked Germans, so we captured them and then we went right through the village to the other end, took these fellows along with us, and at the other end up popped the Intelligence Section, but no infantry platoons. We handed the Germans over to them to take back down and we thought, well, behind us we have a moving barrage and we might as well go on towards our objective, because the others will be about soon.

So the next objective was a line of trenches and then above that a ridge with a little house on it, and this was the house which we were bound for. So off I went, but I only had platoon headquarters with me – you know, we weren't very heavily armed: one fellow had a tommy-gun and I had a Sten gun, and the rest had rifles and bayonets, and, you know, stretcher bearers and wireless operators, not exactly a heavily armed crew. Our sudden appearance sort of caused the Germans to shift out quite fast, and so they did. They went out from the trenches and then they went out of the house, and I went into the house and there were three Italians in there, a man, a woman and a girl, and I said something to them in Italian, and they said, "Si, si," but they stayed under the table where they were.

However, that was all right but unfortunately everybody else, not just a battalion but the whole jolly brigade and the next brigade as well, were held up further down by the Spandaus. We'd gone around some ridges where the heavy machine-guns were and the ravines where the Spandaus were, and we'd gone up between the two so missed them all. So this was a bit of a problem. I waited as long as I could, in the hopes that they'd get up there, and then I had to get my chaps back. So, one by one, I sent them off downhill, and by that time I was the only one there, using my Sten, a funny little sub machine-gun, and fired this thing off every here and there to try and give the idea that there were quite a lot of us still around the house. It probably worked for a while, but eventually I could see them massing, the Germans, and a couple of platoons were getting ready to come over, and they did, fixed bayonets and yelling and roaring and what have you. I seemed to be the only target there, so I dived underneath some brushwood and a sort of orange tree by the house and I lay quite still there, and the Germans sort of rushed all around me and I could hear them saying quite jubilantly, nobody here, nobody here, sort of thing. And there I stayed and that was quite early in the morning, probably about 9 or 10 in the morning, and I lay under this stuff.

I stayed there until it was dark, and then came out, and then I discovered that wherever I went I was walking on Germans. I decided, well, the only thing I could do was to try and find the Seaforths, who were supposed to be over on the other side from me in a town called Minturno, and I decided to make for there. But it was the same there – it was Germans again – and the 17th Brigade hadn't made it either up to the top. So I began to walk down through the woods, through the hills, and it was quite late by then; I must have been on the go for 36 hours, a long time anyway, since I first set out. I probably got careless. I walked down a path and I should have stayed and moved in the trees still, and I walked on top of a German machine-gun post. So they grabbed me and took me down into a little dugout down below where there were – about eight of them down there and three up on top, in the charge of a corporal. They sat me down there on a form and took away my knife and took away my Sten gun, which had German ammunition in. They were very angry about that, most upset – at least the corporal was. Nobody else seemed to worry very much. They were young soldiers,

Hermann Goering Grenadiers, a very fine regiment really, and they found my chocolate, my rations in a tin, and one of them asked if I minded if they shared it, so I said, "Well, I can't stop you." So they shared it out and they were at the point of giving me a square when the corporal said, no, I wasn't allowed to eat, and off he went upstairs again. A short time later I got a little dig in the ribs from one of the soldiers and he handed me over a little square of chocolate. They were only about 19, you know, fine young men those chaps, and that was a very disciplined regiment, even though they did give away chocolate to prisoners.

Then I was taken for interrogation before an officer who spoke with what I think was an Oxford accent, and gave him the usual details – name, rank and number – and he tried to find out what he could by flattery and one thing and another. He was trying to discover something about the regiment I'd come from, and he mentioned that they knew there was a unit in the area because they used to be able to go across the Garigliano River with impunity and all of a sudden they began to lose men as prisoners. He tried to get something out of me, but anyway he didn't, and I was sent off then and put in a place called Frosinone in a sort of a dungeon really, in a jail anyway.

I decided that when they shifted me in a truck that I'd get loose, if I could. So that was the next morning, and I jumped off the truck when we were going up through some trees and I did get away and I met some Italians who directed me to where some of the partisans were. But unfortunately, after a few days, there was another group of prisoners also there at the time, and we were all, I think, given away by the Italian police and back in German hands. So we ended up in a tented camp waiting to go on the train to Germany.

I was duly marched down to the rear end of the prisoners waiting on the platform, and there were some old lags, as we called the chaps who'd been loose, right at the back, and they said, "Stick with us," so I stayed with them. A New Zealander came out of one of the carriages or one of the trucks where they'd been laying straw, and he started whistling "Now is the Hour", you see, and as soon as that happened, these old lags inched their way forward through the others till they were opposite this truck. They got in and I came in with them plus quite a lot more, and before we got going they dug around in the straw and produced a knife, a big knife, and they set to work on the panels of the truck, scratching up and down and up and down so they could cut them and knock them out. The Germans heard us – we were not very cautious. When we stopped somewhere at one stage they heard us, this racket going on, and they stormed inside and they found where the cut had been going and they demanded the knife. We didn't give them the knife, actually, because an Australian produced another – how he had it on him or where he'd hidden it, I wouldn't know – but he had a little pocket knife and he handed this over, so that satisfied the Germans. We were careful then – we sort of smudged over the crack and kept going towards the Brenner Pass.

When we got near there we were all numbered off and there were nine old lags – they were numbered 1 to 9, and then they numbered me number 10. There were about another 20-odd in this truck. Well, we kicked out the panels of the truck where we'd cut – that was in the front of this truck – and climbed out, and the first of the ones that were numbered off, seven of them, got out on the footplate, one after the other, and jumped out in the snow and got going. By which time there was a lot of flak from machine-guns up and down the train, and it came to a stop, more or less, and I had a chap on the footplate on each side of me, and I was sitting in the hole. I was extremely unpopular, but I was hauled out of there by a funny little German who stamped up and down on the ground, and he literally had saliva foaming at the corners of his mouth, he was so angry. He dug this Mauser in my tummy and I stood very still – I thought if I smile at this guy he'll shoot me.

So anyway, they were very cross with us and they marched us off to an empty cattle truck with no straw, no nothing – a cold iron truck, and in the middle of winter – and we went through the Alps and we got to the station on the Austrian side and German land army girls gave us something to eat.'

To return to the short campaign in Sicily, ex-Battle of Britain pilot Norman Ramsay remembered that:

'One morning we were off and we were patrolling over a beach in Sicily where the troops were landing, and on our beach all was well, but the Americans had a very rough time. They walked into a German Division on the ground and also they got quite beaten up by aircraft attacks. The Americans also had their own fighter aircraft, which mistook us for something else and attacked us several times before we managed to convince them that we were on their side. The Germans carried out quite a number of bombing raids over there, and we intercepted and shot down a few German aircraft and that sort of stuff. I was very lucky there, I didn't lose a single person in my flight due to enemy aircraft action, but there were losses when, in dive-bombing attacks, planes were blown up or when our own bombers went too low and were shot down by anti-aircraft fire.'

Naval support for the troops was critical at the landings and of significance in all operations within range of the guns and aircraft of warships.

Lieutenant Commander Roger Hill, DSO DSC, now commanding the destroyer HMS *Grenville* and, once more, in the Mediterranean, has recorded that:

'We bombarded both sides of Italy and saw quite a lot of action. We had some very nice bombarding; there was a line ran down the coast and trains went on this line and we didn't bombard whilst they were coming back from the front, but we did have a go at those going down to the front, and we would fire a burst of Oerlikon shells over the top of the train. And the engine driver I could imagine saying, "Faster, faster!" as he opened up the furnace. When they opened up the furnace, we had a thing on the rangefinder called a stigmatiser, and this would give a perfect range on the fire in the engine, and so then we would blow up the train, blow the engine off the rails. Then there was another place, I think it was called Pescara, where they went into a tunnel, and halfway down the tunnel we would bombard the end of the tunnel where they had gone in, and then we would go down to the other end of the tunnel and we would bombard that, and hopefully trap them in the tunnel. They started getting annoyed about this and they started firing back with 88-millimetre guns, which wasn't very nice.

We bombarded a place called Gaeta where a new German Division had just moved in. Funnily enough, we were going up into an Italian minefield – we had the charts where they had laid the mines, but whether they had laid the mines where they thought, that was the problem. So we went up and then we stopped and didn't move any more and bombarded Gaeta, started a few fires and small explosions. We had some American photographers on board, publicity and so on. They were absolutely furious because they couldn't get any photographs because we had flashless cordite. Anyhow, we had a Polish destroyer, *Piorun*, with us and she went tearing in. We were absolutely terrified she was going to blow up on a mine. So it went on until we got a briefing for Anzio.

We were all briefed for the landing at Anzio. This was going to be the great thing and the tanks would go mad on the plains of Rome and cut off the Germans, and the Germans would surrender and the bottleneck at Cassino would be broken. The only thing about this was, had the Germans had the same briefing, which was quite likely. And then off we went to Anzio, where we got a complete surprise. But they delayed any advance for too long, allowing the Germans time to build up their forces, which resulted in extremely heavy fighting. Eventually Alexander came, a marvellous man, and he took one look at the American General, and he was on a plane next day, back to America, and he put in command a fellow who was the General of the Rangers, and eventually they started to move. They had a tremendous battle there and the original plan never worked, of course, and the Germans, who had retreated from Cassino, went right through Rome and out the other side, and we had to fight them all over again.

Anzio was a very bad thing. Now, I don't know whether I have mentioned this but we had been attacked in the Bay of Biscay on 28 August 1943, I think it was, by these German glider-controlled bombs. It was the first time they had been used, and it was sort of experimental. The chap sat in the aeroplane, had a joystick, and the glider bomb had a green light in the tail and he could steer the bomb, make it go from side to side or make it come down – he couldn't make it go up. It went about 400 miles an hour and had a big explosive in the front, and we had the first attack of this, and we had *Egret*, which had the Captain of the Hunter Group, and *Athabaskan*, the Canadian destroyer, and two "Hunts" and me in *Grenville*. About the first bomb hit *Egret* she blew up and then floated upside down. *Athabaskan* was hit – she had a bomb in her – and then we had the most exciting time, because they had about 16 of these things left and, of course, there I was, the biggest ship left. I found that if I started to turn, the bomb would start to follow me, but the bomb had a bigger turning circle than I did and they all missed us. I could see them sort of turning somersaults and landing in the sea, and I had people on the bridge who were spotting the next one that was coming, and then when it was all over we picked up survivors from the *Egret* and made encouraging signals to the *Athabaskan*, asking her if she wanted to go to Gibraltar or Plymouth. She said Plymouth, so we started off with the survivors of the *Egret*, screening the Athabaskan, and then the Admiral came up and said it was essential we went back, so we thought, oh blimey, we're going to be sunk by those bloody things tomorrow.

The reason why I mention this is that at Anzio, the Captain of *Jervis* – and he had no knowledge of the glider bombs at all, nobody had –he was lying stopped with another "J" Class destroyer, *Janus*, which had just come out from England, and they were bombarding, and the glider bombers used to come over about half an hour before sunset. Anyhow, one of them hit *Janus* and she blew up – very few survivors – and the other hit *Jervis* and blew her bows off. I mean, he was just asking for it, he was just lying there saying "Hit me". The *Bulolo*, the Headquarters ship, sailed for Anzio about this time, which was a very stupid thing to do, so I went round her making smoke. These things had to have a point of aim, obviously, and I made smoke around her. She was very indignant because she said I was spoiling her view of fire or something, when I was saving her. It was so stupid because nobody knew anything about these things. Anyhow, that's what happened – we saw *Jervis* going by at about 8 or 10 knots without any bows, a square front to the ship, so to speak.

Two days later we went back to Naples and there was a signal waiting for me, "Come and see me", from Captain D in *Jervis*. So I went over, completely unsuspecting, which was very stupid of me. He was sitting in the wardroom with all his staff sitting round him, and he said, "Well, I've tried everything, I've signalled the Admiralty, I've signalled the Commander in Chief, I can't help it, I've got to take over your bloody ship."

It was just like being hit in the stomach. I didn't know what to do. I turned round, pretending to look out of the porthole – I was absolutely knocked out, it was simply awful to think that I was going to lose my ship. I was going to get *Jervis*, with no bow.

So the officers rowed me across to my new ship, which was traditional, and with my little dog Skerki under my arm and with my devoted servant, Charley, I went on board *Jervis*. We went down to this wonderful cabin aft – big bed, lovely armchair, big table and so on – which had been built and installed in case Lord Louis Mountbatten were to be appointed to *Jervis* – in fact he had *Kelly*. But *Jervis* was a lovely ship; she had three twin mountings and torpedoes and everything else, but by gosh she was in a mess The Engineer Captain said that all the spare parts were rusty, rust on the deckhead and so on.

Then we sailed from Naples with completely square bows, where the whole of the forepart of the ship had been blown off. She was a lucky ship, they always said she was a lucky ship, and of the nine destroyers in her flotilla the only one left afloat at the end of the war was *Jervis* – all the others had been sunk. Amazing.'

Leonard Thornton recalled his and New Zealand's participation in the Italian Campaign:

'In the meantime I had been promoted to Lieutenant Colonel and appointed to command my old regiment, the 5th Regiment, the Artillery Regiment, and so this was a great pleasure to me now to be back with the guns, as they say, and having my own unit to command. And off we went to take part in the Italian Campaign.

There had been a suggestion that we would do the Sicily Operation, but I think Freyberg felt that we were not quite ready and anyway, he said to me about that stage, "We've done our stuff – somebody else has got to help now," and so he said that we'd not take part in that, and so we didn't go across until after the landing had been made in Italy, the initial landings had been made, and we went over in September/October 1943. We went up on to the eastern side of Italy over into the area of the Sangro. At that stage the idea was to push the German defences back on that coast and swing round across the country and take Rome.

Well, it was a far too ambitious programme and the lie of the country was certainly not appropriate for that sort of operation and the winter was coming on. Anyway, we battled on and eventually we finished up in deep snow just on the other side, northern side, of Sangro, unable to make any further progress, and really the operation then settled down into stalemate. And about that time – we were now about at Christmas Day – somewhere about there or just before, a change of staff occurred in the Division at the divisional level. The then GSO1 had now been in that job for, I suppose, 18 months, and he was pretty worn out and he was sent off on furlough, and so I then was moved up to take over his job, so I now became the Chief of Staff, GSO1, to General Freyberg. And I was with him when we fought that battle at Orsogna.

Well, Monty was about to leave us and take on his further responsibilities in Europe and the Command decided that we would shift the thrust and abandon the eastern side of Italy, and so we were to move secretly around in a big U-turn for the big thrust, which was to occur at Cassino, which was a very strongly fortified position that had been under preparation for months by the German, what you might call, pioneer side of the forces. So it was very heavily fortified and the valley had been flooded and there was wire and so forth everywhere. However, we were not really supposed to take part in the battle to be in the assault, we were to be an "equitation" force – this was Freyberg's great thing, that we were a highly mobile force, we could be self-supporting and all that stuff. And we would come through once the hole had been cut, we could pour through and really destroy the enemy from action from the rear and so forth. Well, the Americans had tried in a very different attack, a very costly attack – I don't mind admitting that we were amazed at the American losses and the way they just simply picked themselves up and went at it again, often with the same battle plan, I may say. The French had tried north of Cassino – there was a French Expeditionary Force there and the British formations had tried at Terracina down towards the coast across what you might call the lower plains of the valley of the Garigliano River. And so really the battle had reached stalemate again, and so it was decided between Mark Clark and my General that we would be drawn into what you would call the assault attack.

At this stage a new slightly pseudo-formation had been set up, to be called the New Zealand Corps; it was really only a name because we did not have any Corps Headquarters. I became the sort of Brigade BGS and I remained with the Division. Freyberg became the Corps Commander and a new fellow – not a new man but one of our most trusted chaps – called Kippenberger, General Kippenberger, he became the Divisional Commander, and so it was in that shape that we fought this battle, the two battles at Cassino. The first attack, there was an Indian Division in there, which was the 4th Indian Division, which was under our command, part of the Corps, the New Zealand Corps. It was the New Zealand Division, the Indian Division and the 78th British Division which were to be available if we wanted them. So the first attack was by the Indian Division up on the mountain towards the monastery, and one of our battalions – it happened to be the Maori Battalion – did an attack across to what we called the Railway Station in Cassino town.

Well, the short answer is that the Indians didn't make progress on the hill above, the Maoris captured their objective and were virtually cut off, because supportive weapons couldn't be got through to them, and really the whole thing settled down. The unsupported Maoris – Maori Battalion – lost considerable numbers and it was an unfortunate knock-back. We had great trouble getting them out, and so we pulled ourselves back and licked our wounds and then, I think, really the operation would normally have been abandoned and they would have developed a different strategy, but the Anzio landing meantime had occurred and there was great anxiety about its survival. They seemed to be only just hanging on by the toenails on to the landing they'd made on the western coast down the south of Rome. And so the whole of that operation was threatened, and it was felt we had to do an attack in order to relieve the pressure on them, but, hopefully, to break through and come in behind and really solve the situation. So, very reluctantly, Freyberg decided that, yes, he would agree to a further attack, but it was a very unpopular decision. By this time, after really weeks, months of very difficult climatic conditions, troops living in miserable conditions which were cold, dirty and so on, there were people who were not in favour of the attack. Now, that was a new experience for me, to find that my brigadiers were reacting in this way – that's very unusual. The New Zealand Division had never had that experience before, and, in fact, my temporary Divisional Commander, this very brave fellow called Kippenberger, had said to me, "I'm not going to do this attack. If I'm ordered to do the attack I shall resign." Well now, this to me, as a Regular soldier, this I found a bit shattering, because that wasn't our tradition at all. I thought he was quite right, between you and me, but anyway he said, "I won't do it." So that night he was called in for a long conference with the Corps Commander, Freyberg, and he came out and said, "Well, we'll be doing the attack because the General has assured me that we will have overwhelming weight of support from the Allied artillery." And he said, I forget, if it was 600 or 6,000 tons of bombs, a fantastic figure, and he said, "They'll just flatten the whole place and we'll just only have to walk through, so I'm going to take it on.'"

Bruce McKay Smith, Sergeant, 25th NZ Artillery Battery, back from furlough in New Zealand, found his unit dug in in the hills around Cassino:

'We were in an area called the Hove dump, which was a dry river bed with very steep rugged sort of country where all the stores were kept for supplying the infantry and various front-line troops, and we were in position above them. Then it became the "Inferno" track because the Germans found out where the stuff was and used to shell us quite repeatedly and caused a bit of despondency. Our observation post people used to go out with the infantry at night in jeeps, loaded up with whatever equipment was required for the front lines. It was always a hair-raising trip. I went out on it twice, which was enough for me. Then we'd come back to our gun positions and generally engage various targets relayed to us by either radio or telephone link. Then our cookhouse, which was down in the Hove dump area, got a direct hit from a German heavy-calibre shell and blew it up, but none of the cooks got hurt, fortunately, for some reason or other – we never worked that one out.

Then they decided that it was enough – we had to alter our positions a wee bit, which we did. Then the Poles started to come down through our lines with all their gear on mules and disappeared into the distance – we never saw them again. Then the Canadians came on the scene. Then a unit which I've never heard of before or since – it was a unit of the Brazilian Army.'

Lieutenant Donald Kerr, NZ 19th Armoured Regiment, arrived in Italy in October 1943 and was soon to experience action:

'At that particular time, the British Eighth Army was fighting a war on the east coast of Italy and we were held up at a place called the Sangro. The Sangro is a big river that comes from the Apennines and flows right across. It was winter time, cold, and we finally got instructions to move. The interesting thing about this was that we moved up into the fighting area, and just at that particular time the 4th Indian Division was responsible for endeavouring to secure a bridgehead across the Sangro River at a place called Perano, and one of their infantry battalions was fighting there and they needed tank support.

As luck would have it, or wouldn't – we'll call it luck – our regiment was close up and A Squadron from our regiment was leading and they had three troops, three tanks in this particular squadron, and they needed an extra three tanks. My troop was the next troop in line, and so I was then attached to A Squadron. This particular action at Perano was the first occasion that the New Zealand Expeditionary Force went into action in Italy, and it was

Donald Kerr

the tanks that went into action, not the infantry. It was quite an experience and quite a bloody action, you might say. We lost seven tanks in that fight – I lost one myself and three of the crew were killed, and my tank was one of the first to even receive a blow. There is one place on a Sherman tank where the armour-plating is twice as thick as anywhere else, and that's where the front section hooks on to the body, and an armour-piercing shot from an 88 hit there and instead of penetrating the tank, it ricocheted up over the top of the tank and took a gouge out of the turret. We were still in action, but my sergeant's tank, which was on the left of me, took the next shot, which, unfortunately, went straight through the turret and killed all the turret crew, the commander, the gunner and the radio operator. Further up to our left, the A Squadron was attacking the village of Perano and they suffered quite heavy casualties there.

That was just the way it went and one of the difficult things that we had in that particular action was that General Freyberg didn't want the enemy to know that the New Zealand Forces were there and ready to go into action, and he put a radio silence on the operation. So you can imagine what it was like in the tank, with the noise and not being able to communicate with the commanders. You carried out your instructions and then you were on your own. We had a very high frequency unit part of the radio, on which I could talk to my other two tanks but I couldn't talk to the Squadron Commander and tell him what was happening. I was given the job of going down on to the river flat and trying to get to the bridge, and things stalled because of the terrific resistance of the Germans with their 88mm guns and machine-guns. However, the attack was successful – we took the Perano village and ultimately drove the Hun from this bridgehead.

Well, the next phase, I suppose, of the tank activity was supporting the New Zealand Infantry to actually go across the Sangro River, which was in flood. It was November and the river was running fairly high, and the infantry got across all right but they needed tanks and we had to try and get across, and they did find a crossing. I can remember going across in my tank and the water was virtually up to the turret. We'd waterproofed the tanks; we had a system of locking down all the hatches and everything. I could still see looking over the top and you could see the driver and the spare driver – their heads were sort of sticking out of the turret – but the water was virtually a foot from them as we went through this Sangro River. Fortunately, in our ford we got through, but further to our left quite a few of the tanks got completely bogged down and you can imagine, with the cold, wet weather, it wasn't a particularly pleasant sort of operation, but that's how war goes.

So their objective was a town called Orsogna, which overlooked the whole of the Sangro valley, and a smaller town called Castel Frentano, which had to be taken first. It was all uphill and you can imagine what it was like, not only for the infantry but the tanks trying to go uphill and up roads that were of doubtful quality, and you were in virtually direct line of fire with all the Germans guns that were just pouring hot metal down on you, and we lost quite a few tanks there. It was that which sort of finished my career for a wee while because we were fighting towards Castel Frentano and I'd been out on a reconnaissance on foot with the CO of our regiment to try and work out a way for the tanks to go. I was coming back to my tank and I'd just got to my tank when a shell rammed the back of it and, unfortunately, I was wounded, luckily only in the arm. I was out of action for two months when they sent me back to Base Hospital, where I recuperated and, as far as I was concerned, action on the east coast was over.

The war in the Orsogna area and the Sangro reached a complete stalemate, and the New Zealand Division, which had not made very much headway over two months, was relieved. They moved across to the west coast to the area of Cassino – the big battle of Cassino was really in operation, and that's where the New Zealand Expeditionary Force, the tanks, the artillery, the infantry and everybody, moved across and prepared to take their part there in trying to break the deadlock there. That's where I rejoined the regiment again when I'd been released from the Convalescent Home.

I joined my squadron again and was given command of N0 11 troop because the commander of that particular troop was a long-serving soldier and due for furlough back in New Zealand. It was very cold and wet, being winter, and there was a complete stalemate. As far as tanks were concerned, or any of the armoured equipment, you could get no movement because the rivers there were in flood.'

Corporal Arthur Gladstone, NZ 27th Battalion, was also closely associated with events around the Sangro River:

'We moved off to the Sangro on our own transport and arrived in the village of Atessa, near the Sangro River, on 15 November. The Company I was with at that time – I had changed from 4th to 2nd Company – were the first machine-gunners across the Sangro River, and we were sent in support of the Sussex Regiment, part of the 7th Indian Division, which were up in the hills. They needed machine-gun support and those of us who weren't actually on the gun line, we had a nightly trek across the river and up the hill carrying supplies for those who were in the line.

However, we were brought back across the river early in December and moved to Castel Frentano round about 3 December. Castel Frentano had been taken by the Division at this time and the advance was pressing on towards Orsogna. On 7 December I went down with jaundice and I was taken back to the hospital in Bari; I didn't rejoin the Division until March '44 in front of Cassino. There the position, by the time I got there, was already static. We had nightly tasks firing the guns in support or low harassment across the Rapido River, but we were not actually in the town of Cassino itself. We operated along the railway line which ran at the foot of Monte Trocchio. Then later we were pulled back to the village of Venafro for a spell and re-entered the line in the area of Terrelle, to the right of Cassino, to the right of Monte Cairo, really up in the mountains, mule track territory.

The infantry were 200 or 300 yards in advance of us – none of us were in trenches, we were all in what we used to call "sangars", which were really stone walls built as high as you could build for your own protection. The area had been occupied before us by French troops, Moroccans – it was littered with every shape and size of tin can possible, and you could only move by night so there was no show of putting your head up anywhere during the daytime because the Germans had complete observation of the whole area. So all the provisioning and supplies had to be handled or hauled up the hill on your back at night, and this meant parties going backwards and forwards and going with great stealth, because you never quite knew when there might be a patrol around or what the circumstances would be. We were also treated with great suspicion by our own troops because any movement through the area had to be regarded as suspicious.

That occupation continued for about a fortnight, and once again we came back to the Venafro area and then later went back into the same Terrelle area; we were told that it was a rest area, a holding pattern. We managed to play bridge by gun team during the day because we could keep our heads down around the gun pit, but that was the only respite we got because our nights were full of activity. So, although there was no great combat going on around the place, there was tension of nerves and on occasion it showed. The spring had just come to the area – there were nightingales, there were fireflies, there were red poppies, and down in the Liri Valley there were cherries. It was quite a remarkable scene really.'

Landing at Taranto was something that Divisional Signalman Harold Greer, 5th NZ HQ Brigade, would always remember:

'It was a wild night of thunder and lightning and as the lightning flashed we could see ships all around us, and it was an experience indeed to be amongst all this convoy in the middle of the night. We arrived in Taranto and we were taken off the ship and "Tiny" Freyberg was on the wharf. We had to march through the town of Taranto to an olive grove where we were camped. We weren't met with very welcome arms from the Italians – some of the boys were spat on, and the atmosphere was a wee bit anti-British.

We dossed down there and we were flooded out with heavy rain and that was the beginning of our Italian campaign. After several weeks there we went up to the Sangro River for our first combat and our first experience of shelling, of German shelling. We experienced the 88-millimetre gun, which

Harold John Greer

had high velocity and you heard the shell scream and land before you heard the gun going off.

The cable we laid was English cable, and quite often we'd lay it and the tanks used to cut it up and we would have to keep returning to mend these faults. As we got closer to Cassino we were given American twist, which was black, and the mud on the road was splashed on to these cables and you couldn't tell the colour, and eventually, after the Americans were there, it was like spider webs along the side of the road, and if a cable had to be repaired you had to go through about 10 or 20 of these lines before you found the live one. We used, if we could, to get a German telephone, which was better than ours, and we used to put two safety pins on the end of our leads, which saved us burying the wire, and we used safety pins to make the connection. Instead of fixing a broken line we used to have to lay in quite extra lengths and, of course, the more we laid in, the more confused it got.

To go back to the Sangro River, it was my first experience of mines. Bob Miller and I were given the job of taking a line to the Sangro River, before the crossing, so that the wire would be immediately on hand, but on the way down the road we came to some crossroads and my friend Bob came back and he said, "Look, we're very fortunate here," he said, "there's a big drain," he said. "We'll be able to take the line in through the drain, which will save us digging through the hard bitumen to protect the wire from the tanks." So we took the wire cable off the back of the jeep and we walked into this big ditch and to the drainpipe and took the line through in the pitch dark at night. At the other side of the drain we were putting the wire cable back on the jeep when we heard an explosion from back where we'd been and we were then scared that the Germans would hear this and would retaliate. However, when we came back there were ambulances about and six men, I believe, were killed by the mines which we had walked through. How we missed walking on them I don't know, because it was a very narrow ditch.

The next morning, on going past, two engineers were lying dead. They'd been sent down to lift the mines, but the German had booby-trapped one mine on top of another mine, so that when they lifted the top mine it exploded and the rest of the chaps were a wee bit reluctant to go down and attempt to take the rest out. We struck more mines as we went up the road; of course, we used to have to put two wheels of the jeep on the side of the road as we laid the cable, which made us a bit apprehensive all the time we were driving.

We did have a bit more fighting until we got to Cassino, and we really hit there, we really hit the hard stuff. During this period I was the driver of a jeep and I drove a jeep from the beginning of the Italian Campaign till the end. Continuing laying wire, we were always conscious of the mines, of course, and I certainly remember the crossroads. The German always had crossroads taped with his artillery, and many times we were sent out to repair wire and it was usually at the crossroads where it was destroyed. He'd be shelling the corners and we'd wait until he'd finished his little anger, and we were always wondering, will we go now, no we won't go now, there could be another shell, we'll go now, and there was always this fear of driving into the corner and we would be stonkered. There was always a tight atmosphere, because there were usually three of us in the jeep and we wanted to get the job done and get out of the road, and sometimes, instead of taping the wire, you'd just join it with a reef knot and throw it up on a bush and come back later to finish the job. We many times had some pretty close encounters with their artillery.

The Americans were at Cassino when we took over, and they were pleased to leave it. We drove up the road near Mount Trocchio and we were standing looking over at Cassino and we wondered why the Americans were hiding all the time, and they thought we were stupid just standing and looking at Cassino. Well, we soon found out why, because the Germans could see us from the Monte Cassino with their glasses – we were quite obvious – so we learnt quickly to keep out of sight. We daren't move and the artillery were continually shelling, with smoke between us and the Castle, so they couldn't see us. Sometimes the smoke would clear and we'd get caught out in the open. It was there that we encountered the *nebelwerfer*. The *nebelwerfer* was what they called the "Andrews Sisters" [a popular singing group of the time] and it was a rocket gun, five rockets in a circle, which was set off with electricity, and they used to scream and that's why we called it the "Andrew Sisters". On one occasion I was in my jeep coming down Route 6 and they let go with this thing and I could hear one landing behind, one to each side and there was still one howling up the top, so I drove to this house where there were a lot of infantry and crashed in behind them and we hid in there until this other rocket screamed overhead. More noise than damage, but very frightening.

We had a few aeroplane attacks there and it always happened after 5 o'clock, and there was always six Spitfires, which used to patrol all day in front of Cassino to keep their air force away, but at 5 o'clock at night it was a routine thing for our six Spitfires to go home for tea, and I think it was 5 minutes after that that the German decided that it was safe enough to come and give us a spurt, a spurt of his machine-guns.'

Major Edward Prebble, in command of a battery of anti-aircraft guns, had now arrived in Italy:

'We were landed just north of Naples – this was shortly after the Salerno landing – and we had no opposition whatsoever. Unfortunately we had no maps of the district and I was ordered to take my Battery to a town south of Naples, without any maps at all, in the middle of the night. I had been to Naples in peacetime on a cruise, and had a fair idea of where we were going, and I managed successfully to guide my troops through Naples and find the right town we were going to. Shortly after that I had to take up positions in Salerno, but we had really quite a quiet time at this particular landing.

I was then attached to the American Army Air Force under the command of Colonel Vogelberg; I should think he was probably an accountant, as he immediately started the bumph war – we had to report everything to him in triplicate. We proceeded up the centre of Italy, eventually arriving at Vesuvius, where the Americans were establishing two airstrips for Marauder bombers. Marauders were going to be used in close support of the infantry. Being a mobile unit, we arrived some two days prior to the Americans. The airstrips were in course of construction, so I deployed my guns for their protection.

When Colonel Vogelberg arrived with his regiment he was a little bit put out and he held a conference at which he had probably about 12 officers, who he introduced to me as his executive officer, his catering officer, his communications officer, etc, and I attended with my Battery Captain, the two of us. He then asked me how many guns I had, which was 18, and it turned out that his regiment, with 1,000 men, had 16 guns, which were designed rather lavishly on the American style, where they had two of everything and a lot of extra vehicles, and, in fact, an ordinary gun pit was more like a small town. Whereas we were designed for mobility and our gun pits contained 10 men only.

Well, shortly after this Vesuvius erupted and this caused small lumps of lava to fall on our camp; these were about the size of cricket balls. Now very shortly afterwards this turned entirely to ash and the ash was coming down probably 2 or 3 inches in a day. I got on to Colonel Vogelberg and asked him what was happening, and he said that we were to stay there as long as the aircraft remained on the runways. I was a little bit worried about the guns, because if the gun pits filled up we would never get them out, so I pulled the guns out of the pits and put them in action on the ground above the pit. The following day I tried to get in touch with Colonel Vogelberg but couldn't raise him at all, so I decided to go and visit him. When I got to the camp, I found that they had all disappeared. They'd left some tents, some vehicles, all the aircraft, but no personnel whatsoever. There were a few Italians scrounging what was left, and I decided that it was no longer necessary to defend anything and I had better look after myself. So we were able to winch the guns on to firmer ground and I consulted the local station master of the light railway which ran round Vesuvius, and he suggested that if we went up the mountain we could get under the trough of the ash which was being distributed, and we would be safer further up the mountain than going down. In any case, the further down the mountain we went, the deeper the ash and the less chance we had of mobility.

There was a vacant train in the station – this was a covered goods train. The bridges had been blown either end, so it had been obviously abandoned there since the Germans had left. I put the troops in the carriages, set up my headquarters in the station itself, and we remained there for about probably three weeks until everything had settled down and the Army was able to come up with bulldozers and graders and make a road for us to get down.

When we returned to the headquarters the guns had all the paint removed by the ash, which of course is really pumice stone; it also took all the paint off our tin helmets, which were now a lovely burnished steel. All the equipment had to go back to ordnance to be refurbished, and the regiment was eventually told to hand their equipment in. It was then decided that as we were an infantry-trained regiment we would be used for reinforcements to the infantry, they having had a very bad time at Cassino.

I was then over the age of 35 and, the cut-off age for majors being somewhere in the lower 30s, I was sent to the Artillery Reinforcement Depot. Shortly after I arrived there I realised what a dead end that place was. All reinforcements which were called for were usually lieutenants or at least captains – senior officers didn't seem to get wounded. They probably had enough sense not to be near the front. Every day on the notice board outside the adjutant's office was a list put up of various jobs which were vacant, such as Pay Corps or any of the specialist things, and if you were a specialist you could get one of these jobs. Well, one day they wanted entomologists. Now, I didn't know what an entomologist was, and I was looking at the board and another officer came to me and he said, "What's an entomologist?" and I said, "I don't know," and he said, "We'll go in and ask." So we went in and asked, and the adjutant said, "Well, I'm pleased you've asked that," he said. "I've got to send two people up to the Medical School at Benevento," and he said, "You are the only two who have shown any interest. so off you go."

Well, we arrived at the Medical School of Hygiene and were told that we were late, the lectures had already started, and that we were to go to hut No 16 where an obvious professor, dressed up as a colonel, was giving a lecture. He said, "You're late, but you'll pick it up very shortly – I've no intention of starting the course again. Take your positions."

There were two desks at the rear with microscopes and papers and pencil, and he continued to lecture. Slides were being passed round, which we put under the microscope to illustrate what he was saying. Well, I couldn't see anything, so I put my hand up and the sergeant who was passing the slides round came down to me and I said, "I can't see anything here," and he said, "No, you won't, you've still got the dust cover on." Anyhow, I showed intelligent interest and eventually the sergeant came to us one night in the pub and told us what all the lectures were about – we were studying the mosquito. But he said there were only two types of mosquito in Italy which we were going to come across and that the lecturer had rather got carried away and told us about all sorts of tropical species which we didn't have to worry about anyway. Anyhow, at the end of the lecture we were passed out and we had a small exam and we had to identify different mosquitoes, but as there were large diagrams all round the room it wasn't very difficult and we had a little help from each other and I passed out as an entomologist. In fact, they never discovered that I wasn't one.

I was sent to the Third District at Taranto and given the title of Deputy Assistant Adjutant General (Mosquitoes), a staff armband, a large magnifying glass, a butterfly net and a frying-pan, a truck and a civilian driver. I was attached to the Medical Unit who had had the mosquito control taken away from them and placed in my hands. I was put in charge of controlling malaria, and by imposing a fairly strict discipline we were able to reduce the casualties considerably.'

CHAPTER 10

Italy: Cassino northwards

*T*he Monastery at Cassino was destroyed by Allied air attacks on 15
February 1944, but it was not until May, when Allied troops attacked
in strength on a wide front, that French troops penetrated into the Liri
Valley behind the German lines. This resulted in the Germans
withdrawing and, on 18 May, Polish troops entered Cassino and the
ruined Monastery. Meanwhile Fifth Army troops, advancing from Anzio,
failed to cut off the bulk of the retreating German troops, but entered
Rome on 4 June. After that the Allies made slow progress north against
strong German resistance, and by the end of the year had reached and
breached the Gothic Line, when it became necessary to call a halt and
await better conditions in spring.

On 9 April 1945 the Allies, with almost complete control of the air and
increasing help from the Partisans, launched their Spring Offensive, which,
despite stubborn German resistance, took them to the River Po and beyond
and left them in possession of Florence, Bologna, Faenza and other major
towns. The New Zealanders were in Venice by 29 April and entered Trieste
on 2 May, the day that the surrender of the Germans in Italy took effect.

Colonel Leonard Thornton, BGS, New Zealand Corps, continues his
account of the campaign in Italy:

'So we then set up the attack and again the poor old Indians, who were up
on these awful heights, rocky heights of Monte Cassino, they were to attack
and take the monastery to give us cover, because from up there everything
we were doing could be seen by the Germans. We were to have come now
from the north end of the town and attack through the town, following our
armour, of course, to sweep through, break out into the Liri Valley, and we
were on the way to Rome. Well that was the theory. This was when the

bombing of the monastery occurred – it had to be done. In my mind, and in the General's, there was no alternative.

The attack on the right flank really didn't take off because the Indians hadn't got there. Not their fault – the conditions were very difficult and they hadn't got organised before the bombing attack. So the bombing attack came in and they weren't ready to attack, so by the time they were ready to attack it was too late, because the Germans had blocked their positions and they were stopped. So our attack went on into the town below this great imposing, what had been a monastery, and fighting at close quarters in the ruins was extremely difficult. We battled on and we battled on and really, with a thousand casualties there, eventually things came to a standstill. I mean, there was nothing we could do, we had to give up, we were not going to succeed, and so we were pulled out and we went into reserve and the whole thing then died until some months later. That was February to May 1944.

It wasn't until May that we managed to get a new attack launched, a much more substantial attack, with the French going through the foothills on our left flank, which really turned the position and Cassino eventually fell. It wasn't actually taken – it fell because they got behind Cassino and the Germans had to abandon it. Although the Poles made a desperate effort there to fight their way through, their casualties really were much worse than ours were, but they never actually took Cassino. It was really abandoned by the Germans.

So that was that, and we went on through Rome, and so the campaign continued up through Florence. We'd had a rest at that time and then we went back into the attack on Florence. Mercifully, the Germans decided not to defend it; they blew down all the bridges and we had a long approach march, with several battles on the way up. And then, when that phase had been completed, we were up against the Gothic Line and we were then switched across to the coast. Freyberg, all the time, wanted to exploit our mobility, you see; he was being frustrated because in close country with continuous narrow defiles and bridges he couldn't deploy the armour, he couldn't make much use of it.

Anyway, we were then switched on to the coast at Rimini with the idea of breaking out into the Po Valley and sweeping across the great plains there. And so this happened; we captured Rimini around about, I suppose it must have been, November or October 1944. And we really settled there to reorganise for a major campaign in the Po Valley, for which we were going to need some more infantry because we found, as I say, that you couldn't use the armour effectively. So what was needed was more and more infantry, so it was decided that we would convert two of our other formations, including my old regiment, the anti-aircraft regiment, and the cavalry and turn them into an infantry battalion so that we'd have three brigades of infantry, and so that took time to bring about.

And at that point I had now been at war for about five years, and General Freyberg decided that I looked tired, but the next day he said, "You look good enough for the next two or three years," and then the next day he said, "You look tired," again, so he said I'd better go on leave. So I was the last officer, I reckon, to go on furlough to New Zealand from the Division.

And during that phase this reorganisation was occurring. They eventually got themselves organised for the great offensive across the Po Valley and finished up in Trieste. And just after the capture of Trieste and the contretemps, the facing between ourselves and the Yugoslavs, I arrived back in the Division from my furlough. I was now appointed as commander of the Divisional Artillery, so I was now Brigadier in Charge of all our artillery.

Anyway, that was that, and so I then really stayed with the remnant of the Division, packing up units, collapsing units, sending parties off, getting them slowly back to New Zealand. It wasn't really until after Christmas 1945 that I was able to get back to New Zealand. In point of fact, what happened was that, because I was a Regular officer, I was appointed there and then to accompany the force which was to go to Japan as part of the British Commonwealth Occupation Force as a staff officer to General Northcott, the overall Force Commander. I was then appointed the Senior British Liaison Officer on McArthur's staff, representing the Commonwealth in Tokyo.

So I left behind my association with the Division. It really was a wonderful experience to exist and to live with a body of men of that kind, and a few women, for all those six years of the war. It was a brave company indeed. They were all resolute, upright and almost without exception strong, good characters, good people, good representatives of our community in New Zealand.'

Another who had witnessed the destruction at Cassino was Sergeant Bruce McKay Smith:

'From the Hove dump area we witnessed the bombing of Cassino, which was a colossal experience because it just went on and on and on, and in the meantime we were shelling as well, and every gun that could fire, I think, was shelling. This went on for, oh, one day anyway, and then sporadically for several days afterwards. Then the turning point came and the attack was mounted and they did break through Cassino after very, very heavy casualties and determined resistance by the Germans. We followed through fairly closely on the heels of the infantry, a bit of shelling and being sniped at, but fortunately not too badly.

The Germans suddenly got into full retreat and we carried on for several miles beyond Cassino and to a rest, what they called a rest area, and we packed in there and had our first experience of being in Italian houses. They were very solidly built places several hundred years old, made of large blocks of limestone, as I recall, and we felt quite happy in there whenever the Germans shelled, although they did drop one through the roof one day, but it didn't do any harm. Our gun positions were a bit more exposed than that, of course. We still had to go out and make sure everything was OK as far as the layout of the gun positions was concerned. We had been fairly well re-equipped by this time after our early stay in Italy. One thing we had, a heavy tank as an armoured observation post. We had two Bren-carriers, as I remember, and we had quite a few jeeps, which were most useful in Italy because the ground was usually wet and boggy and we had a lot of difficulty in shifting vehicles, guns and things around from position to position.

From there on we went to another rest area where the whole regiment got involved in sporting activities, rugby matches, various sports of high jumping and all this sort of thing, athletics, until the time came to move on again back into action. At Rimini we supported the infantry on various attacks, most of them successful, some not quite so successful. The country we were in was divided: it was hilly flats on the coastal side and divided into quite deep ditches and dykes, which the infantry and engineers had to bridge or cross around during the attacks, and fairly dangerous positions they were too, and our artillery had to come up behind them pretty quickly in support.

This went on, off and on, until we came to a place called Forli, which was out on the flat, and there the Germans had dug in fairly extensively. It was a bit of a mess with the Allied bombing that had gone on there, and it was a difficult place to find reasonable sheltered gun positions. So, at night-time, the anti-aircraft units, which had the searchlights by this time, came in behind the artillery units and they depressed their searchlights so that they were parallel to the ground and created what they called artificial moonlight, and this enabled quite a bit of activity on our side because the Germans were, supposedly, dazzled by these searchlights. As a result we were able to pinpoint machine-gun posts and shell them.

I missed out a bit there, about the approach to Rome and Florence. I had an experience there where we'd moved forward with the infantry and we were dug in below Florence and it was a fairly heavily occupied area by our infantry. We were told to go and look into a house to see if it was any good for our battery headquarters. So with two other chaps I went into this house and an Italian family were in the lower part, and they kept on pointing upstairs and I didn't quite know what they meant, but I went up these stairs – it was a very old house – up these stone stairs, and there was a German at the top with a Schmeisser automatic gun and he let fly. I don't think he fired at me, I think he just let fly with nervousness at the roof of the place. So I turned round and I slipped on these stairs and went down on my elbow, which got partially fractured. I don't know what happened to the German, I've no idea, but I was feeling a bit sorry for myself and I was sent to the Regimental Aid Post with this dud elbow.

Eventually I was sent to an evacuation point at Lake Trasimeno, where we went aboard an American DC3, which was a bit of a hair-raising experience, because it had quite a lot of wounded, walking wounded, on board plus several drums of fuel, plus several American Army women. I don't know quite what they called them, but they were there like nurses to look after the sick, but they were dishing cigarettes out all round the place. With these drums of fuel, it was a bit hair-raising. And we were flown from there to Foggia, which was the biggest airfield in southern Italy at that time. I spent about a week in hospital with my elbow being treated and eventually went back to the unit again.'

Donald Kerr, Captain in the NZ 19th Armoured Regiment, saw the bombing at Cassino and was very much involved in the operations that followed:

'I was there to see that unfortunate day when the American bombers came over in their vast numbers and dropped something like 6-700 tons of explosive, and they ruined, knocked the Abbey down because they thought it was being used for observation purposes, but that didn't change things at all.

So the next phase was when they decided they would try and take the town of Cassino. So, to do this, they actually bombed the town of Cassino and it was at that time that we were all involved. We'd been into the outskirts of it; our tanks were around and we all withdrew back about half a mile or more, while the bombers came in and flattened the town of Cassino. Then, after the artillery had followed up the bombs, we all went in again, the infantry, the tanks and everybody, and we could make no progress at all. The town was completely destroyed; the roads that we all knew and had done reconnaissance on, they'd just disappeared. Gradually the various regiments fought their way inch by inch into the town, and once in, it was almost impossible to get out. Our tanks would go in there and stay there and became permanent pillboxes, you might say, and the crews used to take over at night, change crews at night, and you used it as a stationary gun during the day.

The infantry would come along and ask you to do certain tasks, and that's how we lived. You just lived in the tank with the turret down right through the day, the motors running and as much air going through as possible, and, of course, you can imagine, with five men in a tank, the smell and stench wasn't particularly good. With the rattle of the machine-gun bullets on the turret, you couldn't move out and you just hoped that none of them penetrated. The Germans had some tanks in there as well, firing and hitting the odd one of our tanks. One infantry unit was in a house in Cassino, and they heard this motor start up in the next room of this large house; they surmised that there was a tank in there. So they sent a message back to one of our tank leaders and they actually put armour-piercing explosive into that side of the house and there was a German Mark IV tank with an 88-millimetre gun mounted on it. All the German tank crew were killed, but they investigated further and they'd had a process of changing crews around too, through a series of tunnels.

One of the other things, from a humorous point of view, was that it was difficult to sort of carry out the demands of nature when you were in the tank all day, and so when you thought you required to do something you put a shell up the spout, shoot off at something, wait until the shell case cooled down, and then you used that for a urinal and you put it out through the little hatch. That's how you were able to remain reasonably comfortable.

One of the big problems was communications, and the infantry found that all their normal lines of communication, other than radio, were useless. They used to pass messages in to us in the tanks and we were able to pass messages to our commanders who could pass the infantry message to the infantry commanders, which helped.

We had a ferocious battle for the Railway Station, where the Maori Battalion took terrific punishment. The bombing had decimated all the roads and the only way in was along the railway embankment, and the idea was for the tanks to come in after the Maoris, and the Maoris actually made the Railway Station, but because of the shell holes the tanks weren't able to get in and the Maoris were driven out. Ultimately the New Zealand Division were relieved and we all went back and our places were taken by other units, and we left about 20 of our tanks in Cassino because we just could not get them out, and they were taken over by the people who succeeded us.

We all went back to an area called Mignano and regrouped and tried to get our tanks mobile again and in first-class condition, and that's what we did. When that was done we went further back to a place called Pietramelara, where we had about three weeks of real relaxation, and it was from there that the next phase of the Battle for Cassino was fought.

Now, after the period of recuperation the New Zealand Division, as such, was not involved for some time, but one of the English Divisions had the task of trying to break through into the Liri Valley so that we could open up the road to Rome. The Indians and the Poles were still attacking at Monte Cassino, and the fighting was still going on in the town, but the idea was to do a left hook, you might say, and come across the flats and try and drive in up the valley, turn right and cut Route 6, and that was their task. Well what happened, they were short of a regiment of tanks, and we were in, I suppose, as good a state of preparedness as anything, and so our regiment, the 19th Armoured Regiment, was the only New Zealand Unit that was involved in the final breakthrough to Cassino.

The Commanding Officer was told to have his tanks and everything ready to move at 2 o'clock in the morning, and we had to drive this 30 miles at night-time back to Cassino, and that's what we did. It was quite dark and the intention was for us to get into position to be able to assist the regiment and cross the rivers – the Rapido River was the main one – to allow our tanks to support the English regiments. We were there to give armoured support, as and when required. There were two or three salient points which were necessary to be captured so that you could overlook Route 6. They were very heavily protected by the Germans and our squadron was supporting the English troops who had to get into a small town, and they had a very, very hard fight. It was there that one of the English officers was awarded the Victoria Cross in that particular action.

We were on the right-hand side and we had two points to go to, and one was the Hill Point No 55 and the other Point No 50, and this was the critical one because it actually overlooked the railway. There was some very heavy fighting there and it was in the area that, I suppose, our squadron and my troop in particular were perhaps more involved than others. I was in command at the time and found that all the junior subalterns, all the officers of the particular company that was responsible for this attack on this Hill 50, had been either wounded or killed. So I had to get out of my tank and actually took over the command of the British Company and had to co-ordinate the attack on this Hill 50, and at the same time remove all the wounded, and that's what we accomplished. We ultimately took Hill No 50 and there were a lot of German anti-tank guns there. However, we took it and we took 32 prisoners of war. It was, I suppose, quite an achievement.

It was the next day after that, I think it was 16 May, we did an attack on the Route 6 into Cassino, but it was a pretty timid affair because we could hear the Germans during the night pulling out, and when we went forward with the infantry into Cassino and across the railway line, along the Route 6, we met no opposition at all. We had the privilege of being the first troop of New Zealand tanks into Cassino at the final breakthrough, and, in fact, I suppose the leading element of the New Zealand Expeditionary Force, because we were the only New Zealanders there. I can still remember our Commanding Officer of the Company, my Squadron, that was Colonel Parata from Dunedin, myself and others, having a look around Cassino. In the meantime the Poles had actually entered the monastery and I can remember the flag going up on the monastery, the Polish flag, showing that they had taken this obstacle which had cost so many lives, Americans, Poles, Indians, New Zealanders, British.

So we were all withdrawn and the whole of the Fifth Army, including the armoured New Zealand units, pushed on in front of us and we were taken back for relief. We went into another phase of recuperation and getting our tanks in good order again, and we gradually came up behind the Division until the next phase of the battle had to be fought. In the meantime General Mark Clark with the Fifth Army, advancing from Anzio, had entered Rome.

The next movement we were really involved in was the action to take Florence. That in itself was another fight and involved the New Zealand Division, and it was some of our infantry that were first into Florence. I suppose, as far as the 19th Armoured Regiment was concerned, the big battle that we fought was a battle at a place called Cerbaia, and we lost a lot of tanks there in fighting our way up, and again, not unlike Orsogna, we had to fight uphill to get on to the ridge so that you could overlook the Arno River, which really controlled the route into Florence. By that time I'd been promoted to captain, and I was what they call Battle Captain, and so was second in command to the Squadron Commander. I had another troop of tanks attached to me, and we were just a six-tank group held in reserve to do any particular job that was required. We were required to do a job and it was purely a toss of the coin as to whether my troop went first or the other one, but a fellow named Bob McGowan took his troop, went forward and went up the hill and did a great job in taking one of the small towns up there. What happened with him, he pulled his tank in behind the church and took the long leads from the radio and climbed up into the tower of the church, the bell tower, and from there he was an observation post and he was able to observe the German armour and troops coming in. He was in communication with the artillery and able to direct and correct their firing, and they actually broke up a complete battalion of German motorised troops that were assembling to do a counter-attack down the valley. One of the things that worried him was that the church spire was pretty high, and these shells were coming in from the New Zealand 25-pounders and were going right up over the top of the spire he was in and he was hoping they wouldn't hit it. He was awarded the Military Cross for his part in that campaign.

After Florence we went to Pisa and all those areas, but it was still quite a battle and very costly ones as far as New Zealand was concerned. Then, after the Division had been rested, they went further north and into the Po Valley, and that's where all the problems really occurred, because of all the canals and the small tributaries, and wherever you went you there were bridges across these canals, and they were heavily fortified and heavily defended. It was the whole of the Eighth Army going in there and it was a battle all the way. I suppose it's a tribute to the Engineers – they put up this great big bridge when we got to the Po, the Po River, which is a massive river, they put a Bailey bridge and pontoons across because all the other bridges had been smashed, and it was at that stage that the New Zealand Division gradually pushed on to Trieste.'

Signalman Harold Greer continued to be heavily involved in the dangerous task of laying and maintaining wire often under enemy fire. However, he was able to enjoy a spell in Rome during that campaign:

'I was fortunate in having a jeep to drive and, arriving in Rome, I remember going past the Coliseum and driving up the streets and a feeling of great relief that we'd broken through that very strong line. We received a spot of leave in Rome and enjoyed a break in the hostilities. "Tiny" Freyberg had got a canteen for us and we were treated very well. Lady Freyberg used to serve the troops in behind the counter and it was very good time of relaxation. We had a good reception from the Italians in Rome. Of course they realised then that the Germans were the bad men and we were the heroes. Naturally business was the main problem then – they saw us as a source of income and also of food. They were short of food and we were able to barter a bit of bully beef, tins of food.'

A soldier whose service experience in Italy was crucially to influence him was Arthur Gladstone. Following upon the advance to the north of Cassino:

'I have got to say, that at this time, I was not over-enamoured with the life of the soldier. I couldn't see much point in it, and I'd lost quite a number of very good friends. I decided that rather than attempt to contribute to the mayhem, I would attempt to alleviate it and so I set off on my journey as a medical orderly rather than as a combatant soldier. I started to reconcile my new work with the way I felt, and felt that at last I was doing something positive. I was no longer involved in occupancy of the gun pits, but I could take refreshments out to the folk on the guns during the small hours of the morning and during the dark hours of the night, when they were actually engaged in their harassing fire. I found this more satisfying.

Unfortunately, when we moved back to Siena after the River Arno had been cleared, at least on its south bank, and a static line established, unfortunately, as I say, two of my friends from 2 Company came across to tell me that my best mate Paddy Walsh had died of wounds, and I was quite distraught. I am quite certain that Paddy's death affected me greatly. However, life still had to be lived and there was still a lot of it ahead.

We moved away from the Tuscan area early in August and we were promised a breakthrough into the Romagna and over the Po and on to Venice in no uncertain terms. We were going to be the great mobile force and sweep everything before us, and then the rains came. We certainly crossed the Marechia River at Rimini and set off on our trek, but then it started to rain and it rained and it rained and vehicles got bogged on all the side roads and main roads and tanks slithered off into ditches and four-wheel-drive vehicles couldn't cope; the advance became an absolute crawl, and it became slog, slog, slog all the way, house to house, river to river, ditch to ditch through the rain into the Romagna.

After about a month or so of that we were pulled back to a rest area in the Marche and we, the machine-gun battalion, were very fortunate to strike a village right up in the hills, a little village called Pioraco, which depended on a paper mill for its sustenance. The people there were absolutely marvellous; they took us into their homes and that was where I started and determined to learn to speak the language of the people.

Soon afterwards we moved back on to the plains of the Romagna, and this time we moved back into the area immediately south of the city of Faenza; the rain hadn't gone away, nor had the mud. In fact it was almost impossible to move vehicles at all on some of the roads; it meant that we took a long time to get into positions on our particular part of the line, which was south of the Lamone River. Faenza was on the north bank, or the majority of it. The southern part of the town was already in our hands, but at the time we arrived back there was just a holding pattern preparing for the eventual attack on Faenza.

After about a fortnight we were pulled back to Forli for a spell, and then on 16 December the city of Faenza was surrounded and cut off and the German forces withdrew from there towards the Senio River. They didn't go immediately on to the Senio – they had to be pushed – and as a result we left Forli in the early morning of 19 December to go and establish a gun line in the foothills beyond the village of Celle, where there had been particularly stiff fighting on the part of the 23rd Battalion and the Maori Battalion. And we were then to put a gun line in to support the attack, which was to go virtually at right angles to the line of normal advance to clear the area south of the Senio River. We traversed the mud roads with great difficulty and got to Celle just on dusk, turned up a road on the left-hand side which wound up into the hills, and pulled into the first house on the left to gather our gear together because from there to where we were going everything had to be carried.

We moved out early in January to the other side of the Via Emelia, Route 9, towards a place called San Piero Laguna, where we were close to the Senio and in support of the Maori Battalion again. We'd been in support of the Maori Battalion through most of my attachment to this particular platoon. We were in the line there until the middle of January, about a fortnight.

So we were pulled back early in February to the village of Esonitoglia in the Marche, where from machine-gunners we were to become infantry. The Division had need of another Infantry Brigade for some of its envisaged last task in the war, and so the 27th Battalion for machine-gunners became infantry; the Divisional Cavalry had already got out of their Staghounds and were on foot, and the 22nd Battalion, which had been the motorised infantry of the Armoured Brigade, also became part of the 9th Infantry Brigade. We accomplished a period of intense training in Esonitoglia, where we were joined by quite substantial reinforcements from the 3rd Division from the Pacific and the 13th Reinforcements, who were all youngsters, fresh from New Zealand. Amongst them were many young friends of mine, young men who had been at school with me, young men whom I had known but who were, say, two years younger than I was.

Then we were on trucks and going back towards Romagna. We pulled in short of the Senio River for two or three days, and then the Battalion was put into training, backwards and forwards, backwards and forwards, on river crossings and one thing and another because the Senio was still ahead of us. On 9 April the whole show began with the most horrendous bombardment of the opposing forces – the sky was literally filled with aircraft – and from about 2 o'clock in the afternoon it was just one thunderous roar, and when all that had finished the dive-bombers took over and carried on until there was no more light to see what they were doing. Then the artillery took over and the bombardment was absolutely horrendous. They say it was the heaviest bombardment of the war on the Eighth Army side.

In any case, that night we were on trucks on the way across the Senio and our job was the liberation of the little town of Cotignola. In the morning we found that the Germans had escaped – they'd gone, they'd left Cotignola – and a young lad came out of the town under a white flag and gave us the information. As we went into the town, troops from the 58th Division, the Surrey Regiment, actually crossed the river and came in to meet us. So our task, which had been planned as one of great difficulty, turned out to be the simplest, and we just moved forward.

Then we were in reserve until we faced the Sillaro River, where the Battalion really went into action. The evening before the attack, which was the evening of 14 April, Padre Fletcher came up from the CCS and said Mass for the RCs under the olives, and following that event two of my young friends came to me and said, "Arthur, these are our personal things, we'd like you to look after them." I was in a position of doing that because I'd been appointed as medical orderly to the MO of that Battalion, so I was at the Battalion RAP working with the doctor, and so I was in reasonably secure lines. They brought me these things and said, "Look, we'd like you to look after these. We don't know what's going to happen but we know that you'll get them home for us if anything does happen." And I sort of pooh-poohed them and said, "Aw, come on, you'll be OK," and they said, "Well, we know we'll be OK, but we'd sooner you'd hang on to these things for us."

They survived that night, the attack across the Sillaro and the cleaning out of that area, and we moved on to Medicina and the village of Villafontana and confronted the Gaiana Canal, where the remnants of the Paratroop Corps, who we'd been battling with all through Italy from Cassino on, had come to make their last stand against the New Zealand Division. Our boys were the first ones in it across 500 metres of ground with no cover, and these two friends of mine died with the same shell; heaven knows whether it was one of ours or one of the enemy's, it didn't matter – they both died on the banks of the Gaiana Canal.

The Gaiana was eventually overcome with a set-piece battle, but our Battalion had suffered a great number of casualties there. All the dead from that and the previous battles lie in the cemetery of Santa Lucia della Spionate, just outside the walls of Faenza. However, to the Gaiana, it was a very emotional experience as I fancy it would be for any of the members of the 27th Battalion. I know how busy we were in that period at the RAP, and I know of the sacrifice of our adjutant who refused to be attended to and subsequently died of his wounds. "Crash" Ross was a man to be greatly respected, but his feeling was the boys have got to be attended to first. And that was the Gaiana, and really the last battle of the war as far as the New Zealand Division was concerned. From there on out it was chase, chase, chase; we even crossed the Po almost without pause, and whatever ensued between there and Trieste was really only skirmish.

On 25 April, ANZAC Day, I was at last given leave from the Battalion; that was on the day on which they were due to cross the Po, and I was given leave to Florence. I was also told by the Colonel that on my return I would be appointed unit historian for the Battalion, with the rank of sergeant. I set off, supposedly on the journey to Florence, but at Bologna I banged on the roof of the truck and demanded to be let off. I wasn't going to Florence,

I wanted to go back to Faenza, and back I went down the road 60 kilometres and eventually managed to find Antoinietta. That was a fateful moment; from then on I knew that Antoinietta Delmonte and I were destined to spend our lives together.

We had met in a house near the village of Celle where she and her mother were staying with other refugees from the city of Faenza and where my unit was quartered for a few days. We were duly married in the Church of Saint Bartolomeo, the Temple of the Fawn.'

Successes in Italy allowed for a greater degree of aid to Tito and the Partisans in Yugoslavia and resulted in Major Edward Prebble, lately Deputy Assistant Adjutant General (Mosquitoes) receiving a posting of quite a different nature:

'I was then appointed to Force, I think it was called 224. It was at a place called Barletta, which was just north of Bari in Italy. I reported there and I was told that I was just in time, that an LCI [Landing Craft Infantry] was about to go over to Yugoslavia to an island known as Vis. I still didn't know what I was supposed to be doing. Anyway, I went over in this LCI, which was run by a sub-lieutenant and another junior rank. This was in November – there was a snow storm blowing, nil visibility, and I was allowed to sleep in one of the bunks. I remember waking up in the middle of the night and seeing these two young officers peering over a chart saying, "Well, we're just about here – I expect we'll hit the island in a few minutes." Anyhow, in the middle of the night how they ever found their way I don't know, but we arrived in the island of Vis. I disembarked and found headquarters, where I slept the night. I asked the officer there, "Who is in charge?" and he said, "You are," and I realised that this is where I had been sent to look after this AA Battery.

Anyhow, the following day the Colonel of the Regiment had arrived and I reported to him and he put me in the picture. There were two artillery batteries on the island, both anti-aircraft, and our job was to hold the island so that the Partisans under Marshal Tito could be supplied with arms, uniforms, etc, and that he could evacuate his wounded from the island.

While we were there, Tito, the Partisan Commander, asked for artillery support, and it was decided that the only support we could give would be mule-pack mountain artillery. This was a 3.7 inch gun-howitzer which took to pieces and could be loaded on to six mules; six mules per gun. The guns arrived and we had a week's tuition, and the mules arrived from Malta. With the mules came some Italians who had been prisoners and were now liberated, and they were good muleteers. Anyway, this battery was formed and we then took it on to the mainland and supported the

Partisans who were stepping up their operations and who were now strong enough to take the odd small town and hold it for a short time, and thus interrupting the enemy's lines of communication.

The whole of the Allied forces was known as Land Forces Adriatic; we were commanded by Brigadier Bailey, who was on the mainland, and he had Navy, Air Force and Army units. I was then asked to participate in one or two raids and personally took part in several which I considered to be important. If it was a minor raid I sent obviously some junior officer.

Then I had a visit from two members of the British Military Mission who suggested that I took part in a raid on the Peltesac peninsula. Now this was a much bigger raid than any of the previous ones, as it controlled the road which ran from Ston up to Mostar up to Sarajevo, and would deny the garrison at Dubrovnik from having an alternative route. The Peltesac peninsula, the channel running up inside the peninsula, was mined, and we passed through the channel in a Partisan schooner with their swimmers preceding the schooner and placing themselves between the mines and the hull of the boat. I didn't realise the danger at the time, but it was a very foolhardy raid.

Anyhow, we passed through the minefield and got right up inside the channel. It was a moonless dark night and we unloaded the guns by dinghy and pulled them up the slopes opposite the town by ropes attached to the axles of the guns, and assembled them in a fold in the ground, and waited for the signal from the Partisans, who were attacking round about dawn. I think the signal was a green Verey light, I'm not sure now. We had roughly 50 rounds per gun and rations for probably three days, and the party, I think, was of 32 people. When the light went up we started firing; of course, we had to fire from the map identifying the various landmarks, but the target was a fairly large one, the small town at the head of the crossroads. We fired for some time and dawn broke and, I suppose, the Germans realised that they were being attacked with two guns, so they sent a small party out to investigate the forces on the peninsula. Of course we were only 32 at the maximum, so we were very vulnerable. However, we observed the party advancing on us and they were coming up the peninsula and we had no defence ourselves against this party, so I called a conference which included the two sergeants and the other officer with me, and somebody suggested that the only thing to do was to pull the guns out of hiding and put them on the forward slope and open up on open sights, and this we did, and I'm pleased to say that the party who were investigating beat a hasty retreat.

We then went back and continued firing and eventually the red light went up and that meant that the Partisans had captured the town. We had expected to be relieved after this, but the rest of the day nothing happened at all and so, the following morning, I thought it best to investigate because we had no means of getting off the peninsula. So with my batman, who was really my bodyguard, I walked into the town. To my surprise there were no Partisans there at all; some of the inhabitants emerged from their hiding places and we had some difficulty making ourselves known to them and the fact that we were on the Partisans' side and we weren't the Germans returning. Eventually they produced somebody who spoke English. and I told him I was looking for the Partisans and he said that they had all disappeared, but there were two Englishmen in a farm house, and he pointed out where the farmhouse was. It turned out to be these two members of the British Military Mission.

So I went along and they said, "Oh, we wondered what had happened to you," and I told them and they said, "Oh, the Navy are supposed to be picking you up, but I think their vessels have broken down. Anyhow, we'll send a schooner along." So I sent my batman back with a message for the party to assemble at the beach. I went with the two members of the Military Mission to this schooner, which was loading up with all the booty they collected, had taken from the town, including a staff car, and it was a pretty small ship.

We set sail, picked up our chaps with the guns, and were sailing back to Vis when we came across the two Navy ships, sort of assault craft, broken down, so we gave them a tow. We were making very slow progress going up the Adriatic and a storm blew up. This made the vessel rock alarmingly and the skipper thought we might capsize and suggested we sought a harbour to shelter in.

Anyhow, the nearest island was the Island of Hvar. Now that was supposedly occupied by the Germans, but the captain of the schooner said he had information that the Germans had left, so we made for the Port of Hvar and we successfully got into the harbour. I sent a couple of chaps ashore to see if the enemy was still there and fortunately the information was correct; the enemy had at any rate evacuated that end of the island.

At this point I thought it best to try and get in touch with the Island of Vis, the headquarters, and I asked the hotel proprietor at the port whether he had a telephone, and he said yes, and I said, "Do you think we can get through to Vis?" and he said, "Oh yes, no doubt about that," he said, "we go through the mainland." Well, of course, the mainland was occupied by the Germans. Anyhow, we decided to have a go at it and he raised the operator on the mainland and they raised Vis. Well, the telephone in Vis I don't think had rung during the last six months or so, and it surprised everybody at the headquarters. Anyhow, I got through and told them where we were and we would be sailing as soon as the weather calmed, realising afterwards that the Germans could easily have monitored the whole thing. Anyhow, luck was on our side and we got away with it. The weather did moderate and we were able to set sail and the whole party returned to Vis intact.

Shortly after this the Russians broke through from Rumania and the Partisans, who were communists, were more interested in the Russians than they were in the British, and they more or less started to give us the cold shoulder, so it was decided that we should withdraw from Vis, which we did.

Shortly after my return from operations on the Island of Vis and Yugoslavia, we were given the task of cleaning up, as we were one of the few complete units in Southern Italy, the fighting having now proceeded north of Rome. The cleaning-up period is a very distressing type of work; lifting land mines is not everybody's idea of a holiday, and the troops really resented going into minefields where the plans were a bit sketchy, to say the least.

However, I think that the next thing which happened to us, as a unit, was that one day the Colonel, who was a Regular soldier, realised that his life and future promotion lay in Burma or India, where the war was still proceeding, so he had applied for a posting, which came through, and so he called me into his office and said, "I'm leaving and you will be taking over the Regiment." I found myself promoted in one day from second in command to Colonel of the Regiment. It was just about this time that we were sent to an airfield just outside Taranto, which was an old Italian base with some huge hangars where the Italians had built some airships prior to the war, and these had been established in these hangars on this airfield. Anyhow, we were then told that we were to receive German prisoners of war, because in Northern Italy, when the Germans surrendered in the Po Valley, there were some four or five Divisions, probably some quarter to half a million prisoners, and they thought it was too big an operation to be dealt with up there.

We started to build a prisoner of war camp; some officers were sent over from England to show us how to proceed, and a detachment of sappers sent along, and all the materials arriving in the port of Taranto. We put up a camp for 1,000 Germans, and these Germans started arriving by train; we searched them, disinfected them with DDT, because they were all lousy, and put them in this camp, but as soon as the camp was full we were told to receive a further 1,000. By then, of course, we had unlimited labour from the Germans, so we started to proceed and eventually, before I left, a camp of 10,000 had been erected. The Germans were most co-operative; they supplied all the labour, they supplied all the doctors, who worked under our doctor. They supplied all the bath attendants for the washing of the blankets and so forth, and distributed all the rations themselves. In fact, most of the convoys which went out to collect rations and material consisted of a British guard in the first vehicle, the rest of the convoy driven by the Germans, and a British soldier with a tommy-gun sitting in the last vehicle, and nobody wanted to escape because they'd got nowhere to go and they were happy as long as we could feed and keep them reasonably clean.'

Taking part in providing air support for the ground advance in the final months of the campaign was Roy McGowan, now a Squadron Leader and fully operational, after the injuries incurred flying in the Battle of Britain:

'I learned in late 1944 that I was posted back to ops in Italy, and I would go out to Italy and join a Refresher Operational Flying Unit. I went out by Dakota, landing at an RAF military airfield somewhere south of Naples, and was sent to Perugia in Central Italy, well north of Rome, by which time, of course, the Eighth Army from the desert and the Americans supporting them on the western side had pushed the Italians and Germans appreciably north.

In Perugia we had Spitfire IXs, but on each wing we carried, I guess it was a 250-pound bomb. There were no German aircraft in the air – they had a fuel shortage in Italy, they had a hard time with the Allied air forces operating in Italy, and one virtually didn't see a German aircraft. So we would just do Army close support.

So we spent about two weeks practising this type of bombing work, and I was posted to a South African Wing with an RAF Squadron in it. We were on an American base, a place called Pontedera, and it was just between Florence and Pisa. So we were operating from there with these two 250-pound bombs, bombing targets just around the Bomb Line, which was a line dividing the Allied forces from the enemy, and that was changing hourly of course.

We would be briefed on what our target would be – it could be a telephone exchange, it could be a military building of some kind, it could be an airfield. Or information would come in during the night from the Partisans that a military convoy had gone into a little village and was sheltering under the trees, and we'd be briefed on that. We'd go up in sections of four – four aircraft, very loose formation – rising and falling 500 feet to stop ground guns from getting a bead on to us. When you got into the immediate area you'd put your section into a line astern behind you and find the target yourself – some ground fire, but find the target yourself – and then make sure that your three men behind you had also found the target, and then you would go in line astern, you know, a mile interval between each, I guess, and drop your first bomb on the target. It was often possible to get a real direct hit and re-form. If the ground fire hadn't been too intense you would go in the same way and drop your second bomb. They were anxious that you didn't go in under intense fire because the damage to the aircraft would take many, many days to get it serviceable again.

We did some good work with this direct bombing; we didn't see an aircraft at all, a Hun aircraft at all, the whole time. By day the ground transport of the enemy was not moving; it was all moving by night because of this intensive attacking of ground forces by the aircraft. The Americans had their Thunderbolts and their Mustangs, we had our Spitfires, and if a German transport showed itself it quickly would be spotted and it was in trouble.

An unfortunate operation I remember was when we had word that there was a mule train on a low mountain before you get up into the Italian Alps. I was leading a section of four, and yes, we came across this mule train with military men on foot escorting it and loaded with boxes and things, and, of course, it was all supplies and, sadly, we had to obliterate that. On another occasion, I remember, we were told insistently by operations that there were two ambulances going along the road which had to be attacked. We spotted them, we attacked them and they exploded, again carrying something other than wounded.

Not too long before the end of hostilities, a refinement was introduced to this ground support by fighter aircraft. On the UK side an Army man would go in a tank right up to the Bomb Line and he had radio contact with us in the air and he would describe the target that he wanted you to attack – it was visible to him, he was on a bit of high land immediately behind the front line – and that worked out very well. On the American side, where we were operating, that was refined even more in that we had a gentlemen who called himself "Rover Joe", and he was in a light aeroplane and he would be sitting in his aircraft just over the Front Line and he too would describe to us over RT the particular target he wanted us to attack. He made sure that we had it, and then you made sure that your three men behind you had it, and then you went in and you did your attack. These were frequent patrols; we were piling up a lot of hours. If you did a patrol and you couldn't locate a particular target, then the instruction was bomb any road bridge, so you just disposed of your bombs on a road bridge to upset ground transport on the enemy side.

Those operations continued until Kesselring, who was in command of the Germans, surrendered. I think it was about four days before the end of the war in Europe, Northern Europe, so our last operations were showing the flag by flying formations over the Italian Alps where, by that time, all the enemy forces were up in the north of Italy, up in the Italian Alps – flying over there to make sure that they were surrendering and were being escorted south in an orderly way. It was quite amazing to see these German units, still intact with staff cars and so on heading them, and then military vehicles of one kind and another following, to see them coming back behind our own lines still in surprisingly good military order.'

CHAPTER 11

A new assailant:
Japan and the war in
South East Asia

*E*arly on 8 December 1941 Japanese troops landed at Kota Baharu on
*the east coast of Malaya, just to the south of the frontier with Siam
(now Thailand). Quickly seizing the aerodrome there, they advanced down
the east coast, largely as a diversionary measure. The main assault came
from forces landed at Singora and Patani on the Siamese coast to the north,
which advanced into Malaya and down the west coast. With complete
superiority in the air and, after the sinking of the British capital ships* Prince
of Wales *and* Repulse, *of the sea, the Japanese advanced rapidly down the
peninsula and into Singapore, where the British surrendered on 15
February 1942. This was followed, in rapid succession, by the Japanese
conquest of Burma, the Dutch East Indies and island territories in the
South Pacific. In a series of actions in and around the Java Sea, most of the
remnants of the Allied fleets were sunk by the Japanese.*

Something of the unknown factors and consequent uncertainties felt by all
those engaged upon the defence of Malaya from Japanese attack is
expressed in the memories of John Mackie, a New Zealander. He joined the
Colonial Service Mines Department in the Federation of Malay States in
1936, and had enlisted in a volunteer defence force, the Federated Malay
States Volunteers:

'After training and rapid promotion to Sergeant, I was given a sort of
private OCTU course and became Second Lieutenant. I was on leave in
New Zealand when war broke out, so as a member of the Malayan
Volunteers I began to worry and wonder whether I should enquire about
what was required of me – whether I should go back to Malaya

immediately and what the powers that be there were going to do, or whether I should join the New Zealand Army. Contact with Malaya told me that I was not required back there, that I should go on and have my leave, but that I could not join the New Zealand Army without severing my contract with the Colonial Service, and, what's more, I got a sort of rap over the knuckles, saying that I was needed in Malaya because the war production of rubber and tin was vital for the war effort.

So after my leave was concluded I went back again to Malaya and was eventually promoted to State Inspector of Mines of Perak under the Senior Inspector of Mines, and that involved my becoming a Magistrate in the Wardens Court and hearing various mining cases.

But eventually the Japanese intentions became fairly clear; they had gone into Indo-China and by doing that they had obtained for themselves a springboard which was quite close to Malaya, so things began to get a little warm in Malaya. When things started to come to a head, the whole of the British Army in Malaya was on Red Alert, so to speak. The western side of Malaya was largely defended, at that stage, by the 3rd Indian Army Corps under Lieutenant General Heath. The volunteers were mobilised on 1

John Bullamore Mackie (centre)

December. I was in the Perak Volunteers and at that stage I had become second in command of one of the companies in the Perak Battalion. We went into a place called Canning Camp on mobilisation. We had practised for this before, so it wasn't such a difficult operation. The whole Battalion was housed in this camp and we lived there in the dripping rubber for about ten days or more before we got ourselves in order.

Now, I should mention that the Volunteers were not a what you would call a highly trained army unit. They were really set up, in the first place, to control any possible riots in the civilian population. However, we were never called out in a riot role, but I have to stress that the Volunteers were not a first-line Regular Army unit type; in fact we had been trained only on a monthly basis. Most people knew what they were doing with things like Vickers guns, Lewis guns, rifles – they could shoot – but were not particularly well trained in jungle warfare.

Brigadier Moir, ex-Argyll & Sutherland Highlanders, was Commander of the Volunteers and was also the OC of the lines of communication in Malaya, which meant that he had to take command of all the operations going on behind the front line as they developed. We were given the role of aerodrome defence in the first instance, this being to stop the Japanese landing paratroopers and planes, etc, on a number of aerodromes which had been prepared in Northern Malaya for any possible Japanese attack.

Well, the Japs attacked while we were in Canning Camp. They landed at Kota Baharu on the north-east coast of Malaya in Kelantan; they also made a two-pronged attack, landing on the Isthmus of Kra in Southern Siam, and they worked their way westwards and southwards down towards Malaya. Our Army, the 11th Indian Division, had a role which, in defence, required them to advance into Siam at a given signal code-named "Matador". Well, there was a lot of uncertainty, I think, going on in the minds of the commanders in Singapore about this, and the troops were all ready to go into Siam to meet the Japanese coming down, but the British were very wary about going into Siam, fearing it would give the Japanese an excuse to attack Malaya.

So the troops were suddenly then taken away from an attack role into a defensive role when our people decided not to go into Siam in a big way, but, of course, they had to go into Siam to meet the threat, a short distance. So the troops who were defending Malaya were in a somewhat uncertain situation and were not particularly well prepared for the arrival of the Japanese. There were defensive positions in the northern part of Malaya in Kedah, but there had been a tremendous amount of rain in the monsoon, and the defences, many of them had been flooded, so that the situation was not very good from the point of view of defence, particularly when people had been expecting to go on the attack.

However, the Japanese arrived on the scene and attacked on the 3rd Indian Division front, but mainly using as a line of attack the main road south, which ran right down the western part of Malaya. They also had considerable success over on the east in the Kota Baharu landings. The western attacks, with the two prongs I mentioned earlier, were meant to cut off the 11th Indian Division. These two prongs were meant to be a pincer movement which would nullify the troops in the north-west of Malaya, so to speak, but it didn't work that way. Eventually, of course, the 11th Indian Division, very much battered, would escape getting caught in the pincer movement, but they had a rather bad time.

The Royal Air Force had planes stationed in the northern aerodromes, but they were no match for the Japanese, who had innumerable planes it seemed, and also we lost a lot of planes on the ground due, it's thought, to a spy who was an Indian officer, who told the Japanese, by secret radio, when our people were taking off and landing, which gave the Japanese a great advantage and enabled them to do a lot of damage to aircraft on the ground. The Royal Air Force was getting very battered and it was decided that with the limited amount of aircraft available, these should now be based on Singapore, which was a bad decision from the point of view of the troops. So they took off and the aerodromes, which had been specially made there for their use, became useless to the British but of great value eventually to the Japanese. So our role in their protection was no longer needed.

Our Army managed to retreat behind the line of the Perak River in the northern part of Perak State and get a little respite. The troops who had been fighting the Japs were very badly knocked about, particularly from the air. They were getting harassed from the air constantly. Also the Japanese had tanks and we had none, as it had been considered they were not suited to the terrain. However, the Japanese used them quite intelligently to spearhead fierce attacks down the main road and then to use the tanks as strongpoints from which they could harass our troops.

When the remnants of the 11th Division got back behind the line of the Perak River, they were a pretty tattered outfit and fairly well depleted in numbers, so they had an opportunity there to recoup and plan for what they were going to do. They'd lost quite a lot of equipment on the quick retreat south from Kedah, Alor Setar and those places. So in the reorganisation there were two British units in the 11th Indian Division, the 1st Battalion, Leicesters, and the 2nd Battalion, East Surreys. These two had been rather badly knocked about largely through the efforts of the efficient fifth column the Japs were operating then. They'd been spying in Malaya for years and set up units of fifth column all up and down the country, and I think this gave them information about where the various unit headquarters were and that kind of thing. So both the Headquarters of the East Surreys and the Leicesters, as far as I can understand, were attacked, and in one case the Colonel was killed and other officers were taken prisoner.

Anyway, these two British regiments were put together into a single unit, which became known as the British Battalion, and they were still short of men, so our 1st Perak Battalion of Volunteers was called upon to provide two platoons to join the British Battalion. One platoon was given to me, mostly chaps I didn't know – they were from other parts of the country, not Perak – and the other one was a platoon commanded by one of my Volunteer friends, and it was a machine-gun platoon. So we were duly peeled off from the Volunteers and joined the British Battalion, and the plan was that the next British stand would be at a place called Kampar, about 16-17 miles south of Ipoh. It was a good defensive position and there had been time available to get civilian labour and some volunteer labour in to preparing positions at Kampar, defensive positions.

So I was transferred, I think, towards the end of December 1941, and the battalion took up its position astride the main road, which was the access for the Japanese attack on the reorganised Brigade, the remains of the 11th Indian Division. So we got into position and my platoon was put mainly on Battalion Headquarters defence. So we waited there and getting a fair amount of attack from the air and also, before very long, mortaring from the Japanese, who then attacked in considerable force. But they hadn't reckoned on the resistance of the British unit, the British Battalion, who had a pretty good taste of Japanese-style warfare and who defended the position with great heroism. The battle lasted for about four days in all. I can well remember the nights were bright moonlight and the weather wasn't that bad, but there was a lot of heavy metal flying about and a lot of air activity on the part of the Japanese, and none on the part of our people, which was very unnerving, and I think it certainly doesn't help morale if you are constantly attacked from the air and you know that there's not going to be any reply from your own side to that pattern.

The Japanese shelled us, mortared us, sniped and shot at us in every way that you could think of. They made several very determined attempts to get round the Battalion's right flank, which was on the slopes of the hills just to the north of Kampar. There were no less, as far as I remember, than three very severe attacks by the Japanese, and the necessity then was for counter-attacks, and these were carried out with extreme bravery by people of the British Battalion, the Leicesters and Surreys, and also by some of the Company Reserve and, eventually, the Brigade Reserve, which had to be called in. These counter-attacks were extremely bloody affairs and the Japs were beaten back every time, and they had got to the stage where they couldn't get past the Kampar position.

So they then embarked troops in fleets of small ships and towed them down the west coast and landed on the west coast behind the Kampar position, and so threatening our rear and forcing our withdrawal. The Commander of the British Battalion was Lieutenant General Morrison who, among other things, was an Oxford graduate. He was a very fine commander – I have the greatest admiration for him – he controlled the situation and it was his stubborn resistance that stopped the Japs for longer than they'd been stopped anywhere then or later, except Singapore itself.

So eventually we had to withdraw, and the withdrawal took place at night, and I remember it very well. All the companies of our Battalion except one had withdrawn and the last one was late in coming out down from the hills and the rising ground on the right, so the Colonel pulled me in and said that he wanted my platoon up on the main road to cover the withdrawal of the last company out. So he personally came and told us where he wanted us, so we were given this position astride the main road with orders that we were not to shoot if we saw the Japanese. This has often concerned me; I wondered why we were only to use bayonets to defend the position if the Japs attacked. This was a bit deterring because some of my platoon had not been in that kind of action before and, in a way, not really trained for it. It was a bright moonlit night and, with a view up the road about 50 yards or so, you could have seen the Japanese if they'd come down. We were hoping and praying that the final company would get a move on and get out. We could hear the Japanese shouting to each other; they were obviously not very far away. Things became very tense.

My own feelings were, what the devil do I do now? I had a pistol, somebody had given me a bayonet, but I had no rifle and my chaps had been reduced to about 20 or so through wounds and illness. I had very mixed feelings and wondered what would happen if the Japs attacked us. However, the sounds of the company coming down the hill came to our ears and they filed down the ridge track behind us and went off down to Battalion Headquarters where the rest of the Battalion was.

So we stayed there until they got out and the Japanese were getting closer, but there was no sight of them, so they couldn't have been closer than at least 50 yards from us, when we finally got out. Anyway, we got out and we rejoined the tail-end of the retiring Battalion and we'd a couple of Bren gun-carriers with us and we marched through Kampar, which had been shot at and pock-marked and some of the places burnt out, and it was quite eerie in the moonlight doing this. But anyway, we got out and there were various other actions down the country. I eventually got gastro-enteritis and was shuffled off down to Singapore and spent a bit of time in Alexandra Hospital and then to a recuperation camp, not for long.

The Japanese continued on their way down the country making fairly rapid progress until they got down to Johore, where they met the Australians. There were two brigades of Australians stationed there under General Gordon Bennett, and there were some heroics there too; some very good defence responses from the Australians, although not all of them.

I didn't mention the gloom that had been cast over the whole country by the sinking of the two British capital ships, *Repulse* and *Prince of Wales*. They were in Singapore and had arrived in a great sort of burst of publicity about how they were going to protect the country, and, unfortunately, the Admiral who took them round up the east coast of Malaya, didn't have air cover, and the Japs sank them in double quick time, and this cast an enormous gloom all over the country. I think it was one of the biggest blows to morale of both the civilians and the fighting troops in Malaya.

The retreat went on and eventually we got to Singapore, where my platoon and the other one from the British Battalion had been withdrawn back to Volunteer Headquarters on Singapore Island. The British Battalion had got further reinforcements and some of the Volunteers had family, so there was no further need for them.

Then the retreat, of course, eventually got on to the island itself, and large numbers of people had fled down country and had gone on to Singapore Island hoping they might be safe, but of course they weren't. The Japs attacked the island in considerable force and soon, with the poor defence put up in the quarter where they landed, they got through and finally besieged Singapore City.

At this stage I had become an Intelligence Officer in a Brigade commanded by our old Volunteer Brigadier Moir, and we were part of a rather patched-up kind of Brigade placed across the main road leading into Singapore. I think there were troops in front of us, but we were maybe the kind of back stop or something of that sort, so at this stage there was a tremendous amount of bombardment by the Japanese of Singapore from the air with machine- gunning and they were shooting at everything they could see. They were also shelling, as they were close enough to use artillery.

The main thing was that they had taken the two reservoirs which fed Singapore City, and the chief engineer had to advise General Percival, the GOC, that the water situation was so serious that something had to be done to ameliorate the conditions of the population and all the refugees. So a meeting of course took place, which is history, and Percival decided that he would capitulate to the Japanese, I think largely to avoid the Japanese overrunning the city and looting and plundering and raping, doing all the things that could have happened if they'd had to take it by force. He probably did the right thing. My own feelings, when I look back on them, I was sort of taken aback I suppose by the surrender. I thought we had to fight it out, but the surrender did take place.

The ceasefire occurred and the sudden change from this tremendous racket that was going on from shelling, mortaring and so on and the bombardment from the air, the sudden cessation was weird. It created something of a very eerie atmosphere, particularly as Singapore was shrouded in drifting clouds of black smoke from all the burning oil tanks and the rubble from broken buildings. The last days of Pompeii came to my mind.

I didn't have time to think about what it would be like to be a prisoner and to surrender in these circumstances, but I didn't realise for a while that suddenly my freedom had gone and that the Lord knows what was going to happen to all those troops who were bottled up in Singapore. It was a kind of feeling of foreboding. There were rumours about, of course, of the atrocities which had been committed by the Japanese and we were, I suppose, very concerned about this. The thought I had was, well, they can't kill us all, there were too many for that, and it would create such an international uproar that the Japanese would never live it down, but I couldn't have any more thoughts. Things started to happen.

We were told to lay down our arms, which we did; we piled our weapons and left them and marched into Singapore City to one of the Girls' Schools which had been evacuated. I recall that it had been shelled and that a shell had gone through three or four floors on an angle, leaving a gaping hole in each of the floors, and it hadn't exploded, but the detonator must have gone off because the whole of the lower floor of the Girls' School was covered in yellow powder, which I took to be picric acid, which was the explosive that was used. Anyway, there we were in the Girls' School – a bit tattered and unshaven and pretty smelly, I suppose, because there hadn't been much chance to have a bath – waiting to see what would happen. We spent the night and had a reasonably good sleep for once because the racket had gone and we were all extremely tired.

The following day we were still in this position. A couple of Japanese officers arrived on the scene; they just looked at us and went out again. They had decided that they wouldn't bring their troops into the city, but they had a great parade with tanks and armoured vehicles around the city showing that they had taken it. Then we received news that we were to go to Changi and we were not going to be transported there, we had to do it on Shanks's pony. So there you had a tremendous long column of prisoners marching out to Changi with what little they could carry on this 15-mile hike. We passed through some of the areas that the Japanese had been searching for Chinese who were known to have sent money to China to help against the Japanese attacking that country. They caught these poor individuals and murdered them – they chopped their heads off and put them on poles along part of the route that we were on, so it was rather an unnerving sight and perhaps something of a forerunner of what might happen to us. It wasn't very encouraging.

In order to be able to get supplies out on this trek, our people in the Transport Units had dismantled the motors and bodies from a number of trucks, leaving just the chassis and their rubber-tyred wheels, and we were able to load these up with what supplies we had. We had quite a lot of supplies actually in Singapore, but we could only load on these chassis what they would hold, and these were towed by ropes in relays by prisoners going along the road, this very long south-eastern side of Singapore Island out to Changi.

We went all day – it was pretty exhausting – and eventually we arrived in the dusk at Changi. Somebody must have gone on ahead and the people I was with in the Volunteers, the Federated Malay States Volunteers, mostly officers and some sergeants and corporals, were allocated a large bungalow, which was meant for a family of people, so there were something like 140 or so of us sleeping on the floor of this, but it didn't matter, we were so worn out and tired, exhausted in every way, that we just lay down on the floor of this bungalow and we went to sleep.

We had been able to take some gear with us into the camp, personal gear; I had a couple of shirts and some shorts. I found a thin mattress in a house, which was a camp-bed-type mattress, so I rolled this up and I managed to take it with me and a mosquito net, and I was very glad I'd been able to do this. I managed to hang on to these all the time I was a prisoner. They were probably the best things I could have taken.'

Marjory de Malmanche was a London-trained nurse working for the Sepoy Lines Maternity Hospital at Singapore, where her husband was employed by the Harbour Board:

'I was on night duty at the hospital at the time that the Japanese were entering Singapore, and when I got home at 6 o'clock in the morning my husband said, "I have to go and I don't know where I'm going or anything about it except that I've got to go." So we didn't meet again for four years.

Some of us nurses were sent off on a small ship and some of them stayed behind. We embarked in the morning, and late afternoon we were bombed. We had two deaths and several injured. The next thing was we arrived at an island and a lot of the men on the ship went ashore and cut branches and tried to camouflage the ship, and whilst they were away and having a little frolic in the sea, the Japanese came over again and they bombed us well and good. The first bomb went down the funnel and into the engine room. There was only one boat, as the rest were all on the shore with the camouflage crew, so we had to just slide down a rope that the sailors tied on to the ship into the sea and then swim. That one boat was absolutely full of survivors, and all round the outside they were clinging to it too, and there was only one oar, which was being used by an old lady, who wasn't very much good really. So I clung to the boat and said to them all, swim with our legs and push it to the island – we weren't very far away, you see. So we did that and we reached the island safely and scrambled out of the boat. It was a very mountainous island and there were a lot of trees and we started to run up under the trees, and just as we got going the planes came over again and bombed, and our little boat was destroyed and there were a few casualties.

Well, we scrambled up to the top of this quite steep hill, and when we got to the top it was absolutely flat and lying about must have been about a hundred wounded people. Women were going about in their pants and bras, because they'd torn up all their clothing to make bandages. There was nothing I could do because I was wearing shorts and a shirt. So I was really wanting to know where my friends, the two doctors, Dr Crowe and Dr Marjorie Lyon, an Australian, were, so I went over the mountain and down the other side and found them both. Dr Crowe had a fractured skull and blood was pouring down her nose, and Marjorie Lyon had got a belly blast and was haemorrhaging too. Dr Lyon, before she left the ship, had got all the morphia she could find and tied it round her neck, and so it was possible to give some relief to some people who were in great pain.

So anyway, we were on that island for five days and nights and we ate nothing much. We had a biscuit and a third of a cup of water in the morning, and the same in the evening. Then, in the middle of the night, one night we were told to all gather together and we were going to be taken off. I stayed with Dr Crowe and Dr Lyon, and a big sailor, a hefty man, was very good and we had one of the little boats and we put the two doctors and another woman who was very badly injured in the boat, and this man rowed us round the island until we got to a suitable place where they were all gathered waiting to be taken off later in the night.

So they lifted wounded Dr Crowe and the other woman out and made stretchers out of the branches of trees and laid the two badly injured people on those, and then we all sat down and waited. Then a lot of screaming started: "The Japs are here, the Japs are here, coming over with torches!" and, of course, it turned out to be giant fireflies, much to our relief.

Later on the rescue ship came and we carried the two on the stretchers down to this. It was an ex-Japanese fishing-boat, square at both ends, and we all went on that. We set off in the dark and got to the Indragiri River, as we were not far from the coast of Sumatra. So we went up this river – I suppose we were travelling all day up the river – and about 4 o'clock in the afternoon we reached Rengat. We were there for quite a time at Rengat working at the hospital.

The Dutch did not give us any help, but they let us use it. We continued looking after our own wounded. There was one American missionary woman there who was very good to us. She took the two doctors and me into her house and, of course, we were working in the hospital all day. Then we went right from one side of Sumatra to the other in buses and stopped overnight at hospitals, as we had a lot of wounded, and we gradually made our way right across Sumatra to the other side at Padang.

When we were going up hills we had to get out and walk and, in some cases, help to push the broken-down old bus, and at one stage, as we were going up a hill, we heard a sound of heavy breathing and, looking round, we found there was a great big tiger with us. You can imagine, we all flew into this poor old bus and it struggled along. The next day, when we came to another village, we saw the skin of the tiger stretched out to dry, and the headman of the village had shot it.

So after that we continued on and eventually reached Padang, where we were taken in by the Salvation Army. The Dutch wouldn't have anything to do with us really, but the Salvation Army Hospital and Clinic was run by a Canadian couple, and they took us in and we were billeted at that hospital. Of course we had all our wounded with us by that time.

The Matron of the hospital, the Canadian Matron, Dr Lyon, Dr Crowe, another nursing sister and a Mrs Curtis, we all slept in one big room, and in the middle of the night there was a terrific crash and the Japanese smashed down all the doors at once and came in. We all had to get up and be examined to make sure that we were all women and no men there, and Dr Lyon, who had rather a revealing nightgown somebody had given her, folded her arms and was promptly slapped and told to put her arms down. However, after a time, the Japanese had thoroughly searched everywhere and they went away and said we were to stay there and that we nursing people and the doctors were to run the hospital until further notice, but we were not allowed to go out of the grounds.

Well then, after a time, when we got sorted out and we worked at the hospital, we all just carried on in our normal way. Every day the Japanese General on a huge horse and beautifully dressed and everything would take a leisurely ride round the grounds, but he didn't interfere with us in any way.

The Salvation Army people had a certain amount of money and we got fairly decent food whilst we were there. The Japanese seemed to treat the local people quite well, not too badly. We had one little girl about nine years old who had been shot in the leg, but it was accidental, the shooting. The Japanese came in, everybody surrendered, so there were no atrocities actually.'

The naval and air power of the Japanese were experienced by Lieutenant John Hickley RN, First Lieutenant of the destroyer HMS *Encounter*:

'The signal came for *Encounter* to raise steam and sail in company with *Jupiter* to Colombo where we were to escort the battleship *Prince of Wales* to Singapore. The *Prince of Wales* had been sent from Britain to the Far East to be joined by the battlecruiser *Repulse*. These two capital ships were thought, at that time, to be adequate to deal with any Japanese advances. So with *Jupiter* being a few minutes senior to my captain, she led us through to Colombo, where we fuelled and then picked up *Prince of Wales* and so on to Singapore. Arriving there on 2 December 1941, all in one piece, we berthed in the naval base – it was an enormous harbour. So things were very much peacetime, you might say, when we arrived there. I can remember so well, the captain when he came back from the first meeting ashore

John Hickley

248

wondering, in no uncertain terms, how we were going to stop the Japanese advance, and the whole atmosphere in Singapore was pretty slap-happy – all the more obvious to us, having come from the highly efficient operational theatre of war in Alexandria to Singapore, where they really did not seem to realise what was happening. So we arrived into Singapore and nothing seemed to be worrying anybody.

However, with the attack on Pearl Harbor early on 7 December, the fat was really in the fire then, and within a very short space of time the Japanese military advanced pretty damn quickly right down the Malay Peninsula. And there was a scare that there was a landing of the Japanese somewhere on the east side of the Gulf of Siam.

And then *Repulse* and *Prince of Wales* sailed to compete against the Japanese invasion forces, which were thought to be there. And the destroyer escort was going to be supplied by HMS *Express* of the same class as *Encounter*, and one of the old Australian V&Ws, *Vampire* I think it was. The *Express* was fitted with a contrivance on the quarter-deck called TSDS, two-speed destroyer sweep. The destroyer streams these two paravanes from each quarter and it is a method of sweeping mines. I had been in *Acheron* as a sub where we were fitted with TSDS. So the captain of *Express*, Cartwright, he knew that I was available because *Encounter* was in dry dock at the time. He got the captain to allow Hickley to go to *Express* to give them an idea how to run this minesweeping gear. So we duly sailed with the two capital ships at fairly high speed and streamed the TSDS gear, and then it worked for a bit and then eventually it parted, the sweep parted. It didn't really affect the price of beer.'

In fact, the news of the Japanese landings in Siam and at Kota Baharu in Malaya had reached Admiral Tom Phillips in *Prince of Wales* at midday on 8 December, and he had sailed with his two capital ships later that afternoon, intending to attack those transports. There was no air cover. When the force was sighted by Japanese planes on the evening of 9 December, Admiral Phillips turned to the south and headed back to Singapore. That night he received a signal from Singapore reporting a landing at Kuantan, which turned out to be erroneous, but which he decided to investigate with the results now described by Lieutenant Hickley:

'And I can remember the landing at the supposed place was a bit of a red herring – there was nothing there at all – and then *Express* was sent close in shore to have a dekko to see if it was a fact. And we went in very close and, of course, there was nothing doing here. Came back and rejoined the capital ships and within a few minutes we looked into the heavens and saw high-level bombers appearing from the south. And indeed they were high-level bombers and they attacked those two ships, which had been dispersed to act independently, and within a very short space of time they had scored direct hits on both of these poor ships, followed then by wave after wave of torpedo-bombers, which were brilliant. Although they lost one or two, they again scored hits, which very soon reduced the speed of these lovely ships and finally they were sitting ducks. I can remember seeing *Repulse* turn over and go down while the *Prince of Wales* was still afloat but with a hell of a list on, and then more or less waiting for the coup de grâce.

Express went alongside *Prince of Wales* – we even got wires out, berthing wires. It was a question of wounded and those who weren't necessary to start abandoning ship. This was going along fairly well, although being alongside and to see people jump from one ship to another, it's horrific – you miss and you fall between the ships. However, another wave of bombers appeared so *Express* slipped everything and went full astern just in time because *Prince of Wales* then suffered the final blow, which turned her upside down, and there was an empty ocean virtually, with sailors swimming for their dear lives. I don't know how many swimmers we picked up, several hundred, I think, and then *Vampire* picked up what was left

HMS Prince of Wales *with the destroyer* Express *alongside, minutes before she sank. (Imperial War Museum)*

there and we hurtled back to Singapore, pretty quick. I think I am right in saying, after the sinking, a Buffalo aeroplane appeared – air cover! Back to Singapore and back to *Encounter*.

So this is the beginning of the most frightful area of the war, when Singapore was just waiting to fall. So at this stage we operated from Batavia, Cam Jong Piak being the name of the port in Java, our job then being to escort any more convoys coming in through the Sunda Straits up to Singapore; we called it Bomb Alley, pretty frightening really. We went to Sabang on the north-west tip of Sumatra on one occasion to pick up some survivors who had come across from Singapore, and we took a lot of them back to Batavia.

We're now coming along to, this is the end of February – Singapore fell on the 15th and the Japanese invasion fleet was coming nearer and nearer and was sighted in the north of the Java Sea. We had at that stage what I call a bastard force known as the ABCD – the American, Australian, British, Dutch, a mixed bag of cruisers, out-of-date destroyers – to compete with the Japanese invasion forces. Of course, we had never exercised at sea at all; we had a Dutch admiral and we were in action at the end of February in what is known as round one of the Battle of the Java Sea, and I think the action opened up at about 20,000 yards, which was pretty far, even for cruisers. To cut a long story short, *Exeter* was hit and went into Surabaya for repairs.

While *Exeter* was being repaired we went back in *Encounter* to refuel and we made a torpedo attack on a Japanese cruiser, but I don't know whether we scored anything or not. Some repairs had been made on *Exeter* – I don't think she had more than three-quarter power – but we escorted her and an old American destroyer, USS *Pope*. Our job was to try and get the hell out of it, through the Sunda Straits to Colombo, and, sure enough, we were met by a force of, I think it was, four cruisers and five destroyers or something of that nature, and we had a ding-dong battle for about an hour until eventually *Exeter* was sunk followed by *Encounter* followed by *Pope*, and that was the end of that. Another empty ocean.

I swam for about a day and was picked up the following morning by a Japanese destroyer. I think there were roughly about 20 sailors in my group. It was advisable to keep together instead of splitting up, the chances of survival being considered better, and I was lucky to be picked up. We were covered in oil fuel, and I think one of the saving graces, you really might say, was the fact that the sea was mercifully warm and there may have been sharks floating around but they did not like to come near the oil fuel. So that's where I was picked up by the Japanese destroyer and so started my three and a half years as a Japanese POW.'

Sydney Scales, having just qualified as a Sergeant Pilot in the RNZAF, arrived in Singapore shortly before the outbreak of war with Japan, and was not too impressed with the local air force organisation:

'We finished up in our blue serge uniforms standing on the wharf sweating like billy-o in the sun until one of us rang up the Air Force Headquarters and let them know we'd arrived. There seemed to be pandemonium because they didn't know we were coming. Anyway, I was duly posted to 205 Squadron, which was a flying-boat squadron in Singapore where my flying-boat training started, and I was given a commission as a pilot officer. I converted on to Singapore 3 flying-boats, and they were tremendous old machines, designed about 1925 I think, huge bi-planes with four Rolls Royce Kestrel engines, two pullers and two pushers. They were pretty old and decrepit, but although they were heavy they were marvellously soft aircraft to fly, very comfortable.

Following a spell on Singapore 3s we went on to Catalinas, which were a much more modern aircraft, and I was sent over to Ceylon because 205 Squadron at that stage was covering the whole Indian Ocean and had lost two aircraft even before the Jap war started. After a spell in Ceylon we took Admiral Sir Tom Phillips to Singapore to join his flagship HMS *Prince of Wales*, and stayed on there, and then the war came. An Australian Hudson had reported sighting the Japanese invasion fleet coming down to Singora in Siam, and then we took off on reconnaissance and to report its movements, etc. We went up, the weather was dreadful, all cloud, we never spotted it, but the aircraft, another Catalina, following us, skippered by a Sergeant Pilot Webb, he must have spotted them because they were shot down and that was the first casualty of the Japanese War; it was actually before the Japs had bombed Pearl Harbor.

Well, from then on we carried on patrols up and down the east coast of Malaya, out to sea in the Gulf of Siam on anti-submarine patrols and general reconnaissance. The *Prince of Wales* and *Repulse* were sunk on 10 December, and on that day three crews from our squadron were sent down to Surabaya in Java to pick up three Dutch Catalinas. At this stage we'd lost Catalinas and we had more crew than Catalinas, the Dutch had more Catalinas than crew, so they donated three or lent three of them to us. On the way down we flew down to Bandaung in a Lodestar, and then from Bandaung we caught a train to Surabaya where we were to pick up the Catalinas. The train was a night journey and while we were on the train the news came through that the *Prince of Wales* and *Repulse* had been sunk. Now the Dutch were very excited about this, and as we were in air force uniform, the train passengers, they picked on us straight away and said it was all the air force's fault that the *Prince of Wales* and *Repulse* had been sunk. Where was the air force when this was happening, what was going to happen to Java left with no defence at all now – we got quite a lot of abuse. Once we got back to Singapore, we were doing patrols up and down the east coast of Malaya and we used to fly over this huge patch of oil where the *Prince of Wales* and *Repulse* had been sunk. It was very disturbing really to fly over that each time and realise that down under that oil were our two capital ships which were going to save Singapore.

All this time the Japanese Army was coming down the peninsula and getting close to Singapore. And then on Christmas Day 1941 we were doing a patrol up the coast, up in the Gulf of Siam, and we ran across a Jap reconnaissance bomber and we had a running fight with this. It had cannon and we only had .303 machine-guns, and it would fly in, fire off its cannon and move out of our range, and then come in from another angle, and eventually it got us in the fuel lines that lead down from the wing into the hull, and we got set on fire. One chap on the bow gun, an Australian who was manning the bow gun, got shot through the wrist and into his chest.

Anyway, we made a forced landing at sea; fortunately it wasn't rough, so we were able to bang down, bounced a bit and the boys put on their Mae Wests and jumped out. The skipper and I were trying to get the dinghy out of the hull, but it had got caught under the catwalk of the Catalina and, while we were trying to tug it out, the whole aircraft blew up and Dickie and I found ourselves in the water. How we got out I don't know, but we were in the water without a dinghy. There were nine of us in the crew and we had six Mae Wests between us, so we floated around in a circle and held on to each other so the Mae Wests supported us. Before that we had got off a signal to say that we were force landing, with our position, and hoped like hell that someone had got hold of that message. It was a very lonely feeling looking out all round the horizon and nothing there, absolutely nothing, and then the fear arose that in these waters we'd be attacked by sharks. So then I swam over to the wreckage floating round where the aircraft had sunk and managed to get hold of a parachute. So we pulled the ripcord and opened it out and let it sink underneath us, so we all sat inside this parachute. This was our idea of keeping the sharks away. I had rather bad burns on the legs and they were bleeding a wee bit, and we were worried about that, that it might bring sharks, but all it brought was a little fish; it was nibbling away at the back of my knee.

Anyhow, the time went on, we sang a squadron song, discussed the chances of one of our flying-boats coming over, and it was starting to get dark. We'd been shot down about half past eight in the morning so we were there floating round all day, but it was warm water actually, which wasn't so bad. But the bright sunshine was getting a bit tiresome because our shoulders, faces, etc, all started to get burnt. Then just almost at last light we heard an aircraft, and one of our aircraft, a Catalina, flew right over us very low, and it flew over and over, and of course we yelled and screamed and beat the water, and then, after it had passed over us and we were thinking, God, they've missed us, it suddenly did a very steep turn and came back over us and they'd spotted us. It was a most marvellous feeling.

Now it circled us and it dropped water tanks wrapped in Mae Wests, and there was a note to say that a destroyer would come and pick us up in about three or four hours time. They also dropped two dinghies in which there were some tins of food, there were some cigarettes, which were marvellous, some morphine, some flame floats and some flares. We retrieved all those, swam over to the dinghies and inflated them and all hopped aboard, and it was a marvellous feeling that somebody had thought of us and that we weren't forgotten in this huge area of water. The morphine was used on Ray Borchers, who had been wounded, and Dickie Atkinson, my skipper and myself, both of us rather badly burned. Night came and we had instructions in the note to send our flares up from about 3 in the morning. With the fourth flare we saw a little light in the distance. We waited, all agog, and put a flame float in the water to guide them in. Then we heard a "thump, thump, thump", obviously a motor, and we were looking for the loom of a destroyer or something like that, but there was nothing we could see and we were a bit worried that it could be a Jap submarine. But it wasn't. It was a Dutch submarine, K12, and they took us on board and gave us coffee – I remember the coffee, beautiful – and gave us first aid for our burns, etc. They'd finished a tour of duty and they'd just sunk two Japanese ships and were off back to Singapore but had been deviated to pick us up. They were very good to us.

We finished up in Alexandra Hospital in Singapore and were there for nearly a month. At night we used to get up out on to the balcony after we could walk and watch the bombing of Singapore. One night a stick of bombs straddled but missed the hospital. Then, with the Japanese advance down the peninsula and into the Dutch East Indies, the Squadron was moved progressively south until it reached and operated from a place called Tjilatjap on the south coast of Java. While this was going on we were evacuated from the hospital by ship to Batavia in Java. Then I was declared fit for flying and was given a job as second pilot in one of three flying-boats posted to our squadron from Gibraltar.

We took off on my first patrol at first light from Tjilatjap. We didn't have charts of the harbour, and taking off we hit a reef which tore a hole in our hull. We were able to get airborne before much water had entered the plane and were told to carry on with our patrol. Anyhow, we stuffed the hole in our hull with palliasses which we carried on board, completed our patrol and were ordered back to Batavia where there was a Dutch Air Force repair depot. Over the Java Sea we sighted a whole lot of survivors. The sea was dead calm, smooth like a mirror, and there were all these characters floating round on bits of wood, Carley floats and so forth, and we flew quite low over them and of course they were thinking we would come down and pick them up, but we couldn't because we had a hole in the bottom. So we got a signal off to Batavia, we dropped water in stainless steel tanks wrapped in Mae Wests, dropped those and we saw them pick them up. We got a signal from Batavia and they said they were sending out relief for them, and by then our fuel was getting low so we then flew back to Batavia. And I heard later that two Dutch Dornier aircraft and a Dutch Catalina had flown out, landed, picked them all up – I think there were about 170 of them – and they taxied all the way back to Batavia, which was a matter of 60 or 70 miles, I think – a marvellous feat.

So we now had the problem of landing with a hole in our bottom. Anyhow, we circled the harbour and selected an alighting area, and at that time the harbour was full of ships busy evacuating Dutch women and children from Java, but fortunately all the ships were lying to a breeze and the tide and they were all lined up, so that it left a channel between the ships for us to land on. We checked on the stuffing in the hole in our aircraft and had two blokes sitting on it, and when we came in to land we were just about to touch down on the water when a little launch shot out between the ships right in our way. So we had to finish up doing what's called a stalled landing, and the shock of this was enough to jerk all the stuffing out of the hole in the hull and the two lads went flying and she started to fill with water.

Well, fortunately I knew where the slipway was and headed for it while she was slowly filling with water, and got her settled on the concrete just in time. Now that was fine, but the flame floats we had stowed aft had started to ignite on immersion in the water, so we had the crew manhandling them out of the blister compartments of the Catalina and we left a trail of these flame floats behind us as we made our way to the slipway. What we forgot was the depth charges under the wings, which we never thought to jettison, and would have gone off had we sunk.

Then the Squadron was evacuated down to North Australia to Broome and Derby – this was the end of February, early March – and we were left with what was left of the squadron to fly our aircraft out once it had been fixed. The upshot was that it was never fixed because the Japs landed in Java and the Dutch had a "scorched earth" policy and they destroyed everything in the harbour, including our aircraft. So we were left with no way out of Java; the squadron had gone, and we were told to go as fast as we could down to Tjilatjap and try and get a boat.

Well, we got down there but we were too late to get any boats. So that left us in Java, and we finished up in a big convoy of trucks at an aerodrome called Tasik Malaja, and the next thing we knew was that a Japanese motorcycle patrol was going round and round the perimeter and we were all POWs. Then we heard that the Dutch had capitulated and handed over all personnel to the control of the Japanese.'

CHAPTER 12

Hitting back by sea and air

With the Battle of Britain and threat of invasion largely over,
Germany's preoccupation on the Eastern Front and America's entry
into the war, the Allies were slowly able to go over to the offensive and,
while planning for the Second Front, mount increasing aerial assaults and
other operations against the enemy.

The concept of RAF Intruder Patrols evolved, and Flying Officer Alan
Gawith, as an early exponent, recounts his experience in this field of
operation:

'In December 1940 our Squadron, No 23, was selected to do Intruder
Patrols. They were called "Intruder" because, the theory was, if we
couldn't intercept them and shoot them down over England, the radar
people could tell us roughly which airfields they were operating from in
France, and we could get there in time to greet them when they got back to
base and, with a bit of luck, shoot the odd one down. In any case, we could
simply drop our 50lb bomb and be a nuisance by being there. The orders
were, you start off and, with complete radio silence, find the base you've
been sent to, stooge around and look out for enemy bombers. It was fun to
do this because you were completely on your own – you were freelancing,
as it were – and if there was no activity at the base you were sent to, you
would try the next one that was suggested. You had the little problem of
trying to find it for a start in the dark without a navigator and not much
assistance, but you'd already memorised roughly where the bases were in
relation to the first one, and it wasn't too difficult to find the first one.

Over time we sort of buzzed all over France looking for a bit of trade, as
we called it, and then, after we'd found that we could do that quite well,
they sent us some navigators from Bomber Command. These poor

blighters, they were quite useful – they worked out the course to the first port of call, but once we started doing a Cook's tour of Northern France, the navigator didn't quite know where he was. Usually, until they got used to it, we'd have to tell them, well, that's so and so, get us a course to base, and they'd work it out from there, but it was nice to have the navigator. They might have been more use in Bomber Command because we had proved to ourselves, anyhow, that we could find these bases simply with the experience we'd had as night-fighter pilots stooging around over England and finding one's way home when the radio had packed up and that sort of thing.

I should perhaps mention that, during these patrols over England, before we started intruding – it was on 10 October, I think, 1940 – that I saw my first enemy aircraft, and this was a Heinkel bomber coming at me nose-on at high speed. He was heading home and I was heading north, and we missed a collision by a whisker. I took a quick shot but it was wasted ammunition, I am sure; but that was the first time, and I'd been patrolling since 3 September 1939 until 10 October 1940 before I actually saw an enemy bomber within range.

From December 1940 to July 1942 I actually took part in 20 operations over France and Belgium, initially in the old Blenheims which we'd got to know pretty well, and later in Bostons. These were aircraft which had been ordered by the French from America and arrived in our squadron with French instruments. Nevertheless we found them delightful to fly and quickly got used to them, and before very long got some English instruments, which made the navigation a little easier.

The Bostons had five forward-facing Brownings, as did the Blenheims, and each aircraft carried, from memory, eight 50lb bombs, which were really just carried for nuisance value. If there was nothing else to do we just dropped the odd bomb on the enemy base, just to keep them awake and annoy them, possibly do some damage, hopefully. There was one occasion when I jettisoned my bombs because I couldn't find anything to play with and accidentally hit the Communications Centre for the German Fighter Group and put them out of action for the rest of that night, and I think that's why they gave me a DFC.

On two or three occasions I did encounter enemy aircraft. One of the difficulties of engaging an enemy aircraft at night is that it is very difficult to judge relative speeds. You open the throttle to try and catch them while you can see them, and the next thing you're overshooting at such a rate that you really only get a short burst in. One didn't get enough practice to adjust one's tactics to suit the night chase, but, on this occasion, we got a shot in at a Heinkel 111, I think it was, very nearly collided with it, managed to climb over the top of it at the last moment and almost immediately we were rapidly closing on a Dornier 215, I think it was, another bomber, and again we had a short sharp burst of fire at that. We could see hits, but again, with evasive action to avoid a collision, and neither I nor my rear gunner nor the navigator could see what had happened, one claimed a damage or two for that encounter.

One operation I can remember very well was when the enemy had been operating from Caen in Normandy near the coast, and two or three of the squadrons had been over there one night and caused a bit of havoc and dropped a few bombs, and I was ordered to go the following night and I wasn't feeling very well – I had a bit of a headache – but I thought, well, I'll try and cut this short. Crossed over the coast and went on down to a light beacon, which seemed to have some connection with the airfield, turned round there and came back to the airfield at about 1,500 feet, and the lights all came on for me – they thought I was coming in to land. I thought, well, this is great, I'll drop my bombs on the barrack buildings where they'd hopefully do most harm and then get out of it, because I just wasn't really feeling fit enough to carry on with a long patrol. As I flew across the airfield to the barrack blocks on the far side I opened my bomb doors, and the first thing, a cone of searchlights came on to me. I was almost in the apex of it and I immediately dived down, well almost down, a searchlight beam, and the next thing, ack-ack guns of all sizes and descriptions opened up in a circle and it seemed like there must have been at least a hundred of them in a circle right round the airfield firing into this cone, but by the grace of God I was diving down on the outside of the cone of fire.

I flew across the barrack blocks and dropped my bombs and then I flew around the field, just around the outside of the perimeter, with this firing going on up into this cone, and I flew right around about three times at not much more than 50 feet above the ground. It was a fairly light sort of a night, and then I reckon I was several miles out to sea headed for home before the firing stopped, and how much ammunition they used that night I wouldn't know, but I'd learned enough from that experience. I was able to tell my squadron mates, never drop your bombs on the way across the aerodrome, drop them as you leave it, because if that cone comes up you haven't got much chance of getting through.

One of the worries on Intruder operations was the enemy ack-ack guns along the coast. We had to cross the coast and usually we went in at about 10,000 feet, but we varied it, and then, of course, those guns were still there when one was coming out. I remember one occasion when I was patrolling down over Paris airfields very late in the night and I realised the daylight was coming up fast, so I scuttled for home in order to cross the coast quickly. I was flying at about 6,000 feet, and then I went over the coast into a dive, and as I was levelling off just above sea level, about over the coast at a very low height, there was a terrific rush of air and something hit me on the left shoulder, and I thought I'd been shot. I hung on and got control of the aircraft, and then started to explore and I came across feathers – I'd bumped into a seagull – and all was well, I was able to get home with the seagull aboard.

On another occasion, and this was flying Blenheims in the winter, we were sent off to patrol over the Netherlands from Manston airfield on the corner of Kent. It was a night when the weather was not good and the old Blenheim went into cloud at about 1,000 feet, and I was climbing in solid cloud till I reckon I was over the coast. There were signs of searchlights and a bit of activity, but I discovered that I'd badly iced up, and the radio wasn't working – in fact, I think the radio mast had been carried away with ice – and one motor was playing up, so I thought this is no place for me, so I turned round and dived back through this still dense cloud, came out over the Channel at about 500 feet, and was stooging along, nursing this sick motor. Next thing a lot of ack-ack came flying up at me and it was the good old British Navy escorting a convoy through the Channel, and I hastily signalled the letter of the day and fired the cartridge with the colour of the day, but the firing didn't stop and I didn't stop either, I kept going. You don't play around with the Navy – you get out of the way, you can't do anything about it.

Then, of course, without a radio and with a sick motor, it was pretty important to find base. Without the radio I couldn't tell them I was coming, and it turned out later that I had been plotted in as an enemy – the Navy had probably done that for me. The score was, if you needed an airfield you circled and signalled the letter of the day, then the local searchlights were supposed to point to the nearest airfield and you happily wandered in. On this occasion the searchlights wouldn't help me either – not a searchlight went up. So I thought, well, no good hanging around here. I couldn't find Manston. I thought, well, if I set off on a course of 330 degrees I would be still over England if the petrol ran out, unless the motor didn't pack up. So we set off on that course at about 2,000 feet, I suppose – no, it was lower than that – at 1,000, 1,500, and the next thing my crew was roaring at me that we were flying through the Southend Balloon Barrage. That wasn't very funny either, because if you are in a balloon barrage you don't know which way to turn, especially at night. So we had to press on regardless and, by the grace of God, we missed the cables, then one or two searchlights attacked us, but that didn't seem to do any harm and I'd got to the stage of tightening up my parachute harness, getting all ready for a bale-out. All of a sudden some red lights lit up just in front, and I whirled away wondering what it was all about, until I thought, by Jove, those look like obstruction lights, the airfield obstruction lights, and I took a closer look and I could see the Glim lamps. From 1,500 feet, almost over the end of the runway, I side-slipped down – I'd never lost height so quickly in such a short space – turned round when I was pretty close to the ground and managed to land on the runway. I managed to stop about 20 yards short of the end of the runway and under the end was a very high bank, about 30 or 40 feet down on to a roadway.

I hadn't had any radio communication or anything, so I turned round and flashed the letter of the day and gave them a broadside view so that they put a searchlight on me from the Control Tower – I presented my credentials as best I could. They gave me a green so I taxied in and this was about 3 o'clock in the morning and wet, mud everywhere, and I thought, well, after what I've been through I don't want to have to wade in through the mud, I'll drive up on to the tarmac. So I drove up on to the tarmac and a big black shape loomed up in front and I stopped and this was an Armadillo – they put an armour-plated thing on the back of a truck, and this was the airport defence. I reached up and opened the sliding hatch over my head to get out of my Blenheim, and something hard came down my neck and I got marched out, and my crew with me, on the point of pistol, were marched into the Control Room and asked to identify myself. I said, well, you know I've just come off operations; I didn't carry any identification but my dog tags. Well, that didn't suit them and I thought, well, how am I going to identify myself?

Obviously I was mistaken for enemy. I'd been reported by the radar and everything as enemy because my identification gear had all frozen up and fallen off, then I had a brainwave. I said, "Well, tell me who is the Group Controller tonight. Let me speak to him – he can identify me." So he spoke to me; he said, "Where the hell have you been?" I told him what had happened. I said, "Well, can you tell these fellows to take their guns off me because I'm tired and I want to go to bed?" So that was cleared up.

What happened was that about three weeks earlier a German plane had landed there – got lost and landed there. The crew walked into the Control Room, realised they were on a British airfield, rushed out to their plane, climbed in and got away. They weren't going to let me get away, though.'

James Walker, ex-Battle of Britain fighter plane air-gunner, thought he would like a change and transferred to Bomber Command:

'I did my conversion course and then was posted to Squadron 115, a Wellington bomber squadron, as a rear gunner. I did my first raid, a seven-hour flight to Wilhelmshaven, and the anti-aircraft fire was most intense; however, we successfully achieved the bombing mission.

The first bombing raid seemed quite easy, not too traumatic or too difficult. We did, from then on, a number of raids over the Ruhr Valley. Here the anti-aircraft fire was even more intense, and I remember thinking that sitting in the rear turret and watching the anti-aircraft fire coming up at us, was rather like watching a glorified Guy Fawkes display. The tracer, everything seemed to be coming up in slow motion, and then the shells were bursting around us in black puffs, some close, some not so close.

The raids as a rear gunner were rather lonely; the rear turret was unheated, and we had to wear, I think it was, three layers of clothing to keep warm. We were given hot drinks and food to take, but had to be careful we didn't scald ourselves drinking our hot coffee because at a high altitude it didn't seem all that hot, but we quickly learnt, when we arrived home, that our tongues were quite a bit damaged.

Also as a rear gunner, one had to be constantly turning the turret this way and that way, and it was rather tiring, and on arrival at our Base Camp at Marham we would be interviewed by intelligence officers on what we had observed on our trip, and this we found a little bit trying, because we were pretty weary at that stage and these intelligence officers didn't seem to be in any hurry. We had breakfast and then we spent time sleeping. Later in the afternoons we generally did an Air Test on our aircraft, in case we had to fly again that night, and on moonlit nights, when the moon was full, we would sometimes fly three consecutive occasions on various raids.

I remember we did raids over the shipping yards, submarine pens, in Kiel – rather long trips they were, too, and they were dangerous trips – and when we were having breakfast we would be wondering who was not coming back. There was scarcely a night went by when we did not have at least one crew missing – one plane did not return and two of the New Zealanders, with whom I was particularly friendly, were missing. One then began to wonder when our own turn would crop up.

At the end of, perhaps, ten bombing raids I began to feel the strain and I had a feeling that our own time was approaching when perhaps we would not return either. The night that we failed to return was on a raid to Cologne. We experienced engine trouble on the way out but we carried on. The engine that was giving trouble really was of concern to the pilot, so he decided that we would jettison our bombs before the target area, so he chose a bridge somewhere in that vicinity and we unloaded our bombs on this bridge – I think it was over the River Rhine – and then we turned for home. At this stage we got caught in a searchlight cone, which didn't involve anti-aircraft fire, so we knew it was a fighter cone that was working in conjunction with the night-fighting squadrons. Violent evasive action was taken, we escaped, but at the same time a fighter appeared and at that time I discovered that we were flying on one engine. The hydraulic system which operated my turret was out of action and I was faced with the fighter right on our tail and, from memory, he unleashed a burst of gunfire which, I think, was off-target. The pilot then took more evasive action, we lost the fighter, but by this time we were losing height and we were down to a couple of thousand feet, flying on one engine, heading for home. Everything seemed quite normal; the Wellington bomber was quite capable of flying on the one engine so we assumed we would make it home.

Now the next thing that I heard was the front gunner, the nose gunner, who incidentally had to be let out of his turret by one of the pilots, and he began screaming, and I, at that time not realising that we were actually crashing, spoke to him asking him what was the trouble. I received no answer, and the next thing I remember was the "graunch" as we hit the ground. I do not actually recall being injured – I only discovered that later. All then was blackness. I seemed to be regaining consciousness and endeavoured then to escape from the aircraft by manually operating the turret door so that I could just escape out of the turret out on to the ground, which I did. As I dropped I felt this searing pain, and my left leg was rather badly injured, and I experienced this shattering pain, and there again I think I passed out.

The next thing I remember was the front gunner, and this was an unbelievable thing that happened with this particular crash. The front gunner, who was a particular friend of mine actually, he had been in his turret, he hadn't been let out, and on impact with the ground the front turret had been knocked off the aircraft with him inside it. The turret rolled around, he eventually got out of it himself completely uninjured, and he dashed around to see how I was in the rear turret; and the pilots also had got out uninjured. The observer, the wireless operator and myself, three out of a crew of six, were injured. The aircraft didn't catch fire – it was broken into two pieces and the two pieces were separated by some 50-odd feet or more. The pilots came in to assist us; they dragged the injured ones away from the aircraft to the edge of a field and I do not remember being in a lot of pain at the time. It was early in the morning – it was pitch black – but the pilot had told us at the time that we had crashed through tall trees, the trees had broken our fall, otherwise I doubt if there would have been any survivors. So they then went back, set fire to the aircraft – the oxygen bottles were exploding like bombs – and the fire was then noticed by a local village and the villagers came out to assist, and we then discovered that we had crashed in Belgium and we were near the small town of Louvain.

The villagers took us in, gave us breakfast, and then they had to inform the Germans because of the injuries, and to this day I do not know what happened to the pilots; whether they just took off and escaped I do not know, and I have never been able to find out what actually happened.

The Germans came out with ambulances and took us into the Louvain hospital and there I was treated for my injuries. My injuries consisted of compound fractures of the left leg, bones protruding through the skin. I was treated by an Austrian doctor who couldn't have treated me any better if I had been his own son. He set my leg. I was placed in traction, in this bed I had this traction, which was pulling the bones out again to a position where the leg could then be put into plaster. I think it took some three weeks to stretch the bones out again, and then I was eventually put into plaster by this same doctor who informed me that he had a little English, and he informed me that he was not a Nazi, so then I was able to realise why he treated me so kindly and so well. The nurses that attended us in this hospital were Belgian convent nurses, and they also treated me with great kindness. They had to watch their step a little because the Germans were keeping an eye on them; however, they managed to smuggle in sweets and cakes and an English book, which I was very grateful for because I was on my back, I was in traction, I had nothing to do, nothing to read.

I was then moved to a hospital in Brussels. In Brussels I was re-examined and my leg was put into plaster again – it hadn't healed up, it hadn't knitted at this stage, and there was really not much sign of the knitting taking place. So then it was decided I would be sent to Germany; I think I spent a month in Brussels, which included Christmas 1941. There, the German nurses were looking after us in a very civilised and kind way. The fact that we were enemies didn't seem to enter into it at all – we were treated just as well as they would have treated their own, I am quite convinced. I remember at Christmas the German sisters and nurses going through the hospital singing carols, and the Belgian people in the town of Brussels were aware that we were in this hospital and they sent in various gifts for us, bottles of wine, chocolates, and the Germans allowed us to receive them so we had quite a reasonable sort of Christmas. I shall never forget the German nurses going through the hospital and then coming down to our own particular ward, and by this time I think there were about a dozen air force people, pilots, navigators, gunners like myself, in this particular ward, and the German nurses didn't only sing to their own people, they came through our own ward and sang these songs and the German song – I think the carol that they sang in our particular ward was "Silent Night" in the German.

While I was in this hospital I obtained a German grammar and I started to learn German, and I was assisted in this by one of the German nurses. So by the time we reached Germany we had a smattering of the German language.

Pressing on, I was then sent to a civilian prison in Antwerp – why I was sent there I have never been able to find out. At the other end of the ward was a group of Jewish prisoners, prisoners who had been working out on working parties and treated very, very badly, and they had been starved, they had been injured with rifle butts, and they were in a very sorry condition indeed; they had been brought into this prison to try and get them back to a state of health whereby they could be of some use to the Germans again in working parties.

How long I spent there I do not recall, maybe a month even, and then I was transferred through to Germany to an Air Force Camp in Frankfurt. This was a set-up really, and it was a sort of interrogation camp. There was this English-speaking Royal Air Force individual who questioned us and asked us where we came from, what squadron we were with and so forth, but we realised that he was a fraud, and I said to him, "Well, I'm sorry I'm not revealing any of that information." He said, "Oh, you don't need to worry here – I've checked and there are no bugs here or anything like that." He gave up after a while and I was then sent into the rest of the camp. Then after a couple of weeks, I think it was, I was moved through to a camp in Germany, which then became my home for some considerable period, but my leg hadn't really improved.'

In August 1942 British Commandos and men from the Canadian 2nd Division carried out a raid at Dieppe in which certain lessons were learned, but at enormous cost. Eighteen per cent of the 5,000 Canadians landed there lost their lives, and almost 2,000 were taken prisoner.

William Bryson, now commissioned as a Sub Lieutenant RNZNVR, recalled his involvement:

'I joined Combined Operations and I went to Troon for another series of courses, and I was given an opportunity to become First Lieutenant on an LCF, or Landing Craft Flak, especially built for beach protection.

We went for trials off the Isle of Wight and we did a lot of ack-ack stuff. Then the Dieppe raid came on stream and we were sent to Newhaven. We were in Newhaven about a week or two and the Canadian Army and Lord Lovat's Commandos were there, and we were to cover the landings on the beach at Dieppe. We went across there and we cruised up and down the beaches laying smoke and firing at aircraft for nine hours. We were badly damaged – our mast and the galley were blown up, blown apart, but very few casualties. Fortunately we carried a doctor and we kept him busy. We were picking men out of the water who were badly injured, and it was a pretty serious state of affairs, to my way of thinking, that we were putting people ashore and then having to cart them all back again. We went back to Newhaven and they wouldn't let us in the harbour, because it was chock-a-block full of ships with casualties on board, so we lay off outside for a couple of days. We had quite a number of casualties on board and one or two dead, but eventually we got them away and went back to Southampton for a refit and repairs.'

By March and April 1943 losses in merchant ships in the Atlantic had reached unsustainable proportions, with numerous U-boat packs well directed and operated, all but overwhelming escorting vessels. Then, in early May, the scene changed dramatically with fewer merchant ships being lost and a marked increase in U-boat losses, with 41 being sunk in that month. This was the time when the effects of a number of measures taken to combat the U-boat menace became apparent. These included improved radar on escort ships, which, with better use of HF/DF (High Frequency/Direction Finder), extended use of long-range aircraft and the introduction of Escort Carriers, resulted in the earlier detection of U-boats. These, together with improved training in attacking skills, better weaponry and the use of independent highly skilled naval support groups brought about a situation in which the 'wolf pack' tactic could no longer operate successfully. Admiral Doenitz then withdrew his U-boats from the North Atlantic area of operations.

Lieutenant Stanley Jervis, RNVR, now in the destroyer HMS *Oribi*, was very much involved in convoy operations in the North Atlantic at that time:

'I was Second Lieutenant in *Oribi* and took part in those battles in the Atlantic in May 1943 when we destroyed or cut to pieces 40 or more U-boats, and this destroyed Doenitz's U-boat threat in the Atlantic. Wolf packs and all that disappeared straight after that. And of course when that happened, we'd lost our bow when we rammed a U-boat, *U 531*. We rammed it just as it got to the surface, cut it in half. Anyway, it broke in half and destroyed or drowned the entire ship's company. That action earned me my DSC.

And then *Obedient*, another destroyer, an "O" Class destroyer, she stayed with us and we managed to get from the tip of Greenland back into St John's, Newfoundland, at 6 knots. And we were only able to steam at 6 knots because when you hit a U-boat with 2,000 tons doing 20 knots or something it packs a bit of power. And what it had done, the collision, it had wrapped our topsides round so they would form a breakhead against the sea and thus reduce the pressure of water coming in, when under way. We had lost the Asdic compartment, and right up to the bulkhead immediately behind that was open to the sea. The water got in there easily enough, but there was no pressure behind it because the pressure was taken off by the overlapping flanges of the topsides. All the rivets were spurting

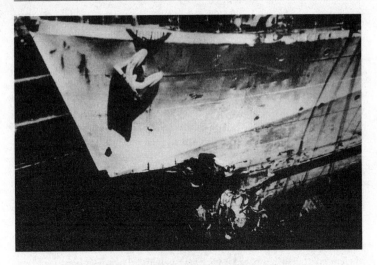

HMS Oribi *in dock after ramming and sinking U-boat 531.*
(Commander S. Jervis)

water, but we got those fixed up and the damage control party shored up that bulkhead with timber planks. Anyway, we got to St John's where they docked us immediately and cut off as much as they could of the old bow and replaced it temporarily and sent us down to the Boston Navy Yard, where we were taken over by two tugs; they pushed us into a cradle and dragged us up out of the water.

The American Navy services were absolutely marvellous. They refitted *Oribi* totally in three weeks. We were out of the water, and they were burning off, by torch, the old bow and it was off in no time. They put a brand new bow on to it – incidentally, they'd got the plans and specifications of *Oribi* from the Admiralty, which were flown over or brought over to the Boston yard so they could get on with our refitting and rebuilding. In three weeks they had repainted every inch of the ship inside as well as outside and gave us anything we liked. Part of my duties was to keep in touch with the American Naval people ashore, or they used to come aboard and ask me what else could they do for us. So they went through the ship and everything we asked for they would do. They replenished the whole of our tool rooms right throughout the ship, they repainted our flat, my cabin, and they did all this in three weeks working 24 hours a day in three shifts.'

Meanwhile, naval activity in the English Channel had continued, and not always to Britain's advantage. Lieutenant Commander Roger Hill, RN

DSO, now in command of the destroyer HMS *Grenville*, around October 1943, found himself working for a while under the Plymouth Command:

'It's difficult not to be critical, but they were mainly reservists from the First World War and a bit out of touch. They would send us along the French coast, opposite Plymouth, looking for a ship from one of the Biscay ports about which they had had a signal from a secret source, and they would send us along to try and intercept it. But, of course, the German destroyers were out too, and they intercepted our radio very much as we did theirs, and we would go along at the wrong speed and the wrong formation.

When Admiral Cunningham was Admiral Destroyers in the Abyssinian business – when I was there in *Electra*, a destroyer – we used endlessly to go out at night and practise catching an enemy cruiser. It was quite simple. You had three pairs of destroyers which acted as reconnaissance and bumpers, and astern of that you had a cruiser, and when the destroyers bumped into the enemy they illuminated it with starshell and the cruiser blew it to bits. Now, if we had had that formation off Plymouth it would have been marvellous, but we didn't. What they did was to send us along in line ahead, a wonderful torpedo target, and the night I am thinking of we went out, we had *Charybdis*, which was a cruiser that had come from the Mediterranean where she had largely been engaged in anti-aircraft work.

We went to the briefing and there were only two other destroyer captains there. One destroyer captain had just taken over his flotilla of "Hunts" and it was his first day in the ship. I asked the captain of the cruiser if I could come back to the ship with him, and went into his cabin and really let my hair down. I said, "It's dangerous, it's the wrong formation, the wrong speed – you should be astern and we illuminate and you bump him off."

"Oh," he said, "I don't really know much about this – I've been anti-aircraft cruiser mainly in the Mediterranean – but we will go and see the Commander in Chief tomorrow."

But that was fine, except that tomorrow the poor chap was dead.

Well, off we went and we went along at 14 knots with the cruiser ahead, me next, the leader of the "Hunts" next and then a whole lot of "Hunt" destroyers and *Roebuck*, another destroyer. I warned the Chief Engineer and I warned the Coxswain on the wheel; I said, "Some time tonight I am going to go hard-a-starboard, full ahead," because I reckoned we could run into a minefield. But when I felt the bumps with my feet, that was the shock waves, they were the torpedoes hitting the *Charybdis*. I went, "Hard-a-starboard, full ahead!" The ship turned very, very fast and we were right in the middle of a torpedo spread, and we had one which missed the bows by about a foot, another missed the stern by about a foot, and then the ship astern of me blew up. So we had the one ahead and the one astern both blown up.

Then I called the ships on the radio and found I was Senior Officer. I didn't mind taking over Senior Officer – someone had to – and I sent the "Hunts" to pick up *Charybdis*'s survivors, but I don't think they allowed enough for the tide, I don't know. I took *Roebuck* and off I went, because I wanted to get at these bloody German destroyers, but was unable to pick up those German ships on radar or visually. I questioned the ships on how many survivors they had on board, and I was really sad to find they had so few, because *Charybdis* had about 800 men on board. They really didn't have very many. Very sad.

A few days later we had a court martial. You always have to have a court martial when a ship is sunk, and they opened the session by looking hard at me and saying, "Now, we are only concerned in this meeting with how *Charybdis* was sunk, whether she was sunk by mine or torpedoes or bombs, and we are not concerned at all with the formation of the squadron or anything else that happened." So I thought, my God, I've been absolutely nobbled, and it didn't take long to decide that *Charybdis* had been sunk by three German torpedoes, and that was it.

On a previous occasion, previous to the cruiser's sinking, I had bumped into, or we, the usual line of destroyers, had bumped into five German destroyers and they had big guns, they had 5-inch guns, and I went off after them and it was absolutely marvellous. I was going to fire torpedoes at last and we had practised it so often, Tony, the torpedo officer, and I. So we went right in at these chaps and they hit us on our aftermast and the shrapnel came down, killed one of the gun's crew, sorry to say, and wounded about 15 others and set the cordite alight – those ready-use cordite in the lockers round the gun – and this made a huge fire aft. A stoker came up to the bridge, and said, "Please, sir, from the Chief Engineer, the ship's on fire."

I said, "Give my compliments to the Chief Engineer and tell him for Christ's sake put the fire out."

He went back to the Chief and said, "They're all barmy on the bridge." Anyway, the Chief succeeded in putting the fire out.

Meanwhile we went on in and Tony and I did what we had always practised before: we set the torpedo sights – he set them, I checked them – we gave the enemy 26 knots and then, in our antediluvian torpedo control, we turned the ship broadside-on to fire the torpedoes. Anyhow, off went the torpedoes, eight of them, and I thought we were in for a marvellous time – we would hit one or two at least and we would go in and board them. Once again I had a party lined up to get the cypher machine, and I just couldn't believe it, because Tony, who had his head in the chart table, was watching the stop watch and he said, "They're passed, I can't believe it."

I said, "No, no, they mustn't have passed."

Years later I was in Cape Town and a friend of mine was having a cocktail party, and he said I would enjoy meeting so and so, he was in destroyers in the Channel, and he introduced me to his friend, and I said, "Which flotilla were you in?" He said, "The 29th," and I said, "There wasn't a 29th," and he said, "Oh yes, there was," and I said, "What class of destroyer was it?" Then I realised he was a German and he had been in the cruiser battle and also this battle. It was really fascinating talking to him. He said that they saw me on fire and they decided to turn towards me to finish me off, and they turned towards me and, of course, by doing that the torpedoes just went on through the lines. They saw the torpedoes go past, and when they saw that they thought we were not so badly damaged as they first thought, so they turned round and went back to France. So, at least I think they, the torpedoes, saved us from being blown out of the water. But, dear, oh dear, I was so sad about that, and I am still sad about it – it was the only time in the war I fired my torpedoes.'

Soon after the Court of Enquiry into the sinking of *Charybdis*, Roger Hill in *Grenville* was sent to the Mediterranean. En route:

'One morning we picked up a clear contact on Asdic with a submarine, which was absolutely marvellous. We depth-charged the submarine for quite some time. The chaps were wonderful with their depth-charge drill – they kept loading and firing – and then we lost contact with her and weren't quite happy she was sunk. About four hours later we found her again, by doing a square search, and had another go at her; we all dropped depth charges on her and, by then, I had plotted the course and speed of the submarine and there was no doubt that he was heading straight for the Biscay submarine ports at about 4 knots under water, so I said, "I must get some sleep," and indicated the exact spot I wanted to be at 6 o'clock that night. So they went on sweeping and I slept and they woke me at quarter to 6.

Half an hour later we picked him up again, because I had his course and speed and knew exactly where he would be. So, then, I think we dropped many, many depth charges on that thing and, of course, I had my boarding party all ready, in the cutter, but he never came up. However, a lot of stuff came up, and it was more than would have been sent up as a ploy, and I reckon we sank him. The next morning we were steering through diesel oil for miles.'

Over Occupied Europe, British then American air activity increased, and John Checketts, RNZAF, was heavily involved:

'The work with the squadron was intriguing also. We used to do aircraft sweeps into France; sometimes as straight fighter sweeps and other times escorting bombers, and a third type of operation was "Rhubarbs", which were done by sections of two aeroplanes at low level in bad weather attacking targets of opportunity. The "Rhubarbs" were very costly to the Royal Air Force really, and were in my opinion a waste of time. Though I flew on quite a number of them, I did not think they achieved much, and to lose an aeroplane and its pilot on such an operation seemed to be an awful waste.

I was shot down into the Channel on 2 May 1942 by a Focke-Wulf 190, and rescued by a Naval launch. We had been intercepted by a number of German fighters and I was watching one that was trying to come round and attack me, and I was shot down by another one, which I didn't see. I can't really describe it adequately, but it was an almighty bang and I was spinning down with part of the starboard wing blown away. I could not make it back to England and had to bale out. I got out at very low level and was in the water for a little over an hour. It was very cold and the Navy rum was an excellent antidote.

Biggin Hill was always looked upon as being a great Fighter Station, and it was. Later we flew the Spitfire IX aircraft, which had a superior performance and could meet the German aircraft on equal terms. The period of escorts and fighting became very hectic and we were doing sometimes three and four sorties a day. The period was so intensely active that we seemed to be flying all the time. We were very successful, too, and during this period the Wing destroyed the 1,000th enemy aircraft shot down by the Biggin Hill Sector. The celebration festivities were fantastic and culminated in a fine ball in a big London hotel attended by 1,000 guests – it bankrupted the Mess.

I was then promoted to command the New Zealand Squadron 485 at Biggin Hill, and we became a very successful unit, and for three months were the highest-scoring squadron in Fighter Command. We lost six pilots during this period and destroyed 18 enemy aircraft. Of the six pilots who were shot down, three survived. Unfortunately I was one of the ones who was shot down after a battle with German aircraft, and I baled out at 10,000 feet, burned and wounded, and I was nursed by French people and fed into an escape line. I came home in a fishing-boat with 12 other aircrew.

I must go back a wee bit because, on 6 September 1943, when I was shot down, we were at that time busy escorting bombers to bomb some coastal targets, which eventually turned out to be the V1 flying bomb sites. The aerial fighting was intense and German aircraft responded to our sorties in some strength. It was strange, therefore, on one occasion in August, when I was in company with the French Squadron escorting Americans to bomb a target near Douai, when we intercepted a flight of eight Messerschmitts and shot six of them down; it was sudden and quick but it was hard to believe that we had been so successful.'

The German battleship *Tirpitz* remained a threat to convoys taking supplies to Russia until September 1943, when she was badly damaged by midget submarines. She remained in Altenfjord in Norway undergoing repairs. A further attack on the *Tirpitz* was being planned, and Lieutenant John Musters, now in the aircraft carrier HMS *Victorious*, took part in this operation:

'After a tour ashore in the Orkneys, I was appointed to *Victorious*, which was a fairly new Fleet Aircraft Carrier, sister ship to *Illustrious*, and I joined her in Liverpool where she had been having a refit, and her new Air Group was training at a Scottish Air Station. We went out into the Irish Sea for working up with them and finally got away to the Fleet Base at Scapa in the Orkneys, and then began some intensive working up for a planned operation against *Tirpitz* at her base in Northern Norway. The intention was to dive-bomb her out of existence, or at least put her out of action. The aircraft which we had to do the job were two squadrons, each of 12 Barracuda torpedo dive-bombers, and we also had two squadrons, each of 14, a total of 28 American F4U Corsair fighters, which were better than any Naval fighter which we could produce ourselves at that time.

We had some intensive work-up and then, in early April 1944, we set sail with *Furious* and, I think, about four escort carriers, which were converted merchant ships carrying a small number of aircraft, and a fast battleship escort plus destroyers and cruisers for northern Norway, in order to carry out this dive-bombing attack on *Tirpitz*. The Barracudas were armed either with 1,600lb armour-piercing bombs, which were intended, if dropped from sufficient height, to get through the *Tirpitz*'s horizontal armour, or a larger number of 500lb bombs, which were intended to mess up the upper deck, knock out the anti-aircraft guns, start fires and generally make a mess. On 9 April we arrived, in perfect weather, from our striking position, which was about 120 miles from the target, which was in Altenfjord, and the first strike from *Victorious* and *Furious* went in and also fighters from the escort carriers provided fighter escort. An hour later, when the first strike had done its stuff and was on its way back, the second strike started off to do exactly the same thing. The second strike didn't have it quite so easy, of course – by that time the Germans had got the idea and they ignited smoke canisters, which prevented the pilots seeing what they were aiming at, except, occasionally, a bit of mast. Some of them did take some interesting photographs of *Tirpitz* under attack, and one of them showed large waves radiating out from the ship's stern, which in the flat calm waters of the fjord could only mean that the whole ship was whipping under the impact of the bombs. It was a fairly dramatic photograph.

We didn't, in fact, sink *Tirpitz*, but they got 14 hits on her and the ship was a shambles, unfit for operations. It took the RAF, some considerable time later, dropping 12,000lb bombs close alongside, to actually blow the ship's bottom in and cause her to roll over. This was in November 1944 when she had been moved to Trondheim.'

Flight Lieutenant George Jenkinson completed his time as a Flying Instructor in South Africa and was posted to Britain, where he was to take part in the intensive bombing of targets in Occupied Europe:

'I was sent to a Pathfinder Squadron where I did my training on the Pathfinder technique and then on to operations, and this was wonderful. When I think back on operations, the first thing that comes to my mind is the Mosquito aircraft and what a wonderful aircraft that was, and those two Merlin engines. My first op – bags of excitement and adrenaline thumping good and truly – was to some target in Germany, and there was quite heavy flak over the target and we were hit a few times by the shrapnel from the flak, but the amazing thing is one could smell the darn stuff.

The worst ones were when the weather was too bad for the heavies to fly; we did trips over Europe to keep the Germans occupied, and we'd either take a load of bombs along or what was called a "cookie" – this was a 4000lb bomb which had no safety device on it, and they had to enlarge the bomb-bay a bit and make it look like a pregnant aircraft to carry the thing. The idea of these trips was just to keep the Germans occupied, so we'd fly over three or four targets before bombing the fourth one, and this was hairy because we were the only aircraft in the sky, and all the ack-ack batteries concentrated on us, and they pumped up a packet of trouble for us. Of course we never flew below 28,000 – it was always 28,000 foot or above – and with Pathfinder technique we had to fly on a fixed course, fixed height, fixed air speed, and we did this for 10 minutes then we'd switch on our control instrument, which would send a signal to the UK which was picked up by the Base Stations. There were two stations. One converted into the distance, and sent us back a sound, either a dot or a dash, and we'd have to keep in the middle of this, and it was a very narrow middle and it took a packet of concentration. The other station was measuring our progress down, knowing our air speed, and so it automatically compensated and worked out the wind speed and direction and gave us the signal to drop our markers at the right time. It's amazing how accurate these markers were.

We would drop markers to give the heavies a flare to line up on. We had

George Richard Jenkinson

to be there dead on time otherwise we were before our Chief, who was Air Vice-Marshal T. C. D. Bennett, an amazing character, one of the earliest real experimental pilots. We had all sorts of techniques again, where we'd set our legs going along with half a minute to spare on each little leg, so that if we were behind schedule we'd at least have half a minute on each leg to catch up. If we were ahead of schedule we knew how to lose half a minute with turns to right or left, so we could usually switch on dead on time. We had to be as accurate as anything.

The other thing was, if there was cloud over target we would drop our markers with the set diverted at the height above the clouds and so, if the aircraft came in from the right direction and they aimed at these markers burning above the cloud, they were pretty accurate in finding the target.

After we'd dropped our markers we had to do a photographic run, which was most probably about 30 seconds or a minute run, still on this fixed height and air speed, and then once a photograph had been taken we would dive off and go like fun, weaving and waving in case there were any fighters around. We usually didn't have much to worry about fighters because we could outpace them – we were faster than the fighters at that height – but the flak was the thing to look out for. In places, Berlin for instance, when you got to Berlin, when you were about 60 miles from Berlin, the floodlights came on and the whole sky was lit up and they'd pin you easily. The floodlight was controlled on you by radar and you couldn't weave away from it or anything. In any case, we had to fly too accurately to do any weaving; we just had to sit there and go on with our accurate flying. A little bit scary when you felt so exposed with all these searchlights, and then, when you'd finished your run and turned off to go home, searchlights followed you and, of course, the flak followed you as well. So it was quite exciting, especially as we were getting near the limit of our duration petrol-wise, and so we couldn't mess around at all.

On one of these trips my escape hatch blew off – I don't know why, when or how. I don't think it was enemy action or anything that blew it off, but this is at 28,000 foot and all of a sudden there was a loud noise, a hissing noise and what have you. My navigator's material all flew out, and for a moment we didn't know what it was, and then my navigator pointed to the hatch missing and it was freezing cold, it really was freezing – 28,000 foot with air coming in through your escape hatch. So we set off for home; my navigator had nothing to navigate with, so we had to call up for bearings to fly, and you know when you're desperately cold like that you become quite euphoric after a while, and I obviously spoke quite a bit of nonsense to the air controller who was giving us the bearings to fly back home because they handed me over to my Home Station when we were close enough. The girls told me afterwards, they said, you know when they handed you over, they said we don't know what your pilot's been drinking, but certainly he's drunk.

As far as specific raids were concerned, there were quite a few. Berchtesgaden was one, and this was a long, long way off, and we had to fly very, very high for that, and Hamburg was another one where, as I recall, we absolutely plastered the place and it burnt down with such fury that everything was sucked into the place and it was an horrific raid. When the weather was too bad for the heavies to go, we'd do our various milk runs, and some of those were the submarine pens on the coast of France and what have you. All very exciting to do them, but, my gosh, the amount of flak we got on these solo raids was quite terrible, and of course doing those sort of raids, again we'd go over a few targets to get the air raid sirens going on those targets and get everybody up and flapping, and then, about the third or fourth target, we'd drop our bombs then.

On one occasion a bit of flak got me in the knee and we really were hit all over the show that night. It didn't worry me much, and when we got back the idea was to keep quiet about it, because if you had to go to the sick bay and have a bit of flak taken out and what have you, you'd be put off ops for the time being, and that's the last thing I wanted. So I kept quiet about it and eventually the bit of flak came out with a little bit of secondary inflammation there – it came out, but it weakened my leg because I limped for a bit, and the muscles became weaker, and it has caused me trouble ever since.'

CHAPTER 13

The second front:
D-Day and beyond

> 'And gentlemen in England, now a-bed
> Shall think themselves accursed they were not here,
> And hold their manhoods cheap whiles any speaks
> That fought with us upon Saint Crispin's day.'
> Henry V, William Shakespeare

6 June 1944 – a momentous day in history. A vast armada of ships of all shapes and sizes lay off the beaches of Normandy, while overhead the air was filled with aircraft, bombers, fighters, gliders. The Second Front, 'Operation Overlord', had commenced.

As all the paraphernalia and men necessary to undertake the greatest invasion of all time were gathered together in Britain, it was remarkable that the enemy remained quite unaware of the time and place of the landing. This, together with the thoroughness and detail of the planning, Allied superiority in the air and the virtual isolation of Normandy by prior bombing, coupled with the procrastination of the German High Command and Hitler's interference, did much to ensure the success of the invasion.

At dawn on 6 June 1944, after a postponement of 24 hours due to inclement weather, the great armada arrived off the beaches of Normandy. Parachutists and glider-borne troops had been arriving during the night and a tremendous bombardment by sea and air preceded the disembarkation of the Allied troops. They landed on beaches designated 'Utah', 'Gold', 'Juno', 'Sword' and 'Omaha', where, it has to be recognised, the effects of rough seas, mines, booby traps and enemy fire took their toll, especially on 'Omaha'.

Nevertheless, by the end of the day all the beachheads were in Allied hands. Over the next few days they were expanded, joined and secured, and some towns, including Bayeux, were taken, although the advance inland

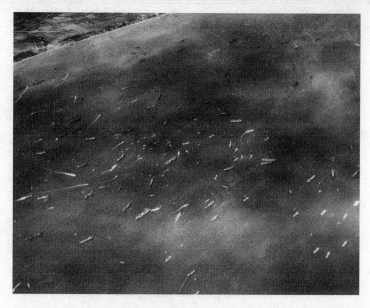

Normandy, June 1944. (Imperial War Museum)

was less than had been planned. By 12 June 'Mulberry', the artificial harbour at Arromanches, had come into use and, together with the capture of Cherbourg on 27 June, this assured the continued build-up of men, material and supplies.

And then, after heavy fighting, Caen was taken on 10 July and this was followed by the American break-out at Avranches on 31 July, the landings in Southern France on 15 August, the German defeat at the Falaise Gap on 21 August and the entry into Paris on 25 August. The stage was then set for the further advance across France into the Low Countries and Germany itself.

There were many sides to the preparation for success on D-Day and then for achievement on the day itself. Effective training in the techniques of towing gliders and dropping parachutists was essential, as explained by Warrant Officer Albert Friend, now back from Burma:

'We then started training, towing gliders, dropping paratroops. Towing a glider was far more difficult than I imagined because a glider pilot, if he is on the inside of a turn, prevents you turning because it pulls your tail to try and straighten you up when you are trying to turn. A good glider pilot would swing out and help you around in the turn; also, a bad glider pilot would go into a low tow position, too low, and pull your tail down, and you were absolutely frantic to keep your speed up and put on extra power. And so a lot of practice and experience was essential, and the glider pilot had a lot of control over the tow, far more control than we in the towing aircraft happened to have. You were supposed to have an intercom between the glider and the tow, but it very rarely worked. Sometimes we could hear them, sometimes they could hear us, but very rarely did we have a two-way communication.

In the Oxford area nearly all the aerodromes were recently built, and there were a number of them, some very close together, so there was always some danger of collisions. The towing aircraft comprised six squadrons of Dakotas in our group, 46 Group operating from Broadwell, and in 47 Group there were Halifaxes, Stirlings and Albemarles. The Horsa was the glider we were mainly concerned with, and it was about the same size as a Dakota, but it was all wood and the brakes and flaps were operated by an air bottle, so that once the air bottle was used you had no brakes and no flaps, but it was always adequate to stop the glider. The Horsa also had nose-wheel steering, so you could steer the Horsa away from trouble. They were made of wood and, at that time, were being built by furniture factories over the country.

At this stage Flight Sergeant Perry, our pilot, was promoted to Pilot Officer, and both Gilly and I were promoted to Warrant Officers. We were then confined to camp together with the paratroopers who were brought in and put under canvas. We joined 512 Squadron in February, and this was the end of May, beginning of June, 1944. Bill Perry and I had already been into the Operations Office and looked through low-level and high-level photographs of the French Coast, and we thought that the best place to land was on the Normandy coast between Le Havre and Cherbourg.

Most of the German forces were in the Pas de Calais area, and their fighter squadrons were in those areas. The bomber squadrons were mainly in Normandy, which we'd been bombing. The Stukas had been withdrawn to Russia, so there were no Stukas. They were pulling back further and further because of our bombing of their aerodromes, which meant they wouldn't be able to spend so much time over the dropping zone and the beachhead.'

Roger Hill was commanding the destroyer HMS *Jervis*:

'Everybody was delighted to get back to Portsmouth, and we went into dock to have the lining of the guns changed because she had been in the Mediterranean all the war and had just shot all her gun linings away. Then we went out to sea and fired the guns and everything was all right and then we waited. It must have been early May 1944, and eventually a chap came on board with a big bag, a big sack of orders, and these were the books for the invasion, and then another chap came on board with another sackful, these were the corrections for the originals – I couldn't believe it. I sent for all the officers, a bottle of gin and a bottle of whisky and some sandwiches, and I said, "Now, we stay here until we've corrected these books," and I passed round all the books for correction and we just ploughed through them, all sorts of things that didn't really matter to us, but this regiment had been changed and that and so on, and we had the whole of the plan of the invasion in front of us. Actually, Portsmouth was sealed off and nobody was allowed to go anywhere.

We all went to a cinema to be briefed on the invasion, and there were all captains and senior officers there, and they had all the charts up and everything, and the First Lieutenants were also going to this meeting, and they thought they had got the wrong cinema because they couldn't get in – all the doors were locked. They found some subterranean way in and they suddenly all appeared from the orchestra pit.

Portsmouth was a most amazing sight – there were hundreds of ships there. Landing craft – every type of landing craft you could find – and all the soldiers started to go on board, and then 5 June, which, of course, was the original date for the invasion. It blew like hell, the sea was a mass of white troughs, very stormy, and we got the signal that the invasion was postponed for 24 hours, and a lot of the ships from the other side of England had already started sailing. If they had put it off for another day it would have meant that there were two or three weeks before everything was right again, moon and tide and so on, and the secret must have come out by then. Anyhow, the next day Eisenhower made the signal to go; they reckoned there was a slight gap in the weather and off we went. All that day the ships had been going by, and we went up and joined them fairly late and we were going fairly fast and passing them on the outside, and we finished up at the head by the time we got to France. It was an amazing sight, all these hundreds of ships.'

Robert William Green, Corporal Electrician, Royal Artillery, was also preparing for the great assault:

'We were moved to Hampshire and the Isle of Wight where we set to with training for assault landing, putting the field guns on landing craft, and going out to sea and coming back, loading, marching up the beach and so on. This went on for quite some long time, gradually evolving better techniques. From there we were sent up to Scotland near Inverness to carry

Robert William Green

on with the training, and it was done in very harsh and unpleasant conditions, and our morale was rather low.

At the beginning of 1944 we were all assembled along with various others, battalions and artillery regiments, in Fort George at Inverness, and all lined up in great military order, three ranks and so on all round the square, and we stood there in sleet and snow for the best part of two hours waiting for Montgomery to arrive. When he arrived he stopped here and there and chatted with the odd soldier, and then, when he'd gone round the four sides of the square, he then went in the middle of the square on a jeep and stood on the bonnet or wherever and said, "Come round here, I want to have a talk with you lads," and the effect was electric. He made no bones about it – he knew what it was like to be a soldier, but he valued lives, he valued his own life, he valued our lives, and when we went into an assault he'd be leading us and he wouldn't lead us into an assault unless he was going to win – he was going to win with the least possible loss of life and injury. To cut a long story short, morale rocketed up, and the whole, you might say, atmosphere in the regiment was as different as chalk and cheese.

Our next move was to be smuggled through the back streets of Portsmouth on to LCTs [Landing Craft Tanks] in Portsmouth Harbour, but it was done in a very unspectacular manner, and there were no crowds, nobody to wave to or anything; it was about, I think, D-Day minus 4. We put the guns, the self-propelled 105mm guns, on the landing craft, four to each landing craft, and two armoured vehicles with them, and then virtually all the regiment was taken back to the camp in Hampshire, and I was one of those left on board. I had to go round all the tanks and guns and vehicles to ensure that all the radios were fully operative and everything was right for the communication side, being the electrician, of course. I was by then a Corporal Electrician.'

Lieutenant William Bryson, RNZNVR, received his first command in time for some training in readiness for D-Day:

'My next appointment was to go to Bristol. They were building LCT 7096 Mark 3 Star, and I was to stand by while it was being built, and that was for the D-Day operation, no doubt. A week later they commissioned it and I signed for it and the girl from the office cracked a bottle of wine over its bow, and so she was launched. Then we went to Portsmouth, did a lot of training around the Isle of Wight, loading up and unloading, and eventually we went to the River Orwell up at Ipswich, and that was our D-Day establishment up there. We were locked in there just prior to D-Day, and no leave. We were told by a senior officer that he was expecting at least 50 per cent casualties in our crowd.'

Wing Commander John Checketts was now in command of a Wing comprising a Canadian, Polish and RAF Squadron at an advanced landing ground at Horne near Gatwick:

'It was interesting working from the area because we were accommodated under canvas and did the normal flying and escorting bombers and fighter sweeps from there. It was quite obvious that the invasion was not far away, and we did a lot of interdiction work against bridges, German traffic and escorting bombers to isolate the area. We had no idea where the landing would take place, but all the paraphernalia for the invasion was being assembled at Selsey Bill; huge concrete caissons and material for landing on a foreign shore were towed there, ready to be despatched over to France. It was an exciting period and we were very busy. Strangely, we did not encounter much opposition from the Luftwaffe, but I think this may have been in part brought about because of the long-range fighter escorts used by the United States Air Force into Germany, which caused the Luftwaffe to be dispersed back into the home territory, at the expense actually of covering France. There were German fighters there, but not in the numbers there had been previously, and those we did strike did not seem to be so aggressive as the earlier models.

We flew Spitfire VBs and missed flying the Spitfire IX aircraft, which were comparable to the German types, and found that we did not have the performance we would have liked in escorting bombers at altitudes in excess of 10,000 feet. However, the Spitfire IX Wings from the Second Tactical Air Force were always flying above us. We did not see any German aircraft of consequence during this period. It was an exciting period, really, and the build-up to the invasion unfolded before our eyes. It was tremendously exciting to be called to the briefing by the Air Marshals for the invasion on that morning in June.'

A vignette of medical preparations for D-Day is provided by Captain Leo Hannah, RAMC, back from the Western Desert:

'I returned to England on the strength of a General Hospital and we were sent down to Malmesbury in Wiltshire, and were billeted in a big country house, and went into training for the attack on Europe, D-Day. Some of us were detached to be Medical Officers on Tank Landing Ships, as it was thought that casualties would be very heavy and the Hospital Ships would not be able to cope with them, and some would have to be brought back by Tank Landing Ships, which were heavily supplied with stretchers and medical equipment. There were three Medical Officers on each Tank Landing Ship. These were American ships and were real ships, not just open craft, and were very useful. We went down to the Isle of Wight to become familiarised with these ships and practised getting casualties on and off them under varying circumstances.'

Corporal Charles Teague, Ulster Rifles, was also being prepared for 'the Day':

'We did our invasion training up in Scotland mainly at Inverary on Loch Fyne, and we used to go out on boats and practise climbing up the rope ladders on to the boats, running up mountains and so on. We came down from Scotland to assemble for the invasion and we went to camps on

Charles James Teague

Ashdown Common, within easy distance of London docks. Eisenhower came and reviewed us down there, and he walked round with Montgomery, who, at one time, was my Brigade Commander. We were just waiting; all the vehicles all lined up, waiting our turn to go.'

Then the hour came: D-Day and its aftermath. Warrant Officer Albert Friend, RAF:

'We took off on the 5th, late in the evening, and we took the first wave in; they were paratroopers, we had 18 paratroopers. They were Royal Engineers and they were to blow up the guns at Merville. One of their members had a Bren gun, which was folded into his kitbag, and they all had kitbags with weapons and explosives, and these were attached to one of their legs by a long lanyard, so that the kitbag landed first and it relieved the weight on the parachute, so that slowed their descent. We had a container of anti-personnel bombs, so we dropped that on the coast to simulate a bombing raid. Towards Le Havre – we could see Le Havre – and by Le Touquet, just over the coast near Le Touquet, an aircraft crashed and there was a big fire and I thought it was probably one of the Germans. Anyhow, we had no idea who it was and we had 23 seconds to run from the coast to the dropping zone, and we were flying 115 knots, and to descend we had 15 degrees flap on and we were descending at about 100 feet a minute and, at the end of the 23 seconds, the green light came on. Out went the First Lieutenant followed by 14 more, but the 15th member dropped his kitbag and the Bren gun was too wide to go through the door – he'd dropped his kitbag inside the aircraft. He tripped over and went head first and out through the door, and of course he was dangling by his legs because the kitbag was jammed in the door. The only thing I could do was to lever up the gun so that I could let it out of the door, which took a few seconds to do. So number 16 went out after him and number 17, and then the red light came on, so number 18 held back; the red light was on and I pushed him back and reported that I had a hang-up to Bill, and said we had one more paratrooper to go because the red light came on before I could get him out. He was a sergeant bringing up the rear.

I then had to pull in all these static lines and Bill was going in a circle to the east, a routine circle to the east over the German lines, and I was too busy to notice what was going on below – I was trying to pull in these static lines, and the slipstream was trying to pull them out, and I was trying to pull them in. I couldn't get a grip on the shining aluminium floor – I was sliding backwards and forwards – so the paratrooper took his 'chute off and his pack off and helped me with pulling them in. We pulled in the static lines and put them out of the way and I said, "You're not ready." I was horrified – he had his 'chute and his pack off and he started to put them on when the green light came on. He didn't jump because Bill considered it was too dicey getting back in the stream between other aircraft, and so we turned and flew back home.

We had to stand by for a supply operation that evening and our aircraft had rollers fitted in while it was on the ground, so that we could push out the supplies. We were supplied with four Army Service Corps men who would push out the supplies, and I thought that was a waste of manpower because there was no problem pushing out the supplies when they're on rollers – I could have done that myself, on my own. They were elderly men and I asked them if they had any parachute training, and they said no, so I told them how to use a parachute.

Then we were away and were on a descent, and we were just approaching the coast when flak came up. Flak came up from below, a heck of a lot of it in jets, and Bill must have thought it was Germans, so he turned to starboard, which took us over the British ships – there were only about 1,000 ships and I reckon at least a hundred of them were firing their 20mm guns straight up at us, and it was all tracer, it was like flying through a forest of tracer.

Bill kept descending and put the green light on so as all the supplies went out over the dropping zone. We also had ammunition in containers, which the First Officer was supposed to drop. He thought he'd dropped them, but we had a hang-up. We didn't know we had a hang-up because the bomb rack was underneath and there was no way we could see that we had a hang-up, and it was a load of grenades which hadn't dropped. Anyhow, Bill couldn't avoid all the flak – he was standing the aircraft on wing tip – and all the time Gilly was plotting our position very calmly, and flak was going up everywhere.

I went back into the cabin to look aft, and the aircraft was lit up by the amount of tracer. A shell came up by my left foot and departed over my head, and I could see the starlight through the hole. We'd been hit several times, but we didn't know how many times; most of the shells had gone through the starboard wing. These were British shells, they were all 20mm because we were over Sword Beach practically, and Bill and Gilly were saying, "Turn on to 010," and Bill said, "I can't turn on to 010 – the gyro's toppled, the magnetic compass is spinning" – he was flying through a forest of tracer. So Gilly said, "Turn right," so he turned right just as we were hit again, and we flew north out of all this flak. We were lucky – seven aircraft were shot down, but not us, although we had a badly damaged wing which we couldn't see because it was dark.

We flew back to Broadwell and I thought, well, I wonder if the undercarriage has been hit or whether a tyre has burst, so I braced myself for the landing, but it was a good landing and no problem. We had to have the wing changed because it was so badly damaged – how it stayed in one piece is beyond me. Luckily the shells hadn't touched the controls to the flaps or to the aileron, but the shells had damaged at least two of the spars that kept the wing stiff. So we were unable to fly it for ten days.'

Lieutenant Commander Roger Hill observed the bombing from his naval perspective:

'For the whole of that day and night, Bomber Command came over and bombed all the beaches, and I think they were so scared of hitting the ships there that they went too far inland and I think they actually missed the defences on the beaches, and then, in the morning, hundreds and hundreds of American B24s came over and they bombed, and then there was a period of about 15 minutes when nothing happened, and then the cruisers and *Warspite* and *Rodney* opened fire and we opened fire. They had taken aerial photographs of the whole coast and, of course, they had to take them of everywhere else as well so as not to give away where the landings were to be, and we had these pictures of where we were to bombard, and we had a group of 88mm guns which we were to knock out. As we came in to the coast we saw them, opened fire, hit them straight away and knocked the things out, and then we had a sort of general bombardment. I didn't fire quite as fast as I could have, as I remembered the tanks coming down at Salerno and the destroyers going in and taking them on, and I thought this might happen, so I wanted to preserve as much ammunition as I could. Anyhow, we bombarded steadily and then the assault went in and all these landing craft went in – wonderful to see them.

The extraordinary thing was that even at this time the artificial harbours started to arrive and these little tugs, each towing two bits of harbour, they had these huge great concrete pontoons and these were to make a breakwater, and they started to arrive and be put in place, although, in fact, we were still getting a certain amount of shellfire from the shore. Talking of that, we really didn't notice it, but we had one really big shell which arrived about every 2 minutes, and I overheard one sailor say "Fucking cheek!" It never changed – it always landed in the same place, as though they were firing it without looking at us to make any corrections. There was quite a lot of small stuff around, but we didn't take much notice of that. Anyhow, the landing craft were landing on the beach and I was watching them through binoculars, when suddenly I saw one of them catch on fire – a shell burst among them – so I trained my binoculars along the edge of the shore and came to a hill, and on the side of the hill I saw flashes. I said to Gerluykens, who was called "Glop", our gunnery officer, a Belgian – wonderful chap – I said, "Quick, Glop, you've got to knock these out," so we went. We couldn't take the minesweeper – had to take a chance on it – and so we went along the coast until we were almost looking straight at these guns as they were firing and we opened fire. They were in a very clever place – they had grass over the top, so couldn't be seen in aerial photographs, and they had been unspotted until then. A few days later, when one of my officers went ashore and went up there, he found there were 35 holes in the concrete front of the guns and the ground all round was all churned up with our shell fire.

Then we had a chap called a Bombardment Liaison Officer aboard the ship, and there was another BLO ashore who kept in touch with the ship, and he would call for fire, and all the charts we had, charts of the sea and the shore, were all gridded, so they might say "014272" and then we would put it on the chart and we would open fire. We would only fire one gun just to get the right range, and when they said "KKK", which meant the range was right, we would fire a second gun, and we had some very, very nice shoots, and when the Army was held up at strong points we would fire and they would break through and so on.

The best one we had was a few days later. We got the order to fire on a church tower from which the Germans were observing, so we carefully laid the whole thing out and we fired one gun and the answer came back, "KKK". We had hit it straight off, and then we fired all six for about 2 minutes, and then they came back with "Tower's destroyed". Another one we had was a call for fire just past our extreme range, and we had been responding to their calls for fire after about 20 to 60 seconds or something, and they came up with "Why haven't you fired?" I said, "It's not deep enough – I can't get the ship near enough." Eventually I had about 6 inches of water under the ship, and when we fired the gun the ship sort of went down and hit the bottom; anyhow, we were able to fire the two forward guns.

It was a fairly harassing time because at night the German E-boats attacked, and there was this chap Peter Scott, he was tracking E-boats from a radar ship, which came out at night, and directing Motor Torpedo Boats [MTBs] on to them. It was very, very interesting to see E-boats coming in, and we would let them pass and then they – the MTBs – would attack them on the way back, and if any got through, we destroyers would have a go, and this happened to us several times.

We used to do about 12 days on the French side, and then go home for about two days and fill up with ammunition. A barge would come alongside with all the ammunition for our ship and water and oil and food. We had one delightful day when we were ordered to look after a crowd of minesweepers which were going out to sweep mines off Le Havre, where they had some big coastal guns on the top of the cliff, and they started firing at us, and a Canadian destroyer, who was the senior officer, signalled "Gunfire" and I replied "Yes – in a major war, too"! The wind was just right so we made smoke and covered the minesweepers, and so I told them to keep moving fast and changing course and speed, and as long as the Germans kept firing at us they would be all right. I suddenly realised that the minesweepers were on a steady course and they started shooting at them, and the outcome was that the minesweepers said, "We think we will go home now," so I said "Fine" and then we tore up and down and our shells were hitting the cliffs, bursting just below the guns, and then we turned to go back. The minesweeper chaps said, "You shouldn't have done that – there are a lot of mines about there – you may have touched one off.'"

In command of Landing Craft Tank 7096 was Lieutenant William Bryson:

'Force L we were. We were taking the Seventh Armoured Division to Normandy, H hours plus 12, and we were carrying high octane petrol. We went over there and, by the time we got there, all the big stuff had stopped and it was an anti-climax that I'd never thought possible. We hit the beach; the idea was you lower an anchor a certain distance out, from a big winch, and as you hit the beach you lower the ramp, you lift the mortlocks – mortlocks are an extension to the ramp – and they gave a better angle for craft leaving. We got rid of our Seventh Armoured Division, and coming off the beach we must have hit a mine or something, a little bit of a bang aft and the A bracket on the prop was useless.'

Patrolling over the beaches as the landings took place was Wing Commander John Checketts, RNZAF:

'I flew out before daylight with 130 Squadron to cover the first part of our patrol over the beachhead, and was astonished to see the size of the fleet of ships approaching the Normandy shore. The reaction of the Germans in coastal defence, as far as anti-aircraft fire was concerned, was secondary only to the stupidity of the Royal Navy, who shot many of our aircraft down. Their attitude to aircraft was one of hostility, and it annoyed us intensely. In fact, we had to do our patrols, in many instances, behind the German lines because of attacks by our own guns. However, I did manage to damage a German Focke-Wulf 190 on the second morning; in fact, I think I shot him down, but by that time I was so short of fuel I could not stay to see what happened.

I lost some pilots and it grieved me to lose these men because they had become good friends. I liked the Polish and Canadian boys very much, and 130 Squadron, with its mixture of nationalities, was unique. I was fortunate, really, to command such a conglomerate of lovely people, and it was really a very competent Wing. We flew very hard during the period of the invasion, and after the break-out did a lot of ground strafing.'

In a Landing Craft Tank was Corporal Robert Green, Electrician, Royal Artillery:

'The message we got, a written message wishing us luck and so forth, was somehow cold comfort, we found, and off we went. It was a sunny day in the early afternoon when we went out past the Isle of Wight and the sea was choppy. As we went along in the late afternoon/ evening, the water became rougher and the tank landing crafts are most uncomfortable things, flat-bottomed barges which just slammed down on the waves every so often and jerked and rocked about and gave, you might say, an uncomfortable ride. Sufficiently bad it was, that most of those on board were seasick. I wasn't, but I remember getting a camouflage mat and lying down on that and putting a blanket over me or whatever, and I slept for several hours by the side of one of the guns. As the light came in the morning somebody said, "Cuppa cha," and about three of us were the only ones who attempted to drink that early cup of tea, about 3 or 4 o'clock in the morning. Not long after, the coast of France came into sight very dimly on the horizon. There was high thin cloud over us and the sea was quite choppy. We could see this huge armada around us and behind us, and it was really a most marvellous thing to see, and a wonderful, you might say, comfort or encouragement to us to be anything but alone.

Anyway, from about 7 miles out the guns started firing on to the coastal defences. The only things in front of us that we could see were two or three Landing Craft Tank on which were the rockets, and these rockets kept shooting off in flashes of yellow flame, and where they landed you could see the cloud of smoke and so forth come up. They fired until we were in about a mile off the shore, and then behind us the infantry were in their small boats following in to land. We turned back out to sea and, after the infantry fellows passed us, then we joined in behind and followed on heading to the coast. By the time we beached, shelling was really starting to take its toll; a landing craft just to the right of me was hit and another one, further along, the cabin at the back went on fire and so on, and things were at first really very lively.

We landed into quite shallow water fortunately and went ashore. I was in a White armoured half-track and the four guns from our LCT were just in front of me as we came ashore. They started firing on the beach as soon as they could, and we parked at the top of the beach with them and we found that, whereas we'd been in our half-track expected to communicate between the batteries and the regiments and the regimental headquarters, we found the other landing craft had been hit, so the other control set, which worked from regiment to division, had to go back to England, so our half-track took over both jobs. So we had a double role to play that day, all of which went well, and the only hitch came when the aerial was shot off one of the sets, and, of course, broadcast failed there and then. It was easy enough for me to do that repair, anyway.

On the beach at this time everything was going on, from rifle, machine-gun fire to land mines going up, to shells landing on us, and it was a real baptism by fire. I was remarkably surprised, not ever having been a pugilistic boy or anything, to find how cool I was, and, though I say it myself, I went about my job as diligently as I would have done at any time.

You didn't take chances; you dug yourself a bit of a slit trench for when there was nothing to be done, and on one occasion I had to get up and do some job or other out of the slit trench and came back and found two other soldiers in it, so went and dug myself another.

Anyway, the long and short of it was, the guns went off the beach after maybe an hour, and the Royal Engineers had laid tracks through the sand dunes, but the half-track stayed on the beach as the radio communications were all right and the less people clogging up the roads the better it was basically, so we stayed on the beach until about, it must have been, 1 o'clock in the afternoon. It quietened down as the forces moved inland a bit, except that the shelling resumed from time to time, and there was one attack, when a couple of German fighters came down and strafed the place; however, we survived all right and eventually moved inland.

The next thing I particularly remember was, it was in the afternoon, and we were in an orchard and the airborne soldiers came in on our left and we saw all these huge array of parachutes and the gliders coming down, a most remarkable sight indeed, and, of course, very heartening for us because we were on the very left of the line – we were virtually against the Orne River. Our job from that point was, in fact, to cover the airborne forces with artillery fire. The half-track joined with two other vehicles, which consisted of the Regimental Headquarters, and we moved twice more, the last move ending about 1 o'clock in the morning.

Then the guns were firing, the yellow chandelier flares were hanging above us, the bombs being dropped on us, butterfly bombs and whatnot, and the enormous racket of the anti-aircraft guns, and every fifth shell was a tracer, so the night sky was like Guy Fawkes Night at its best. However, eventually they said, oh well, now is the time to get in your blankets and have a spell – we'd been awake, most of us, from about 4 o'clock the morning before, I suppose. Anyway, I lay down on the blanket there, I got a groundsheet and a blanket out, and lay in a bit of a ditch and I shook to death, frightened, scared stiff. I remember saying to myself, as I sort of pulled the blanket over my head, I remember saying that won't do you any good at all, just straighten yourself up now or you'll never do what you want, and I sat up there and then and I looked round at everything that was going on, and I accounted for everything that was happening and every noise, and I said now you're in the best place you can be, shut up and go to sleep, which I duly did. From that time forward I was never once concerned for my own safety more than being properly prudent as any good soldier would be anyhow.

The next morning the light came and a Messerschmitt came diving down out of the cloudy sky, and the next thing we know was a Spitfire on its tail and a great stream of black smoke came out of the Messerschmitt and the

Spitfire disappeared back into clouds, so we couldn't have had a better start for D plus 1. There were snipers still about and we had to turn on the guns and shoot into a church tower, a sandstone church tower, where snipers were being active.

In the middle of the morning a half-track turned up at the Regimental Headquarters telling me that a radio on one of the tanks was not functioning, so I pile into this Bren carrier with my bag of tools and off we go and see the Highland Div men marching in sixes outside, up the road and towards the front. It was slow rising country and as we got on to the top of this rise, there's a Sherman tank looking as good as ever and perched on the track; the driver has his mirror and he's frothed up his lather on his face and he's just getting his razor out having a shave, and I say to myself, what am I worried about? Anyway, before you know where you are, a salvo of shells came over and landed on us; I shot into that tank as fast as you know how, slammed the lid down on top of me and got stuck into the radio. Once inside and with the radio, nothing else seemed to matter; I found what was wrong with the set and I had to re-solder a part of it, and so that meant getting out of the tank, getting the blowlamp going and heating the iron and then climbing back into the tank again. The driver was in his slit trench just in the lee of the tank while I was heating the iron up, and when it was hot enough I got into the turret of the tank and got him to pass the hot iron into me. We soldered up the joints, with the tank closed, I might say, and tested through the radio, and it's all working OK. So I quietly climb out, and by then there's no more salvos and I get back in the Bren carrier and go back to Headquarters and my half-track, but this experience of being able to do the technical things, despite what was going on, was really an outstanding surprise and I was most grateful for it for ever. Through my time right up until Bremen and the ceasefire, there was only one set I was unable to fix, and that had a big lump of shrapnel right through the middle of it, but all the others I was fortunately able to fix up.'

What most impressed Squadron Leader James Hayter on D-Day was:

'...the enormous amount of shipping and the huge formations, the American bomber formations and the British formations – I think the biggest formation I had ever been in close quarters to would be 600 bombers, which was pretty impressive. They released 200 gliders and we went down with them and watched them land; it was pretty depressing when they had some pile-ups.

Around D-Day, we were doing close Army support to gliders, bombers, and then when we landed on D-Day plus – it was quite a few days after D Day – we landed on a landing ground that they'd made for us and we continued doing close Army support with the Canadian Army. We were mainly strafing convoys. "Mary" Coningham, the Air Officer Commanding, had told us to shoot everything that was behind enemy lines, and one night a parachute was on my film, and then a day or two later there were ambulances coming out of Le Havre, but we'd been told that they were carrying ammunition or troops and we were to attack them, which we did.

We strafed a lot of convoys, trains. What we got I don't know, but I know a lot of the claims were pretty outrageous, and in the end you really couldn't tell what you'd destroyed, if you'd destroyed anything. So we only had Squadron claims, we didn't have individual claims, because it was impossible to claim anything really, but we did strafe a lot of stuff – how much damage we did is a debatable point.'

Landing late in June, Corporal of Signals Robert Brown, Brigade HQ, 59th Infantry Division, was immediately involved in the battle for Caen:

'Of course, Caen was supposed to have been taken on D-Day, and it didn't fall actually until some time in early July, so we watched this spectacular

Robert Alfred Brown

bomber raid on Caen. I think there were about 600 or 800 bombers, both British and Americans. Unfortunately, the Americans had the habit of dropping their bombs on the wrong people and we suffered quite a few casualties. Actually, I've been shot up and bombed more times by Americans than Germans, but that's all part of the war.

A bridgehead was forced over the River Orne by 176 Infantry Brigade, and we were on the far side in the bridgehead there and it was quite desperate really, because the enemy were counter-attacking, and on the radio sets the battalion was reporting that Tiger tanks were attacking and it was a vicious counter-attack. We were asking for Typhoons to help us out because we were in danger of being surrounded. It was at this stage that I had some grenades lined up on the top of the radio sets just in case, and I was going to pull the pins out of the grenades and run for it, but, however, it didn't eventuate and the counter-attack must have died out and we were able then to advance from this bridgehead, but that was quite dramatic at the time.

Well, after Caen was taken the Americans were doing very well on the other flank and this was the beginning then of the Falaise Gap, the pocket, and we took part in this, the battle of the Falaise pocket, and I remember I was on the radio set for about 30 hours during this battle, and somebody would bring me some food or a drink, but I must have lost the use of my legs – I had to get somebody to lift me out eventually.'

Corporal Robert Green RA had also been involved in the struggle to take Caen:

'We spent a long time in front of Caen where the German armour was drawn into that Eastern Sector, and we went over the Orne River and Canal and the Pegasus Bridge to an attack by two armoured divisions at Fort Chalon heading south-eastwards. This generated a furious battle, with very little forward movement indeed, but much more German armour came from the Pas de Calais and so on to stem our action. This was the key to letting the Americans break out in the west, but even armour from the west was brought into this in front of Caen and Chalon, and the fighting was static and quite fierce, of course. A 500-bomber raid which came, I think, in July, in front of Caen, virtually had no effect on the Wehrmacht, and they came out into assault, into attack, and repulsed the advances made by the infantry after the bomber attack was over.

As the battle developed we moved westwards to go via Flers and Vire, helping to close the bulge to keep the pressure on the retreating Germans going out of the Falaise Gap. As the line shrunk we were dropped out of the line and we were moved to Bayeux, where we handed in the self-propelled guns and got back our old 25-pounders, much to the sadness of the gunners, but we had a long way to go and mobility was important.'

Providing air cover for the beach landings and operating further inland was Squadron Leader John Gard'ner, who found that he had more than enemy action to worry about:

'I was posted to 219 Squadron, who were operating out of airfields on the East Coast of England, and our task there was to cover the beachhead landings and the push-out following the landings in Europe. I had been converted at some stage on to Mosquitos and was now engaged in night-fighting, again operating in all types of weather, and I had this frightening experience of lightning. The lightning caused St Elmo's fire in aeroplanes, when your whole aeroplane would light up and you'd get this enormous great sort of flash of light. This frightened me far more than ever meeting an enemy aircraft at night-time. We were controlled from the ground – they had sort of radar control units that had moved over on to the Continent – and we were being led to intercept anything coming over, actually from Germany, I suppose it was, over towards London. Again, during that period I didn't see a thing. Coming back to the St Elmo's fire, this was a sort of a big sheet building up on your windscreen, and the tips of your propeller would start to glow blue, and you could find this blueness getting brighter and brighter and, after one or two of these things, you knew exactly when to close your eyes, because if you didn't and the thing flashed, everything was blank – it was pink in front of your eyes, your instrument panels, everything had disappeared. Luckily it only lasted for a few seconds, I suppose, but it seemed like eternity because at that point you had no idea which way up your aeroplane was, and that, to me, was a most frightening experience.

Eventually, with 488 Squadron, I was posted across to Amiens in France; this was about three weeks after D-Day. Amiens had been bombed but the runways had been repaired; there were no buildings left on it. We were actually billeted in a chateau off the edge of the airfield, and I recall all the windows were just sort of papered up or had sacking over the windows – there was no glass or anything. It was as cold as hell; it was in the middle of winter and we had our camp beds. I recall there that we had kerosene stoves to keep warm, and we used to sort of heat up our shaving water by putting an empty tin of milk, or whatever it was – you'd put it on top of you heater thing there and you had hot water for shaving in the morning. Always correctly dressed.'

In Normandy and beyond, mines, booby traps, snipers and hidden 88s were a constant menace, as Corporal Charles Teague explained:

'The Germans were clever at booby traps and they had delayed mines at the side of the road and booby traps in doors and things like that. In one village in France there was a sniper that was in a church steeple and it was one of the civilians pointed out where he was, and they just blew the steeple up, blew the whole lot up. There was another instance – we were in this orchard and this gun, 88mm gun – we didn't know where it was firing from – and it did quite a lot of damage. Actually we'd been working on a Bren gun-carrier and my mate Reg Goodrick, he'd left his tools under the Bren gun-carrier and went to pick up his tools just as a shell came over the top and blew the whole lot up, including Reggie Goodrick. They sent a spotter plane up and he noticed that this 88mm gun was on a mounted goods truck, and it was going into this tunnel at night. It was firing each side of the tunnel and then going back in again and you never saw it. What they did, they ordered a couple of these rocket-firing Typhoons, and one Typhoon came at one end of the tunnel and the other at the other and they shoved a rocket in each end of the tunnel and buried the whole thing.'

As the campaign in Normandy developed, Lieutenant Commander Roger Hill still had much with which to occupy himself and his ship's company, this time in the vicinity of the Channel Islands:

'Next thing that happened was, we were attached to an American Admiral, who was then at Cherbourg, which had been captured, and he said to us destroyer captains, which was me and Bill Churchill of *Faulknor*, and he said, as he puffed on his cigar, just like the Americans on the films, "I want results," and he sent us in to the Channel Islands, which had a tremendous amount of radar control and big guns, 8-inch and 11-inch, all round the Islands. I didn't see any point, at this time of the war when we were winning, losing men and *Jervis* in such an unnecessary procedure, but he felt that ships passing between the Channel Islands, with their German bases, should be sunk. Anyhow, we went in and I went in at 25 knots and, obviously, they had us on their radar, because they fired and I immediately went hard a-starboard, full ahead, and from then on all their shells arrived just in our wake and the difference of speed from roughly the 25 knots on their plotting table to the 32 knots we had increased our speed to made all the difference. "Glop" shouted at me, why couldn't we fire back, and I said we can't fire back, this is part of England, we can't shoot back. He was terribly upset because he could see the flashing of the guns. We had to keep on for about 26 minutes to get clear of the strait between the mainland and

Alderney. Anyhow, all was well and we got a bit of shrapnel aboard and that was all.

Anyhow, we got in next day, and then the next day we saw an island which was called Roches d'Oeuvres, and we sent a party in with machine-guns and so on to capture it, and when it was half way in, Bill Churchill signalled, "Come back, it's too dangerous," so I made the recall, and then I said, "No, we can't see anyone there," so he said, "All right, have a go." So I said to him afterwards, "Why did you call me back?" and he said, "My doctor, he came on the bridge and he said he could see men walking about on the island." There wasn't anyone there at all. Anyhow, they went ashore and they hoisted a flag and a note to say "Captured by HMS *Jervis* on such and such a date", and there were no Germans there. Anyhow, the boys thoroughly enjoyed their trip ashore.

And there was this island, the name of which I forget, and the American Admiral said, "We must test the defences of that island." But how the hell do you test the defences? So we went there and I laid a long line of smoke and then we got the other end of the smoke and opened fire on the island and they fired back at us, which was very unfair, so we dived into the smoke and then we said to the Admiral, "Defences active, enemy defences accurate" and then we went back to Le Havre and passed the battleship *Malaya*, which was on its way to bombard that island, which resulted in its surrender after numerous telephone calls had been made to the German Commander. They were completely cut off and in a hopeless position.'

CHAPTER 14

The campaign in North West Europe and final victory

The advance across Europe to the Rhine and beyond continued slowly but inexorably with opportunities lost and inevitable delays to allow for refuelling, replenishing, refitting and so forth. Brussels was occupied on 3 September 1944 and Antwerp the next day. There was the setback at Arnhem in September, then on 16 December the Germans attacked in strength from the Ardennes and, with history repeating itself, caught the Allies off their guard. They made considerable progress but were unable to sustain their advance and were defeated. On 22 March Patton's Third Army was across the Rhine to the south, and on the 23rd Montgomery launched his major offensive across the Rhine near Wesel, preceded by a massive artillery and aerial bombardment. By 25 April the Russians were in the suburbs of Berlin, on the 27th they met up with the Americans on the River Elbe, on 30 April Hitler committed suicide, and a signed document of unconditional surrender became effective on 8 May. Such an outline sets the scene for the reminiscences of the men who were there.

Corporal Robert Brown was on the rapid advance through the Low Countries:

'Up through Belgium, we missed Brussels and we headed straight up towards Holland. I was still a radio operator, now with the 128 Field Regiment, and we were working with the guns, mainly on fire orders and map references and the shells and setting up programmes for them. We'd be out during the day. I used to go out in a jeep with the radio set and the forward observation officer and we'd look for targets, and set our targets for a programme during the night when the guns used to fire – harassing fire mainly, to keep the Germans on their toes, to keep them jumpy. We also used to try and locate other German batteries and try and eliminate them. We were firing 25-pounders.

Anyway, we finally got to a place just outside of Liege and this was our first experience of the V1s, or the flying bombs, the "buzz bombs" as they were called, and we could hear these things coming and we were just in front of a reasonably high hill, and lots of these buzz bombs didn't clear the hill and they crashed into this hill and there were these terrible thunderous explosions as these blessed V1s burst.

Anyway, it was while we were in Liege at the time of the Ardennes Offensive, the Battle of the Bulge as they called it, and I remember making our way down – I was in the half-track, with the radio in the half-track – and making our way down over these icy roads, and there was snow, and trucks and vehicles were slipping off into ditches. Every now and again some of the guns would be unlimbered and they'd be firing a few shells into this Bulge, and we finally got to a little place called Marche, which was about as far as the Germans had penetrated.

Then I was detached from the outfit, although the guns were probably with us, because I found myself up on the island, which was on a piece of land between the two rivers, the Maas and the Waal, and I was posted to an element of the American 101 Airborne Division. We were part of the force striking north through Nijmegen and heading for Arnhem, but we just were not able to relieve these Airborne forces over in Arnhem – they had to make their way back, what was left of them.

Anyway, I was with this American outfit and they used to send out fighting patrols every night and you could hear the shells, they'd be bursting, and these villages changed hands every night – one night the Germans would be in and the next night the Americans would take them back again – and you could hear the shells exploding on the icy ground and they made an uncanny sort of terrible metallic sound. The Americans used to carry out these patrols and they'd always bring some dead, two or three of their dead, and lie them just at the back of my half-track, and these poor fellows would be lying out there with a blanket or a groundsheet up over them. I remember, you know, the wind would take the groundsheet off them and their poor faces, white faces, would be looking up – oh, that wasn't very pleasant.

While we were there the Germans must have zeroed in on us, because they had these *nebelwerfers*, which were these multi-barrelled mortars, and one night they zeroed in on us and these blessed mortar shells, we were in an orchard, and they were exploding all over the place, and I thought to myself, well, this is it, if one of these hits this blessed truck we're in for it.

Then things quietened down – we were getting ready for the Rhine crossing – and eventually we made our way down to the banks of the Rhine. I remember they had smokescreens along the Rhine there, trying to hide what we were doing. Supplies were coming forward, and then bridging equipment. Then it was our turn to move forward and I think it was one of our battalions, the 1st Gordons, was the first over the river, and then we followed suit. It would be a pontoon – they bridged it during the night, the engineers bridged the river during the night – and then we were over the Rhine.

Just one small incident I remember, we'd moved into a location – it was a farm and there was a barn there – and when we went into the barn there were six young dead Germans lying there, and we took them out. They were quite young. We took them out and buried them, and we had a padre who must have come over, a young padre, and he was quite upset seeing these young fellows. In fact, he was quite tearful really, but, anyway, we buried them, and it's quite ludicrous really, because after this, that evening, in the same barn, we had a cinema show, a comedy.

After the fighting over the Rhine we were then heading, the 128 Field Regiment and 51st Div were heading towards Bremen in northern Germany. I remember this must have been just before the end of hostilities and we were taking part in an attack and I was using a remote control – the set was still in the half-track – and I was just sitting in a ditch with a remote control and we were under fire and there were shells, and there was mortar bombs and small arms fire, and there was a tap on my shoulder and this man, he was a corporal too, he said, "I'm your relief, you know," and what a relief! "I'm your relief – you're going on leave." So I didn't waste any time – I said, "OK." I collected my kit together and what I had, and it's amazing because just a few yards, a bit further back, things were much quieter; so, anyway, I was on leave. Then during my leave VE Day occurred.'

Warrant Officer Friend continued to be very much involved:

'As our forces moved forward they built aerodromes or repaired aerodromes, and we just went forward with them taking fuel for the tanks, 25-pounder shells and mortar bombs and ammunition, and we brought back wounded. Five days after the Seventh Army had taken Brussels we moved into the aerodrome there. The Belgian people couldn't do enough for us. If we went into a bar they bought the drinks, and if we went into a restaurant they paid for the meal. We travelled on trains and public transport free – everything was paid for. I found the Belgian people all seemed to be well fed; none of them were starving like they were in Paris.

We continued supplying the forward troops with fuel, etc, as they moved up into Holland. When Antwerp was finally taken we flew in there. On the aerodrome I watched a V2 take off from about four or five miles away, and it went straight up with a corkscrew type of trail behind it and up into the clouds and disappeared in the high clouds, and then, a little while later, there was a fantastic explosion. It had landed just outside the aerodrome – it landed at supersonic speed – so not only the explosion of 2,000lb of amatol, there was also the sonic bang when it landed. I thought that was quite close so I went out to see where it had landed and it had landed in a backyard with a very large house, three-storey house with attic windows, and the house was still standing and the V2 had landed about 50 yards behind the house. I went back to the aircraft waiting for casualties to be picked up and I got into the aircraft and another V2 landed and the aircraft bounced, it was such an explosion – the aircraft bounced from the ground, probably from the shock wave from the supersonic barrier wave that precedes in front of the rocket.

Then we were posted back to Broadwell from Brussels to prepare for the Arnhem operation, and because of the distance we had to move up to Suffolk, or it might have been Essex, to get nearer because we would run out of fuel, flying all the way from Broadwell. The first stream took paratroopers mainly; they flew paratroopers and landed almost without any opposition at Oosterbeek, just to the west of Arnhem. We went in on the third stream of gliders and the Germans were better organised by then and there was far more flak coming up, mainly 37mm. We crossed the Rhine and dropped the glider at Oosterbeek and then flew back to Brussels.

Anyhow, at Broadwell we had loaded up with panniers to drop across over Oosterbeek, and we had ammunition, mortar bombs and anti-tank ammunition to take to Oosterbeek, and before the operation we also had four Army Service Corps men. So I had to brief them on the use of a parachute again because none of them had been taught how to use a parachute. So I told them that you won't need the parachute because it's never happened to me and it's not likely to happen to you. Anyhow, off we went and we flew across Holland up the corridor that the Seventh Army had made from Eindhoven up to Nijmegen, and then across a stretch of ground between the Lower Waal and the Rhine. Crossing the Rhine we started to drop our load, at about 2,100 feet. We dropped our load and turned left to come out, and I looked out of the door and there was a German half-track with a battery of 38mm guns on it, and they were firing off at us. There was nothing I could do because we had no guns to fire back, and we were at 2.000 feet, and one of the shells they fired hit the wing, just inboard of the port engine, and immediately there were flames coming out of the hole where it hit. It was just above the front spar, very close to the port engine, and it had hit the fuel tank, the main fuel tank, and the filler cap, which was on top of the wing and was screwed in and restrained by a chain, that flew out like a champagne cork and flames came out of that hole too, blue flames that stretched backwards.

So I went up front and somebody had told Bill that we were on fire and the port engine was on fire, but the port engine wasn't on fire, it was a fuel tank, and he'd stopped the engine and flew a bit, and he was still trying to go on with the starboard engine. I said, "We've got the main port fuel tank on fire," and we all put our 'chutes on and I checked the four Army Service Corps men that their 'chutes were correctly on. The map reader had the little fire extinguisher, which he was pumping in through the hole in the wing at this enormous fire out of sight, and I had to laugh at him, because it was a silly effort, what this tiny brass thing was squirting in, because everything he squirted out went back into the slipstream – none of it reached the scene of the fire at all because the fire was inside the tank, the fuel tank.

I thought, well, I'll wait until we cross the Lower Waal – I didn't want to swim in the Lower Waal – and I watched it go by and Bill was still climbing and I beckoned to these Army blokes to follow me, and the map reader came up behind them to make sure they all got out, and I stepped off the aeroplane into space. I turned my head around to see the aircraft disappear behind a cloud, and I saw another aircraft streaming fuel from the starboard auxiliaries, but it wasn't on fire. Then I pulled my ripcord and my 'chute snapped open and it seemed to pin my shoulders so that my arms could hardly move, and out of the cloud came a Stirling, and I thought it was coming straight for me. When I saw this Stirling coming for me I waved my legs because I could wave my legs better than I could wave my arms, and he banked away from me and I waved to him as he went by and continued on about 2,000 feet towards Oosterbeek.

I could now hear firing, because in the aircraft you don't hear the gunfire, and I couldn't be sure whether they were firing at me or firing at the Germans, or the Germans firing at the British. I could hear this machine-gun fire and I had the impression I was the target, because it was a beautiful clear day – there was just this odd cumulus around, otherwise it was perfect.

I couldn't see any movement, I couldn't see any gun flashes or anything, so I then released the straps and straightened up. Below me it was a potato field that had been harvested, but I never saw anybody until I got in close to the ground, and there were the population on the ground then. As I got nearer the ground I braced myself for a landing and I pulled on the straps just as I got near touchdown, and it was a perfect landing.

I didn't know where the Germans were, and I pulled in the canopy as fast as I could and rolled it up under my arms, and I still had my flak helmet, and under the flak helmet were my earphones, and I heard one of the Dutchmen say "Boches", and I thought he thinks I'm a German, so in my battledress blouse I had my forage cap, so I brought it out with the Warrant Officer's badge and I showed him the Crown over the Albatross RAF, and that satisfied him. Up and behind me came an armoured car – one of these Humber four-wheeled armoured cars – and the commander of the car got out, he was a lieutenant, and because I was expecting to see Poles on the ground, paratroops, I asked him if he could speak English, and he said, "Seventh Hussars." So he said, "I could give you a lift back to the lines," and I was just about to get in the armoured car and the Burgomaster arrived in a Model A Ford, the American Burgomaster. So I thought the armoured car would bring the 25-pounders or the 88mms on to us, so I thought I'd travel in the Burgomaster's car – it's probably a lot safer, they won't fire at a Model A Ford when they could fire at an armoured car. So the armoured car went off ahead and I travelled back in the Model A Ford with the Burgomaster to behind our lines.

Eventually I was taken to the tank laager, the Seventh Hussars on the other side of the village nearer to the German border. We were housed in the Commandant's caravan and the CO, a Colonel, gave over his bed to me, and I was a Warrant Officer at the time and he shared his champagne – he had this champagne bottle, had some beautiful food, good corned beef sandwiches. What happened to the rest of our crew I don't know, because when I jumped out the four Army blokes still hadn't reached the door behind me, but they were coming my way and I assumed that they were all right.

Anyhow, they laid on a jeep for us to go to the American, I think it was the 82nd Airborne Division Headquarters, which was a farmhouse in an orchard, and off we went to this farmhouse. Going into the farmhouse, I noticed there were three paratroopers lying down on their bellies aiming their guns through the hedge across the paddock, and across the other side of the paddock were the Germans firing in towards the American Airborne Headquarters, local headquarters I suppose. We moved into this orchard – it was September and the pears were all beautifully ripe, so I climbed a tree to fill my battledress blouse with these pears – and the German across on the other side was firing at me, but, of course, he couldn't see me because I was up amongst all the foliage and the bullets went phut, phut, phut through the branches and I took no notice of them at all.

The Army were there in force and there was no accommodation for us, so we were then taken to near the aerodrome at Eindhoven and the RAF Regiment had moved into the aerodrome and they were disorganised. I couldn't find anywhere to eat – I'd had nothing to eat apart from my pears. Anyhow, there was no accommodation, so I slept in the middle of the paddock with my canopy for bedding. I woke up covered in dew in the morning and repacked my canopy the best I could, and went to look for breakfast. I thumbed a lift from a little Chev 15cwt; this Army chap took me to where he was based to the east of Brussels, probably about 30 kilometres to the east of Brussels. I had breakfast there and I was served by a sergeant, because I was a Warrant Officer First Class by the Army standards, and I got a beautiful egg and bacon breakfast, and tea served by a sergeant who was calling me "sir". I thought, gosh, I'm in the wrong force.

I then got a lift and they dropped me on the outskirts of Brussels. I got on a tram, which got me to a road leading down to the main Railway Station. As I walked down the road, who should I see but the map reader, Frankie Marriott. Frank and I then went off to the aerodrome to get a lift back to Broadwell. Once there, I took my parachute to the parachute section to be repacked, and when I handed my parachute over they said, "Where's the ripcord?" and I said, "Oh, I must have dropped it," and they said, "That's seven and six."

Then I went to the Orderly Room because they'd posted a "missing believed killed" telegram to my mother, and I asked them to get another telegram off to my mother to show that I was all right. So we then got "survivor's leave" and off home I went. Then back in Broadwell, where I learned that Bill and Gilly had tried to belly-land the aircraft, but they crashed well south of Arnhem and the aircraft burst into flames and they were both killed. They were taken to Ede between Arnhem and Amsterdam and were put in the cemetery there, so they are now buried side by side in the cemetery. I wrote to Gilly's mother in Allahabad and explained what had happened to Gilly. I went and saw Bill's father in Farnham and I explained to Bill's father what had happened to Bill.

Then it was back to Brussels again on supply-dropping operations; we'd got to the Elbe by then. We were then told to liberate Denmark, so we flew to Luneburg to pick the Signal Corps jeep, which was loaded, on to our aircraft with members of the Signal Corps, and we flew north to Copenhagen. We had an escort of 12 Spitfires and six Tempests, Hawker Tempests. The Spitfires left us over the Baltic Sea because it wasn't the Germans they were worried about, it was the Russians, because the Russians would fire at just about anything they didn't recognise as their own.

We flew into Kastrup, the civil aerodrome for Copenhagen, and as we circled over the roads, below us was the *Prinz Eugen* and two destroyers of the Kriegsmarine, but the Kriegsmarine hadn't capitulated – it was only the Wehrmacht and the Luftwaffe in Schleswig-Holstein and in Norway and Denmark that capitulated. This was before VE Day.

So we turned over to the north and landed north-west to south-east on a long flat runway; we were just three Dakotas and we were at No 3 in the stream and coming over the anti-aircraft posts. All these were manned, but they weren't aiming their guns at us – all the barrels were low, but they were all manned. Behind us landed the six Tempests and we were directed in by Luftwaffe ground crews, three abreast – marvellous to be directed in by Luftwaffe.

When we were flying over the town we saw all these Danish flags popping up and people moving into the streets in huge numbers, and by the time we landed this swarm of people – must have been half the population of Copenhagen – they were swarming towards Kastrup. Kastrup is on an island, but it is connected to the mainland by a short causeway, so it is more an isthmus than an island, and these people were coming in hoards down the road. No buses, no cars, no bicycles, because the Germans had taken all the transport, and they arrived at the gates and the Germans were still manning the gates – the Luftwaffe was guarding the gates.

The Luftwaffe Commanding Officer in his greatcoat and heavy Luger held by the barrel with the butt down in the correct fashion was waiting to be disarmed. I was a Flying Officer by then and he was senior to me, and our highest rank we had there was a Squadron Leader. So he did the necessary.'

At an earlier stage the 59th Regiment RA had reached the River Seine, and John Campion, a Sergeant in that Regiment, recalls:

'We crossed the Seine at a little place called Les Andelys and from there we moved fairly quickly because the Germans were getting away as quick as they could. I think it was at a place called Coleville – that was rather an unpleasant place we were in – and while I was there the German Air Force, what was left of it, decided to strafe our position, so, like everybody else, I got my head well down. I shared a hole with a batman, and when the German planes went away we looked up and the poor old batman got an awful shock – he found he'd dropped his officer's kit on a pile of cordite. The cordite from our guns came in bags, and somebody had been very careless and the result was that the officer's kit went up in smoke – I don't know how the poor batman got on. But anyway, that was a quite unpleasant position. We even had an infantry anti-tank gun sharing a position with us and we had tanks also. We didn't like them there and they didn't like us where we were, because we both attracted German gunfire, but eventually we got on the move again and started off on our way to Antwerp.

The Germans were still holding Antwerp at the time and they were holding up in the port, but we moved on before the place was actually taken and the only memorable thing about Antwerp was when two of our men, the only ones to desert, decided to leave their rifles propped against a wall and make themselves scarce, and we didn't see them again until the end of the war. Unlike the First World War, all they got was two years' hard labour. Anyway, the rest of us moved through Holland. An incident rather amused us in Holland. We were moving through one place and we came across banners which had been set up across the road, and in very large letters were the words "Welcome to Marshal Montgomery's Glorious Soldiers". A lot of the girls turned out, jumping on the footboards, jumping on the engines, and so on. They had all been throwing flowers on to the vehicles, but some of our officers, being spoil-sports, made us remove all the flowers.

Later, of course, we crossed the Rhine; that was almost the end of our job as gunners. We were given occupation duties and once again our vehicles were taken to ferry ammunition forward. The Germans had moved back and were taking refuge in big ports like Hamburg. Our first occupation duties were guarding a Polish displaced persons' camp – very dull and rather dreary job – but we were protecting the Germans against the Poles, I think.

After this DP camp we were then sent to the town of Bochum on the edge of the Ruhr district, and were simply acting as policemen, sending patrols out in the evening and at night to see that curfews were observed. But one job we had, which nobody ever liked, was battlefield clearance, they called it, where you had to go out and around collecting unexploded ammunition like hand grenades, anti-tank missiles, things of that sort, and mines. Unfortunately, I had the job on one of these, taking a party out to collect them. We were getting quite a big pile when it decided to explode. That was the last of my active war in Germany. I spent the next five weeks in hospital.'

Squadron Leader John Gard'ner, now stationed at Amiens, continues his recollections:

'I was with 219 Squadron when I had my first operational success. I was on a night patrol over Holland and at about only 5,000 or 6,000 feet, as I recall it, I was vectored on to an aircraft, and I was flying a Mosquito and we caught this thing up, and just realised it was a Focke-Wulf 190. He never saw us coming, and I got into a nice position behind him, fired off a short burst, whereupon this aeroplane in front sort of twisted over and went plunging straight down and hit the ground.

I was operating out of Amiens just for a few weeks before we moved up to Gilze-Rijen, which was still all night patrol, and I recall one of the sorties that I was on there out of Gilze-Rijen, when my radar operator told me that we were being pursued by something which whizzed past us. It overtook us and went past us so fast that all I could see was a sort of ball of light, or there were two balls of light, and I believe that that was one of the first times that the Germans had used the twin-engined – I can't quite remember what the aeroplane was called – but it was the twin-engined jet aircraft that they were starting to use for night interception.

My time with 488 Squadron at Gilze-Rijen was a period of, well, lots of patrols, and it was during this time that I was flying up over the Rhine area when suddenly the anti-aircraft guns let go, and one shell went off really close just ahead of us, and it flipped my aircraft over on to its back and there was the smell of cordite. I realised, when I got the thing under control again, that the starboard engine was overheating and that we'd been hit. My radar operator said that he felt uncomfortable and felt under his bottom and he found a piece of shrapnel that had come through the fuselage or through the engine and had just lodged in a position that he was virtually sitting on it. Despite fog there was no trouble, on the one engine, landing at Brussels/Melsbroek aerodrome. The next day the Germans came over and they strafed the aerodrome and destroyed a large number of Allied aircraft on the ground, including my own Mosquito.'

Corporal Robert Green had little to commend his winter on the Maas:

'It was a cold, cold, dreadful winter and the Dutch we found relatively unco-operative and unhappy and difficult to communicate with, because we didn't speak their language. The earth roads, all were frozen stiff, and you could move about on them while that happened, but when the thaw came it was impossible to move other than on the sealed roads. There were regular exchanges of fire all through this winter where we were, and we had to live in as secure conditions as could be found. You couldn't have a dugout because the water table, the ground water, came up so close to the surface that you'd be lying in water, so you were in barns, buildings, anything you could find, or even in the lee of them.

On we went from there down on the west side of the Rhine to join in the assault over the Rhine, and this was very notable as the biggest artillery barrage that was ever put together. There was everything from the heavies, mediums, field guns onwards, lying almost wheel to wheel on the west bank, and the firing started in the late afternoon, went on continuously into the night, and covered all the time while the actual crossings were made by the various regiments.

I well remember one poor lad, who was reinforcement to us, and it seemed so sad to me. We were at the Regimental Headquarters in an old farmhouse and I can see him to this day, sitting on the foot of the stairs, crying his eyes out, and I said to him, "What's the matter, Martin?" and he said, "I can't stand it, I can't stand it." So I said, "Come outside with me and listen to it and look at it – every one of those is going the way we want it, every one of those is helping to preserve our lives." The poor lad he just wept more and I just left him there.

We crossed the Rhine in the very early hours of the morning. The field guns were all on a pontoon bridge, which was a marvellous feat by the engineers. The battles immediately on the east side of the Rhine were very tough. From after, perhaps, ten days we headed up north-eastwards and came back into Holland, and we went through and we were the first troops, I believe, in Enschede. From there we headed eastwards across to Lingen to eventually finish up in Bremen at the time of the German surrender.'

Charles Teague also recalled the crossing of the Rhine:

'When we crossed the Rhine it was night and it's a swift-flowing river, and this pontoon, it was a pontoon bridge, and the river was so fast and it was bulging a bit in the centre with the flow pushing it. When we went across there, our lorry wheels were just like within the bridge, it just gripped the lorry wheels and that was it. The water was lapping over the bridge with the weight – there was only three of us allowed at one time across the bridge because there was shelling – they were using 88mm and everything. That was one scary moment – I've never been so scared as I was that night, never.

Then we went towards Bremen – this place was called Nordhorn where we were – and there was a naval prisoner of war camp there in between Bremen and Nordhorn, and in this camp they were as thin as rakes. Oh, they were in a bad state, those guys were. Also in the square at Nordhorn there were a series of wooden huts, and there was three-tier beds down each side, and there must have been 14 or 15 or maybe more in a hut, and to walk down in the middle you had to walk sideways, and there was a bucket at each end which was all they had. These huts were full of displaced persons, Latvians, Estonians, all kinds of young women – they were just young women in their 20s or 30s, really nice-looking young women. Some had their hair all cropped and they were wearing sacks, all sorts of things, mostly sacking. When we liberated them, they came out into the centre of the square and one or two played their guitars and what have you and they were doing folk-dancing in the square. A lot of them had got anything they could lay their hands on – broom handles, shovels, anything – and it was like a residential area round about at the top – big houses, huge houses – and they went and smashed windows and doors and what have you and came out dressed up, dressed up with all civilian gear and what have you, everything – came out and started dancing, and I'll never forget that, dancing in the square.

This is at the end of the war on the River Elbe. The Russians were on one side of the Elbe and we were on the other, and there was a bridge going across, and on this bridge there were Russian guards on one side, and we were on the other side. One of our trucks had broken down on the Russian side, and I went to get this truck, and when we eventually got this truck back, when we looked in the back, it was full of displaced persons who had got in the back of the truck in order to get away from the Russian zone. What they were doing to get across, they were swimming the Elbe, and if the Russian patrols saw them they would take pot shots, shoot them on sight – these were Germans getting across to the other side away from the Russian soldiers, and this is what they used to do, just shoot them.'

The first attempt to cross the Rhine in September 1944 was remembered by Lieutenant Harold Lander, Royal Armoured Corps:

'This was when Montgomery had his plan to outflank the Germans and end the war by Christmas by capturing the bridges at Nijmegen and Arnhem. There was one road which any Dutch officer who went to the Dutch Military Academy knew the stock answer in their exams – you do not attempt to go by that road because it stands miles in full view, huge ditches on either side, once you're on it you can't get off it, but that was the road the British Army went up; consequently the Germans on either side could easily knock out vehicles. So the reason we were sent up there, and we slept in tents by the side of the road, was to defend this corridor, as it was called.

The next big event that I recall was an operation called "Clarkeforce". Nobby Clarke was the Brigadier of our Tank Brigade and we were an independent Army Tank Brigade – we didn't belong to any division – and Nobby used to go around looking for jobs, and he found a job. "Clarkeforce" was an operation to clear the hinterland of Antwerp and West Holland – this was after Arnhem, of course – and we set off from Belgium; actually we were under the command of the Canadian Army, the Canadian Army on our left and the Americans on our right, and the operation lasted about ten days. Anyway, we captured the little town of Wouw on 28 October and I have vivid memories of what happened that day. My troop was the first to enter into Wouw. There was fierce opposition. I had my own tank knocked out and I took over my sergeant's tank and carried on. What happened was my troop was leading the attack and we were going up this road with huge ditches on either side in this flat terrain. What we used to have to do was to try to hide behind hedges.

One day during that operation, before entering Wouw, I had to escort a platoon of infantry who were in Bren gun-carriers. We set off across this field with the Bren carriers and as soon as we emerged from behind these huge hedges into the field, two German self-propelled guns, which

Harold Lander

were ahead in the village we were trying to capture, opened fire. Some of the infantry were wounded, I think, and the Bren gun-carriers just turned round and went back. I didn't want to present my rear to these German guns, because the rear of a tank is its weak spot, so I went forward to the next big hedge. My corporal was ahead and we were spotting, trying to find exactly where these German guns were, when we got word that we had to go back. So I didn't fancy that much, but anyway we made it.

Then the Germans launched their Ardennes offensive and Montgomery sent us and most of the British Second Army down to the Ardennes, and we went down, crossed the River Meuse at Dinant, and we went into the Ardennes. We had great fun with the tanks on the snow in the Ardennes, and a number of tanks lost their tracks because once you got on a slope the tank acted as a sledge and went down sideways, and when it stopped at the bottom the tracks broke. Anyway, we became quite expert at turning into the fall and powering our way out of it, and we had Christmas there down in the Ardennes. We fed on turkeys which were looted off an American convoy that happened to pass us whilst we were at the side of the road – trucks loaded up with turkeys and goodness knows what. Anyway, we were waiting for the Germans to come, but the Americans managed to stop them before they reached us, and so that was that.

Our next big operation was the Reichswald Battle – that was in February 1945. The night before the battle we slept in tents and there was the biggest barrage of the war that night, greater than the barrage at El Alamein, and there were rocket-firing things just behind our tents you know, whooshing off. Eventually we managed to get to sleep, despite the noise, and what woke us up was the sudden silence when it all stopped, when the barrage stopped about 5 o'clock in the morning, and off we set trying to get into the Reichswald. There was a valley in front of the Reichswald, and we had to cross this valley and go up to the forest, and it was a quagmire. Tanks were getting stuck in it and eventually we managed to get my troop across. Well, trying to get through the Reichswald, the Germans had snipers in the trees and their favourite target was Tank Commanders. We had orders not to stick our heads out of the turret. It was impossible to direct a tank without seeing, so we wore our steel helmets, but we lost a few Troop Commanders all right.

Then when we got to near the main road, which was going north-south, there'd been an attempt to go down this road by the Army, but it had failed because towards the southern end of the forest was the Siegfried Line with its concrete emplacements. So the next day my troop (we were working as detached troops, but attached to an infantry battalion, I think it was the 2nd Black Watch) and another troop from my Squadron to our left, had to advance down the road, and there was a creeping artillery barrage which was going to advance so many yards each minute, and I had under my command a troop of Armoured Engineers.

We set off down the road, the corporal's tank in front and then me and then the sergeant, and we went down this road with this creeping barrage. Infantry didn't like having tanks near them because they reckoned the tanks attracted fire, so they kept well out of our way. We had to be on the road – we couldn't go into the woods – and we eventually came to where three

'Mail from home': a quiet spell for Lieutenant Lander and his tank crew during operations in Reichswald, February 1945.

huge trees were across the road. I called up the Engineers troop to come and deal with these trees, but we had no response – couldn't see them behind me and I couldn't see the troop sergeant either, and so the corporal said, "I think I might get across," and I said, "Well, have a go," and we managed to get across. So we cut across these trees, and then the infantry came to us – we had telephones on the back of the tanks – and they said, "There are these pillboxes – can you come and have a go at them?" So off we went and blasted these pillboxes, and the Germans came out without incident. Then we came down to the village, slowly, the village of Hekkens at the bottom of the Reichswald, and emerged from the woods. The infantry had to clear the houses at either side of the road, and they said to us, "Can you cover us or give us a few bursts?" So I said to the corporal, "You do that side and I'll do this," and again a few rounds from our guns and the Germans came out and surrendered, so we cleared that village and captured that route. Then we took up defensive positions there.

Then my troop, having been in the lead for some days, was put into reserve. However, the leader of the troops taking our place reported his tanks weren't fit for the next advance, so we were pulled out from our well-earned rest and we had to carry on and take part in this attack on the town of Kessel. It was at this town – we were in the square – and whilst we were unloading our spent shells and reloading with fresh ammunition – I was stood on the back of the tank – the Germans mortared the town. Unfortunately a mortar shell fell just behind my tank and the splinters from this mortar shell went through my legs in various places and that was that for me for some time.'

CHAPTER 15

Prisoners of war in Italy and Germany

*T*he life of a prisoner of war must have been one of profound frustration, nagging uncertainty and, in most cases, discomfort to aggravate body and spirit. To be out of touch with family and loved ones over a long period of time, not knowing how they were faring, especially if they were subject to enemy action, and without being of any material assistance to them at such times, would have been a worry. Not to know when, if ever, their captivity would come to an end must have been an extra burden. But such concerns and worries are not obvious in the accounts of the seven men who contribute to this chapter. Perhaps this tells us something about the resilience of the human spirit. As it happens, there is a sense of optimism and underlying humour as well as an acknowledgement of the occasional kind and humane treatment received at the hands of a few of their captors.

Rex Thompson, driver in the NZ Army Service Corps, was taken prisoner in Crete while awaiting evacuation on the beach at Sphakia in May 1941.

'Our prison camp had been our 7th General Hospital, which the Germans had bombed prior to the invasion, and they'd strafed and overrun it after the invasion started. There was just an ordinary six-wire fence round it, and it was on a little peninsula which was about two or three miles west of Canea towards Maleme. We made little bivouacs out of torn tents there, and the Germans occupied what buildings were there. And while we were in this particular camp, generally speaking they treated us all right, but food must have been short because it was very meagre.

Our bivouac was not far from the sea. But to get out of the camp, which we did two or three times, you'd swim out very quietly – it had a wire fence into the sea which you could get round. You always knew where the guards were, so you knew when you could get out round the end of the fence. The last time we went out – we went out at night of course – and we went up the valley where there was a vineyard. And daylight came and we were walking out of this vineyard and a little Cretan girl said good day to us and took us up to the town and put us in a cave on the hill behind the town or village, and a little crippled Cretan boy came up, brought us some food. We learned that the week before we were there the Germans found a couple of our lads in the village being looked after, and as a result they shot all the menfolk who were there, and the women had to bury them and there was just this little crippled boy left. So after that we didn't go out because of that, but the hardest part was getting back into camp, because we never knew where the guards were. Anyway, they never seemed to miss you.

After a while the Hitler Youth Brigade arrived for overseas experience, and they put them more or less in charge of the camp. And they were really little horrors and caused us a lot of discomfort and threw their weight about. And on the inward side of the compound, the road we'd passed, it was just a bit higher than the fence, and this particular morning a Cretan lady, quite an elderly lady, walked past and she had a bag and bread in it, and so she threw some over the fence. There was a general scuffle for it; one of these Hitler Youths gesticulated to her and told her to get off, but she just looked at him and threw another loaf over, and he climbed up to her and she's just picked up another loaf and he clubbed her down with the butt of his rifle, and she was out for quite a while. It just about caused a riot – they had to fire machine-guns over our heads and Lord knows what. She eventually got up and the boy had disappeared; then she looked around and she put her hand in the basket, threw over another loaf, probably the last one, and staggered off on her way.

After that some of us were transferred up to Maleme, and the Germans had asked for mechanics so we thought a change was better than nothing, so we became mechanics. Actually I was one, so we went up there and the German troops up there were Austrian/Bavarian Alpine troops. They treated us very well as equals, and fed us – first time I had goat meat there, and it was good, too. On one particular day – it was getting on for Christmas; I had seven months all told on Crete – and we were in a tent, quite a few of us, and the sun was shining and a cat walked around the side of the tent; you could see the outline of it. They were scavengers, just as much as we were, and one of the boys had a spike there; he threw it through the tent and nailed the cat. So we didn't know what to do with this cat, so we buried it, and we got to thinking about it, and it was why can't we eat it? So we dug it up, skinned it, and as soon as you cut the paws off the darned thing you couldn't tell the difference between a cat and a rabbit, and so he butchered this thing up, we brewed up and it was a darn good feed.

Then they sent us over to the airstrip where the British had left these six-cylinder Lister diesel lighting plants, and two of them were still in their boxes, so they had us assembling these darn things. Once we had these things running we could not bear to see them go to Rommel in going order, so we decided to cause a diversion and three of our chaps got cracking in a mock fight, kicking things round, and while that was going on the guards were trying to break them up, so we slammed some valve-grinding paste in the oil.

After that things went much the same until Christmas-time, when they decided to ship us out of Crete, so we went aboard a transport there and headed for Salonika. We had a few days in a POW camp there, and then we were herded into cattle trucks – they just had a little barred window in the front and rear on opposite sides, and it was midwinter there. They had straw on the floor and they put 41 in the wagon I was in, and only 39 could lie down. And so we headed into Germany and we soon found out that if you did lie down you had to put something round your head because when you woke up your hair would be frozen to the side of the truck. They used to stop once a day and let us out – they'd stop on the line near a paddock somewhere, a comfort stop – meantime you made your own arrangements. And they hand-delivered bread to us; it was still frozen of course, and a lot of chaps got "crook" with that. The idea was to cuddle it for an hour or two and thaw it out. We had four deaths on the way, and after that we could all lie down. And it was not a very pleasant trip; 14 days is a long time to be locked up in a truck.

We eventually ended up at Lamsdorf, and were baled into the compound, and most of the chaps were in summer gear coming from Crete. We were there about a week and the rations were poor, but they were not bad, I suppose, but it was so very, very cold. And one incident there that I remember very well was the Russians, who were virtually just next to us, and we were told the Germans used to let the alsatians in on the Russians every now and then for a bit of sport. But this particular morning, this Russian, as the dog went to grab on to him, he just grabbed his front paws and broke both legs. They said you could hear the dog howl for a while, and within minutes the dog was skinned and eaten.

We'd been there about a fortnight, maybe three weeks, when they called for volunteers for the coalmines. They wanted 40 volunteers and I happened to be near the end of the line, so they just cut off the first 40 and we headed to the coalmines. We got to a place called Buthen and we arrived into the camp which was occupied mainly at that stage by Dunkirk boys, and there would be about a hundred there. And from then on we became coalminers. Our billets were rooms with double-deck bunks with wooden slats and 20 in a room, and that included all shifts – there was morning shift, afternoon and night shift – so the ability to rest was not great. However, the mine itself was a very modern mine, round about 9,000 tons a day, and there were all sorts working there. We never had our guards down the mine – they left us at the top of the shaft – but there were shift bosses, they were all armed of course, and we were under their control.

As regards the work we had to do down there, we were rather fortunate because the Dunkirk boys had been here quite a long while before us and they advised us on the procedure – to do as little as possible. Your first job normally was to be assigned to what they called filling. That meant you were filling the trucks with loose coal and doing that all shift – they were eight-hour shifts. When you first start down there, you're not supposed to be coalminers, so when you get a shovelful you just throw it over the wagon, anywhere at all, but not in it, and if we did that, they told us, we'd get abused, but to stick to it. So we stuck to it and we got abused, and when the following morning arrived and they were allotting the jobs, the German would just about throw his hat down and say, "Don't want him, he's no good," and that went on for a while, so we got shifted to helping people doing other jobs.

And everything round the mine was very modern. As a result of our poor performances on shovelling, most of our chaps ended up on controlling shakers and conveyors and endless ropes, and helping the people servicing and running new shafts in the mine, which led to a lot easier life and a lot more time to yourself. It also gave you plenty of opportunity for a bit of sabotage.

Pretty easy days, too, because you'd done so much work and decided you had done enough for the shift, and you'd go over and have a bit of a snore-off. The shift bosses were easily identified because they had reflectors, bright reflectors, on their helmets, and you could see them coming a long way. So you were normally safe as long as someone was awake.

And the next thing was, of course, after the shifts came up and we had a really good hot shower, plenty of soap and back to the barracks, where the guards were waiting for you and they would search you. It was amazing what came in on the feet of boots and stuff like that – it was just amazing what got in the camp. The Commandant, German Commandant, was named "John the Baptist", and he was a very sadistic anti-prisoner sort of a chap. But he was not very well liked even by his guards – he used to drill them round the perimeter of the camp outside, and some of the lads used to take a delight, when they were marching outside, in singing out "Halt!", and everyone would halt and the sergeant would be marching on by himself. He'd go mad and demand an inspection, and it didn't matter what time of the day, afternoon or evening, it was.

And this particular time it was cold, and once you got into your hut, you stripped off because one thing we did have plenty of was heat – you'd coal for the stoves – and when they arrived on the search I was standing with my back to the stove pipe, and when they came in for inspection you had to stand to attention. Everybody had to get out of bed, stand to attention, and this particular day there was one chap in the top bunk there and he was just a bit slow coming to and didn't quite see why he should get out of bed. So he was asked quite politely why he was still in bed, and he says, "I'm too tired to get up." With that they took the side of the bed and gave it a pull – all the slats fell through and he fell through, and then they set about wrecking the place. And one of the guards there shoved me as he went past and I went up against the almost white-hot flue pipe, which worried me for a long while. Then, of course, the usual routine after that sort of racket was another inspection in 20 minutes' time, and that filled in quite a bit of the day. He was certainly not a popular person.

After about two years – might have just been a little bit over – quite a number of us were transferred to Katowice, which is in Poland. And there was a mine there at Sosnowiec, very close to Katowice, and it was quite primitive; they even had ponies, pit ponies, and it took us a while to get used to it. The German camp there was quite good; the Commandant was known as the Wolf and acted very much like one. It was the same procedure there when we went down in the shaft – we had no guards and we ended up much the same as we were doing in the other mine, except that there was no machinery. The work was not so bad, but the air was, and I was carted out a couple of times, and once you got out you vomited for a day and a bit, and then you were sent back to work again.

And after the second time I thought, well, there's no future in this, so there was a chap from Gisborne, a friend of mine, and we decided that we would do something about it. So we bound a handkerchief around my finger and he gave it a belt with a pipe over a metal plate, so I went up in the lift and the old Commandant was there, and he takes a look at me and asked what was wrong. So I said I think I must have broken a finger, and he shouts out, "Sabotage, sabotage, left hand, left hand!" So I informed him that I'd been in Germany long enough to know all that; if I'd done it myself I would have done my right hand, which he more or less accepted, so I was taken in to Katowice to the doctor there and they put it in plaster of Paris and sent me back to camp and I was sent to a hospital which was run by British doctors and was well inside Poland. I was very, very fortunate, in so much as the doctor I saw had been a Harley Street specialist, Dr Carmichael. And he had a look at it, stripped the plaster off it, stuck a couple of splints on it, and away I went and it seemed to be quite all right.

It was very nice there – Red Cross parcels and nice beds and good food – and after a fortnight or so I worked out that I was just about due to go back, and thinking of how I could prolong my stay there, when Joe Stalin's cobbers all arrived on the scene and we had to evacuate. That was Christmas Eve they evacuated us, and we set off, I don't know, it must have been about a hundred of us all told, and the first day's march was between the German artillery and their front line – and midwinter, of course. There was snow everywhere, and from just about the first week, I think, we slept in football fields, 2 or 3 foot of snow, and by huddling together and that we managed to survive. And that went on until we got to the Oder River, crossed that, and we had three days in a hospital there while they fought to keep the Russians from crossing the river, which was frozen over. And round the back they had these 12-barrel mortars about every hundred yards, and we always knew when there was an attack on because these things could fire two, four, six or 12 barrels at a time, and a regular din.

Anyhow, after that a train took us to Sagan. We had a few days there and then continued on the march, and we went south to Regensburg and back up towards Springburg, and there were a lot of casualties. We had a few Russians joining us and odds and sods when we were on the road, and the Germans at that stage were quite trigger-happy, and if you stopped and the boys scattered around in the paddocks or anything like that to ease themselves, they'd fire at them and they didn't seem to worry whether they hit them or not. On top of that, when we got to Germany we only had the stuff we stood up in. I was very fortunate in getting a new pair of boots when I was at Sosnowiec, and I received the only parcel I ever got from home, which included a set of green hide soles which the bootmaker there, the chap who did the boot repairs, put on the new boots. Fortunately for me they saw me right out – some of the poor beggars went right through their boots, and it was sad to see, even blood marks in the snow as they were struggling along.

So the Germans, apparently, really didn't know what to do with us. They had the British and Americans arriving from the coast and the Russians pushing in the other way, and so we eventually ended up at Stalag 9, which had been an American prisoner of war camp, but they had been evacuated. And from there we went on, round about 16 to 28 kilometres a day, and by this time they were putting us up at night in barns or whatever on farms. As soon as we were led off into the courtyard where buildings were, a few of us would hop into the building and try and make a nest, and the others would sort the area out and see what was available, what we could pinch and what we couldn't.

Eventually, well we had two or three days' rest in one place, and eventually we got to Bad Ulm, which was up on fairly rugged country – had been a health resort round there – and we arrived about 14 March and spent the rest of the time there. And there some of our planes used to come over and they took quite an interest in the place, so we grabbed toilet paper and laid stones on them with the letters POW on the ground. When they came over they'd dip their wings and carry on. While we were there the Gestapo or the storm troopers arrived to shift us. We had virtually nothing to eat and there was a German doctor there, and between the German doctor and one of our doctors, they jacked up a couple of cases of meningitis and they issued a proclamation that it would be dangerous for the German public to have us roaming round amongst them, and so we were allowed to stay there.

At one stage we were marching down a long valley – just can't remember where it was – and these planes started to go over about 9am, and they kept going over, continual roar, right up to lunch-time. And by that time the vibrations from the planes was so great, the whole ground appeared to be shaking, just like a large earthquake. I think it was when they were bombing Hamburg or one of those big raids that went on about that time. And on the air business I would like to compare the American bombing with the RAF. I had occasion once to go into the main camp, the main Stalag, which had been transferred from V111B to Stalag 344, and during the trip we passed two places; one was a conversion coal-to-oil factory, which had been attacked by the RAF, and another was a factory of, couldn't tell what it was, but the Americans attacked that factory, and they got the factory all right but they got the town and countryside for miles round it as well. The synthetic oil and fuel place was amazing – we went right past that, very close to it on the train, and it was a complete write-off, everything screwed up like benzine tins, and there was a lawn along one side of it, a road, a lawn and houses, and the only thing hit outside the target was a bit of meadow by the houses.

The battle for Bad Ulm, which took place on the flat, but which we couldn't see, was being fought, and eventually taken. And I think it was 1 April that an American tank arrives up at the main gates of the prison camp with about 14 or 16 GIs behind it. By this time, of course, any ratbag guards had taken off and there were just a few Germans, the better ones, there, and when we saw the tank coming in and that they were more or less ready to capitulate, we said, well, it's your turn to do the chores now, boys. The tank pulled up and they had the turret open and an American officer was there in the tank, and we were all clustering round, and first thing he said was, "Well, boys, if you've got any grudge deals to do, get 'em over with before we get organised."

But we were taken down to the airstrip hospital and looked after there for a week; we were very weak and thin by then. I myself was just over 6 stone when I got to England, and normally I'm about 11 stone. And the food they fed us from their point of view was very good, because it was gradually getting us used to eating; however, we were not anticipating a slow start on to food again. So they went out and raided the American food dump that was alongside, and some were not feeling too well next morning.

About a week later they flew us out on a C47 – we know them here as DC3s – and we spent most of our time on the trip over putting our heads in buckets because we'd over-eaten, and they flew us to a town just north of Le Havre. There they deloused us and set us up in uniforms, and we were there for a couple of days, and then they flew us to England.'

Captain George Arthur Brown, 20th Battalion, NZ Infantry, had been severely wounded in the fighting in Crete and had been taken prisoner and flown to Athens:

'I was then put on the back of a truck and I think they must have toured Athens trying to find a hospital. We reached one prisoner of war hospital and apparently I wasn't to go there, so I was taken to another one, and I was dumped on the floor at the entrance. Somebody came and took my water bottle away from me, and I lay there and I lay there and I lay there. People came along, looked at my docket and did nothing about it, so I called a couple of them over and said, "Look, how long am I going to stay here?" So then action started. And I found out the reason for the delay was because they had to carry me up six flights of stairs to a ward.

Then the doctor came along and, after examining me, he said, "I'm afraid you'll have a dot and carry one," so I immediately knew that that was having a leg off. Then I said, "Hell, doc, I want to run a pub when I get back to New Zealand," and he said, "Well, you've got gas gangrene and it's got to come off." So I was taken away to the theatre, and after the operation I was put into what they called the "dying ward" – it had two beds in it. A couple of blokes died while I was there; the third one that came in, he had a chest wound, he was a member of the Welsh Regiment on Crete, and he kept me alive by telling me the history of his regiment, getting hold of a mirror and putting it in front of me so that I could look out to the sea.

After a few weeks there, with dressings stinking like hell, two New Zealand doctors came along and they said, "We've got a few eggs and a few tomatoes – we're going to carry you up to our quarters and give you a fine meal," which they did. Then, when I was able to be moved, I was taken to the Officers' Ward, which was on the top floor of the building, and it had a sun-deck on top, so I used to go up and lie on the bed on the sun-deck, expose my stump, which was still raw, to the sun, and I think that's how I made a steady, rapid recovery.

After quite some weeks we were told that we were moving to Germany. We were put on an Italian hospital ship in Piraeus Harbour with German guards on board, and I and several other officers were put down in the bowels of the ship in two- or three-deck bunks. And I knew a little bit of French, and in my faltering French, when our meal came round, I said, "Are the officers expected to eat here?" Our meal was instantly whipped away and we were gathered up and taken up to a stateroom with cabins on either side and a dining area in the middle, and I found myself sitting at the head of the table with a fairly elderly Italian nurse standing behind me with her arms on my shoulders. I had my first bath on board that ship – a friend helped me into it and helped me out – it was great. There were no lavatory pans as we know them – they were all squat. Imagine me trying to squat on one leg, which I did anyway.

All round me were very healthy-looking blokes, and I wondered who they were until we got talking on deck and we found out they were supposedly German wounded from Crete. Some of them spoke very good English, and they said, "Where are you going?" and I said, "Oh, we're en route to England."

"Oh, you get to England, we'll bomb you and you'll lose your other leg."

However, we took that in good spirits and we said, "You know, we have an old saying, 'He who fights and runs away, lives to fight another day'."

We had a Roman Catholic padre on board who spoke very good English, Italian, and he took messages from us that he said he'd send through Vatican radio to England. I sent a message to my aunt, my mother's sister – she didn't actually hear it, but somebody did hear it and passed it on to her.

When we reached Salonika the Italians put another meal on for us, and as we were waiting on deck this lovely stewardess came along and started stuffing white bread rolls into our shirts, and I said, "Oh, we don't want these, we're going to England."

"You'll need them," she said. "We know the Germans."

Now I spoke about these healthy blokes in the toilet; they marched off in full battle order off the hospital ship, formed up off the wharf and away.

We were put on trucks and taken to a prisoner of war camp which had previously been the old Turkish barracks, derelict. I think I had a mattress, I was carrying a blanket – the place was filthy. Chaps had been there for weeks or months with dysentery, beriberi, malaria. The shortest way to the latrines was through a room and out of a window, and the route was lined with faeces. I was pretty fit, but after a while there I started to use that window.

I had adopted a sergeant of our battalion who had been very good to me in Athens hospital, showering me and helping me upstairs, and I wanted to stick with him – Jim Hesson from Alexandra (now dead). Word came that we were going to Germany, so I said, "Jim, you and I will stick together," but, no – Jim had his arm in a pair of plain splints but he was put in a cattle truck. I waited for a couple of days and I went on a hospital train – beautiful, white sheets, food came regularly. I had a little bit of money left. We stopped at one station in Yugoslavia, and there was fruit for sale; I beckoned the German orderly with some money to buy fruit, which he did, and I was able to get enough fruit for our carriage.

Eventually we reached Germany and we stopped off at Ulm, and the German equivalent of our Red Cross were on the platform – there were Germans on the train too, serving out eats. I put my head out of the window and one of the nurses said something to me, and I said, "Ja, ja," and a drink was brought me, and a big fat German in uniform came along, took it out of my hand and spoke to this girl, and she did look crestfallen.

Then we went on and we reached the town of Rottweil in Bavaria. It was late at night and we were told to get dressed and went out and there were armed Germans on each side from our carriage out to the road with fixed bayonets, and we were put on trucks and taken to a hospital where we had the ground floor, the French had the second floor and the Serbs and French had the top floor. My clothes had been taken away from me and I'd been given a pair of long-johns and a singlet; it was autumn and I froze all night. It took a long while for any Red Cross food parcels to reach us, but when they came and when parcels started arriving from New Zealand, we were a pretty happy lot.

Some of the troops were taken away to officer camps, which left four amputees, three with legs off and one with an arm off – two New Zealanders, an Australian and an Englishman – and we travelled by train to the north of Germany to a place called Rotenburg, half way between Kassel and Frankfurt. We had to change trains often and we had an old German guard with us with a rifle, and on some of the changes we made we carried his rifle while he carried our gear. At one station we were put in wheelchairs, with our wooden legs stuck out in front of us, and we passed a German troop train with officers and NCOs on the platform saying goodbye to their girlfriends and wives, and we threw salutes at every officer we could find. We thought, you poor devils, you're going to the Russian front. Occasionally we saw parties of Jews, and very occasionally we could slip them a piece of chocolate or a cigarette because the Germans were so wary. I think at one stage on our journey we were on the Berlin Express – we had a lovely compartment, the guard was with us and we'd just handed him a piece of chocolate – and the door was flung open and a German officer came in and we thought that guard had had it. But he questioned him, who we were and where we were going, and left him in peace; he didn't say anything about the chocolate. So we arrived at Rotenburg late at night and they wanted me to walk, and I said no, I wouldn't walk, it was too far, so the commandant got his car out – it was a little Opel – and two or three of us squeezed into that. That was a pretty good camp. The senior British officer was Brigadier Nicholson, who was in charge of the troops at Calais and who refused to surrender, thus helping matters at Dunkirk.

Then I think I said that my eyes were getting bad, so they sent me to Klosterhiner where there was an eye doctor. While I was there I used to go and take a blanket out and lie on the lawn and read, and the British doctor in charge put an order out that only the orderlies and staff were allowed to use the lawns. So the patients said, "What do we do about this," so I said, "Well, I'll break it." So next morning I took my blanket and my book and settled myself on the lawn; the guard looked at me and said nothing, and along stormed a German officer outside the wire. He must have been a Prussian because he had a sabre cut on his face. And he roared at me in German and I took no notice until I heard a round being put in the breech, and I gathered everything up and went. Next day we were allowed on the lawn.

We were given the offer, would we like to go back to Rotenburg or would we like to go to Spangenberg? So I decided I'd go to Spangenberg. It was a good camp – we were allowed out into nearby fields to get away from camp atmosphere. From Spangenberg we got word that we were being repatriated. We eventually reached an assembly point and were taken down to the railway station. We officers were given a carriage that was half sleeping berths and half lounge. Food was brought in regularly and the German accompanying the food I recognised as the German who was our orderly from Athens to Germany, and who bought the fruit for me in Yugoslavia. I had a few photos of myself taken in hospital, in German hospital garb, and got somebody to tell me what the German words were for "Thank you for what you did for me from Athens to Germany two and a half years ago", and signed it with my rank, number and unit, and I hope that helped him.

Sometimes of an evening we'd have a piece of chocolate given to us – that was a special present from the Führer. Another evening we had tomato sauce, which was a special present from the Führer. It was quite a pleasant journey, and we eventually reached Marseilles. We officers were put in, I think, it was a building called the Queen Victoria Hospital – it still had a British caretaker, although the hospital was closed and had been opened for us. The men slept in beds or bunks in the barracks in the garden.

After a few days we went by ambulance down to the port, and I forget the name of the German regiment that had the skull and crossbones on their hats – SS – but they were there to carry our bags or what luggage we had, which they did. I can't remember what the accommodation was like – oh yes, it was an Italian hospital ship with a few German deck officers and army officers, and we were put in a cabin of about three. We had access to a bathroom with a bath – that was lovely. We ate in the same dining saloon as the German and Italian officers – they were at one end, we were the other end – we didn't mix; but here again we got special presents from the Führer, it might be a couple of cigarettes or a piece of chocolate. We passed through quite a pleasant time and then we reached Barcelona, and the British ships had come over from Egypt bringing the German wounded for repatriation and protected personnel, and we had blokes like myself, "Unfit for Military Service", and a lot of protected personnel. And so we sailed for Alexandria.'

Corporal Keith Newth had been wounded and taken prisoner during the battle at Sidi Rezegh in North Africa and, after some rough and ready treatment there, had been shipped in a hospital ship to Italy:

'I was taken to a POW Camp, Camp 057, almost at the border between Italy and the Brenner Pass, and it was from there that I was to be repatriated after about six or seven months. I was then taken down to Altamura Hospital where we were being repatriated from. And it was there, on the day that we were coming home, that I had this confrontation with the Italian orderly for fighting with a one-legged Aussie. I did my top, belted the orderly and took the Aussie back to his bed. For this I was put in a dungeon for three weeks and stopped from coming home. And they let the boys in at half past one in the morning to say goodbye to me on their way back. That was the toughest night I think I've ever spent. They tried to send me from the hospital to a prisoner of war camp and punishment camp, and the nuns, well they ran all the hospitals in Italy, and they wouldn't let them send me, and they kept me at the hospital there right up until Sicily fell. I was in that hospital then, thanks to the nuns and the Mother Superior – I wasn't a Catholic, but they couldn't have been nicer.

When Sicily fell they wanted the hospitals for their Axis wounded, so we were sent up to Simona, and that was where we escaped from. We had had word the Allies would be up to release us out of camp. After two days we realised there was no sign of them, and the Jerries had come in to take over the camp, so we took off over the Apennines, three of us, and we took a few Red Cross parcels with us. People were going in all directions and the Jerries sent some of their troops up to bring them in, so we went off down to the village of Caramanico and hid down there. And two girls came along to pick up wood and we went out and said to these girls that we were British prisoners and we'd escaped from the Simona camp, and they said, "If you wait till dark we will come up after dark and pick you up and take you down to our homes." So they did, and took us down to this old farmer's place in Caramanico, and because the Jerries were going in and out of Caramanico all the time, we daren't poke our noses outside or even let the neighbours know.

And we were there for months with them, and then we decided to take off, and there was a doctor in Caramanico and his sister who got us civvy clothes, burnt our uniforms, and got an alpine trooper to guide us through over the Sangro River and put us on the way down towards Pescaro where we knew that the British were. We had with us a Fleet Air Arm pilot, an American lieutenant and two Tommies, so we finished up with eight of us.

We were on top of a very high hill and up there was on old monastery, which had been or was being renovated. Well, in this building we found that there was a place which the workmen had been using as accommodation. There was a fireplace in it and so forth, and so we took this over. From up there we could see down at the bottom the British on the one side of the river and the Jerries on the other side. And we had one man walking along the perimeter every morning just to watch the movement and make sure the Jerries weren't coming our way. And up there, there were two shepherds and they had quite a large mob of sheep, and they killed a sheep for us and we gave them a chit to give to the British to pay for whatever they gave us.

Well, they were very good to us, those chaps, but worried because Jerry was taking all the young Italians through to Germany and putting them to work. So we decided if these boys, when we got to a village, if they'd go in and make sure there were no Germans in the village, and arrange for us to sleep there, we would see them right when we got through to the British lines, and make sure they were treated right. And this worked all right until one of our boys, actually another Kiwi, he got into the dungeon of this old church and there were a lot of skulls and bones down, there so he brought a couple of crossbones up and put them on the mantelpiece over the fireplace we had in this hut. And when these two Italian boys came back, they just crossed themselves and took off. And at half past eight that night, just as we were going to go into bed and two of the boys went out to relieve themselves, we heard, "Hands up." Doug, the other Kiwi, and I hid behind the chimney and in came a paratrooper; he was bristling with ammunition and guns, and there were eight of them.

"Come, come," he said, so we thought we'd better come – it didn't look too good.

We went out with him and the officer was with them. He said, "There's only six of you – where are the other two?"

I said, "No, there were only six of us here."

"I'm sorry gentlemen," he said, "I know there were eight of you."

He was told about us by these two Italian boys who had got the breeze up and went down and brought this platoon up from the village. He spoke perfect English, this German officer, and he said, "I know it will be easy (it was pitch dark) to escape going down off here," so he said, "Anybody who tries to escape, they'll be shot."

And old Bill Wilson, the American officer, said, "Well, what are you going to do, boys?"

We said, "Don't worry, Bill, we'll play ball."

Well, climbing down in the dark, they were slipping and sliding, and every time somebody slipped they'd feel a Luger stuck in their back. Well, we got down on to the road eventually and started, and this officer said, "Oh well, we might as well be cheerful, so let's sing as we walk along. What about some songs?" Somebody said what about "Hanging Out the Washing on the Siegfried Line" and he said that's taboo, but he started off with "It's a Long Way to Tipperary".

So I said to him, "Where did you learn to speak such perfect English?" and he said, "Before the war I was at university in Chicago."

And we were complaining about the cold, and he said, "Don't worry, boys," that's what he called us, "once we get down to headquarters, do you like German schnapps?"

I said, "No."

He said, "Well, that'll warm you up," he said. "We'll make sure that you get some schnapps when we get down there."

So then a motorcycle came along and he stopped him and sent this boy into the village and sent back two cars to pick us up. The two boys that sold us, he took them in one car and we were put in this other car and taken down to the village

And they'd taken over the Padrone's house – that's the mayor of the village – for headquarters, and I'll never forget, it reminded me of the old spy pictures you used to see. We went upstairs and there were big double doors, and he threw these doors open and here was a huge room with four or five settees around it and tables set in a big U. And there must have been 20 or 30 German paratroopers there and we were in civvy clothes and one chap came over and he said, "Are you Englanders?" and we said, "No, we're Kiwis, New Zealanders." "Oh," he said, "New Zealanders are good chaps."

And the officer said, "Well gentlemen, we're having a dinner tonight before we go into action tomorrow and you are to join us." He said, "You other ranks sit down here," and he took the officers with him up to the top table. Well they had pork, they had mashed potatoes, it was a fantastic meal, and we hadn't had anything decent for quite a while, and we had this wonderful meal. And sure enough a half bottle of schnapps came round for us, which really warmed us up. And then in my pocket – as I said before we were in civvy clothes – in my top pocket there was a cigarette case which a Yugoslav prisoner had made for me in the prison camp from an aluminium

Italian dixie. It was sitting there and he picked it up out of my pocket and there was nothing in it, and he just took off and I said to the other boys, "Well, that's the last I'll see of that." Within five minutes he was back, put it in my pocket, and I took it out and opened it up and it was full of cigarettes.

And when we'd finished this meal, we hadn't had a chance to have a decent wash or anything all the time we'd been on the move, and I said to him was there any chance of having a wash and clean up. He took us in a room; he said, "I'm sorry gentlemen that I haven't proper beds for you – my men are using those."

We went into this room and here on the floor were all the guards; they'd been on duty and they were going to go on guard duty later on in the evening. And he said something to them in German and they turned round, opened their packs and handed us soap, toothbrushes and toothpaste. I'll never forget that evening. We went to bed and when we got up in the morning we had a beautiful breakfast given us and he said, "I'm sorry gentlemen, today you will be taken back to headquarters and you will find the German troops are the same as your own – front-line troops are genuine and the further back you go, you get what you call the shit." And he was quite right.

We took off in the cars and finished up at the railway station. Standing in the railway yards was an ammunition train which the Allies had blown up and was quite a mess. After that, I can't remember how long, we were taken in to cattle trucks and taken off and through the Brenner Pass by rail, and finished up in Renzberg, about 35 kilometres from Munich. And it was a transit camp where we were taken to there, and while we were there it was turned into an NCOs camp. And that's where I stayed until I was repatriated.

I left Germany on 5 January 1945 in a Red Cross train. We went up to Anneberg – we were in a Duke's castle in Anneberg which the Jerries had taken over. We had waiters at the table and we were treated like lords. We all felt the idea was that we would forget about the bad times and say, when we got home, that Jerry wasn't a bad sort of a chap. I remember that paratroop officer, he said, "We should not be fighting each other," he said, "we're in the same boat, we've got the Italians and you've got the Yanks." But he said, "Germany and the British should never be fighting."

The camp in Renzberg – Stalag VIIA was our camp – there were 75,000 in the camp, 45,000 Ruskies. It was a huge camp; it was on the edge of the Black Forest and the Camp Commandant had been a prisoner of war in Dover during the First World War, and he couldn't have been more pro-English. Whenever the Gestapo came to do the camp over, he sent his guards in, they pulled the floors up, hid anything we were not supposed to have, put them down, dust them over. The Gestapo would do the camp over, and then after the Gestapo had gone, they'd pull up the floorboards and give it back.

We were taken by train and then came right down through Anneberg, and that was the place where the V1 and V2 rockets were being made, and Jerry had blown everything up. We came through there to Lake Constance, and we pulled up on one line. There were three lines – there was an empty train, there was our train and then there was an empty line on the centre. And a train drove up this empty line; it was full of German ex-prisoners of war. Some of them wanted to cut our throats, others were very friendly and gave us magazines, and they went out of that train into the empty one on the side. We got out of the one we were in and into the one they'd come in; we moved 200 yards under an overhead bridge and there was, "Where are all the Kiwis?" And it was Ace Wood's sister there and she was handing us out cigarettes, chocolates and Lord knows what. Just within a distance of 200 yards we were from prisoners of war to free men.

And we came then, right down through from Lake Constance, down through France, and the Kiwis for some reason or other were taken to a hospital in Geneva. And each man had a nurse to himself. My nurse was Gabrielle, and, oh, she gave me quite a number of souvenirs to bring home to Lorna, who is now my wife. We went and sat on the station to go back to Marseilles, and we sat until midnight, a beautiful clear night. And all the Swiss guards and the nurses came on to the train with us, and as the train was due to pull out of there, and there was snow everywhere, and they were singing their yodelling songs. It was out of this world – a clear still night and all these beautiful voices yodelling. We Kiwis, we all started up with "Now is the Hour", but we only got about four or five lines and we choked.'

Reginald Ralph Urwin, after being rescued by the U-boat that sank his ship, had eventually arrived in Germany and his prisoner of war camp:

'I was registered in the Merchant Navy side of the camp and given a number and clothing and so on, and was allocated a barrack to live in, in one of these huts. Once I'd got to this place, a lot of the chaps were around wanting to know what was the latest news, what was happening in England at the present time, how the state of the war was, and so on. There was lots of questions they asked me, which I afterwards thought was a bit superfluous because I learned that they had radios in the camp, illicit radios, and it wasn't until my attendance at the final, the ultimate reunion of the prisoners of war, the Mulag Prisoners of War Association dinner, that I realised that.

One chap came up to me and said, "I know you, you were a plant," he said. "You were the plant in the camp."

And I said, "Hey, hey, hey, why do you call me that."

"Oh," he said, "we always thought you were a German," and they did – this is a fact – and I couldn't believe this. He said, "Your story was just too silly for words – you were the only one off the ship, the only member of the crew off the ship," he said. "You came here on a German submarine and you were put into this camp and we couldn't accept that, we couldn't believe it," and they always considered that I was a German spy, and to me, when he told me that, it was just dreadful. Looking at it in restrospect I realise now why I couldn't get on to a football team, I couldn't join in the sports – there was always an excuse, silly little niggly things, you know, and I didn't sort of feel accepted. No, it was a strange, strange feeling, but I got on with it because I thought that was the norm, and obviously it wasn't.

The camp itself, we did pretty well, we used to get a parcel, one parcel a fortnight from the Red Cross, and this consisted of the basics and the odd treat, and this used to last us over the following fortnight until another issue. As the war went on and it progressed, it got slowly worse and it got that there was a parcel between two men, and then three men, and then the parcels dried up at one stage towards the latter stages, because the Germans couldn't guarantee the delivery of them and they couldn't guarantee the safety of the pick-up people – the prisoners who used to go down to the station to load these parcels on to trucks and bring them back to the camp.

At that time we were pretty well situated there as far as observation went; we were between Hamburg and Bremen and we used to see these air raids or the effects of them anyway, fire storms and the bombing. We could hear sometimes some of it – we could see the searchlights and these thousand-bomber raids. The planes used to come over and we were in the flight path of some of these raids and we knew they were taking a bit of a pounding.

This went on for a while, as I said before; I couldn't do anything much about getting in touch with the Escape Committees or anyone. I was about 17 then and I was full of life and I didn't want to be behind barbed wire, and I thought, well, if I could get out I would. Anyway, I was fortunate enough at one stage to be picked for a farming gang – this was chaps who used to go to the surrounding farms and give a bit of a hand on whatever they were doing.

At that time the Germans, I think, were on a ration of about three or four cigarettes a day, and we used to get tins of 50 in our parcels and not everyone smoked in the camp, so there was an abundance of cigarettes around inside the camp. Of course a lot of this was used for business with the guards. There was chocolate and soap, which was another good medium of exchange. It brought fresh eggs in there, we got milk and cream in the camp. We brought it in and, of course, as I said before, the guards at that time were only on a very minimal ration of cigarettes and the way we used to get them in was to hold a couple of cigarettes in our hand as we came through the gate, and when the guards came to search you, you gave them these cigarettes and they invariably let you through, in a lot of cases. You got the odd very thorough guard that would search you and he would really go over you with a fine tooth comb and he would throw your cigarettes on the ground and stamp on them, and then you knew you were going to be done and he'd do you. For that you'd get a mandatory seven days on bread and water in the camp's prison.

I got into this farm commando, "barrow commando" as they called it. The first thing I thought of when I went out there was to try to escape, and so I managed to take out some stores. We used to concoct an escape ration which consisted of chocolate; we melted the chocolate, mixing in raisins and prunes and stuff like that and then resetting it. So we did this sort of thing and I made up a batch of this and took it out of the camp and stashed it away, hid it against the day when I would have a go. Anyway, the time did arrive one day that the farmer asked me – and we were allowed free rein pretty well because we were sort of on parole, but I'd never promised that I wouldn't attempt to escape or anything like that – well, the farmer asked me to go up the road to help this other farmer with a job. I said, "Right, OK," so I picked up my escape gear and went up this road to give a hand on this farm, but I took a deviation and didn't get there, and I was pretty well on my way to Zeeland. I think there must have been Army manoeuvres or something going on, because I'd been about three to four hours tramping across paddocks, through ditches, down hedgerows and trying to keep away from the main thoroughfare as much as I could, and I ran into a bunch of Germans which was unfortunate. I was lucky – I was able to drop my gear, all my escape stuff, and I just dropped it in a ditch close to where I was, and it was a dead give-away. I was surrounded by these people virtually. How the hell I got through them I don't know in the first place, but I dumped everything and I had no recourse but to walk out. I told them I was lost and was looking for such and such a farm that I was supposed to be helping. They took me back, they asked me where I was from, and I told them the camp, I told them the farmer. They took me back to the farmer, and the farmer verified my story.

It was probably some time about August when I thought I could have another go. I'd got a compass that had been made in the camp and a very rough sort of map, and two of us thought we'd have a go this time. We got all our stuff together and got it outside the camp, got it through the guard at the gate and got it outside the camp, and we got it all ready to make a run at the first available chance. Round about this time, I think it was haymaking, it was a haymaking exercise we were supposed to be going on, and we thought if we can be set for that when the haymaking season was at its peak, we stood a reasonable sort of chance.

So we got all our stuff together, went away on this farm to help with the haymaking, and round about lunch-time everyone had their lunch and you sat where you wanted to, and so Reg and I decided we were off. So we took off and we sort of ambled slowly away just with our hay rakes as if we were going down to the bottom paddock to do some hayturning or something, and we had out little bits and pieces stashed about us and we just kept going. We just kept walking, walking, and there was no sign of any pursuit or anything like that, so we sort of rushed to a bit of a forest there and we stopped just to have a check and see where we were and checked the map, checked the compass – right, we'll head for Zeven. So we went to Zeven and there we saw what appeared to be a Post Office or something like that, and we pinched a couple of bikes and with the hay rakes over our shoulders and on the bikes we just wandered quietly over the town, not too slowly but, you know, we were worried because we'd heard that if you were caught thieving anything in Germany you were shot, you know, and we'd pinched these bikes, and it wasn't in the plan at all – we didn't intend to do anything like that.

We didn't have any means of identification, we didn't have any false papers, anything like that – all we had was our prisoner of war tags, which we kept, and just as well we did. We got outside of Zeven and we holed up; we had a few nights under the stars and we travelled during the day and we got through as far as Gelsenkirchen, which was almost on the German border. We got to the outskirts of Gelsenkirchen and we thought, well now, it's a big place, a big city, and we thought, well, we've got to get through this place, and we can't get through on bikes and we can't have hay rakes, so we dumped the bikes in a stream just before the outskirts of Gelsenkirchen and dumped the hay rakes and then we just wandered in on foot, just quietly, unassuming – hopefully we were being as inconspicuous as we possibly could.

Then there was an air raid warning sounded and we wondered what the blazes we do now, because we could see people rushing, everything was suddenly dropped, and people were rushing off in all sorts of directions, so we followed them to an underground shelter which we got in to. We got in line and went in there. We were in there for probably half an hour or so, I suppose, but we didn't hear anything, didn't hear any bombs or planes or anything. We were coming out and at the top end of the passageway on the way out I could see this chap and he was checking papers. We thought we'd try and brazen it through anyway. So we said we were French workers working for a farm; we'd been in here to the market and we'd got caught in the air raid, but unfortunately there was a Frenchman behind us and he started to speak to us in French and he completely blew us away and we were stranded – we couldn't talk to him. This German guard picked up on this and I think, perhaps with a little aid from the Frenchman, who was probably a volunteer worker, he was not impressed. Anyway, the game was up as far as that went – we couldn't answer this guy – so then he called someone from the door of the shelter and asked him to take us in hand, which he did, and they took us down to the Gestapo Headquarters.

The first thing that we did then after that, after we realised that the game was up, was to get our identification tags out double quick, because we'd heard about the Gestapo and we didn't like what we heard, and so we gave them our ID tags and it was only a couple of phone calls and it wasn't long before a couple of chaps arrived from the prison camp and took us back to the camp. The raid, by the way, was a false alarm – I was wild about that. We were interrogated – for that you got 28 days solitary confinement, that was a little bunker place outside the camp by itself, and you were on hard rations for 28 days.

Then we were called for by the Camp Commandant, who was almost in tears. He was elderly and a nice chap whom I liked. The camp, by the way, was manned at that time by burnt-out ex-naval men, and they didn't have a lot of time for Hitler or his methods, and they were pretty sympathetic to us. So this old Camp Commandant, anyway, had a bit of a talk to us and he said, "You know you really shouldn't try this again because you might get shot and the war is so close to an end that it would be silly for you to do anything like this ever again." He said, "The war is almost over." This was in early autumn 1944.'

Randal George McMurtry, a Captain in the Wiltshire Regiment, had been captured by the Germans in Italy and has already described his experiences up to the time he finally arrived at his prisoner of war camp in Czechoslovakia:

'It was only a small camp – about 1,900 prisoners – and in it were Stirling, the SAS Commander, and a Captain Gardiner VC and various people like that, a mixture of people who'd been proper nuisances to the Germans, what with escaping and that sort of thing. There were also a lot of university professors and teachers and they grouped us all together in this one place. The university people were tremendous – a bonus to us as prisoners. Otherwise there was very little to do there. We had a "walk around stooge" who basically was just watching out for Germans, so that the people who were manning the radio and maybe planning escapes and what have you could have early warning of their presence. There was a very big escape planned for Maristrubo, but it was discovered by the Germans and as a result of that I remember Sikhs were implicated and probably shot, but we were shifted out of the place to Germany, fast by train. As we went through Germany we were handcuffed. So the first thing we found out very quickly was how to undo those things. In our carriage we all undid them all at the same time, and demonstrated that we no longer were wearing them whilst the guards sort of looked in consternation; then they laughed, but then they asked us would we please pretend they were on when we got to a station because of the SS. So we did that. What brought the SS buzzing around was we had a home-made duplicator there and we'd been throwing out leaflets all along the line about what a waste of time it was carrying on with the war, it was won and so on and so on. Of course once the SS got hold of the news they were very angry, and they stopped us at a station and ordered us all off, and then the German Commander, who had this quite strong manner, he said, "No," he said, "if you take them off it's your responsibility – some of them will escape."

So we were taken on into Germany and ended up at a place near Brunswick. It wasn't a safe place because it had a flying bomb site on one side and there were tank works on another side and an airport, so it had all these targets around it. And we got used to having the British coming over at night in their Mosquitos and they seemed to let the bombs go before they got to the camp, and they'd go over the top of us and then bomb targets on the other side. They were very accurate and they never hit us. By contrast the Americans in their Flying Fortresses coming over by day hit us and killed one or two prisoners, so that was just our usual experience of the Americans I guess, one of those things.

So with a friend of mine, the two of us had the idea of getting out of there and we contacted the chaps who brought the food in, who were slave workers of different nationalities I suppose, and some of them were French. We contacted two Frenchmen who wanted to go to Britain after the war, and we arranged to change clothes with them and get out, and we'd start moving towards the Army. That was put on hold and then stopped by a senior British officer.'

This decision was later rescinded and Captain McMurtry escaped as planned, joined up with an American armoured column and eventually arrived back in London in time for VE Day.

James Ian Walker, rear gunner in a Wellington bomber shot down in Belgium, has already described his experiences in hospital in Brussels and Germany. He was then sent to a German prisoner of war camp, where the compound fracture of his leg was still causing trouble:

'I was still in plaster up to the hip, and shortly after arriving at this particular camp the wounded and injured were examined by a Swiss Red

Cross party who were, at that time, establishing numbers who could be repatriated in an exchange for German injured. My leg was quite unsightly at the time; the plaster had been removed for them to have a look at it and it was rather raw-looking, and they placed me on this repatriation list, and that was only after some four or five months of captivity. I became concerned myself that the leg wasn't knitting, and having some nutritional knowledge, and as the Red Cross parcels which were coming regularly contained tins of cheese, small tins of cheese, I decided that I would try and exchange other things with the other prisoners for cheese. So each issue of Red Cross parcels I managed to get about seven tins of cheese in exchange for various items that the others wanted, and I used to mix this cheese with the German ration of potatoes that we had each day – I think it was two or three potatoes. So I would mix this up, mash it all up together, put it in a dixie and used to heat it up on the hot water pipes in our bathroom, our shower room, so I had an evening meal then of cheese and potatoes. Eventually this did the trick and my leg started to knit again and the bones healed up and the plaster was removed, and I then took all the exercise I could and got things working again, got the knee working and the ankle as far as it would go, walking around the camp, and became quite fit again. The camp life itself was not as bad as you may expect; it was no picnic, but we had entertainment and, being NCOs, we didn't have to work. We had our Red Cross parcels coming more or less regularly, we had a library, and we were able to exercise in the precincts of the camp. So life passed reasonably quickly; we had letters from home arriving and I then began to think about the possibilities of escaping.

I then became friendly with a Scottish infantryman, and he had similar ideas to me, so we decided we would make a few plans and endeavour to get out of the place. At that time we had to be particularly careful that we kept our plans to ourselves, because in the camp, if anything such as an escape took place, the Germans would come down very heavily, and all the privileges would be stopped and Red Cross parcels stopped and all the rest of it. Anybody who was contemplating escape had to keep it to themselves otherwise there were individuals in the camp who would enlighten the Germans to what was going on. So we kept it pretty much to ourselves; we had one or two people that we knew we could trust implicitly. We made our plans and we put dry rations aside, realising that there was an opportunity of getting out of the camp in a certain area. The camps at the time were an inner camp surrounded by a high barbed-wire entanglement, a no man's land in between where the guards patrolled, and then a high barbed-wire entanglement on the outer, so we had two entanglements to get through.

We had decided that daytime was our best chance of getting through. The guard in our particular part of the camp was the person who opened the gates to let out a party of prisoners removing rubbish from the camp, and it was during this time his segment of the camp would be unguarded. The time during which the guard was away from this particular area appeared sufficient for us to breach the entanglements and get out of the camp.

So the day arrived which suited our plans, and I think it was mid afternoon and we had a helper helping us to breach the inside entanglement and then to pass our luggage through to us with our bag of dry rations, and then there was the dash through the no man's land to the high entanglement on the outside. The only way we could get over that was by climbing one of the posts. We climbed the entanglement, tearing our hands rather badly on the barbed-wire, and over the top, dropped to the ground, and then disappeared into the bush that was not far away from the camp.

Then, of course, we had to put as much distance between us and the camp as possible, not knowing whether our escape had been discovered; if it had, we knew that we would be tracked by dogs, so the first thing to find was somewhere where we could cross water and endeavour to put the dogs off the scent. We did find water and crossed the water and we kept going till nightfall, not seeing a soul, no people around, and we then decided we would hide in some area of undergrowth, which we did. We rested there for some hour or two until it got dark, and then we set off. Our plan had been to travel at night. We had compasses and we had maps, which we had obtained in the camp. We carried on all that night and became very, very thirsty walking, and it was summertime, it was August, the weather was fine and warm. So we then were faced with hiding up in the daytime, and we wanted to find a spot where we could hide and it was also handy to water so that we could take water into our hiding place and also know where water was to fill our water bottles for the evening and the night-time trek.

We managed to do that on most occasions, and we had some interesting experiences during the time that we were out enjoying this freedom. We hid up one day in a cornfield, a huge cornfield, and on the outskirts of it they were beginning to harvest, but we hid up in this cornfield on the other side from where they were working, and I didn't realise at the time that we could have been eating this stuff and saving our own rations. We spent the day there in this field – we could hear the Germans talking to one another and calling out and their machinery going – and then in the evening we began our walk again.

We were heading towards Belgium, and all sorts of noises we would hear in the night. The dogs, if we got close to a village, would start barking and disturb the villagers, and we'd walk for seven or eight hours. Another night we could find nowhere to hide but in a brickwork factory – well, it wasn't a factory, it was a place where they stored their bricks and evidently dried them in structures that were 2 or 3 feet high or even higher – and the only place we could find to hide was in these small kilns, but we had to lie on these bricks, which was terribly hard. There were one or two workers coming round, but we were hidden from their sight. We could hear them speaking French, so we debated whether we'd make contact with them because we thought that maybe they were French prisoners or workers that had been brought from France. So, eventually, we decided to risk it and so we made contact with these French people, and sure enough that's what they were; we had to just trust them, of course, that they wouldn't enlighten the Germans, but they seemed very friendly and they brought us food and brought us bread and they were really quite amazed and very excited that we were there. So the day went on and nothing transpired, no Germans came, so we realised that they were going to be of help to us. Indeed, they came, and we were about to set off and one or two of them came over and gave us directions and food and wished us well on our further journeys.

Another night we found beet, beetroot fields, sugar beet – the Germans grew a lot of sugar beet to make their own sugar – and we thought we'd try those for eating, but they were a bit of a mistake. I didn't eat much of it but my Scots companion had quite a good feed of it and it upset him very much and he came very ill with it.

We contemplated trying to board a train, and we actually went into one particular spot where we thought we might be able to get on a train, but it didn't look very safe, so we carried on. Then I became concerned about my Scots companion who was so ill, and I thought I'd better try and get help for him. So then I – my own leg wasn't standing up, the one that had been injured wasn't standing up very well to the continued walking – and so I thought the best thing to do was then to make contact with the Germans. So then we reported to a Police Station; we were treated rather badly and eventually we were returned to our former camp. Again we were treated badly and they threatened to shoot us. In the end the Germans gave up, gave us two weeks bread and water, and we were kept under close observation.

Two months later the first repatriation came to take place; my name having been on it, the Germans, I suppose, were glad to get rid of me, and I was on this repatriation party. Several members of the camp met up with a Swiss Red Cross train, which took us down through France, down to Marseilles. The exchange took place in Barcelona. We boarded the ship the Germans vacated, we went to Alexandria and then back to New Zealand by hospital ship, arriving home on 14 December 1943.'

Sergeant Pilot Trevor Teague RNZAF, flying his fourth mission in a Lancaster bomber over France, was shot down but landed safely by parachute and spent eight days attempting to make the Spanish border before he was captured. His short time in a prison near Paris gave him the worst experience of his life:

'Very close to my cell somebody was very obviously being tortured and given a good beating up. The terrible blood-curdling, ear-piercing screams of pain and terror that no words of mine could ever describe continued on and on, and by this time I was really riled up with frustration at not being

Trevor Raymond Teague

able to do anything at all to help. The screams finally subsided to a mere whimper, the thudding was going on, and then there was an unearthly silence. Whether the victim had succumbed or lapsed into a merciful state of unconsciousness I've got no idea, but I've wondered through the years just what would have happened if a Jerry had come into my cell at that time, because I was so riled up I'd have been very hard pressed not to do something extremely stupid; fortunately, perhaps, for me, nobody came in. I do know that I prayed hard and long that those sadists would die long, lingering, agonising deaths themselves. Volleys of rifle fire early morning need no explanation from me – this was an evil place.'

Then en route to Germany by train Trevor Teague experienced a more humane side to his German captors:

'We finally got going on the train. It was one with a long corridor down the side and compartments. Jerries had to stand in the corridor while we sat down in the compartments, which I thought was only proper. In the compartment that I was in was a very badly burned American airman. We ascertained from him that he was in a Flying Fortress which had been shot down. His face was bloated, his hands were burnt terribly, his flying suit had all the wiring – it was a heated suit – the wiring was all dangling down and he indicated that he had had no medical attention whatsoever and he was in a terrible state. One of the Jerries in the corridor opened the door, had words with our guard, and he was finally let in to our compartment. He had a little bottle of some sort of ointment or something, and this Jerry very, very gently smeared this preparation over the Yank's face and hands, a most humane gesture from one enemy to the other. Some of us shook the Jerry's hand before we left, but we certainly all showed that we appreciated what he had done.'

Trevor Teague was later to take part in that terrible forced march from the Polish border into Germany just ahead of the Russian advance:

'It was in the middle of January 1945 and there was snow on the ground and quite a blizzard blowing when, at 2am, we set off on the march to the west. It was very cold, we were ill-fed and ill-clothed. However, we trudged through this snow; we stayed in a barn the first night, or it might have been late afternoon, and we were sort of packed into this barn. You didn't bother changing clothes or anything – you were just as you were, and I was silly enough to sit up at one stage and the surrounding blokes all filled up the space that I had for my legs, so I had to sit up all night; some of the blokes stood up all night.

It was extremely cold and we used to sleep with our boots on because they'd have frozen in the morning and you wouldn't have got them on again; some blokes had taken them off and they had to slit them to get them on. The fluid in our knees froze so it was a very painful experience starting off getting up in the morning. You sort of slept in what they call the foetal position with your knees up, and used to rub them to try and get them going, but it was extremely painful. At one stage some of the blokes had had enough and they said we're not moving. And then the Jerries got the alsatians out and stuck them in the barracks they were in and these poor beggars came out screaming with pain, sort of hopping with their knees bent until they could get their knees working again. We'd walked through snow and ice and rubbish for about 250 kilometres before we got into cattle trucks and we finally jolted our way to Luckenwalde, 30 miles south of Berlin, where we took off all our clothes, put them in a delouser and had a hot shower. Berlin at this stage was being heavily bombed, and night after night our barrack blocks shook with the bombs 30 miles away, an experience I'd slept right through.'

Eventually, after a far from comfortable time with the Russians in control, Trevor Teague was released and flown to Brussels, where he attended a concert in which a young English girl got the biggest applause of the evening when she sang a very popular song 'Don't Fence Me In'.

Sapper Alex Rodgers, wounded and captured in Crete, began his captivity in hospital in Athens:

'I was in there for quite a few months having treatment, and from there I escaped and went out in the hills 12 or 15 miles away from Athens and hid out in the hills there. The Greeks, they were fantastic, they couldn't do enough for us, and we knew the consequences if they were caught, what would happen, and they knew too. They were good, they looked after us – there were quite a few of us at this stage, there were about five or six in our group. We didn't want to get to be a burden, which meant moving around the countryside from place to place, and we slept up in the bush at night-time.

One particular time there we knew the Germans and the Gestapo were having a big blitz on the Greek people round about who were looking after soldiers, and we were sitting on this hill, there were three or four of us, and there they had this Court Martial sort of thing there with the civilians: a couple of men digging their own grave, and then they just shot them, so you see what those Greek people were made of – they sacrificed everything to look after us chaps. We never forgot that. Fantastic people.'

Alexander Rodgers was recaptured by the Germans and for the rest of the war was to experience difficult times as a prisoner of war:

'We were in prison in Salonika for a time. I've never seen rats as big as what they were there. At night-time when you were in bed you'd feel something running over you – bloody rats – and if it wasn't that it was cockroaches, there were millions of them. Seven thirty at night everybody had to be in the barracks, and we weren't allowed outside no matter what the cause was. There was one particular case there where one of the POWs was taken ill and the orderly thought he'd shoot across to the Officers' Quarters to get a doctor to come over, and even though it was only 8pm they shot him down. The poor old ill soldier, he died too, because he didn't have treatment. There were a lot of Hitler Youth chaps – they were bad, very bad, they didn't give two hoots. The tucker was poor, practically non-existent, but we got used to it after a while – we didn't carry any surplus fat.

When we left Salonika we were loaded on to these cattle trucks – there were 60 of us to a truck. It only had straw on the floor, a little porthole window, and we were on there for 12 nights and 13 days. Some of them were very sick – they had dysentery and they were given very little water. Sometimes the Red Cross would be there with a cup of soup.

We eventually got to the prisoner of war camp on the Polish border, Stalag VIIIB. There were thousands of prisoners there of many nationalities. It was winter and some of us were still in our light clothing, and no blankets or anything, so they said if you volunteer to go on a working party to a paper works in Czechoslovakia they would supply you with clothes. So we managed to get some clothing and a blanket and they sent us out on this working party. There were 35 of us, and instead of going to this paper works we finished up in this big Industrial Area Steel Works, where they were making all these toboggans and heavy artillery stuff for the Russian Front.

So there were a few of us there and we were working outside and it was snowing and cold. We started work at 6.30am and went on till 6.30pm, so we said we're not putting up with this sort of thing. I said, I'm not doing any more work for this lot – they might as well shoot us as starve us to death. So we had a meeting there – right, we go on strike. So next morning the Jerry guards came to take us to work and we said, "We're not going." Well, then the fun started – we wouldn't go, so about five hours later out came the Gestapo and they put us through the paces. The next morning they had us out of bed about 5 o'clock in the morning. These Jerry officers came along, lined us up, pulled their revolvers out and they said, "Right, fall out those who are going to work." So out of 35 of us, 30 went back to work and five of us stayed there. Well, did they give us the works. They kicked us around the room and butted us with their rifle butts and old jackboots. Anyway, the long and the short of it was we were sent back to Stalag V111B where we were marched up before the Commandant and we were given three months in solitary confinement for sabotage.

Eventually we were moved to Stalag 303, a new camp down in the Bavarian Alps just out of a place called Hohenfels. It was up in the hill in the centre of a sort of a triangle; there was Nuremberg at one point, maybe about 70 kilometres away, and then there'd be Regensburg, that would be about the same distance, and then Munich. Now these British and Yank planes during those daylight raids used to come right over the camp. The same at night-time – you'd hear them and watch them down over Nuremberg with the searchlights going, and then with the vibrations of the bombs they'd dropped, you could feel the ground shake under you, and that was what, 70 kilometres away.

With the Germans on the back foot, they thought they'd empty the camp, take us on a march over to the Black Forest, and what we heard through the grapevine was that they were going to hold us as hostages until the Yanks came. I said to my cobber Alf, "I'm not going on it," so he said, "What are you going to do?" I said, "I'm going to go AWOL for a bit," and he said, "How?" So we said we'll dig a hole underneath the hut and hide in there at night-time.'

The Germans did decide to evacuate the camp but Alexander Rodgers and his friend concealed themselves in a hole they had dug under their hut and were left behind. They then made their own way towards Nuremberg, met up with the Americans and eventually were flown to England.

CHAPTER 16

Operations in South East Asia and Japanese defeat in Burma

*A*fter the Japanese had overrun Burma the situation was extremely grave. India had little in the way of effective defence and the surviving ships of the Eastern Fleet had withdrawn to a base in East Africa. However, the Japanese halted their advance on the Chindwin River adjoining Assam, and there followed a period during which the British were able gradually to build up their forces in India and carry out air strikes against the Japanese. Then, in March 1944, the second Chindit operation was launched. This succeeded in establishing temporary bases inside Burma and disrupting Japanese communications and supply routes by blocking off the railway, road and Irrawaddy River at a point where they ran close together, blowing up supply dumps and generally harassing the Japanese occupation forces in the area. Eventually, and following upon the Japanese defeat after their abortive attacks on Imphal and Kohima, the Allies were able to re-occupy the whole of Burma. In addition, SEAC (South-East Asia Command) was planning to make landings in Malaya and mounting ever-increasing sea and air attacks in the region. All this came to an abrupt end with the dropping of the atom bombs.

Sergeant Albert Friend, Air-gunner/Radio Operator/Navigator in the RAF, following his spell of duty in Malta, flew to India and was then engaged in operations against the Japanese in Burma:

'I was posted to Asansol to 60 Squadron, which was flying Blenheims into Burma, which necessitated flying into the advanced aerodrome at Agartala, near the eastern borders of India, to refuel. From there the usual thing was for us to attack big Japanese aerodromes. We'd take off from

Agartala and the Hurricanes didn't have a long enough range to fly to Mandalay without long-range tanks, and with them they were hopeless at manoeuvring, and if they dropped them they obviously couldn't get back, so they were told not to mix it with the Japanese. So we didn't get much in the way of fighter protection. So we flew to Schwebo, which was north of Mandalay; we were eight aircraft and again we were tail-enders, being all NCOs still, still sergeants, and we attacked Schwebo from the south-west to cross the runway obliquely. We only had two guns and I think they were .303, and on the ground were 14 Japanese planes. They were Nakajima 43s (Allied reporting name: 'Oscar'), but we called them Zero Ones because that was the official way of regarding them. Two of them got off, got airborne before we put a bomb right in the middle of the runway.

The flak was very accurate – one shell burst immediately ahead of us, possibly between 5 and 10 yards ahead of us because you could smell it, you could smell the explosives – but we weren't hit with any shrapnel. Then, of course, these two Nakajimas came up to attack us. We had no fighter escort and we turned back towards the west again, and I watched these two Nakajimas come up. The first one continued to climb above us and the second one closed on us slowly from the south-east, but he was heading more to the south than towards me, more towards the Australian crew, our wing man. The other one went up and up and, of course, I had to put the periscope on to look up at him, but my guns would only elevate to about 70 degrees and I couldn't follow him any more, so I had to ignore him and he went straight over the top of us.

So I then brought my sights down to this other plane, and I estimated the range at about 550 yards, and he was closing slowly but he wasn't closing towards me, he was closing to the south. I kept my sights on him and kept trying to calculate the amount of bullet deflection I'd need because I'd calibrated my guns for 250 yards, and I thought that's too far away and I wanted it less than 300 yards before it was worth firing anything. He continued to move closer, but to the south, more to the south-west, not towards me at all, and I thought to myself is it worth firing, and I was just about to fire and the aircraft above me went whoosh through my sights. He passed my tail about 10 yards astern – very, very close – and I looked around for bullet holes and there was only one small round bullet hole in the port wing, I couldn't see any others. This first Nakajima had dived down and then he climbed up to the north of us so he was on the starboard side, and the other one took up position on our port side, and they did crossover attacks, and I couldn't fire at any of these attacks from the port side because the Australian aircraft was between me and him.

So I concentrated all the attacks on the starboard side, and he started his attack and he must have been at least 500 yards away from under our wing tip because, as soon as he came in firing at us, I thought to myself he's not allowing for deflection or bullet drop, because they were using telescopic sights, and I thought how stupid can you get. With telescopic sights you can't put accurate deflection on, and he was opening fire far too early, which was ideal for me, but I wasn't going to fire at him until he got within 300 yards. He was firing at me and I was looking down his nozzles and I knew he couldn't hit me because he wasn't allowing for deflection – he was looking down his telescopic sights. When I opened fire he broke away, he broke away under the tailplane, but that area was where I couldn't fire the guns. So when he went under the tailplane I had to tell the navigator that he'd gone under, but he was on the ball, he could see him, so he gave him a burst. I thought, gosh, he's not a very experienced flyer because he didn't get close enough.

I was looking round for these aircraft because one of them had dropped his starboard wheel down, half way down, and I thought he'd been damaged. I called him "Peg Leg" because that identified one of them from the other, and I couldn't find this Peg Leg, and I was looking around and I looked down and there was the other one with both undercarriages up coming up below the Australian aeroplane. He was coming up from underneath and the Australian aeroplane was an old Blenheim without ventral guns. Anyhow, when he came up I got my sights on him and I put my sights just ahead of the pilot and I fired about seven rounds, because the other gun's firing mechanism failed. You needed two hands to control the turret and you needed the feet to move the guns left and right and the handlebar to turn the turret and the twist grip to raise and lower the guns, so working the guns wasn't exactly easy. So I only fired about seven rounds and he went down, and I reckon I probably hit him, even wounded him, maybe killed him, and down he went, and he'd already hit the Australian aircraft, but the Australian aircraft was maintaining its position so I assumed it was all right.

After the Schwebo raid we were moved to Jessore, which was nearer to Calcutta and nearer to the Japs, a lot nearer than Asansol. So we operated from a beautiful concrete runway, and the control tower was the top of a banyan tree, a very tall, very mature banyan tree, and we had to climb to the top to the control tower, a long snaky ladder going from branch to branch to the top of the tree.

When we raided Magwe we had a Hurricane escort, six Hurricanes close escort, and I think about nine high cover. They all had long-range tanks, clumsy 200-litre long-range tanks, one under each wing. At Magwe we had 24 aeroplanes, and the first 12 were Mark V Blenheims with which 103 Squadron had been equipped, and these had a Bolton Paul turret on and the ventral guns were fired by the navigator lying down, whereas in the Mark IV he had to use a periscope to fire the guns.

The Mark V was a better aeroplane – it also had more armour-plating – but it suffered from a very poor rate of climb, so they always led and we always flew behind, and I was still tail-ender. On the bombing run we bombed Magwe, and again there were 14 Nakajimas on the ground on the photographs when we counted them. We bombed from north to south, and at the southern end of the strip was a Battery of two 75mm, and they shot Number 2 down, one of the 103 Bomber Squadron's Mark Vs, with one shell. The pilot must have pulled back on his stick, because he went up in a mass of flames in a half loop, and he came down towards me but to my port side, and he shot past me vertically, still a mass of flames with no 'chutes coming out. I didn't follow him down because there were two Nakajimas on their way up. These two Nakajimas, they reached our height and the Hurricanes never moved. Somebody from the front of the Squadron fired a Verey to bring down the top cover, but the top cover never came down. Obviously they were in radio contact with the close escort, and the close escort probably said, "Oh, there are only two of them – we won't need you. We'll call you when we need you."

These six Hurricanes were spaced out behind us and the two Nakajimas, one took up a position to the south of us way over to port, and I estimated his range at 450 yards, the other one was south-east of us, behind a Hurricane. He wasn't aimed at the Hurricane – he was too busy looking over his shoulder, probably expecting to be attacked from behind, because there was top cover there but the top cover didn't come down. The Hurricanes never changed their position – they kept flying steadily on the same course – and I wanted the Hurricanes to get out of the way so that I could fire at this Nakajima. Somebody ahead of me was firing at the Nakajima but his empty cartridge cases were hitting my turret and one of the empty cartridge cases broke the Perspex – it bounced off but it broke the Perspex. We flew along for about 10 minutes and the Nakajimas weren't going to attack us – they were too wary about the Hurricanes above and behind them – so eventually they turned round and went home. Well, we got an escort, but two Nakajimas were with us too. Anyway, back at base they saw the hole in my turret and they said, gosh, you were lucky. I didn't tell them it was only a cartridge case bouncing off; they thought it was shrapnel, but I kept quiet.

I actually flew a Blenheim once. I wasn't allowed to; I only took over the controls if the skipper wanted to have a stretch, but there was no way he could fly continuously, because he was stuck in the seat and seven hours at a time is a long time. To go to the toilet he had to get out of the seat – the Blenheims were really out of date. They'd phased them out in England, sent them to the Middle East, and then phased them out in the Middle East, but we still had them.

Squadrons 5 and 155 now had P36s – Mohawks they called them – and they had a longer range, so they escorted us on a raid to Prome, which was too far for the Hurricanes, but we had a Hurricane escort at first, part of the way. To get to Prome we had to fly between Magwe, which was a fighter 'drome, and Akyab, which was a forward 'drome, but it could have fighters on it. Here the Japanese had a supply base alongside the Irrawaddy, the railway and road. There were a lot of new huts – the photographs showed a lot of new huts, big bamboo long huts – so we bombed these huts and there was no flak, no interception, and we started some big fires there.

After we left Jessore we went close to the Japs, we went to the south-east of Chittagong to an aerodrome called Dohazari – dirt aerodrome, just a narrow strip on the bend of a river, it was all alluvial soil. We had no flak [anti-aircraft guns] there to begin with, no early warning, but when the Japs raided Chittagong they flew over the top of us, and when they flew back they flew over the top of us. They obviously knew we were there.

The first visit was from 27 twin-engined bombers, they were Kawasaki twin-fins, and about 15 Zero Ones as escort, and they bombed us. Bombs started falling, and as we had a lot of soft alluvial soil there, the bombs went in and just dug themselves in about 6 foot down, and we had no bomb disposal squad so the armourers had to do it. We were digging down to these bombs, digging deeper and deeper holes to get the bombs out of it, and these bombs were made in America. They had been captured in the Philippines to be used against us. It doesn't say much for the American bombs, because they didn't go off. We built pens around our aircraft and each aircraft had a pen that we taxied the aircraft into, and where they could be maintained, bombed up, refuelled and protected on three sides from bombing.

After we had been visited and bombed one morning by 12 Nakajimas, I went down to the aerodrome and I saw the CO and I said, "Now we should go to Magwe because those aeroplanes must have come from Magwe and they'll be landing without any fuel," and he said, "We can't do that," and I said, "Why not?" and he said, "We're standing by for an Army operation, Army co-operation." So we missed an opportunity there.

We would get a lot of local flying – it was fairly local because the Army wanted us to attack these targets – and one of the targets they gave us was an officers' billet, a Japanese officers' billet on the Mergui Peninsula just north of Akyab. He said that the billet south of that was where the "comfort women" were billeted. We were not to bomb that billet, only the army officers' billet, and it was only 15 yards away.

We flew south of Chittagong on the Bay of Bengal and there was no aerodrome there and I looked over the side and there were these Hurricanes climbing up, and I said, "Where the heck are they coming from?" I was looking over the side and I saw a Hurricane come out from under the trees, tear down the beach and take off – they were using the beach. These Hurricanes came up to escort us down the coast of the Arakan to just north of Akyab. We flew down to bomb these billets that the Japanese were supposed to be occupying somewhere in the Mergui Peninsula, and we were tail-enders again. Eight aircraft – one had turned back so there were seven aircraft – and we bombed from 3,000 feet because we wanted accuracy. We not only missed the hut where the comfort women were but we also missed the officers' mess, because we were so keen to keep our bombs away from where the comfort women were, but we bombed the other billets to the north.

We circled back over the Bay of Bengal and the Hurricanes were above us and we went down to strafe the Japanese on the ground. I couldn't see any movement, but we were tail-enders, and we were in a turn to come back for another run up the peninsula, strafing from inside the peninsula, from the inside not on the outside where the huts were, and the lead aircraft was down to about 50 feet and we were strung out line astern. The navigator said, "Who's that firing at us?" and the tracer was coming from where the Hurricanes were down over our starboard wing. I looked up and there was a Nakajima firing at a Hurricane and another one firing at me, only his deflection was hopeless because we were in a turn and he was firing behind us over our starboard wing. The two Nakajimas then made high tail towards Akyab and I never got my sights on them until they were out of range, so I didn't fire at them and the turret was so darn slow.

We flew General Slim down to Buthidaung and there were several strips around Buthidaung and we had code names for them, and the strip he wanted to land at was in Japanese hands, and we said, "Oh no, we can't land there, we will have to take you to Lyons where there is another strip." We landed at Lyons and there was a staff car waiting, so obviously that's where we were intended to go. Anyhow, we asked him, "Why don't you operate over the hills?"

He said, "You can't get over those hills, it's too steep and it's thick jungle."

I said, "The Japanese operate over the hills."

He said, "No, they can't get their equipment over, they can never get their equipment over, it's far too difficult."

And that's exactly what the Japanese did. They came in behind our troops that were advancing down towards Akyab and cut the troops off, but that was later in the piece.

The Japanese pilots I considered to be not very good at their job because, after all, we were attacked for over 20 minutes by two and we only got one bullet hole in and we were tail-ender. If it had been 109s and that had been Malta we'd have all been shot down, I'm sure of it. The Germans were the professionals, we were the amateurs, and the Japanese were handicapped by the wrong equipment.

When the Squadron was re-equipped with Hurricanes, I was posted to 31 Squadron which had Dakotas with twin Wasp engines. I was also promoted to Flight Sergeant and flown to Kharagpur, west of Calcutta, which was the base for 31 Squadron, to gather information on the equipment on the DC3.'

With the changeover to Dakotas, so the nature of Albert Friend's activities changed from dropping bombs to dropping supplies to troops scattered over areas of Burma, a tactic that precluded the need for troops to withdraw as had previously been the policy when threatened by encirclement. A major recipient of these supplies was the Second Chindit Expeditionary Force, the greater part of which had been flown in by glider in March 1944, with the purpose of cutting Japanese communications and supply routes. Lieutenant Christopher Rooke had joined the Chindits, serving in 77 Brigade under General Mike Calvert, prior to the commencement of the Second Chindit Operation:

'Finally the day arrived for our departure. We were up at 4am, got equipped, put on our packs. We marched to the airfield where all the gliders were drawn up. I was due to go in P1, "P" standing for Piccadilly, which was our destination, and "1" standing for the first glider that was going in. This consisted of the Brigadier and other officers who were due to go in that particular night. However, they found the glider was too full, so I was told to go off and find some other glider. I remember going down the line and wondering which one to take. However, I decided on one which I thought was the most comfortable as it had a jeep in it and no other passengers at all, so I and my Gurkha batman took our seats very comfortably in the back of the jeep.

We took off, started taking off rather late, because it had been discovered that Broadway, to which half the gliders were going, had logs drawn across the actual chosen strip and they didn't know whether the plan of our attack had been divulged and the Japanese had some good idea of where we were going. So the attack was delayed while they decided whether the attack should go forward. Eventually it was decided that they would go forward and we took off as night was falling. It was an odd thing being towed by the Dakotas because two gliders were being towed by one Dakota, and we had to get over the Arakan Yomas, which rose to about 7,000 feet, I think, and

Christopher Charles Kirshaw Rooke

fires had been lit at the top of the ranges so we could see that we were well below the Arakan Yomas as we approached. It seemed to take a long time to get altitude because the air pockets were quite marked, and suddenly you'd find yourself dropping several hundred feet almost before the Dakotas started pulling you upwards towards the ranges. We were lucky, we got over quite safely and headed towards Piccadilly.

When we came in finally, my glider came in to the landing strip and we were told to look out. I didn't hear what the pilot was actually saying, but I gathered that I had to get into the back of the jeep. I was in the front seat at the time, but unfortunately my batman had decided to sleep stretched out in comfort in the back seat and wouldn't move in time. So I was caught standing up when the glider landed, and cut my head open. The plan was that when the gliders landed everybody would disembark and push the gliders to the side of the landing strip. Unfortunately logs had been drawn out on to the airstrip and these had left furrows, so that when the gliders landed the wheels came off and the gliders were stranded in the middle of the landing strip. This would have been all right if communications could have been established with Headquarters, perhaps to stop the gliders coming in one after another, but the communication gliders, as well as the medical gliders, had gone astray, so that one glider would come in and crash into another glider which had already landed, and that the casualties were quite heavy before we'd even started coming in contact with the Japanese.

It was a bright moonlit night and after we had got out of the glider we were rushed into the jungle, and my first task was helping with an operation. The doctor had set up his surgery, if you could call it that – it consisted of a groundsheet on which he had to amputate the arm, a badly mangled arm, of a soldier who had come in. He had no anaesthetics and I remember I had to hold the arm while he operated. The man was only semi-conscious and he kept on calling for his mother. The operation had to be performed under candlelight. We had no blood plasma and so he asked me to go across the airstrip to collect some plasma from a doctor on the other side of the airstrip. It was quite a weird sensation because it was bright moonlight, I could hear the planes going overhead, but one couldn't see the gliders coming in until they were fairly close, and then you saw their outline clearly coming in, and the next moment you'd find a glider flashing past one and disappearing into the darkness beyond – it was quite nerve-racking.

By the time I got to the other side of the airstrip I was halted by someone challenging me in a foreign language and shoving a bayonet in my chest. I gave the password but that was not enough and I was marched off with the bayonet behind me into the darkness, and I thought this was it, the Japanese had caught me. It was, however, a member of the Burma Rifles and he took me to the Company Commander of the Burma Rifles who gave me a good swig of whisky because he thought I needed it, which I did. I collected the blood plasma and went back across the airstrip. By this time they had managed to get some communication back and the planes had stopped coming in, so it was a much easier passage back. By the time I got back, however, the patient had died.

I then went to try and find my batman with whom I'd left my pack. I couldn't find him and finally I found my pack at the base of a tree, and he was up in it, I don't know why, so I told him that he was there to guard my pack, not to be up the tree. I went back to try and help the doctor with other casualties, but about 4 o'clock that morning there was no more that could be done and I went to get my pack and my bedding only to find not only Budiman gone but my pack gone as well, and I thought this time the Japs had really caught him as well as the pack. Finally I found him up another tree – this time he'd dragged my pack up as well.

From there, the next day I went out on patrol expecting to see Japanese round every tree; in actual fact there was nothing there, but when I got back Wingate had flown in and when I went to give my report for my patrol, he asked me how things had gone with the landing. I told him that I'd knocked my head and he insisted on examining my head and ordering me to go to the doctor about it, saying that on no account should I disregard any injury in future. He had a very great concern for every one of his men, and this inspired, I think, tremendous loyalty from anyone who served under him. People may have disagreements about his general strategy, and certainly he was able to carry all his information in his head, which left his commanders in doubt if anything should happen to him, but he certainly had the quality of inspiring loyalty and affection amongst people who served under him.

About two days later, when the rest of the Brigade had been flown in, we divided up into columns and started our march towards our destination, which was a position on the map where a hillock dominated the railway line and road which went from Central Burma up to Mogaung and Myitkyina. Our intention was to cut communications for those Japanese regiments serving in the north of Burma from reinforcements to the south. Being virtually in charge of the rearguard was a trying experience because you had to wait behind for every mule that threw its load or anything else that happened which caused delay, so you were constantly trying to catch up the rest of the column, which just marched on. As a result, we used to arrive in camp late. On one occasion I remember we arrived in camp about two or three hours after everybody else; we had no water, couldn't light fires, because it was dark, and we could hear water at the bottom of this hill, but we couldn't go and fetch any, and it was a very uncomfortable and rather hungry night as a result.

We proceeded on, and I was ordered to go ahead and get in touch with a Gurkha rifle column one evening, and we made contact with them but further information came down round about the middle of the night which required me to go and find the Gurkhas. It was pitch dark with no moon, and we had to cross a great paddy field to get to the Gurkha positions; we halted there, did our stuff, and then had to find our way back. Of course, my own platoon had been left behind. As a result of this I missed the battle next day because I waited there, while the column came through, and joined the end of the column as I was in charge of the rearguard. I never got to the battle at all and came in at the end, much to the annoyance of the Brigadier – I think he felt I should have been there.

From the "Block" [a fortified position established in the jungle] our technique was to cut the Japanese communications, but we were able to do more than this at one stage because the Japanese Headquarters had a telephone line that went from the northern Headquarters down southwards, and they were constantly on this telephone line, which we discovered, and since we had an officer with us who spoke Japanese, he was able to find out what they were talking about all the time. Unfortunately, they must have tumbled to this sooner or later because the conversations suddenly stopped.

It was uncomfortable in the Block because the Japanese came up and were constantly attacking us, and since we had no artillery and were confined in an area about 800 yards in circumference, at the most, they could concentrate their fire, their shellfire, on us for long periods of time. The first attack came in, I remember, one night and the battle ensued most of that night, and the South Staffs repulsed them.

I had a lucky escape the next morning because the Brigadier gave me a message to take to the Colonel commanding the South Staffs. I asked a soldier who had been wounded – he had a bloodstained bandage round his head – if the part of the base of the hillocks which we were defending was clear, and he said yes. So I decided to go round there, and on my way I found one of our food dumps had been overrun and the Japanese had torn out all the food from the packets, but they'd left packets of cigarettes there. The actual dump was in a little depression, so I jumped in and collected the cigarettes as I thought the troops who had been fighting all night would be grateful for them. The Japanese must have thought that I had cottoned on to them because suddenly four of them jumped out, no more than 2 or 3 yards away, and dashed off into the jungle which lay beyond a little space behind them. I couldn't help laughing at the time to think how I was completely oblivious of their presence there, had my revolver through a lanyard and was completely unprepared for any sort of action whatsoever, and that they had been sent to gather information, which they could very well have gathered straightaway from me, I should think.

Thereafter I got myself attached to a platoon of the South Staffords as they had lost an officer there, and I found this great to get back to actually doing something with troops. I wasn't happy with the Gurkha company I'd been attached to because I couldn't speak Gurkhali, they couldn't speak much Urdu themselves, so I found myself very out of touch with the Gurkha troops, whereas getting back to British troops again, one could relieve tension and things with a joke, which one couldn't do with Gurkha troops.

I also remember, while I was with them, that the Japanese launched an air attack on our positions. We couldn't defend ourselves at all, of course; they just came in and dropped their bombs. I was actually in an open trench about a couple of feet deep – it hadn't been covered in or anything – and I noticed that there was some flame-thrower fuel near a fire which had been started by one of the bombs which the Japanese had dropped, setting light to some straw just next to this flame-thrower fuel, so I dashed over there to try and put this out, but as I was putting it out I heard another plane coming over and had to dash back about, I should say, something like 20 yards into my slit trench. I heard the bombs go, and just made it back and threw myself into the slit trench when the bombs went off in the tree. I was buried alive virtually with debris, but not to any great depth, and the soldier who was occupying another branch of the slit trench – it was in a sort of L-shape – said, "Are you all right, are you all right?" then, "Are you dead?" My lungs must have been collapsed a bit because I couldn't get any answer out to this, until I finally made it through the debris and came up and said, "I don't think so." Unfortunately we lost our Jap-speaking officer – he was just only a few yards away but his lungs had been collapsed in the bombing. Perhaps if we'd known more, had more medical knowledge, we might have been able to save him.

It was quite hairy in the Block because we used to get supply drops. In the initial stages they used to come in and have certain things which came down by parachute, but unbreakables, like barbed-wire and bales of hay for the mules, would be dropped free – they called them "free drops" – and it used to be quite nerve-racking when you heard a twang of the barbed-wire no more than 15 yards away from you, particularly as they used to bounce up again and go dong, dong, dong as they repeatedly jumped. In the first nights we were very exposed as we hadn't dug down sufficiently deep or got our trenches covered in, so it was quite dangerous and one person was killed by a bale of hay landing on him.

Once the Japanese started attacking us they were able to mortar us at night quite badly. They had one thing which we nicknamed the "coal scuttle", which was a great big mortar; it was an 8-inch mortar and this used to make an extraordinary buzzing sound, so we used to hear it coming and this proved quite nerve-racking.

I'll revert back to the planes, because when we were being attacked and we had got in touch with Headquarters in Burma and explained our predicament to them, that we couldn't answer back to these attacking planes, they flew in four Bofors by helicopter. The helicopter was a write-off, but we were able to drag these Bofors up to the top of the ridges of these hillocks. The Japanese knew nothing of this and they came in as bold as brass to attack us at nought feet, and we let loose at them and we gather that we knocked out eight of their planes, and, as a consequence of this, they never came near us again and it quite depleted their air force in the area; of course, they didn't have many planes in Burma.

A sad thing that happened to us was that a new officer arrived to take over the platoon, which I was temporarily in charge of, and they were ordered to help or reinforce a platoon which had been under constant attack up on one of the hillocks which I knew fairly well, because the Gurkha company to which I was attached had occupied it before, and I knew that the whole route up to this particular position had been booby-trapped.

So the next morning I volunteered to take this group up to these particular positions, which were now held by 200 South Staffords. The person in charge of them was a man called David Scoley, a delightful officer. It was quite nerve-racking going up this particular little track between the booby-traps because I wasn't quite sure of it, but David would yell out to me from the top saying, "Now stop, turn right and go." We also heard that there was a Japanese sniper at the top there, so it was quite a worrying little trip up. At one point I remember the platoon behind me piling up while I was pausing to decide quite where I was going, and I remember an odd line of "Horatius" coming into my mind, which I quoted, and that was "And those in front were shouting back, while those behind start crying forward", and I quoted this and we giggled the whole way up to the top of this hill, which David was holding. David greeted me with the words, "Ah, Chris," he said, "I'm so relieved to see you – we've had a horrid night." He was that sort of person. He got the immediate award of the MC after this, but was killed a little later, and that was very sad.

The next sad thing that happened was when we got to the top I had no more duties with the platoon, whom I'd got to know fairly well, because their new officer had arrived that night. He was married, had two young children, although he was pretty young himself, so he went off to the left flank and after about 10 minutes or so I heard shots. One of the men on the left flank came over to me and said, "Will you come over, sir?" He said what had happened: this young officer, getting up and trying to shoot at the sniper, he'd been hit himself and three other men had been hit, so I told them to get their heads down and got the people out. Unfortunately the officer died.

After that, when we actually left the Block heavily booby-trapped, we marched north again towards Mogaung. By this time the Officer in Charge of the Brigade Defence Company had been killed, and I was acting as Platoon Commander under the eye of Major Girling. We went up into the hills on one side of the plain, which divided the big valley, the Mogaung Valley, and another Brigade was putting down another Block further to the west.

By this time, of course, Wingate was no longer in charge because he had been killed. Oddly enough, I met him that afternoon, the afternoon that he was killed. He had come to inspect the Block and talk to the Brigadier in charge of the West Africans. My slit trench was on a path fairly close to where the Brigadier had his trench. Anyway, I decided I would cook myself a cheese toast, as we'd had what was called the luxury drop, which consisted of bread – of course, we lived on K rations and it was really monotonous, but they did have a tin of cheese in them. Because we had this bread I decided a cheese toast would be just the job. The bread was pretty mouldy by the time we got it, anyway, so it was good to toast it, but I then put this processed cheese to cook in my mess tin, to cook under my little fire. Wingate passed and he came over and asked me what I was doing, and I said I was cooking my cheese toast, and he was quite interested in this ingenious idea, but after he'd been talking to the Brigadier for about an hour or so, he came back. By this time I was still cooking my cheese toast, so he came over and looked at it, and in the process of cooking it had got stringier and stringier, and he said, "I don't think you're doing a very good job, Rooke," and that was the last I saw of him because he caught the plane from us back to what we called the "Stronghold", and was flown out and was killed in the hills that evening.

To return to our advance towards Mogaung, we ran into very heavy monsoon weather after this and the pathway became very muddy and the conditions were pretty appalling. One of the Gurkhas in fact committed suicide on our advance early in the morning when it was pouring with rain, and even the mules got fed up and when we started going up into the hills they would quite often commit suicide, or attempt to commit suicide by throwing themselves off the pathway. When we eventually got to the top the weather changed, and we had to look out for another Block that had been put in across the other side of a river which ran down the valley separating us from another line of hills on the other side. It was badly conceived, because there was no support from the platoons from the other brigades to stop the Japanese coming in, and the Japanese brought heavy artillery down to shell these positions. They had very, very heavy casualties and eventually had to withdraw, which was a pretty tragic business, as some of the wounded had to be left behind. I am not sure, but the rumours were that they had to kill off the very seriously wounded because they daren't leave them to the mercies of the Japanese.

When we were up on the mountain there, I had to guard the approaches to the Brigade and I thought that the Brigadier had allowed me to use my initiative over the business from the instructions that had been given me by the Column Commander, but this was apparently not the case and he was furious with me because I put my platoon in a different place. However, that was rectified and I was up there trying to spot the artillery which was firing at this Block and, funnily enough, we couldn't do this from that position, but I went up to the position which I had chosen, one hot afternoon, and managed to spot them, so I was able to come down and was rewarded for this by being told to take a platoon down that night, down into the valley, and attack these guns the next day.

I took a platoon down to the village, which we entered late in the evening, and since it was unwise to go into the villages – or certainly put up there in the night, because they could be easily ambushed – I withdrew the platoon up into the jungle, where we spent the night. Unfortunately it was leech-infested and the monsoon broke out and it was one of the most uncomfortable nights that I have ever spent. The next day we waited for the rest of the Company to come down under Major Girling and another Engineer Officer, who was to blow up any guns which we found. However, the next night we spent in the jungle again and it rained yet again and my orders were virtually to put these guns out of action. I had no idea what one had to do. The only knowledge I had of putting artillery out of action was taking their firing blocks out, and I didn't know how to do that, or else from my reading of earlier campaigns, that you do what the Lancers did and spike the guns – I didn't even know how to do that. I was ordered by Major Girling to cross this river. I was to attack the positions while he gave covering fire, and then the Engineer Officer would come in and I hoped he'd know what to do with the guns. I was very unhappy with this situation, because we only had a platoon and I presumed the Japanese would be there in force, guarding these guns, so I was quite thankful that when we tried to cross this river Major Girling and this other officer were swept down the river, and decided that it was not feasible. The next day – the Block had actually fallen that night – we were ordered back up the hill to rejoin the Brigade, which we duly did.

When we rejoined the Brigade we proceeded on our march towards Mogaung. My job now was as a Point Platoon for the rest of the Brigade. I proceeded fairly carefully at the beginning, but was told by the Brigade Commander that I was to disregard care and advance as quickly as possible; in fact, it was my job to be ambushed, as a warning to the rest of the Brigade. However, nothing happened until one night when we came to a sort of crossroads of tracks, and there we were told to halt for the evening. I was joined by a platoon from the South Staffs and the next morning the Japanese caught us, just as we were "stood down", and three of the South Staffs were killed in the action. As a result of this we were told to hold our positions while the rest of the Brigade went through.

I rejoined the Brigade, but at the end of the column this time, which was much more comfortable. We bivouacked for that night and the next morning I prepared my platoon to take over the leading positions again, but the Brigadier informed me that another platoon had taken over this task and I was to rejoin at the rear of the column again. I was very lucky because the leading platoon ran into the Japanese within 5 minutes of starting our advance, and the officer in charge of the platoon was killed.

We proceeded onwards and then we came to a position where the track took a right-angled turn. There were two little hillocks which were occupied by two village huts and I felt, rather firmly, that the column could be split if the Japanese managed to hold one of these hillocks, so that we could not advance forward. I had the temerity to inform the Brigadier of this when he came down the column, and got soundly ticked off for not using my initiative this time, and I was told to use it. So I went back with a platoon and positioned two sections to cover the advance of a third section. Unfortunately, the Japanese got on to one of these little hillocks before this and opened fire. I hadn't counted on advancing with only one section, but fortunately some members of the South Staffords joined me. We tried to get round behind the Japanese and so prevent them from escaping, but we ran into elephant grass

and couldn't do this, so we had to make our way back towards the column again. As we tried to cross the little pathway which led up to the Japanese positions, I noticed that we weren't fired upon, so I decided that we would go up towards the Japanese positions.

When I got to the top, we went over the brow of this hill and I was met by the Japanese, who were only about 3 or 4 yards away, and I was fortunate to get away with it, but I had my rifle at the ready and I fired a round at them before retreating back over the ridge and getting the platoon up in line so that we could charge them. I yelled "Charge!" but this was evidently a bit early because no one was quite ready for this order and I found myself on my own on the other side. I fired another round and got back again very smartly, being no hero myself, and this time prepared properly and threw a grenade and ordered other people to throw grenades as well. This must have been fairly successful because the Japanese retreated – we discovered later that their leader had been killed.

However, the Japanese had learnt by our example and started throwing grenades back, and one landed just behind me and I went out like a light. When I came to, I was worried because I found myself on my toes and all my clothes were actually in shreds and I was bleeding fairly profusely from the wounds which I'd received. These weren't too serious, but going up on my toes worried me because this is what I'd seen people do when their testicles were blown off. Anyway, I dropped my shorts, opened my legs and asked the corporal next to me to see if they were all intact, and he said it was all right. However, after we got back I spent the rest of that day on a stretcher being carried to one of the jungle huts, and I was always grateful for those who had this unenviable task that afternoon. Fortunately our attack had stopped any further Japanese attacks, and we reached our bivouacs, I think, without any further interruptions. I spent a very uncomfortable night that night because I hadn't been able to urinate, I suppose because of shock, so when I woke up at night desperate to urinate, I couldn't do so because of all the wounded who were beside me – when I tried to move, they of course cried out. In the end, since we were in just a jungle bamboo hut, I let myself do so, thinking all would be well because, being a bamboo hut, there were gaps in the bamboo floor. I forgot that some people might be sleeping underneath on the ground, so there were some pretty horrific cries from below.

Anyway, one thing that happened while I was there was that one of the Hong Kong Platoon members came over to me and said that they were going to torture a Japanese prisoner whom we had captured. He was part of a patrol which was in our neighbourhood. After we had left the village, evidently, a Japanese patrol had come in and spent the night there and moved off the next morning. The Kachins had come back to the village and found this poor chap fast asleep, and had taken him prisoner and brought him in to us. I don't know how the Hong Kong Volunteers had got hold of him, but I had to get up and somehow get to the platoon to stop this going on, but I remember it being rather a frightening moment, standing between this Japanese and the Chinese volunteers, so I was glad when that little incident was over and I was able to return to my little stretcher in the cow shed where all the wounded were lying.

It was very uncomfortable there because we were lying on stretchers, but these stretchers used to close in on one from the side because of the weight of the person lying in them. Also the stench of blood was appalling after a few days. While I was still there Michael Almond was brought in – he'd been wounded badly and it was hoped that one of the American planes would come in and take him over to Myitkyina because that was the route by which our wounded were evacuated. Unfortunately the plane couldn't get back because night overtook this plane and the pilot couldn't make it, and Michael died during the night – he was later awarded a VC.

After a few days I thought I could rejoin the Brigade, which was about a mile and a half away. It was a very hard journey for me, I found, because I got hold of a bamboo pole which I used as a sort of support to help me get back there, but my leg was giving me quite a lot of trouble and it took me about an hour and a half to cover the trip back there. I was again kept in the hospital there for a bit, but managed to rejoin Brigade Headquarters.

One of my troubles now was acute constipation and the awkwardness for me, with my injury, to use the facility available, which was a slit trench. After a bit I could contain myself no longer, and went to the nearest slit trench, where you have to hold your hands behind you, but I had to hold out my leg and I couldn't squat over this wretched trench, but I sort of pivoted myself on a sort of tripod consisting of one leg and two arms behind me. I'd hardly settled myself when there was a plop beside me, and I felt this, and the plop was very hot, and I realised it must have been an unexploded Japanese shell which had landed beside me. I managed to get off that rather uncomfortable position I was in rather rapidly, and informed the Brigadier about this, and the slit trench was later abandoned. By this time I found I couldn't move very much and the Brigadier ordered me out. So I went back this time by horse, but it proved to be an equally uncomfortable journey because I could only put my foot in one stirrup and it seemed very odd trying to stand up on a horse while I made my way back.

From there I was ferried by light plane to Myitkyina and transferred to a Dakota and flown back to India. When we landed the first thing that happened to any Chindit who returned was to have all your clothes taken off you, including your boots. I was very annoyed about losing my boots because they were New Zealand boots and were the best boots I ever had, and I had worn them in thoroughly. However, even they had to go. I was then transferred into a hospital and it was wonderful to feel safe for the first time, see attractive nurses and sleep in clean sheets. Of course, the first thing they had done was to put us in baths and pretty well boil us for a bit to get rid of any dirt. I was there for about two days, and I still couldn't move. Finally a little pimple came up on my leg, which burst, and about two cupfuls of solid pus came out, and after that my leg felt fine and I was able to get up.'

In early 1944 British forces were poised to advance into Burma to re-open the overland route to China with a direct attack across the Chindwin River, a secondary one in the Arakan, and the Chindit Operation. To forestall this the Japanese opened up their own attacks in the Arakan and on Imphal and Kohima. They were partially successful and the British troops in the Arakan were cut off initially, and eventually the British advancing from Imphal into Burma were withdrawn to Imphal. While the British forces were well supplied from the air, the Japanese had no way of replenishing their supplies, and by June 1944 it was the Japanese who retreated with their forces in disarray, and the British started their advance through Burma and the Arakan to final victory in Burma.

William Seeney, who had served as a Lance Bombardier in the Artillery in the 'Phoney War', was now Lieutenant Seeney, Royal Engineers, serving in India and Burma:

'Eventually we arrived at Chittagong. We were there for a few days and then along came two or three jeeps, and there were about ten of us RE subalterns, and we were taken to an airstrip and there was our old friend the Dak, the Dakota, otherwise known as a DC3. We eventually arrived at Imphal and, for a man like me, it was quite a shock, because we'd come from what was relatively peaceful conditions to a battle, but, fortunately, the battle was getting towards its end and the Japanese had really extended themselves just too far to attempt to get into Northern India by way of Imphal. The Japanese were being held and, what is more, they were weakening and the 14th Army, on the other hand, was being strengthened quite considerably. It was rather scary because it was action the whole time in one place or another, but time passed and it's an odd thing, you know, you do settle down and keep your head down. That seemed to be part of my wartime experiences, keeping your head down. By this time I'd become a pretty experienced sort of a soldier.

We were all becoming pretty experienced soldiers; we could bivouac wherever we dropped or, with a bit of luck, we could find a deserted village. When it was decided the time was right for us to move down the Arakan, it seemed at a very casual rate. We didn't push it, there was always opposition, we were always in contact with the enemy, but we could just as well be a bit careful; we didn't have to go in "boots and all" and take casualties when it really wasn't necessary, because the pressure we had on the Japanese, by this time, was evident. We just kept moving, and it is a blooming long way from Cox's down to Ramree, and we walked the whole way, for God's sake.

However, we eventually arrived at the final assault on the Island of Ramree, which was a sort of combined operation. Whilst we were on Ramree the 14th Army arrived at Rangoon and one could say at that point the operation in Burma had finished, although there were plenty of other Japs about.

So then we took a breather and ended up at Bangalore. The place was chock-a-block with troops and everything was done for us. They gave us two or three weeks to do just nothing, just to relax, which is what we did. By this time, I might add, I was a Captain, and at times I was Company Commander when the boss was away, and I remember going with our motor transport people down to a depot which held all these vehicles and it was unbelievable, the place was full of brand spanking new vehicles of every kind you could imagine, and, I might add, all the way from the United States of America. At that time we were really spoilt – clothing, we could just get as much as we wanted.

By this time we'd been nicely fattened up and got rid of the effects of the anti-malarial drug, mepacrine, which made us yellow. In Burma we were all yellower than the Japs! Then, of course, we just naturally began to speculate as to what was going to happen to us. We just speculated as to where we were going and, of course, as is usual in the Army, there were always rumours going round, and the main one was Malaya. The very thought of going on a job into Malaya to continue this war – and when you think of the distances and the areas concerned, it wasn't particularly to my liking... Another thing – I must add this – was the luck I'd already had – it couldn't keep on, surely.

But, before that happened the news came through that the two bombs had been dropped on Hiroshima and Nagasaki. We were told they were atomic bombs, they were special bombs, but we didn't know much more about it than that. Then the Japanese capitulated some weeks later, and that was the end of the war. What a lovely feeling.'

Albert Friend, now flying in Dakotas, resumes his account of his experiences in Burma:

'Anyhow, I was passed out by the First Radio Operator as being capable of operating the equipment, so my next move was to Agartala, which was nearer to the Japanese, where we dropped supplies to our forward bases. The most supplies we dropped were to Tiddim in the Chin Hills, south of Imphal; we dropped tons and tons, day after day after day, 25-pounder shells, mortar bombs, rice, sugar, bread, barbed-wire, attar, food for the mules. Besides Tiddim we supplied Falam, another hill-top base, and also Haka, but mainly Tiddim, and usually we dropped 7,500lb on a trip and we could do up to four trips a day, and there were about a dozen aircraft doing the same thing.

We never had trouble with the Japs, although it was very close to the Jap-held territory, and our supply-dropping aircraft had Vickers gas-operated guns out of the escape hatches on either side of the aircraft in case we ran into trouble. We had no armour-plating, no self-sealing for the tanks, and occasionally, when the Japanese fighters moved in, we got a Hurricane escort, but as soon as the Hurricane escorts failed to find any Japanese fighters they took them away again. So most of the time we had no escorts whatsoever. There was always cloud in the area because we started dropping in September 1943 and it was just after the monsoons. Towards December the weather was improving, but quite often we arrived over the dropping zone and found that we couldn't drop because of cloud covering the hill tops. We sent out probes to check that each place that we dropped was clear of clouds, and if the probe came back and said no drop today because the clouds were covering all three dropping zones, we had a day off, but otherwise we worked very hard. Mainly it was free drop – a bag of rice would be inside a bigger bag, so that if the bag broke it broke into the bigger bag, and the same with attar and flour.

The only things we dropped by parachute were the 25-pounder shells, the mortar bombs, small arms ammunition, and anything that was likely to break.

We also dropped things that weren't on the manifest. If they wanted toothbrushes they just wrote toothbrushes on the ground and we packed them ourselves – we paid for those – and we also dropped magazines and newspapers because they weren't on the manifest either. So besides the official supplies we had our own personal supplies, and we used to drop little messages to them as well. We got good response from on the ground – they put out ground markers to show they were pleased with what we were doing.

When the Japanese went round the back of our troops going towards Akyab they cut off our troops at Tong Bazaar and Coppie's Bazaar, so we then flew down there to supply the troops and laagers with 25-pounder shells and mortar bombs and their food for the day. In the Akyab region the Japanese fighters were more active because the Royal Engineers were strengthening the bridges across the creeks to enable our tanks to go down there to fight the Japanese. The British were far better off with heavy weapons, the 25-pounders. All the Japanese had were light mountain guns.

The Japs came over the hills with mules, and if they ran out of food they killed a mule and ate the mule. They always assumed that they would capture British supplies by going into the rear, and probably they did, but it was never reported that they had. On one occasion we were dropping supplies and the Japanese came over to attack the British. They sent over 14, somewhere between 14 or 16 Zero Ones, or Nakajima Ki43s, and some of them were bombers and some of them were fighters to escort them, and there was a lot of kerfuffle going to the north of us, so we decided to get out because we only had the Vickers guns out of each window. In order to get out we flew to Nykidauk Pass, which was a narrow pass with the hills on both sides of us, higher than our altitude. The starboard gun was manned by a Canadian, Dinger Bell, and I manned the port gun, and I sat half in the aircraft and half out so as I could have a good view, and Jim flew the aircraft out to the Bay of Bengal and went up the coast, sneaking up the coast away from the action. One of our aircraft, because there was more than one in the operation, flew north, and he was shot down, so we did the right thing – we flew away from them and to the Bay of Bengal and up the coast to our base.

Back at base, we continued flying backwards and forwards to Tiddim, Falam, Haka, and when Wingate's deep penetration column went into Burma from Kohima in the north, they crossed the Chindwin and we had to supply them from the air. We did it at night and we relied on a weak radio signal; we used to call up "777 777 777" and when we got a weak reply "555 555" we knew we were in the vicinity and they knew we were in the vicinity, so they lit a triangle of fires, then we dropped adjacent to the fires, which sometimes was successful, but it depended on their dropping zone; sometimes the dropping zone was at a very awkward position. One of them was in the bend of a river, and at night we had to avoid high trees and at the same time had this small target, so we couldn't go too low and we couldn't go too high, otherwise we'd overshoot.

Anyhow, the only other occasion that was significant was when we were off to supply Wingate's forces and there was a waxing or waning moon and there was a definite haze level. Above the haze level the air was calm, below the haze level the air was rough, and I thought Jim was worried about night-fighters, although the Japanese weren't active at night. We were flying below the haze level just above the ridges, and most of the ridges were north to south, and we were flying west to east to find the Wingate column, and we flew over one ridge and were hit by a down-draught. I was sitting in the right-hand seat because we never had a co-pilot, we only had one pilot on board, and I tried to assist him to pick the starboard wing up because the starboard wing dropped. I thought it best to put over to port, but the starboard wing wouldn't come up and we were dropping into the gully, and it was getting darker and darker and we, both of us, tried to pull the aircraft up, but it still fell, both of us pulling on the stick and trying to right the plane, but it still went down, down, down. Eventually, of course, we hit solid air and we climbed out. We'd hit solid air and we climbed out and the navigator gave us a new course to steer and Jim turned round and flew west, and the navigator said, "Look here, we've got these supplies for the Wingate forces – if we don't drop them they don't eat," and Jim said, "Ah no, it's too dangerous, the wind is hopeless for dropping supplies – we can't possibly drop them on a small dropping zone with this wind blowing," and we went back to Agartala. We landed at midnight or just before midnight, and I was told that I was posted to England and that I should pack my bags and catch the early mail plane at 8 o'clock to Dum Dum. So I had a few hours sleep, I didn't have much to pack, and I caught the plane to Dum Dum and was flown by a British Overseas Airways Armstrong four-engined plane to Delhi, and from there in various planes, finally arriving at Lyneham in Wiltshire.'

The situation and operations in the East Indies theatre of war have been touched upon as far as the Army and the RAF have been concerned. The Navy also had a role to play. Richard Begg, now a Sub Lieutenant and navigator of the destroyer HMS *Paladin*, attached to the Eastern (later to be known as the East Indies) Fleet based on Trincomalee in Ceylon, had memories of Naval service in the area:

'HMS *Porpoise* was a mine-laying submarine and she had been laying mines off the Japanese-held port of Penang right down in the Malacca Straits, and she'd signalled on 9 January 1945 to say she'd laid her mines and was coming home and that was the last that was ever heard of her. The Japanese didn't report her as being sunk, so no one really knew what had

Richard Campbell Begg

happened. *Paladin* was ordered to sail down her likely course of return in an effort to find her. So we went across the Bay of Bengal and down the Malacca Straits towards Penang, but we could find no trace of her whatsoever so we returned to harbour.

Soon after we got back to Trincomalee we started exercising bombardment procedures. We had an Army Officer called the Bombardment Liaison Officer on board, and we used to anchor alongside various parts of the coast and bombard targets ashore. Then, towards the end of January 1945, and with three cruisers, *Newcastle*, *Nigeria* and *Kenya*, we proceeded to sea. We went across to Burma, still held by the Japanese, and for the next couple of months we took part in the operations in the Arakan area of Burma, where, with the Army, we were involved in reclaiming territory which had been lost there. The 15th Corps of the 14th Army was advancing down the coast and we were providing bombardment support.

We bombarded a small island called Cheduba, which was just to the south-west of the large island of Ramree, on which the Army was in the process of landing, and which was held by a large Japanese force. Anyway, the Marines from the cruisers were given the job of clearing the Japanese from this island of Cheduba. So we anchored off Cheduba, bombarded the beach, and the Marines landed in fine style and very shortly afterwards Cheduba was ours. The small Japanese garrison had evidently taken off shortly before.

After that we went up a river, or chaung as they are called – this was the Kaleindaung River between Burma and Ramree Island, which was being invaded by the 14th Army. Our job was to anchor up this river and provide artillery support for the Army and also to prevent Japanese troops from getting across the river into Burma as they withdrew from Ramree. This was another navigational headache for me, because this Kaleindaung River hardly appeared on the chart at all. The inlet was on the chart, but that was all, and that was at the top left-hand corner of the chart and it showed quite a few hazards, but once beyond that we were off the chart completely and it was just a matter of keeping to the centre of the river, taking soundings and hoping for the best. Before we got off the chart there were a couple of reefs which extended diagonally across the river – about 50 yards between the two reefs – and these reefs were under water, you couldn't see them, but you had to go from one side of the river to the other side between these two reefs, and it meant turning on bearings and one had to allow for the tidal flow to calculate the correct course.

So we quite successfully managed to cope with this the first few times we went up or down this river, but on one occasion, coming down-river, we altered course a little too late and next thing we knew we could actually see the fangs of this horrible reef just under the surface of the water and we were drifting right down on top of it. Our Captain, Lieutenant Cundall, was very good; he managed to get the ship away in the nick of time by some skilful ship-handling and we were through. Somehow or other I had

HMS Pathfinder *anchored in Kaleindaung River prior to the air attack.*

Landing craft on the Kaleindaung River.

misjudged the speed of that tide, but the thought of being wrecked on that reef in Japanese-held territory was indeed worrying.

Anyway we were up there for about two months and this was called "Operation Block". Our sister ship, HMS *Pathfinder*, was anchored just round the corner from us and there were some small landing craft and motor launches scattered up and down the chaung as well. They were all stopping the Japanese getting across.

Then one afternoon I was down in the charthouse and it was a lovely afternoon. I think we'd got a bit complacent by that time. The Japanese weren't reacting very much to our presence there, and suddenly there was a loud screaming noise, a terrific horrible noise, and then our alarm gongs went so I shot up to the bridge, but I found my way was blocked by a lot of our sailors who were trying to get closer to the deck in a little structure called our plotting house. It was made of wood and you had to go through this to get on to the compass platform. The bridge was an open bridge and I found my way was barred by people hitting the deck inside this little shelter, which was a really bad place to shelter, because of the danger from wooden splinters.

Anyway, I managed to get through, got on to the compass platform, and just as I got there there was an enormous explosion and a mass of water cascaded from alongside the ship on the port side of the bridge, and I could see a plane leaving us about bridge height and going on towards *Pathfinder*, which was around the corner. It had been a very near miss – the bomb had just missed the ship. So I arrived on the compass platform and found it deserted except for the gunnery officer, who was at the telephone there trying to contact the guns to get them to open fire, but no one seemed to be opening fire and he wasn't having much joy. Then there was another horrible noise; I looked up and there was another plane coming in, straight at the bridge, straight at us, firing its machine-guns, and the gunnery officer took a dive into the little recess between the front of the bridge and the compass platform and I grabbed the phone, quickly realised there was no one answering and, deciding discretion was the better part of valour, shot on down to the charthouse to collect my tin helmet. I got down there very quickly and paused for a few seconds because I thought a bomb was about to hit the bridge above. It is interesting to reflect upon what one thinks about on these occasions. I'm afraid my thoughts were all completely self-centred: I sort of thought it seemed such a pity, here I was, too young really to have experienced much of life, and there was a bomb coming straight down at me. However, luckily for us he had expended the last of his bombs.

Anyway, I went back on to the bridge where everyone seemed to be gathering again, and the Captain was standing behind the binnacle saying, "Get the anchor up, get the anchor up," and no one seemed to be doing anything, so I clambered over the screen in front of the bridge, went down to B gun deck and down to the fo'c'sle trying to work out in my mind how the winch worked for weighing the anchor. Luckily I met the Chief Stoker, and between us we managed to get the anchor up and the Captain weaved the ship around a bit and then we dropped the anchor again and that was it. We were all ready now, but of course it was a bit late, the enemy had come and gone. HMS *Pathfinder*, round the corner from us, also received a near miss, which did much more damage. She was in shallower water and in fact she had to be withdrawn and that was the end of her career as a fighting ship.

What had happened was that the Army had reported that two planes were attacking them ashore at Ramree and could we please get the Air Force to get them off – they thought they were our planes. We tried to deal with this, evidently, but couldn't get through and the next thing was that these so-called friendly planes were mounting this attack on us.

Well, life continued up the Kaleindaung River, and one occasion I recall was when we sighted a small dinghy in a mangrove swamp on the Ramree side, the Japanese side, and I took the motor cutter in to fetch it and I took a few of our sailors armed with Sten guns. We got half way across and our ship suddenly started sounding off its siren, and we dithered around for a bit wondering what they were at, but we hadn't really arranged any signals in code. Then we pushed on, and just as we were approaching the shore there was a burst of machine-gun fire, and we could see spouts of water coming straight at the boat. Looking a bit closer I saw one of our seamen had opened fire accidentally with his Sten gun, and the machine-gun fire was actually going in the reverse direction. So we all breathed a collective sigh of relief, got in, grabbed the boat and came back to the ship. In fact, they had thought they had seen signs of life on the shore and the siren was really an attempt at recalling us.

Then the Japanese would try and get from Ramree Island to Burma, usually at night-time in rafts or dinghies or canoes, and we would often pick them up and show them up in the searchlight or our signal lamps and shoot at them with the Oerlikons or rifles kept up on the bridge for that purpose. The main mayhem was done by the troops in the landing craft and the motor launches, up and down the river, who really killed a large number of Japanese crossing that river. It was a macabre sight, all those bodies floating face downwards in the water – there were hundreds of them – swept past the ship on the outgoing tide and back on the next incoming tide. We even got to recognise some of them as they came back and forth, a sort of grisly dawn to dusk parade.

Very few of the Japanese being pushed towards us from Ramree surrendered. One who had been captured was persuaded to journey to and fro in a motor launch, up and down the chaungs, with a loud-hailer exhorting his comrades to surrender, but none did. Those who succeeded in getting across the river still had a horrific journey ahead of them, and most would have perished.

Well, eventually we sailed down that Kaleindaung River for the last time, very pleased to do so, and collected HMS *Pathfinder*, and together we sailed back to Colombo. *Pathfinder* went back to the United Kingdom and was scrapped. We went into dock to have some of the superficial damage we had suffered repaired.

I suppose it was in April 1945 when we embarked a number of commandos, Army Commandos with their kayak canoes and equipment, and we exercised landing them at night. Our motor cutter would tow the kayaks with these commandos in and drop them at a certain spot; they would paddle to the shore, land and carry out sabotage exercises, and then they would come back to the canoes, paddle back to our motor cutter, which would take them in tow and bring them back to the ship, and then we would set sail again. We did that a number of times.

The reason for this became obvious when we finally sailed some time in April with HMS *Roebuck*, another destroyer, in company, and we went to Chittagong where we refuelled. We must have taken on more fuel than *Roebuck*, because when it came to leaving Chittagong there was a sandbar at the entrance, and the gap in the sandbar through which the ships used to go would change fairly frequently, and we'd both come in quite well through the gap in the sandbar designated on the chart, but on our way out *Roebuck* went out all right but we suddenly stopped and shuddered and the plates ground together, a horrible feeling, and we were aground on the sandbar. Again our skipper did some very good adroit manipulations of the helm and speed, and we managed to slide off. The only damage was to the Asdic dome.

The other thing that happened was that the Officer of the Watch had been very conscientious and had entered in the ship's log book in indelible pencil the time and the annotation, "Ship aground on sandbar". We decided that it would be far better not to commit ourselves to this, and so it was taken out of the log. I found it extremely difficult with indelible pencil – I couldn't rub it out, but managed to remove it eventually with the help of a razor blade, and we made the notation that we had probably hit a whale. This would be seen in a more favourable light than grounding the ship would have been, and we really didn't want, at this stage of the war, to put everyone, including ourselves, to the worry and expense of an enquiry or worse!

So anyway, we continued our trip down the Japanese-held Burmese coast until we arrived at a port called Tavoy, and here we arrived just before midnight on 18 April and we anchored. We were a bit late but we sent the motor cutters in, towing the kayaks inshore, and there we were; we sat and waited in this enemy-occupied harbour. We looked at all the silhouettes and shadows we could see around us and wondered what they were and whether the Japanese were conscious of our presence, knowing we had to get away before first light in order to avoid any obvious sighting and reaction on their part.

Midnight came and the early hours, and this had a great significance for me because this was my 21st birthday, and someone said "Happy Birthday", and I wasn't feeling like having a happy birthday, but anyway, I will always remember this happening on my 21st birthday. The time wore on, and there were no alarm signals. If we had seen Verey lights going up, that would have meant they were in trouble, but we didn't see any; on the other hand we didn't see our men or boats either. Time went on and they were supposed to be back, and the dawn was breaking in the east and still no sign of them, and the whole of the ship's company was getting very edgy, and we never had so many people keeping a look-out – everyone was peering away towards land to see whether they could pick up the motor cutter returning. Eventually she appeared, towing the kayaks, and we got them on board. The motor cutter was hoisted in the normal way. We cleared lower deck and it was hoisted manually with all the sailors running along the falls, and I've never seen a motor cutter lifted with such verve and enthusiasm – she really shot aboard – and we turned and we steamed out of that inlet as fast as we could, anticipating Japanese aircraft, at least, would be taking action against us.

The day went on and we didn't have any form of retaliation, and it was a great sense of relief. Unfortunately the landing had had to be aborted because it was found they were too far out and they couldn't get in in time to get ashore and do any damage – there just wasn't time. They had to turn round and get back to the motor cutter and get back to the ship, so the whole thing was a waste of time anyway. So back to Trincomalee, where we had a belated celebration of my 21st birthday plus also my promotion to Lieutenant.

Our next operation was fairly soon after that; we went to sea to escort Royal Fleet Tanker *Olwen* as Force 69 to take part in an operation called "Bishop". This was a covering operation to give protection for the forces engaged in Operation "Dracula", in which troops were to be landed near Rangoon. The Japanese still had some heavy cruisers about in Singapore, which could be expected to disrupt proceedings, and they had their aircraft operating from airfields in Burma and on Nicobar Island and so forth. So the East Indies Fleet (its new title) comprising a battleship, cruisers, escort carriers and destroyers, with Admiral Walker in command, sailed later in the day as the main component of "Bishop". This force also had the added task of bombarding and bombing Japanese bases in the Andaman and Nicobar Islands and generally disrupting Japanese coastal shipping.

We, in Force 69, made rendezvous with the Fleet to the west of the Andamans and the destroyers took it in turn to oil from *Olwen* while under way, and then the Fleet continued to the east while we escorted the *Olwen* to and fro round the rendezvous area. The next day the *Paladin* was relieved of her duties of guarding the tanker and we joined the Fleet, and so later on that day we were in the vicinity of the North Andaman Islands, and the day following took part in the bombardment of Port Blair in the South Andaman Islands. We then spent some time attached to the Fleet to carry out air-sea rescue duties, which involved us in cruising off places being bombed by carrier aircraft. This we did in various parts including off Cap Nicobar, and so we finished that sortie and went back to Trincomalee.

It was while we were returning to Trincomalee that we had the great news that Germany had surrendered, and we all listened to Churchill's speech on the compass platform and followed this up by splicing the mainbrace, which was a thing almost unheard of in a ship at sea in wartime. The celebrations for VE Day were short-lived. Early on 10 May the major part of the East Indies Fleet put to sea to seek out and destroy enemy ships which were about to evacuate their troops from the Andaman and Nicobar Islands. This culminated in a brilliant but not very well-known destroyer action when the 26th Destroyer Flotilla torpedoed and sank the Japanese heavy cruiser *Haguro* in the Malacca Straits off Penang. Of the five British destroyers involved, *Saumarez* received hits which caused casualties, some fatal. Later *Virago* also sustained deaths and casualties as a result of air attack. Our role in *Paladin* in this operation was to escort the tanker, the Royal Fleet Tanker *Echodale*, eastwards across the Bay of Bengal to rendezvous with the Fleet and refuel ships as necessary.

However, our mission was somewhat enlivened when we received a signal from the Admiral saying that we had been reported by Japanese air reconnaissance and we were to expect attack by Japanese suicide planes. To emphasise that he expected the worst, Admiral Walker ordered another tanker to sea with our sister ship HMS *Penn* in escort. In fact we managed to avoid any such confrontation and arrived at the rendezvous with the Fleet some 200 miles south-west of the northern tip of Sumatra later in the month. Then we were detached and returned to Trincomalee.

The next interesting episode occurred after we had officially become a member of the 10th Destroyer Flotilla. HMS *Tartar* was the Flotilla Leader and other ships included *Eskimo*, *Nubian* and *Penn*. All these ships had had fairly recent refits, including the provision of up-to-date radar. *Paladin*'s radar was completely outdated – largely useless for detecting aircraft or for navigational use – so in this respect we were the lame duck of the Flotilla. So when, in early June, we sailed for the first time as a Flotilla to carry out anti-shipping sweeps between the Nicobar Islands and Sabang, an island just to the north of Sumatra, we sailed in line abreast with 5 nautical miles between ships, with *Paladin* tucked somewhere safely in the centre, in view of her radar deficiencies.

It was then, during that night, that we received a copy of a signal for Captain D in *Tartar* instructing him to detach one destroyer to go to the Batu Islands to pick up an espionage party. That destroyer was to be in position well within the island group by dawn on 9 June. We sensed it was going to be us and, sure enough, in the early hours of the next day we were leaving the Flotilla and were on our way. We'd already located where the Batu Islands were, having had no idea up to that time, never having heard of them. They were just to the west of Sumatra and almost on the equator, which put them about south-east of our point of departure from the Flotilla. So we decided to travel down parallel to the coast some 150 nautical miles to the west so as to be out of enemy radar range and hopefully air reconnaissance as well. Then, after dark on the evening of 8 June, we would alter course to be at our designated position within the Batu Group of islands by dawn.

This required some rather exacting navigation. I've already described some of the difficulties that I'd had with navigation and some of the errors, but this is one of which I've always been rather proud, because almost up till the time from sailing we'd had no signs of any stars nor the sun – it had been completely overcast all the way – and so we were travelling on dead reckoning, estimating our position as a result of the course we had sailed and speed and not allowing very much for currents because we really did not know what they were. So, towards evening of the last day before we turned in to our rendezvous, I had already been working out alternatives, that if our dead reckoning position was correct we'd be all right, if it was in error to the north then, at 2 o'clock in the morning, we should be just about aground on the coast of Sumatra, which jutted out a bit at this region, or if we were further south than we thought we were, then we would not have sighted land even at 6 o'clock. So I worked out these possibilities and went up to the bridge with my sextant towards the estimated time of sunset – because we had no sun visible – and hopefully looked around, and to my joy one star suddenly made its appearance and I was able to shoot that star, and then another one appeared, and then another – I got all three and then the skies closed in again and there were no more stars. So I went below and worked out our position and found our dead reckoning position was fairly spot-on, and felt very relieved – at least we knew where we were.

So round about 2 o'clock in the morning we sighted land as we thought we would, and steered parallel to the coast to the east, and I was able to do some pilotage then, not that I recognised anything ashore, because it was dark anyway, but what one could see were the silhouettes of the hills and the mountains on the shore, and I was able, by taking the largest-looking, the highest peaks, to take bearings on them and work out our position from the charts, so it was fairly straight sailing then. Of course there were lighthouses about, but none of them was working, and there were no recognisable features except for these mountain-tops, which worked very well. So, at 6 o'clock in the morning, there we were, right dead-on, in position and looking hopefully towards where the espionage party were supposed to be, but of them there was no sign.

We spent the morning cruising to and fro looking for them; we even stopped a little fishing-smack and interrogated the fisherman, but he couldn't speak our language and we couldn't speak his. So time went on and we were getting a bit anxious, because we weren't too far from Singapore, which was just over the other side to the east of Sumatra and fairly close flying from the base there, but no one seemed to do anything, and later in the afternoon we turned to the west and sailed out to sea again.

We were back there next day, but still no signs of that espionage party. We were then ordered to rendezvous to the west with Force 64, which was

South East Asia: HMS Paladin *about to refuel at sea from a tanker.*

a Fleet Tanker escorted by HMS *Penn*, and relieve *Penn*, who would take over the search. We then refuelled from the tanker and then we had to go back to the Batu Islands to relieve *Penn*. Still no sign of that party, so we were ordered to rendezvous with the submarine HMS *Trident*, who continued the search. The espionage party was never found and it was discovered later on that it had been betrayed to the Japanese, and all its members killed.

Then on the afternoon of 19 July we slipped and proceeded as Force 63 on what was called "Operation Livery". The Force comprised the battleship HMS *Nelson*, flying the flag of Vice-Admiral Walker, the cruiser HMS *Sussex*, escort carriers *Empress* and *Ameer*, and the destroyers *Rotherham*, *Racehorse*, *Raider* and ourselves. Also included were the ships of the 7th Minesweeping Flotilla, and our operation involved crossing the Bay of Bengal and getting up towards the Island of Phuket off Siam, under Japanese occupation. "Operation Livery" was a diversion to mislead the Japanese into thinking that the proposed landing to retake Malaya would happen there. The minesweepers were to clear the area of mines and this involved sweeping fairly close inshore where the minefields had been laid. During this time the major part of the Fleet would lie further out to sea providing cover for the minesweepers and bombing and bombarding Japanese installations ashore. Two destroyers were with the Minesweeping Flotilla to give close support.

Then on the evening of 24 July the minesweeper HMS *Squirrel* had struck a mine and had been seriously damaged, with seven ratings killed, and she had to be sunk whilst the rest of the Flotilla continued to sweep. The next day HMS *Paladin* and HMS *Raider* were detached from the Fleet to take over the close escort of the minesweepers off Phuket. So far there had been no obvious response from the Japanese to these activities right on their doorstep. However, towards evening I went up on the bridge to check our position and I noticed a rather old-fashioned-looking aeroplane flying at very low level and quite slowly, a few hundred yards off our port beam. I could see the pilot quite distinctly in the cockpit, and there was a great purple emblem on the side of the plane. It had crept up unnoticed by anyone. I hurriedly pointed it out to the Captain, who was standing alongside me, and he immediately ordered the guns to open fire. Before they could do so, the plane turned away and flew off towards the south-west, where bigger game in the form of the "County" Class cruiser *Sussex* had fortuitously appeared on the horizon and obviously saved our bacon.

Then suddenly there was a clatter of noise from our starboard quarter and, looking round, we saw yet another Japanese plane flying towards us and quite close, but being pursued by a Hellcat fighter from one of the carriers. This time we were ready for it, and we opened fire and our fire went between the Japanese plane and the Hellcat, so much so that the Hellcat had to veer away and the Japanese turned to port, came round, turned to port again, and came straight at us. Between us and the Japanese plane there was a little minesweeper, *Vestal*, and for some unknown reason the Japanese plane went straight into the *Vestal* – ignored us, the bigger ship, and crashed his plane on to the upper deck of the *Vestal*. The whole ship exploded in a mass of flame and was obscured for a while, and then, when the flames cleared, there was *Vestal* still afloat with the Japanese plane suspended on its upper works.

The other ships of the Minesweeping Flotilla began steaming in circles round *Vestal* picking up survivors, and at this time the first Japanese plane had reached the *Sussex* and we saw it going straight into its stern, which appeared to dissolve into a mass of flames, and we thought, oh gosh, she's hit it, but *Sussex* steamed on and the plane, a ball of fire, fell into the sea. They'd just got her before she got them and the cruiser was all right. So this was the first episode of kamikaze action which the ships of the East Indies Fleet had had, and it was the last, because this turned out to be the last operation by the Fleet before the Japanese surrendered.

Admiral Walker then ordered the surviving ships of the Minesweeping Flotilla to retire at high speed to the west, and we joined them, but were ordered back to sink *Vestal*, which was still afloat. This was easier said than done, but we eventually managed to get her to sink and then rejoined the Fleet. "Operation Livery" was completed and Force 63 went back to Trincomalee. Fifteen men were killed in *Vestal* as the result of this attack.

I flew over the site of this action many years later and thought of *Squirrel*, *Vestal* and their dead, still lying there as all those holidaymakers disport themselves on the beaches nearby, completely oblivious of the high drama and sacrifices made on their behalf so many years ago.

Flying Officer William Scott, as second pilot of a Liberator bomber, was involved in long-range bombing missions across the Bay of Bengal:

'On arrival in Bombay we went to the transit camp at Worli where you got used to eastern ways, I suppose you could call it, and waited for your next posting. I suppose I was there for about a fortnight and was then transferred to my Squadron, which was No 203 Squadron, which was a Squadron attached to an organisation called the Indian Ocean General Reconnaissance Group. I went down to a place called Madurai in Southern India by train, an interesting journey, hot and sweaty. In Madurai I was introduced to the crew of the Liberator. My Captain was a Flight Lieutenant and the crew consisted of ten – air-gunners, navigator, wireless operators and so on – and we did there a little training in low-level

William Lindsay McDonald Scott

bombing. Our role was going to be anti-shipping strikes – in other words, to go out and attempt to sink Japanese shipping by low-level attack. This low-level attack was literally on the deck. We had a radio altimeter which would get us down quite happily to 25 feet, and that's the sort of height we would attack from, and the object of the attack would be to come in at very low levels as I've said, pull up over the ship, release our bombs, and try and get out of range as quick as possible.

Doing this in the Liberator of course was quite exciting because, while it was a lovely aeroplane to fly, it was nice and comfortable, it really wasn't the sort of operational-type aeroplane that, say, a Lancaster or something like that was. However, it could take a lot of punishment and that was a happy thing to think about. Well, we trained there in Madurai for a while and then I was sent down to Colombo to learn to recognise shipping, so I became the Squadron's expert on shipping and ship recognition. It mainly consisted not so much of Japanese warships as of local trading schooners and things like this. Well, of course they were important at that time because they were the ships that were carrying supplies for the Japanese forces up and down Burma and the Malayan Peninsula.

The object of the exercise was to sink ships, and the place to sink ships was around Northern Sumatra, the Nicobar and Andaman Islands and up and down the Malacca Straits. That was the sort of area where we used to go and look for shipping. The round trip would take us about 15 to 16 hours, probably cruising at 140 knots or something like. They were armed with four 0.5s in the front turret, two 0.5s in the mid-upper, four 0.5s in the rear turret, and side beam gunners, again 0.5 Brownings. We carried overload tanks down the centre beam, and then in the bomb-bay alongside the overload tanks we would carry 500lb bombs and occasionally depth charges, and so off we went to war in this configuration.

Our own operations – I only went on five or six – and the first one was against the harbour in Sabang in Northern Sumatra, and there was a fair amount of shipping in there. Well, the tactic we used, at the time, was three aeroplanes would set off on the raid and would come in in formation into the harbour or against a ship and drop our bombs. Front gunners would open up first and then bombs and rear gunners. My own personal recollection of that first raid was that we went in at the right sort of level, the Captain pulled up over the ship and kept on going up, and I was shouting to him, "Get down, get down, get down!" but the other two – we were leading the group of three – did the right thing, but one of them got shot down and that was the sort of pattern for all the operations we undertook. We lost one out of three every time.

We got hit with small arms fire on several occasions, but nothing very serious. My own personal bit of injury was, it was a bit of a panic in the back because somebody had been hit, well only mildly wounded, and I, as second pilot, co-pilot, was sent to the back to enquire what was going on. As I walked past the wireless operator the top hatch fell on my head, and to this day I have a blood-stained flying helmet – which was my only war wound, I have to say.'

The dropping of the second atom bomb on Nagasaki brought the war against Japan to an abrupt end. Lieutenant Begg in the destroyer HMS *Paladin* was in Colombo on 15 August, VJ Day:

'The official celebrations included the traditional splicing of the mainbrace, in which all hands took part, and in the evening all ships in the harbour switched on their lights, and searchlights wreathed through the sky, a fine sight, and "V for Victory" sounded off on the ships' sirens and added to the general effect. We were once more at peace.

At 1845 on 30 August *Paladin* slipped and proceeded to sea with the cruiser *Nigeria* and destroyers *Rotherham*, *Racehorse*, *Redoubt* and *Nubian* in company. We proceeded to the east at 20 knots to take part in the re-occupation of Japanese-held territory. We eventually joined the Fleet, Vice-Admiral Walker flying his flag in the battleship HMS *Nelson*, and the French battlecruiser *Richelieu* was also in company.

On 3 September we proceeded down the search channel which, hopefully, had been cleared of mines, to Penang, where we oiled and spent the next few days. It had been decided that "Operation Zipper", in which our troops would have been put ashore, if the war had continued, should take place anyway in the same fashion as laid down in the Operation Orders, but, of course, there would be no naval bombardment or air attack and, hopefully, no response from the Japanese. So at 0400 on 9 September *Paladin* proceeded from Penang to take part in "Operation Zipper". By dawn we'd anchored in our bombardment position close to the beach south of Port Swettenham, the landing duly took place and we were heartily glad it was not the real thing. The tanks and vehicles, many of them became caught in the mud under the sandy beaches and some of them are still there to this day. The position would have been very different if the landing had been resisted. In addition to the natural hazards and resistance on the beaches, the Japanese had collected a formidable number of suicide motor boats and planes which would have created havoc amongst the anchored naval bombardment vessels and other ships of the invasion force.

Then, later in the day, we weighed anchor and joined the flagship, HMS *Nelson*, and other ships, including some of the 10th Destroyer Flotilla, and proceeded to Singapore. At 1955 on 11 September the 10th Destroyer Flotilla, with the destroyers *Relentless* and *Saumarez* in company, sailed down the search channel, and by 2238 were anchored off Singapore City. We were amongst the first British ships back in Singapore and Penang.

One little episode I recall: I had borrowed our previous Captain's bicycle, which was an old crock that had remained on board after he left, and went for a ride round Singapore. There was no transport available so this was a good way to see the island. I cycled round and admired the spacious gardens and large houses and went out and passed a couple of prison camps, and, at one stage, I passed a car full of Japanese officers, all attired in smart uniforms, and who looked in my direction and saluted as I wobbled past on my decrepit bicycle. I responded with a salute, which was as coldly polite as I could make it, in conformity with official orders. Then

Above and above right Admiral Mountbatten strides into the Municipal Chambers, Singapore, for the formal signing of the surrender, 12 September 1945, followed by the Japanese under officer escort.

Right Japanese 'Top Brass' being escorted to the signing.

I rode to the Raffles Hotel and had a couple of glasses of water, because there was nothing else available there. They had trestle tables and forms to sit on and water and nothing else.

Then came the morning when the Surrender Ceremony took place. We landed a platoon of seamen to take part in the proceedings and I landed and went down later, as a spectator. There were thousands of people outside the Municipal Chambers where the signing was to take place. I managed to get in the second row of spectators and so had a good view of proceedings. Lord Louis Mountbatten arrived and inspected the guard and then disappeared into the building. The Japanese top brass then appeared, each man having two senior British officers as guards, one on each side. They were marched into the building to the jeers of the crowd, and suddenly there was a burst of what sounded like machine-gun fire on the outskirts of the crowd, and for an awful moment we thought the Japanese military had had a change of mind. There were, in fact, far more Japanese soldiers than British in Singapore at this stage, although they were being bundled across the causeway to Johore to await collection by our troops coming down from the landing beaches. However, it turned out that the musketry was only fire-crackers being let off by the jubilant Chinese.

After the signing the Japanese were led away and Lord Louis appeared and gave a very spirited speech. Then, as the Combined Services Bands played "God Save the King", a Union Jack, which had been kept hidden for years by the POWs and used for funerals, was slowly hoisted, whilst we all saluted and remained at the salute as the bands played the National Anthems of all the Allies. A memorable occasion indeed.'

CHAPTER 17

The war in the Pacific: with the Americans, fashioning victory from defeat

*P*arallel with the struggle to clear the Japanese out of South East Asia was the still larger-scale endeavour to overturn their dominance in the Pacific. With the war in Europe over there was an ever-increasing flow of ships, planes, armaments and men arriving in the Pacific at a time when the reverse was happening to the Japanese. Many of their island garrisons had been bypassed by the flow of battle, and, with their supplies drying up, they were suffering from malnutrition and disease, yet they still fought on with great tenacity. Air attacks, especially of the kamikaze variety, were becoming the order of the day as the ships of the American Navy and the newly arrived British Pacific Fleet drew closer to the shores of Japan. Squadrons of planes of the New Zealand Air Force had been operating with the Americans from airstrips on Bougainville, with Japanese troops in close proximity, for quite some time. So here are the accounts of these events as told by men who experienced them.

When Gerald Burton qualified as a Sergeant Pilot in the RNZAF he served for a time as an Instructor and Test Pilot at Ohakea, then, with Japan in the war, he was posted to No 7 Squadron on reconnaissance and anti-submarine patrols operating from the top of the North Island:

'We only had old outdated Vincents and Wildebeests. That is how tragic the situation was in New Zealand – they became our first line of defence. They used to carry two 250lb bombs, one under each wing. So that's how desperate New Zealand was for aircraft at that time. I was then transferred to another General Reconnaissance Squadron at Gisborne on the east coast of the North Island and was there for over two years before we eventually got advanced aircraft, which was the famous Grumman Avenger, and at that stage we started our training on the Avengers and were reformed ready to go overseas into what became 30 TVF Squadron. I had, by then, been commissioned as a Pilot Officer, and later during my service in the South Pacific was promoted to the rank of Flying Officer.

Brothers Gerald and Jack Burton undertaking pilot training.

New Zealand's Home Protection: an obsolete Vickers Wildebeest.

Then the Avenger: Gerry Burton's 'Pride and Joy'.

We were to fly from New Zealand to Norfolk Island – being single-engined aircraft we had to do it in about three hops to get to Bougainville, where we were eventually heading for. We left Whenuapai heading for Norfolk Island, and I've never forgotten – I suppose it's one of these vivid things you have in your mind looking back over the years – because we headed off from the top of the North Island and got well out to sea. I took one look back at Ninety Mile Beach and the Three Brothers and I thought, well, is this the last time I'll ever be seeing my beautiful New Zealand. We were escorted right up from Auckland – we couldn't navigate ourselves, so we had an escort aircraft – and we had a night in Auckland and then a night at Noumea, and then we arrived at Espiritu in the New Hebrides. Here we continued more advanced training; that was about half way to our destination. It was in early 1943.

From there we were escorted until we went on to Guadalcanal where the great battles for supremacy had been raging. We just overnighted in Guadalcanal before we flew on to Bougainville. On our arrival at Bougainville I began to wonder whether I was in the Army or the Air Force – there seemed to be shells flying in all directions. The Japanese ran a semicircle up in the jungle, and Bougainville comprised three airstrips, which the Americans had built. Torokina, which was a fighter strip, was right down at the beach, and about half a mile inland they'd carved out of the jungle a second airstrip, which was known as Piva One, and another half mile further into the jungle they'd carved out Piva Two, which was the one from which we were to operate. This was surrounded by Japanese in the jungle and in a direct line only 300 or 400 yards from our strip. At night, quite frequently, there would be rifle fire, and bullets would shoot sometimes through the top of our tents; that's why, I say, I began to wonder whether I was in the Army or the Air Force.

The Japanese had been causing so much trouble with firing, mostly at night, and I remember on one occasion they hit the bakehouse and destroyed that, so we were out of bread for about a week. On another occasion, which seems funny now when I look back on it, we'd just come back from a raid on Rabaul and we'd all gone down for a swim, down to Torokina Beach, but, of course, up there you didn't bother to wear anything, you just went in the nude, and the Japanese decided this was a good occasion to land a couple of shells out in the bay, and I've never seen so many nude bodies disappear out of water so fast in all my life, as we scampered up the beach to get out of the water where a few shells were being dropped.

Well, we started our bombing and the first raid we did was just one round the perimeters of the airstrips to try and locate some of these Japanese hideouts, and they had a lot of vegetable gardens and things there. Well, I was flying Number Two to our CO and he couldn't dispose of any of his bombs so I was the next one to drop; I managed to drop three out of the four, so I claim that I dropped the first official bomb of 30 Squadron on operations. The instructions were that if you did not discharge all of your bombs you were not to come back and land with a bomb on board – you had to fly out to sea and try and get rid of them – and if you did not get rid of them you were instructed to ditch the aircraft and get back the best way you could or you'd be picked up. Well, I wasn't very keen on this, and I think I flew for about 20 minutes, I rocked, I almost stalled the aircraft, but once you opened your bomb-bay there was a little panel that your crew from the back could see whether your bombs had gone, and they said, "No Gerry, it's still there, we haven't got rid of it." Anyway, finally I did get rid of the thing. I still don't think I would have ditched the aircraft; I think I'd have closed the bomb-bay doors and gone back and hoped for the best, even though it was against orders.

I do remember on one occasion, and we had one 2,000lb bomb on this particular occasion, and the last thing I used to do was check that the bomb-bay doors were operating successfully. Because of the heat that used to be generated on the aircraft, you couldn't put your hand on any part of the aircraft or you'd burn yourself – the crew used to wait outside until the last minute. I'd done all my cockpit drill and I'd given them the thumbs-up and they'd pile in the door and get on board and we'd taxi out for take-off. On this occasion they were both standing there and I checked the bomb-bays, but there was something wrong somewhere when the bomb had been put on board. The next thing I saw was my crew disappearing about a quarter a mile away down the revetment. I was trying to call them back, but they wouldn't come back; they were just pointing and waving their arms and pointing at the aircraft, and I thought what on earth's wrong? So I just left the motor running and I got out to have a look myself, and there was the bomb sitting underneath the aircraft. The only thing then, of course, was to abandon the aircraft and get a replacement aircraft.

The biggest worry I always found was at take-off time, because there could be up to 24, 50, 60 and on one occasion over 96 aircraft, which used to take off in pairs. You'd taxi out from the revetment, down to the end of the runway, get lined up, and you would be waved off two at a time when the two aircraft ahead of you were actually airborne. I found this the most worrying time of the lot, because with all the aircraft fully loaded with petrol, fully loaded with bombs and assembling down at the end of the strip, it always amazed me why the Japanese never shelled the strip at that time. There would have been absolute chaos if they'd landed a couple of shells; they would have destroyed half of the aircraft taking off. I was always very happy to be in the air and on our way. But strangely the Japanese never tried it while we were there, thank God, otherwise probably a lot of us wouldn't have survived.

Most of our air operations on Rabaul were on Japanese airstrips and on Rabaul harbour itself. Rabaul, of course, was up until that stage the biggest Fleet base that the Japanese had when they were desperately trying to recover Guadalcanal from the Americans. Looking at the war in Europe I often wonder why the war in the Pacific always seems to have been looked upon as a secondary war. I don't think a lot of the world ever realised that some of the biggest naval battles of any war took place in the Pacific, in the Battle of the Coral Sea and the Midway sea battles.

There was one night when the rumour was that the Japanese were going to try and make a breakthrough and attack our three airstrips, and the American Admiral, Bill Halsey – they called him Bull Halsey – was a bit fed up with this and came in with a cruiser, which sat out off the bay where we were at Bougainville, and decided to open up on the Japanese. Well, for about an hour there was just this blast of heavy shells coming from this cruiser and landing only 3-400 yards the other side of our camp. It sounds quite humorous today when I look back on it, but I was terrified. By this time, of course, we were in foxholes outside our tent – we weren't there sitting watching the great display. I was terrified that one or two of the shells might not quite make the distance and might land in our camp. The next

Final attack by 30 Squadron, RNZAF, on the Japanese fleet base at Rabaul.

morning they told me they cleaned out about 500 Japs and just flattened half of the jungle around there. A lot of the boys went up to see it after the shelling but I just wasn't interested in seeing dead bodies or anything else; I was quite pleased still to be alive and where I was, but it was quite an occasion and a night to remember.

I would just like to mention something about the Avenger. We were very happy with it, it was a wonderful aircraft, and one of the things about it, it would take terrific punishment. Any that were hit, provided they weren't hit in vital areas, still seemed to be able to fly and get home, which was something that we valued very much. From our point of view one of the few problems was they were never really built for steep dive-bombing, which, ultimately, we were using them for. We had started training for glide-bombing, but eventually got on to steep dive-bombing. They were never really built for use on the land as we were using them. They were really the outstanding carrier-based torpedo aircraft at that time. Consequently, they had very small wheels for a very large aircraft, and one of the problems we had using them on the land was that we were occasionally bursting tyres, and this was due to the very hot conditions and that we were taxiing them too far from our revetments to the taking-off strips. Having been a carrier-based aircraft, of course, they were airborne in a very short run and there was no trouble.

As for our attacks on Rabaul, we were using them really for fairly steep dive-bombing and we had a maximum diving speed of 350 knots. Now, the Avenger had folding wings so that they could be parked below deck on aircraft carriers. So there was the danger that, at very high-speed dive-bombing, if you got over 350 knots there was the possibility that the wings could fold back in the air, which, of course, would have been a major disaster. Fortunately we never lost any through this. We did lose two aircraft of our Squadron over Rabaul; tragically; they were shot down by a twin naval gun which the Japanese had brought down from Singapore and had right alongside one of the major airstrips at Rabaul. They caught two of our aircraft and it completely blew the wing tips off both of them. They just didn't have a chance.

The Japanese had also brought down radar- or radio-controlled guns from Singapore and set them up round a place we knew as Hospital Ridge in Rabaul. It was one of the real hot spots and the Japanese were able to operate these guns from tunnels that they had built into the side of the hill, and unless you got a direct hit on the guns your bombs would slide down very steep hillsides into the jungle and would have no effect at all. Mainly we were operating on the airstrips to try and keep those unserviceable, so the Zeros and fighters could not take off.

I remember, on one occasion, we were attacking one of the airstrips. If you did not get on to number one target you always had a secondary target you had to find. Well, on this occasion the Americans were leading the attack and through very dense cloud, through a small hole in the clouds, they managed to spot the secondary target and led us into the attack. Well, this was all right for the first half-dozen aircraft that went through – it was only a small hole in the clouds. Our particular squadron were fairly well back amongst the aircraft attacking at that stage. We were back about midway, and it occurred to me, I thought, well, Gerry, by the time your turn comes to go through that hole in the cloud the Japanese will have just peppered the whole of that hole. I could never understand why they never did it, because if they had aimed their anti-aircraft fire just at that one small hole in the clouds, they'd have copped practically every aircraft that went through it. Fortunately, thank God they never did it and we got through it safely.

Well, after having done your attack, the idea was to keep down low to about 1,000 feet so that any Japanese aircraft couldn't get down underneath or behind you, and then shoot straight out to sea, and you formated on the first friendly aircraft you saw. It didn't matter whether it was American or whether we formated on our own or not, but it was just to gain protection. If there happened to be fighters about, at least you had two or three aircraft together that could try and fend them off. I remember, on this occasion, I shot out to sea following instructions, and couldn't see a friendly aircraft anywhere. Anyway, I eventually spotted one and formated up and we finally got our whole Squadron together right out to sea and came back quite safely.

There was another occasion coming back. We were about 50 miles from home and we had a fire in my cockpit – all the electrical equipment began to smoke. I called the aircrew to grab the fire extinguisher; I said, "We've got a fire on board." I called the tower, told them we were about 50 miles from base, that I had a fire on board, and if I could make it I'd like permission to be the first to land, and my air-gunner down the back, he grabbed the fire extinguisher and tried to get up the little tunnel in the aircraft, but he got jammed with his Mae West and all his gear on. He tried to operate the fire extinguisher and it wouldn't operate, and he said, "Gerry, it won't operate, I can't get it to go." By this time I'm getting pretty anxious because the smoke was getting more dense, and I said, "Well, have a look at the instructions and have another go." By the time he'd read the instructions the thing was ready to operate all right. The instructions said to strike the knob and wait so many seconds or a minute or something before operation, and of course the whole thing went off all over the aircraft, and by the time we got it pointed at the fire the extinguisher had extinguished itself, so that didn't help, but fortunately, very fortunately, the fire just seemed to go out of its own accord and we got back quite safely.'

Another man to experience war in the Pacific in the RNZAF, but in quite a different role, was Airman Allan Carson. His preference was to be an Observer, but for health reasons he served with Operations and Intelligence:

'I was on Bougainville for three months as the clerk to the Station Intelligence Officer. I suppose this time on Bougainville was one of the periods I will remember for the rest of my life. We were camped in a great high grove of trees, sandy ground close to a wonderful beach, Empress Augusta Bay, miles of a wonderful surf beach, and it really was a very pleasant physical environment. The only thing was, at that time there were three airstrips on what you could call a toehold on Bougainville. There were thousands and thousands of Japanese throughout this big island, and there were two bomber strips, Piva One and Piva Two, and Torokina virtually on the beach. The New Zealand Air Force Fighter Squadrons operated from Torokina. The toehold I mentioned was really bordered by a perimeter which extended from the coast around in a semicircle to further up the coast, and that was guarded by United States Army and Marines and they simply kept the Japanese at bay.

I will always remember in March 1944 news came around on the grapevine that the Japanese were planning a push to dislodge this toehold of three airfields under their noses, and one morning without any further ado they began to shell the bases. This went on for about a week and it was miraculous we had no casualties – shells fell in and around the airstrips and into our camp, but there were no casualties. The Americans then set out to really settle the Japanese in this area, and I had the opportunity with my CO to go up to the perimeter, and it was a terrible sight to see thousands of casualties. Japanese casualties were enormous and they were simply buried in pits with bulldozers.'

Back in New Zealand, Allan Carson, having attended an Officer School of Instruction and having been promoted to Pilot Officer, was posted to No 19 Fighter Squadron as Intelligence Officer:

'No 19 Squadron was forming up and, on 25 October, the Squadron was posted back to the South Pacific; we had a period of familiarisation at Espiritu Santo, and we then moved to Emirau, an island in the Mussau group, practically on the equator, and we were the first New Zealand Fighter Squadron to take up duties there from the Americans. The tour of duty at Emirau lasted for just under three months, and I will always remember this period. The pilots were engaged mainly in carrying out patrols over Rabaul, and, of course, Rabaul was really the vital focus point in the South Pacific for the Japanese. They had built up a great base with a natural harbour, Simpson Harbour, and they established five airstrips surrounding the town of Rabaul. They had gradually, over a period of time,

Allan James Carson

been made unoperational – the airfields were bombed to smithereens. There were hundreds and hundreds of Japanese aircraft at Rabaul, and for the last two or three years of the war none of them ever left the ground. The aerial combat which engaged RNZAF pilots earlier in the war came to an end.

The RNZAF shot down 99 Japanese aircraft, but they didn't get the century, that was where it ended, and from that time on the Japanese were simply kept neutralised. They had no opportunity to do anything by sea – the Solomon Islands had all been occupied, Guadalcanal, New Georgia, Bougainville. It was the maintenance of patrols over Rabaul to see that they didn't get any of the airfields operational again or mount offensives of any kind that then engaged the fighter squadrons which rotated and maintained patrols over Rabaul.

My squadron, 19, they went off every morning on a dawn patrol and every evening on a dusk patrol, and this was their main occupation. They also carried a 500lb bomb – we were using Corsair F4U single-engined aircraft – and the lads took off with a bomb which they dropped on what we called a target of opportunity: bridges, Japanese gardens and the Japanese, of course, in and around Rabaul who were coming close to the point of starvation because they had no further supplies from Japan or anywhere else and they were living off the land.

From there we went on our next tour of duty to the Admiralty Islands, again very close to the equator, and the airfield was on the island of Los Negros, and again these patrols were maintained over Rabaul. At the Admiralty Islands there was a huge natural harbour protected by a great circular coral reef, and towards the end of the war that accommodated most of the British Pacific Fleet. There was a floating dock quite close to our base, and the only excitement I suppose really at that place was when a Japanese torpedo-bomber was launched from a Japanese ship of some kind and he attempted to drop a torpedo into this floating dock. However, it didn't come off.

We maintained our patrols, and while there, while at Los Negros, we became aware that things were happening on the other side of the world, and on 8 May we were just actually waiting, listening to radio news and signals coming through that the Germans were about to surrender. On the following day the war ended and the Station had a holiday; we went out, some of us to look at a British cruiser, and then in the afternoon, just to add to the excitement, a great water spout came in from way out to sea and destroyed several buildings within 100 yards of the New Zealand Camp.

We ended that tour on 4 May and returned to New Zealand shortly after the end of the war in Europe. The squadron, as usual, reformed. We had few casualties, we did not lose a pilot as the result of enemy action, that's to say anti-aircraft fire, and there were no aerial combats as I've mentioned earlier. The fellows came under anti-aircraft fire when they were doing their patrols and dropping their bomb, and several of them came back, of course, with holes in their fuselages, but we did not lose a pilot.

We reformed, as I say, at Ardmore, made up any deficiencies in the numbers – usually a squadron was 24 pilots – and we set out again on 30 June and travelled up via Tontuta in New Caledonia, the usual stopover in Espiritu Santo, and then we were posted to Jacquinot Bay. This was a base on the main island of New Britain, quite a short distance, minutes flying time, from Rabaul, and we continued these patrols. Then in August news comes through about a new bomb dropped on Japan equal to 20,000 tons of TNT, two-thirds of Hiroshima demolished. Now again, over the next few days, we all just simply sat and waited. The daily routine continued, and on 15 August 1945 the unconditional surrender of Japan was announced.

Patrols really became a formality now; we were required to keep in touch and to cover practically all movements in and around Rabaul because we realised that although there had been a formal surrender there would be hundreds if not thousands of Japanese who wouldn't even know that this had happened, and, of course, any active hostility would have been quite tricky. But on 18 September two Japanese fighter aircraft, Zekes, the famous Zero aircraft, and a reconnaissance plane, a Dinah, landed at our strip. I was ordered by the CO to escort these pilots back to Rabaul. So one of my colleagues and I in a Catalina flew up with these four Japanese pilots, and I'll always remember my feelings at that time as a 22/23-year-old and here we were, hot and sweaty and in khaki shirts and shorts, and here were these Japanese pilots dressed to the nines, obviously out to make the best of this ignominy of surrender. I always remember one of them had a very, very nice white silk scarf wrapped round his neck. Anyway, we escorted them back up in this Catalina and had the experience of landing on Simpson Harbour, a graveyard for so many pilots who were shot down into and around Simpson Harbour.

Anyway, after they went ashore a lighter came out to the Catalina and the next thing we realised, these hard-cased Aussies were passing up what we thought at first were some bundles of washing, and suddenly we realised that these were two or three little French nuns in their white habits, yellow, I suppose. They'd been in captivity – this is September 1945 – and these women had been in the hands of the Japanese since very early in 1942, and they were followed by several Sikh soldiers who had again been prisoners of the Japanese. I'll always remember one of them, he was obviously dying, he was passed up on a stretcher and we made room for them in the Catalina and we flew back to our base, and of course these people simply went straight into an Australian Hospital that had been set up.'

Lieutenant John Musters RN, who has featured in previous chapters, was still serving in the aircraft carrier HMS *Victorious*:

'In July – I'm not sure, June or July '44 – *Victorious* and *Indomitable*, another modern Fleet carrier, were sent out to the Far East to join the Eastern Fleet as part of the build-up for the Pacific Fleet, which was not very far ahead. We passed through the Mediterranean, a thing we couldn't have done earlier – by this time of course Italy was out of the war – and down through the Suez Canal, down the Red Sea. Going down the Red Sea we had some practice dive-bombing attacks on ourselves by our Barracuda squadrons. Two of those Barracudas broke up in mid-air with disastrous results, killing the air crew, and that was an absolute shocker. The Barracudas had done extremely well in the *Tirpitz* operation and there had been no reason to suppose they were not, in fact, safe aircraft to be dived steeply with a load, but these accidents in the Red Sea changed people's attitudes.

Although we didn't do any more dive-bombing with those aircraft, we did still have them as torpedo bombers, and at the Eastern Fleet's base in Trincomalee we had one dummy torpedo attack by Barracuda squadrons on the Fleet in harbour, which could have been quite a useful practice for later on. Disaster struck them again, when two Barracudas collided and crashed, killing their air crew, so they were not very popular aircraft by that time.

We did various operations in the east in the Indian Ocean as part of the Eastern Fleet, carrying out air attacks on Japanese outposts there and in the Nicobar Islands and the western tip of Sumatra, Sabang and one or two other such places. Those were not very eventful – there was not a great deal of opposition.

In January 1945 the Eastern Fleet reached the point where the British Pacific part of it could be transferred to the Pacific in order to take part in the American onslaught which had now passed the Philippines and was about to be launched against Okinawa as the final step before the main attack on Japan proper. So we, with the rest of the ships which now constituted the British Pacific Fleet, travelled just south of Sumatra, and on the way the four carriers did a two days' bombing strike on the Japanese oil refineries at Palembang, which is in south-east Sumatra. The first day's strike went quite well and caused lots of fires amongst the oil tanks. The second strike was not so good; Japanese fighters were waiting and the carrier force lost quite a number of aircraft. By this time we had been rearmed with American Avenger torpedo-bombers, which could be used as shallow dive-bombers, though they were originally intended as torpedo-bombers, and these aircraft were used at Palembang.

From there we moved on to Perth in Western Australia, and then round to Sydney, where we spent a few weeks in final preparations logistically and planning for the operations up in the Western Pacific. From Sydney the whole force, the four carriers plus, I think, we had by that time four fast battleships and quite a lot of destroyers and some cruisers, we all moved up to the Admiralty Islands, an island called Manus, which was a fuelling stop and the final stop before we went into battle with the Japanese in the Taiwan area.

From there we sailed north and started bombing operations against Japanese-held islands in late March. The phase of operations at this stage was that the Americans were about to assault Okinawa and carried out heavy carrier air strikes. The British Pacific Fleet, which formed the equivalent of an American Task Group with four carriers and four fast battleships plus cruisers and destroyers, we had the mission of attacking airfields and then keeping neutralised some islands between Taiwan and Okinawa with the purpose of preventing the Japanese from staging aircraft, particularly kamikaze fighter-bombers from China through Taiwan, to join the Okinawa battle. They would need to stop for fuel in the Sakashima Islands, two of which, called Myako and Ishigaki, had airfields on them and which the Japanese wanted to use, so our job was to beat up any aircraft we found in or around those islands and keep the airfields cratered with bombs so they couldn't be used. Well, we did this on a sort of prolonged assignment – two strike days flying, perhaps four bombing strikes several times for each of two days escorted by fighters. We also had patrols of our own fighters at various points overhead to protect ourselves. Well, this went on and off; we had two strike days and then two replenishment days.

At dusk after the second strike day the whole force would beat it out to the pre-arranged rendezvous with our Fleet train to replenish with oil fuel, aviation fuel, bombs and any other ammunition we needed. There were replenishment aircraft usually available from an escort carrier which carried them; food, stores, whatever we needed to keep going. Mostly it was a matter of fuelling, both oil fuel and aviation fuel, and the Fleet train was not purpose-built – it was tankers taken up from civilian trade which had no equipment for replenishing ships at sea except what could be extemporised. They lacked the accurate station-keeping, accurate speed, accurate course equipment which made it a reasonable proposition to fuel from them, so it was a pretty hairy job for the carrier and other warship captains to fuel from these things, but they did it. I know our captain in

Victorious, Michael Denny, said that his two replenishment days were much more exhausting and nerve-racking than two strike days of occasionally having the odd kamikaze attacking us, and I could see exactly what he meant. So that was the pattern: two replenishment days and then back into the strike area for the air strikes in accordance with a pre-arranged programme.

The formation we used was American, and it was the obvious common sense one for operating two or three carriers because it was a circular one. You had a cruiser in the middle that was guiding the Fleet, the four carriers equally spaced round an inner circle of, I think, 1,000 yards radius – it might have been more, but I think it was 1,000 – and a slightly bigger circle, filling the gaps on a 1,500-yard radius circle, you had the four fast battleships *King George V*, *Duke of York*, *Howe*, *Anson*, and outside everything you had the other cruisers, not many, two or three, and about 16 destroyers. The destroyers were asked to form, I believe, a 4,000-yard circle. The advantage of this is that, whenever you needed to fly, which was every half-hour or so, to launch or recover aircraft the whole force would be turned together and you would all maintain the same compass bearing and distance from each other. Of course, you would be steering whatever course was necessary to go into the wind for the carriers to launch or recover aircraft instead of moving in line ahead, which would be much more laborious and take four times as long.

We expected the kamikaze attacks, which had been going on against the Americans by that time since about October '44, and sure enough, on 1 April, we got the first detection of a group of aircraft coming in from the direction of Northern Taiwan and fighters intercepted some of them. The Japanese had the practice of breaking up the formation once they got to about 20 miles out and just in sight of the force they were supposed to attack, and then they would carry out single attacks independently, preferably using cloud cover in order to get close in without being sighted, occasionally getting a sight of us in the cloud gaps. Then each Kamikaze pilot would try and line up on a carrier, preferably coming in from aft with the length of the flight deck as his target area, making a hit rather more likely than if he came in from the side where he could easily have dropped short or over.

The first attack on 1 April, I saw one of them dive into *Indefatigable*, which was one of our carriers. There was something rather nasty about it, which we got used to afterwards, but seeing this deliberate crashing and then the fireball and explosion was a very upsetting sight, I think. It didn't do any vital damage because all our carriers now had armoured flight decks, which as far as I know were 3¾ inches thick, covering the whole of the hangar below, between the for'ard and the after lift wells, and also there was some on the side of the hangar, as well as the side of the hull. That armour had been just sufficient in the case of *Illustrious* when she was heavily bombed in the Mediterranean by the German Air Force in November 1940. They made a mess of her but they didn't get through her armoured flight deck, which undoubtedly saved that ship, and of course it saved a lot of ours later.

Anyway, *Indefatigable* had some casualties from bits of splinter from the aircraft being blown into the island. Incidentally, the kamikaze aircraft were usually fighter bombers, naval fighters with code names, Zeke or Zero, occasionally the Army Oscar fighters, which were of much the same performance, but not as fast as our Corsairs and our Seafires, which were a naval conversion of the Spitfire. Very manoeuvrable, and they carried a 550lb bomb.

These Japanese fighter-bombers were relatively light aircraft and the penetration which they achieved with their bomb when they hit in a 30 to 45-degree dive was not as much as a free-fall armour-piercing bomb, which would have been dropped from, say, 2,000 feet. The American carriers, which were much more numerous than ours – they had about four Task Groups there, each of about four or five carriers and fast battleships, etc, to suit – they had the armour lower down below the hangar deck; the flight deck was unprotected and just light steel with wooden planking to make it more comfortable to walk on. Of course hits by kamikazes on them did appalling damage and they burnt like torches, but they never lost a Fleet carrier, although many of them were hit. They did lose one or two light Fleet carriers, or one, anyway, earlier in the Philippines battles from a kamikaze hit. They were smaller ships built on 10,000-ton cruiser hulls. The Americans were quite astonished that our ships stood these hits and they couldn't really believe it when we reported that such and such a carrier had been hit and it was operating aircraft as though nothing much had happened half an hour later, which is how it went.

We all went down to Leyte Gulf in the Philippines after, I think, about six weeks of this operation to replenish, do a little maintenance, have a breather. The Americans had been rather reluctant to have us around at all before, but when we went down to the Philippines they found it necessary to detach a bunch of light fleet carriers in order to carry on the work we had been doing, the flights in the Sakashima Islands. After Leyte we went back for a second wave, same targets. On 9 May we got hit ourselves in the late afternoon; raiders were detected coming in fairly high and the fighters at the appropriate height were sent off to intercept. That lot turned away and didn't do anything very much, but they had diverted our attention up to 12,000 feet, or wherever this bunch had been performing. Meanwhile, the real threat came in from low down, and they weren't detected by radar until just about the time they were being sighted and they came in quite low. When they were, I think, about 10 miles from the Force, they climbed quickly into cloud cover, and after that it was not possible to carry out individual detections by our fighter directors. There were lots of targets milling around among our own fighters. Then one of them slid down with *Victorious* in its sights, and the Captain, looking out over the starboard wing bridge, saw that the thing was going to, well, it was certainly going to hit, so he sung out to us on the bridge to lie down, which we did reasonably promptly, and I tried to see the thing hit. I heard a sort of roar not quite the same as our guns, which had been thud, thudding away out there, and then a sort of orange glare as everything blew up.

We bent our heads over the parapet and through the windscreen, which was hit, and saw it was a bit of a mess with smoke and muck, and somebody said he'd found the pilot's boot. But he had made a hole in the flight deck just for'ard of the armour on the port side and smashed the catapult, which had its rails flush with the flight deck for launching aircraft if we needed to do it that way. Also he'd smashed his way into the port for'ard 4.5-inch group of four guns and put them out of action and caused casualties in those enclosed gun- mountings. We had a supply of big steel plates all strapped

A Kamikaze aircraft about to crash on the Victorious's *flight-deck. Photo taken by R. Jolly from the Signal Bridge on* HMS Victorious, *9 May 1945.*
(Fleet Air Arm Museum, Yeovilton)

against the side of the island in order to mend holes caused by these sort of things, and the flight deck repair party ran up to one of these things, just ran for'ard with it, took it to where the hole was and spot welded it into place so we could continue to launch aircraft, so that didn't take very long.

While they were doing this another attack came in, and she came in low from our starboard side at about a 30-degree dive, hit the flight deck aft of the island and had gone straight through a couple of Corsair aircraft, so they were write-offs – one of them was just broken up. That did no particular damage to the ship, but it had got a couple of aircraft. I should have said, before our first encounter with kamikazes back in April, the Fleet had been turned together by an emergency turning procedure which was done when an attack was close in, by voice radio using a simple code, so the Fleet was kept turning every 3 minutes to starboard or to port in order to make it more difficult for the dive-bombing aircraft to line up on the flight deck. We were turning to starboard under normal tactical helm of about 20 degrees when the Captain saw one of these planes coming in on our starboard quarter, and quick as a flash he ordered full helm to be put on to sharpen our turn, and that worked. In fact, he dodged the kamikaze because the thing sort of whistled across the flight deck in its dive – its starboard wing tip just hit, touched our port side – and the whole thing went into the sea with an enormous splash and a hiss and a roar and we had smoke and spray about four times as high as the mast, and this was duly photographed by somebody else and looks impressive. It was all rather sort of tricky because we hadn't actually been so close to one of these things before. That was before we got our hits in early May.

Well, this thing went on until some time in June, when the whole Force was withdrawn. Okinawa had been captured by the Americans by this time, so that phase of the operation was over. So we went down to Sydney to see the bright lights and have the hole in the flight deck properly repaired and so on.

The final operation was to be an onslaught against the Japanese Air Force on the mainland of Japan itself, for which we duly sailed north via the Philippines in July, and these were called the July/August Operations, and I'm sure they had a proper code name. We had our part in the sort of American Air War plan, which involved air strikes against Japanese airfields in Kyushu and across the Inland Sea looking for any of their warships that might have survived; there hardly were any. Japanese aircraft were very difficult to find because they had been preserving them for the sort of final defence of the homeland and they had put them in sort of barns and up country lanes and disguised in all sorts of places, so we really had to look for them. We admired the Americans, who had done a ceaseless onslaught on Tokyo and other cities, and this went on, usual pattern, two strike days, two replenishment days, until the early August when the atomic bombs were dropped and everything ground to a fairly quick halt, but we still had to be briefly on our guard until we got out the operating area in case we had some die-hards who were not going to give up. And that was that.'

Brian Prendergast has previously described his role in 'Operation Pedestal' when he was an Ordinary Seaman. Later, as a Sub Lieutenant, RNVR, he entered the Submarine Service:

'I was appointed Third Officer in charge of guns and torpedoes, and we did quite an extensive period of working up before we did our first patrol in early 1945 off Bergen in Norway; it was uneventful, and then we were ordered out to the Pacific. We spent VE Day in Malta, then proceeded to Trincomalee and then on passage to Subic Bay in the Philippines, where there was a British submarine flotilla under overall American command. We did our first and only patrol in the South China Sea, mostly on the surface, but keeping a sharp look-out for aircraft. We stopped an Indonesian lugger working for the Japanese and intended to sink it by gunfire. I was boarding officer and ordered the crew into canoes, which were lashed to the deck; they got away all right but unfortunately one of them capsized and left the crew struggling in the water. The Captain ordered me to throw them a line and we had to haul them back on board

Brian Prendergast (right) in the submarine Spearhead.

the lugger. The Captain could hardly fire on the lugger and sink it with men still aboard, so we pulled away and left them to it.

We'd one other adventure before the war finished. Some time in July we went to Borneo to pick up a midget submarine or X craft, XE4, which we towed to Saigon. We stopped the tow on a very dark night off the mouth of the Saigon River and the X craft continued into the river and grappled with a telephone and telegraph cable which ran along the river bed. We made rendezvous with them the following night. We had a spare crew on board and they changed over in a rubber dinghy. The Captain, Max Sheehan, came aboard bringing a large piece of the cable with him as proof of their success. We took the X craft back to Borneo and then resumed our patrol.

After a few days we were astonished to receive a signal telling us of the first atomic bomb, and later the second and the Armistice. We returned to Subic Bay and almost immediately were sent to Hong Kong. There was a rather disconcerting state of affairs for a day or two with the Japanese flag still flying over the dockyard. When the surrender was signed aboard *Duke of York* the flag was hauled down and we rounded up Japanese prisoners.

We tied up alongside the dockyard wall and ran our diesel engines to provide power to run dockyard machinery and other essential services. The colony was absolutely deserted after the Japanese were rounded up and repatriated, and it took several weeks for the Chinese to return from the interior. Shops were very slow to re-open, and unbelievably we had to convert our US dollars to yen before the Chinese would do any business.'

CHAPTER 18

Prisoners of war
in the Far East

W*ithout comment, an account of the experience of four people is presented here.*

Captain John Mackie of the Federated Malay States Volunteers has already recorded how he became a prisoner of war held in Changi camp at Singapore:

'So there we were, and we lived on what rations we'd brought in for a while, and then the Japanese managed to organise rice for us and we even got about a cubic inch of meat from the food store in Singapore, which the Japanese didn't want to use apparently, and there was quite a lot of meat in the store, so they dished this out and we got this cubic inch a week of meat, and what with our own stores and some rice and this bit of meat, we survived for several weeks. We had a bit of tobacco and stuff that we'd brought in with us.

Our quarters were very cramped but we managed to survive and get ourselves reasonably well organised. The British had set up a Headquarters in Changi Camp called the Southern Headquarters. This was the Command for the Prisoner of War Section under the British and was the liaison with the Japanese, who very soon began to demand large working parties to go and clean up Singapore and so on. So those parties were hived off and put into other camps in the Singapore area, which had been used by mainly Indian troops, Army Service Corps troops and Motor Transport troops and so on before the war. Thus the numbers decreased somewhat in our camp; the people that were sent were other ranks mainly, with NCOs and a few officers, although they weren't keen on having officers amongst the people on the working parties. There were many tales of how these officers were being beaten up and given a very hard time by the Japanese as they tried to keep the conditions, for their own troops, reasonable. The Japanese were well known for beating people up and it was very hard for the officer in charge of a group because if he tried to protect his troops he got beaten up harder than the troops got beaten up, and there were many brave officers to whom that happened, and if it hadn't been for them I suppose the troops would have had a harder time still.

I had some involvement with a secret radio. We had a radio set in our outfit and we had to operate it clandestinely because it was well known that if the Japanese found you had a radio set you could lose your head, which was the general punishment. So I was put in charge of hiding this set which I did by digging a hole in the bank near a place where we did our ablutions and the hole was big enough to take the radio with its batteries, which we wrapped up in a gas cape to keep it dry as far as possible. The news had to be disseminated very carefully amongst the troops, and this was done, but eventually the batteries ran flat and we couldn't get any more, so I then was relieved of this responsibility.

After six months in this POW camp the Japanese decided they would pay us. We'd been in disgrace, of course, up till then, because the Japanese regarded anybody who surrendered as less than the dust and regarded us as cowards, certainly not imbued with the spirit of bushido, so we were nobody. Rank didn't matter – even a General was treated like a third class private. So they paid us and they gave us 20 dollars in some Japanese currency that they had had printed, no doubt, and it was a pretty useless sort of currency, but we were able to spend it in the sort of canteen we had available, and we were able to get a few things with it: a little bit of soap, tobacco, but nothing much. The other thing was that all badges of rank had to be removed in the case of the officers. I was a captain by this stage and the way the Japanese distinguished between officers and other ranks was we were allowed to put one pip on the pocket lapel.

Everybody had to salute every Japanese – it didn't matter whether he was a third class private or colonel, he had to be saluted – and if you didn't have a hat you had to bow, and the regulation bow was supposed to be 15 degrees from the waist, not a deep bow. If you bowed too deeply you got whacked for doing that, if you didn't bow enough you got whacked for doing that, so most people tried to wear some sort of headgear and salute because the idea of bowing didn't appeal to most British troops.

In the early days when I was in Changi we didn't see too many Japanese about and it wasn't until later on that we had regular Tenko parades, and I can recall the early ones very clearly indeed, because when we were formed up in two ranks to number off and get checked for numbers, we did it in the British way; if there was an odd number there was a blank file left at one end from the rear rank at the end. But this didn't appeal to the Japanese because when the front rank numbered off, the Japanese doubled it and they got one too many people, so there was a lot of slapping of faces and swearing by the Japanese.

One of the favourite things the Japanese did when they got angry was to take off their sword – this was in a heavy scabbard carried on chains on their belt – and they would clank the chains and wave the sword in its scabbard in the air and occasionally belt people with the sword in its scabbard, which tended to be rather painful.

Of medical services we had practically nothing. There was a hospital in the Changi area called Roberts Hospital, which I suppose had been the hospital for the troops, the Regular garrison of the island. The Japs allowed us to use this as a hospital, but they supplied very little by way of medication and equipment so the medical officers had a very hard time trying to deal with the influx. That takes us on to what started to happen not long after we had gone on to the rice diet pretty well entirely – rice and sweet potatoes and tapioca and stuff like that which the Japs supplied us with, usually in relatively small quantities, so that we really weren't well fed at all, and the one cubic inch of meat disappeared too after a while. However, the diet then reacted on people so we had considerable outbreaks of dysentery amongst the people and various forms of stomach upset, and this was hard to combat because of the lack of the right medicines to treat it.

The other thing, of course, which began to appear medically was the various deficiency diseases, the main one being beriberi, which resulted in swollen ankles and other parts, and was disconcerting when faces became swollen and you couldn't recognise people. Another manifestation of beriberi was a very painful thing which affected the testicles; they lost their skin, looked like skinned tomatoes, and were very, very painful indeed. They were known as Changi balls or Changi goolies, to use the rude expressions. The only thing that was really needed was a little bit of vitamin B, and somebody managed to unearth, maybe through local people who were sympathetic in the population, they unearthed a supply of Marmite, which they gave to the hospital. It only required two or three teaspoonfuls of this Marmite to restore the people with the Changi complaint back to reasonably good health. So the medical side of it was difficult – it always was in every place I was in.

We had a special parade for one of the Japanese Generals who came to inspect us. This was odd because we were all told to face away from the road as the great man passed. We were not supposed to look on him; that might have tainted him, I suppose, in some way or other. Our morale was never bad really, it was amazing, and, I think, it was mainly due to the ability to receive news from the BBC, which we knew to be the real news. The Japanese provided all manner of propaganda to emphasise the successes they were having, which undoubtedly they were at that stage.

After about six months or so they decided that all the senior officers of colonel and above would be removed from our camp and taken elsewhere, so General Percival and all the brigadiers and the other generals and people right down to the rank of full colonel were winkled out of the camp and taken away.

A very terrible incident, I suppose you would call it, took place in early September. We were told that we had to sign a piece of paper which put us on our honour that we wouldn't escape or attempt to escape. Now this, of course, goes against all military codes that I know of, and certainly civilised ones, because it's the duty of every British soldier to escape if he possibly can. If we didn't sign it all manner of terrible things would happen to us. So this, as you can imagine, created great debate, and in the end we said we wouldn't sign. So we were all rounded up, marched out from where our quarters were into this one area of Changi known as the Selarang Barracks. It had a large parade ground and was surrounded by three-storey barrack buildings, and something like 25,000 troops were put on this parade ground and in the buildings.

Here we were guarded by Japs who had machine-guns, and also they had by this time recruited a number of Indians from our Army into the Indian National Army, which was an outfit created by Chandra Bose. So there were our former Indian soldiers guarding us, and obviously if we made one attempt to step over the boundaries of the parade ground or the buildings, we would be shot and we didn't have any reason to doubt this.

So the buildings weren't big enough to hold all these troops, so many of us had to camp out on the parade ground, which was a tar-sealed normal type of parade ground. The main problem came immediately with lack of toilets. The only thing to do was to start digging up the parade ground, so there were squads put on to digging large trenches on the parade ground, which they did, and there were these 25,000 people all using the trenches, so they were rapidly filled up and others had to be dug.

So there we were, and there we remained for four days, swearing that we wouldn't sign this thing, but there was no doubt about the intentions of the Japanese, and I'm sure they would have annihilated all of us if we hadn't agreed. So eventually the senior officer present finally gave us instructions to sign it. So we all signed it and we all said that we wouldn't take any notice of it. Dysentery had started to break out in quite a big way, so that we'd have been killed off by diseases anyway if we hadn't been shot by the Japanese. So we returned to our usual quarters.

In October 1942 we got a shipment of Red Cross food and clothing and stuff like that from Portuguese East Africa from Lourenco Marques. We did get things like hats and boots and some shirts and also food, canned goods.

Guavas I remember were among the things we got, but there was condensed milk and cocoa and other stuff, and I think each of us got about 6 pounds of this, and it was very welcome indeed at that stage because the food supply was not at all good Also round about this stage we were allowed to send a 25-word card, postal card, back home. I think we had two chances to do this between February, when we went into the bag, and April 1943 – two cards I think we sent. I think mine both arrived home eventually. We had no word from home, of course, at all.

The Japanese had a system of sudden searches. They would turf everybody out of the quarters and they'd have to wait outside in the hot sun while they went through the quarters looking for anything suspicious. If they found anything they would take it away to their headquarters and examine it, and if there was anything suspicious about it, the responsible persons would be called up and it wasn't a very pleasant experience, I believe, if you were interviewed in that way. We were warned not to keep diaries because of these searches, because they could easily involve people getting into trouble.

One curious thing happened to me during a search. We used to get very little warning of these searches, but we got a little on this occasion and we had the problem of getting rid of a radio that we had, which was a small mantle-type radio, a valve set, and it was in a cardboard box with some other gear, and it was handed out through the window of one of the huts to me and I had to take it along the side of the hut and give it to somebody else. While I was doing this I was confronted by a Jap guard, and I thought, here goes, I'm for it this time, but the Japanese soldier, he delved into the box and he grunted to me, "Tobacco, you got tobacco?" and I said, "No, no tobacco," and he looked, no tobacco, and passed by, and it's a bit hard to understand people like that. They were pretty well known for this sort of thing, being a bit clueless at times.

Recreation of course was not regarded as being a particularly good thing in view of the poor diet we were on. People did kick a football about and that sort of thing, but mostly for relaxation. We had the odd concert and it's amazing what the British soldier will do when he's pushed to get a concert together – one can only use the word "magnificent". Some of the concerts were absolutely staggering. They'd gone to enormous bother to get clothing, female clothing for the female impersonators particularly, and make-up and so on for them, and they were extremely popular, of course, the female impersonators, and got tremendous encores. There were some very good singers and musicians amongst them and they'd managed to acquire instruments from somewhere.

Another thing that was started up was the Changi University. People got together and organised classes in just about everything you could think of, and I took advantage of this in order to study Pitman's shorthand, which I thought might be useful. There was electronics and mathematics and that was interesting, because the mathematics classes were run by Lance Bombardier Oppenheim, who had no shirt and a ragged pair of shorts and pretty rough sort of footwear, and I can still see him standing there in front of a piece of ordinary three-ply material and he had a lump of chalk – not a stick of chalk, but a lump – and he was writing out differential equations and all sorts of things on this. He was an extraordinarily good mathematician, I believe, and later on he became Vice-Chancellor of the University of Singapore, I think it was, or perhaps Malaysia.

By this time, after eight or nine months of imprisonment, people were beginning to die in increasing numbers. The sick were put into Roberts Hospital outside our main camp area and the funerals took place from there. Not far away from the Changi camp was the big new civilian jail that had been built, I think for 600 or 700 prisoners, but there were, I think, something like 2-3,000 civilian internees in this jail, including quite a lot of women. Now, they had to send out working parties to collect food from the local villages and so on, and of course we had to do the same sort of thing, and we would, under guard, go round to the villages nearby and buy material with whatever money one could raise. Some people still had some original Singapore dollars; the locals weren't very keen on taking the Japanese variety, which wasn't regarded as very reliable as money.

Anyway, the people from the jail and our people out on these foraging parties often met, and with the ability to divert the attention of the guards, they could sometimes pass notes. Some of the fellows in the POW camp had womenfolk, wives and so on in the jail, so this helped, but it was a risky business. Occasionally the Japs would allow the husbands in the POW camp to visit the wives in the jail, and they were all paraded outside the jail under supervision, of course, and they only had about half an hour or an hour every two or three months.

As far as work was concerned and activity, I myself became involved in what was known as the wood-chopping party. The Japs provided some firewood for the cookhouses in the form of logs, and these had to be sawn and cut up and so on for the cookhouse fires, and that was really my main job, I guess, with two or three other people from our section. It was hard work but one did it, I think, mainly with the idea of contributing something to the general community pool, and also to keep reasonably fit, because although we weren't getting much food, it wasn't a bad idea to keep your body functioning properly.

Now I go on to another rather unusual sort of activity in a POW camp. The powers that be decided that it wouldn't be bad if we had 100 or so people trained in unarmed combat in case there was an opportunity to take the Japs in the rear if there was a frontal attack by our forces, or to use it for escape purposes or something of the sort. So they called for volunteers, and I volunteered for this rather odd occupation. The course for each group of 20 lasted, I think, about 10 days or a fortnight, and it was a painful experience because we had people who were well accustomed to teaching unarmed combat. I think they were Australians, from recollection, sergeant-majors, and there was a mixed bag of officers and other ranks in this thing, and we had to forget all about rank and everything else. Each party of 20 was divided up into the doers and the stooges, who alternated from time to time. The doers had all kinds of fabricated weapons supposed to be rifles and knives and clubs and things of this sort, and as a stooge you stood there and were attacked by one of the others, and you had to disarm him. We did have one or two broken bones on the course, but I think at the end of it most of us were fairly proficient and confident, and there was a final passing-out parade when we had to demonstrate our prowess to a group of senior officers who had thought about this wonderful escapade. We did this in an area which was guarded by our own people in case the Japs intruded.

We had our first Christmas, of course, in 1942; it wasn't a very merry occasion, but we sang carols, had some church services, exchanged a few small presents and things of that sort. Oddly enough the Japs gave us some rice wine to celebrate either Christmas or New Year. It wasn't particularly good stuff, but at least it was a gesture.

Since the middle of 1942 large parties had been mustered and sent off by the Japanese to various destinations, which were never disclosed to us, but in the end we found that the preference for the Japanese was Thailand to work on the railway they were putting through to Burma, and the people on that had a terrible time. Other people were sent off to Formosa and Japan. The Japanese said always, when a party went off, that they were going to far better camps than the one we were in, that they would be well looked after and well fed, and naturally we knew them to be the liars that they were; there was nothing true about any of these things they said.

In April of 1943 my own turn came to be put in one of these parties. Again, we didn't know where we were going, we got very short notice, and were only able to take what we could grab in a hurry. I managed to take my old leather suitcase with odds and ends in it and my mosquito net and my thin mattress rolled up. We were all mustered in Changi camp, a thousand of us, including half a dozen or so officers, of whom I was one, and we were put in 3-ton trucks, open trucks, 40 at a time, and driven down to the Singapore dock area. There we all congregated in the hot sun and waited all day to embark on what appeared to be a 3-4,000-ton old Jap rusty tramp for our voyage to an unknown part. It was now April 1943.

This was a bit upsetting, of course – well, one wondered what the hell was going to happen and where were you going. Anyway, after nightfall we were all marched on to this thing; all the other ranks were put down below in terrible conditions in very close quarters with wooden bunk systems built up so that there was very little space between them, and they just had to lie on these bunks. The officers were not put down below; we were allowed to stay on deck in a small cabin, which was, I thought, not too bad. The latrines were built over the side of the ship, and people were allowed up from down below in groups to use the toilets or latrines. The weather, fortunately, during the entire trip was quite good, otherwise we might have been in a parlous situation. There was quite a lot of dysentery amongst the people on board, so the latrines were well used.

The Japanese officer in charge was not a bad sort of a chap really – he was not a vicious type at all – and we were able to talk to him; he had some English and he did listen. Eventually we were able to get the chaps down below up on deck in groups for an hour or so to get air and see what was going on, but they were pushed down again and came up in relays. We wondered where we were going, but of course it became pretty obvious before long that we were sailing pretty well due east from Singapore and we came to the conclusion that we were either going to Borneo or some place in that direction, and it proved to be true – we were actually headed for Kuching on Sarawak.

So the voyage went on, the food was terrible, the conditions were bad, and I think after four days everybody had had enough, but we arrived in Kuching and were unloaded, not in Kuching itself but at a landing place, I think, up the river. We were all disembarked and there they sprayed us with some disinfectant as we went past a staging point. I still managed to hang on to my old case and belongings, which was fortunate for me.

We were then taken in trucks to the Batu Lintang POW camp, and this had been the barracks for an Indian regiment pre-war, the garrison for Kuching. The huts were, I suppose, something like 100-odd feet long and perhaps 15 feet wide, and they were built of wood and had a thatched roof. The windows were just open spaces with hinged shutters that could be shut if there was a lot of rain. So they weren't that uncomfortable.

We were split up, of course – the Japs had all manner of people in separate enclosures in this camp in the main barbed-wire perimeter. The Jap guardhouse and the Jap quarters were at the top of a sort of rise, and all round the rise were other enclosures in which the biggest was the British other ranks section, which, I think, had 1,600 in it in total. The other people in the camp were Australian officers, there were some Dutch officers, there was a fairly large group of about 260 women and children, a lot of whom were nuns, and there were the wives of various government officials. There was also another section, about the same size, of male civilian internees who were government officials and planters and others.

There were some Indians from the 2/15 Punjabis, who hadn't been enticed by the Japanese into Chandra Bose's Indian National Army. They were given a hard time by the Japanese but they resisted and remained loyal to the British flag. They were under the command of a Subadar who was a fine fellow indeed and I think was decorated after the war for the stand that he put up. This fellow, in spite of being constantly bashed by the Japanese, if he met a group of ragged British POWs, officers marching around the camp doing various chores, he would always call his group of about 50 to march to attention, and he would give them eyes right and salute the British officers, and thereby he got bashed well and truly by the Japs, but he did this every time. It was, I think, a very morale-boosting sort of thing for us as officers.

I was put in the British officers' section, where there were about 120 of us, and the section was enclosed in barbed-wire inside the main perimeter. I went into the quarters to see where I was, to put my bed down, and the first person I saw was a chap named Captain Ron Green, and I had been with him during the Battle of Kampar, where he had been quite badly wounded. Ron made a space next to him for me and so I immediately had a friend who knew the ropes – he'd been there for a little while. So they got me some bits and pieces to make a kind of bed and I roosted there for the whole of the time I was in the camp.

Well now, I think I've mentioned that in Changi, the Tenkos that we had were a bit of a shambles, with the counting of heads creating a little bit of histrionics amongst the Japanese at times. But when we got to this camp, Batu Lintang camp in Borneo, the Tenkos were then run very strictly by the Japanese, usually a sergeant or a sergeant-major, and we had to make all our orders in Japanese and count in Japanese. This caused consternation, of course, amongst people who could only count up to ten in Japanese, as you had to count up to 20 at least. Then there was a great deal of face-slapping and bashing of people who couldn't count properly and quickly enough, so that you had to learn. They led to all sorts of funny things happening. We had one officer, Captain Clarke, who was a magnificent physical specimen although he'd fined down quite a lot, about 6 feet high, and Nobby had to take the Tenko parade. So everybody was drawn up and a Japanese sergeant known as the "sailor", who used to harangue us at great length waving his sword about, took this parade, and Nobby had to line everybody up and get them going and he had the whole parade of 120 of us there and he had to give us some sort of a command in Japanese, but he didn't really know any Japanese and his comment to the parade was, "Can anybody here speak Urdu?" and of course the Japanese took great affront at this and he was belted by the Japanese guard on the jaw. The Jap had to jump up and hit him because Nobby was a bit angular and it was a wonderful sight to see this Japanese whacking away at Nobby's jaw, jumping up to do it, and then retiring nursing his hand with Nobby still standing there and sort of unperturbed. This is the sort of thing that did raise our morale a bit. Resistance to the Japanese was a good thing if you could muster it.

Well, at this camp we were much more dominated by the Japanese and the guards were all pretty vicious and there were frequent beatings up. This was the sort of thing we hadn't had in Changi much, so it was a changed atmosphere. Colonel Suga was in charge of all the POW camps in Borneo, but Lieutenant Nakata was in charge of our particular camp and he was a rather nasty person who did not like British people at all, or anybody who wasn't Japanese for that matter. He had all his guards and people tuned up the same way so you didn't have to step out of line very much to get a beating.

The water supply was not unreasonable. In our particular camp we had a standpipe with a shower on it and a couple of taps in concrete tubs, so were able to do a little bit of washing, although the soap supply was pretty well non-existent, but we were able to get our clothes washed and have a shower, and the water was only turned on I think for an hour each morning and an hour each afternoon. So you had to be quick and there was no screen round it, it was a completely public bathing facility. The latrine system wasn't bad; we had a group of latrines under a thatch enclosure with buckets, and you kept the products and used them in the garden. We had an area in the camp that we dug up and planted sweet potatoes and beans and papayas and tapioca and so on.

For accommodation in the huts we just had rough beds lined down each side of the long hut. There had been no lighting originally, but I was told that it had been put to the Japs that it would be to their own advantage to have lights in the huts because if they came down at night they would be able to see what was going on, a shrewd move. Anyway, the Japs said if you want lighting you have to put it on yourself, so they got barbed-wire and bailed it along the rafters of the huts and used broken bottle tops as insulators, and hooked it up to the camp electricity supply. So we were allowed, I think, three 40-watt bulbs in each hut.

There was a hospital in the camp – it was down the road from the Japanese headquarters almost opposite where the womenfolk were camped – and it was run by two or three medical officers, but they had a terrible job because they had no medicines much to do anything with. People suffered most of the time from rather bad ulcers on the legs and feet, and these were terrible, really bad things; some of them got extremely large and deep and there were no antibiotics of course in those days, only sulphur drugs, which sometimes became available in small quantities Well, the hospital was the place where the news was exchanged in the camp. There was one secret radio and it was in the British other ranks camp operated by some men from the Royal Signals, and they passed the news through their sick parties into the hospital and the medical officers in hospital judiciously doled it out to people on other sick parades to take back to the other sections of the camp.

However, we had a canteen as in Changi, but it was not a very prolific sort of canteen. We got the usual bits of peanut toffee and some gula molacca, which was a sort of fudgy-type sugar substance which comes from the coconut tree and is boiled down to make this substance. Oddly enough we got rations every now and then of something which we were absolutely surprised at – one was prawns. We got several sacks of prawns on one occasion; they were dried and we kept them as long as we possibly could, because they were a very good source of protein. Other things we got which surprised us were turtles eggs; I don't know whether the Japanese didn't like them or not, but we got quite a lot of them on two or three occasions, and Sergeant Roberts used to make a wonderful cake using these turtle eggs. Funny things – they have a musky flavour and are regarded as a great luxury in peacetime by some people. Things like coconuts and plantains and some vegetables came in the canteen and we had to pay for these, of course, from the Japanese pay we got.

The cookhouse fires had to be kept going, of course. We were surrounded by rubber plantations and I became a member of the wood-chopping party, and we had to go outside the camp to get the wood, cutting down rubber trees. We cut the trees off about, say, 2 or 3 feet above the ground surface because that was the easiest way of felling them, because rubber trees are a bit like willow trees in texture. After we had cleared quite a large area around the camp the Japanese made us dig out the stumps and use those for firewood. It was a terrible job because the rubber tree has a long tap root which goes down 8 or 9 feet at least. It was remarkably hard, dirty work which was always subject to Japanese "shveido", which meant "get on with it", and if we didn't get on quickly enough we'd get a rifle butt in the backside and kidneys or somewhere, or get belted by the Japanese over the face with his fist. So there was always encouragement to get on with the job.

Actually, on one of these occasions I got my worst beating in the whole camp, in the whole time I was a POW. We had marched back to the top area where the Japanese mustered us after being on an outside fatigue and I was in the front rank of our group, and for some reason or other the Jap guard had taken a dislike to me and he called me out and picked up a branch that we'd brought in, which was, I suppose, a couple of inches thick and about

5 or 6 feet long, and he hefted this up and tested it, and then he "whung" it and hit me on the head with it. I thought my last day had come when I saw this coming, but you couldn't do anything. If you flinched or avoided it you'd only get worse punishment, so he felled me like an ox, and I was out for several hours as a result of this, and the others carried me back. The Colonel complained bitterly to the Japanese, and I don't know what happened, but the guard was never seen again. Whether he was disciplined I don't know, but anyway it took me quite a long time to recover from this, this bashing. I had bruises all over my face and head for weeks afterwards and I had headaches after that for quite a long time, which dragged over into the peacetime afterwards.

Surprisingly we had a library. One or two people, civilians in Borneo and particularly in Labuan and Kuching, had quite substantial libraries and these had all been brought in to Kuching and we were allowed access to them. There were a number of Japanese prisoners of war in New Zealand, in Featherston, and there was a fracas, and in fact quite a number of them were shot while trying to overcome the guards, and this got back to the Japanese and for a couple of months we were barred all books except bibles. Church parades we were allowed to have, more so earlier on than later, when they became a bit difficult to administer. In our particular case the Japs allowed in one Anglican and one Roman Catholic clergyman. The RC was a Dutch priest. They also allowed the Bishop of Sarawak to come into our camp and conduct the Sunday service every fortnight. This Dutch priest, Father Leo, he took little notice of the Japanese and he had his little church service in the end of the hut, and it consisted of a Mass lasting about 10 minutes, and the rest of the hour he was allowed, he spent in passing over what was known as the gen from local sources, all the news from round about that he could muster. He would have got very badly punished if he'd been caught, but, of course, they thought he was taking the service.

The Bishop of Sarawak was defrocked by the Japanese shortly after this. He was seen passing some eggs over the wire to a sergeant for the sick ORs in the men's camp. The Jap guards saw this and they were both whistled up to the Jap headquarters and put in the guardhouse, and they were separately queried and the sergeant, who had been beaten up a good many times, knew that the best thing to do was tell the truth and he told the Japs that the Bishop had given some eggs for the sick men in the camp and that was all. When they questioned the Bishop he said he hadn't passed anything over the wire at all, and the Japs of course immediately realised that he wasn't telling the truth and for a Bishop to be a liar was a great thing for them to uphold in front of the rest of the camp, so they publicly defrocked him and said that he wasn't allowed to be called the Bishop any more, just mister.

We were again allowed to send out some 25-word postcards as in Changi – I think there might have been three or four in all, over the period of 2½ years I was in this Batu Lintang camp – and eventually we did get some mail and this was all years old, just suddenly appearing after 18 months or so, in bunches. All well censored, of course, but it was wonderful to get news from home. One would read them over and over again, which most people did, and they regarded them as great treasures. We got one Red Cross issue during the whole time we were in the camp in Borneo. These were United States PK rations, I think they were called, and there was one of these boxes of rations, which were not very large, for each six men, but nevertheless we got some fresh coffee, which was something that people hadn't had for quite a while, and Spam was another thing, of course, which we didn't know anything about, and some butter in cans and things like that. It was nice to get them but they didn't sort of help very much at all towards our feeding – a little bit of protein maybe and something nice to taste.

Now in the camp there was a chap named Lieutenant Bell, Frank Bell was his name, he was, I think, Royal Artillery, an ack-ack gunner. He was a Cambridge man who had graduated in modern languages, and Frank decided that it wouldn't be a bad idea to set up a sort of university in our officers' section of the camp. It was strictly against the Japanese rules – we were not allowed to meet in groups of more than two or three, we were not allowed to conduct any kind of courses in anything – but Frank roped in various people to take courses. I got roped in to take a course in navigation and astronomy, which was relatively popular and which I conducted for a term or two. He had the whole thing well organised, being a university man, and he was teaching several languages: French, Spanish, Dutch, even Russian, which he had to teach himself. I took the courses in conversational French and in Spanish, and we used to sit around in the evenings trying to talk French and Spanish in these conversation courses. The Japanese didn't know anything about this; it was dark and they couldn't see us, and they couldn't understand anyway, most of them. So the university went on, and those of us who took courses finally passed out of them, and Frank went to all the bother at the end of typing up diplomas for us on rough paper that he found in the Japanese office after the surrender, on the Japanese headquarters typewriter. I still have as a very valued possession my Diploma from the University of Kuching.

Colonel Suga was our overall commandant. He was an odd character; he had had some education in the United States and could speak English not badly, but every now and then he would harangue us and have us all on parade outside the Japanese headquarters and he would always start his harangues by saying, it was something like, you must look after yourselves and keep your healths in good order, or words to that effect, always saying how well the Japanese were looking after us and what have you. We didn't believe him very much, of course. But Suga seemed to be fond of children; he was a man, I suppose, in his 60s, a bit tubby for a Japanese, and he used to take the children from the women's camp out on rides in his large black car, which he'd inherited from some British government official I suppose, and he would buy them sweets and so on. So a bit hard to fathom, Suga – he didn't seem, on the surface, to be a bad sort of person, and he used to go away looking at the other camps in Borneo. So Suga was something of an unknown quantity to us – we didn't quite know what to make of him.

There was a woman in the camp who became a well-known author – her name was Agnes Keith. She was in the women's camp; she had her small son with her and she kept notes and eventually wrote a book called *Three Came Home*. She, at great risk, kept notes to write this book, and Suga used to have conversations with her. He'd call her up to headquarters and query her about various things. She got badly beaten up on one occasion by Nakata, I think, so she didn't escape either. At the parade attended by the Australian General, in command of the troops who finally released us, Suga stood on the outskirts, a lone figure. Agnes Keith was the only one who went up and spoke to him. But I've jumped ahead of myself.

One night, when we were all asleep except for our man on guard duty, all of a sudden – this would have been about 2 or 3am – there was a shot which woke everybody, and our spy reported that there were lights on near the Jap headquarters, so we got ready for some sort of trouble, wondering what it was. Eventually the party of Japanese, about half a dozen, I suppose, came down; they had candles to light their way because they couldn't get batteries for their torches. Everybody was ordered out of their huts and paraded up as for Tenko – everybody clad in horrible old things, sarongs and what have you, that they used to sleep in. Then the Japs ordered everybody to pull up their sarongs or whatever garments they were wearing and to bend forward. Well this was a rather curious order, as you can well imagine, and everybody wondered what was coming, and they proceeded then with their candles to bend down and peer at all the horrible backsides that were exposed, and most people had scabies and various forms of diseases, and they must have been a horrible sight, very thin too. So they inspected every backside with great care. Then we were told to go back to bed, so we did that, wondering what the hell this was all about.

We found out of course, eventually, that what had happened was that the shot had been fired at someone who had stolen some sweet potatoes from the Japanese Q store up near the top, and he had to get back into his own camp through a double-aproned barbed-wire fence, and he had to get through in a hurry and the Japanese had argued amongst themselves that this no doubt was the best way to get a scratch on the backside, so they inspected everybody in the camp. I don't think they inspected the women, but they inspected all the men in every camp for scratches on the backside, and the remarkable thing is they caught one fellow who was the culprit by this method, and he got a very bad time.

Well, at this stage I think we were about six months before the end of the war, and air raids had started to take place in Borneo. The first sign of this was half a dozen very large planes flying very high – they were Flying Fortresses, I believe – and they flew over the camp at 20,000-odd feet and the Japs loosed off at them with some ack-ack, but I don't think they could get near them. Then we heard rumbles as they dropped their bombs on, I believe, the port area, where there were some Jap ships, and that was the beginning. From then on we got raids every now and then. We were made to dig slit trenches and every time there was a warning for a raid we had to get into these trenches. We were not allowed to look up; we were not allowed to raise our heads above the ground level. If we did we were accused of spying and passing messages to the aeroplanes, which, with typical Japanese sort of logic, didn't seem to make sense. This was, of course, a big morale booster to us to find that at last the tide had turned and the Japs were getting "what-ho" from our Allied forces.

So the raids continued. We were forced into our slit trenches every time and I can recall on one occasion someone must have looked up or done something. We were all paraded in the nearby rubber plantation and we were stood to attention and we were not allowed to blink – if you blinked you got beaten – and so it was very difficult to stand to attention rigidly in the heat with the Japs and quite a few of them walking up and down the rows, standing there peering at you so that if you blinked you got walloped. So there wasn't much encouragement to blink or to move in any way.

They also, at this stage, began a rather ominous exercise. There was a Japanese sentry path right round the exterior of two sides of our camp, and on three occasions, I think it was, all of a sudden Japanese arrived with a machine-gun in each party, two or three parties; they mounted the machine-guns at the corner of the barbed-wire fence and stayed there, and we were ordered into our huts. Now somebody had heard that this was one of the Japanese tactics for killing people off – they shut you up in your hut and machine-gunned the hut, and then burnt it down – so we didn't know whether we were going to be shot up or not. However, we were let out and everybody breathed a great sigh of relief, as can be imagined, and it happened on another couple of occasions. We didn't know whether they were going to shoot us or not, and it was very upsetting.

Finally, of course, the time came when the war was over, at the time when we were unable to work our secret radio because the Japs had turned the power off. We didn't know whether they had done this deliberately or whether the powerhouse had been bombed. Anyway, we had no radio for a month or so, and at a pretty crucial time, but they got it back working. It was a remarkable piece of work because they made a generator, in this period when there was no power, out of bits and pieces, and you wouldn't believe the way it was done, and it was operated by a machine that had been devised for mashing up tapioca root in the men's camp, the ORs' camp. This had a wheel like a mangle on it and the wheel could be disengaged from the mashing machine and used then to wind the generator, and it had to be wound at a regular rate by hand to generate enough power at the right voltage to operate this single-valve set, with one earpiece, but it was done and it was got going again just in time for us to hear the news about the atom bombs being dropped on Japan and the fact that the Japanese had finally surrendered. We got no word of this from the Japanese, of course.

However, there was great jubilation all round when we heard that the Japs had surrendered, but this happened in the middle of August, I think. So we had no word from the Japanese. They gave no signs that they'd surrendered, but, after a while, they relaxed some of their regulations; they gave us a bit more food and some mosquito nets were handed out and things like that.

After a while our people came over, the Australian Air Force, and dropped leaflets. As these leaflets came down the Japanese ordered us all back into our huts, and we were not allowed out until they'd gathered up all the leaflets. However, one bunch of a hundred or so of these leaflets had fallen in a tree in our particular camp and they hadn't noticed. So after we were all allowed out, one of our blokes shot up the tree and got the leaflets, and these were instructions to the Japanese as to what they were to do about us and themselves. They were in various languages and had been dropped all over the place. Again, the Japanese didn't realise we had got these, but before long, of course, the pamphlets were all over the camp. The leaflets instructed the Japs to put strips of calico across the top of the Japanese headquarters hut in various patterns in order to let the people in the aircraft know what their reply was; they were unable to communicate by radio apparently.

So we waited anxiously for two or three days to see what the Japanese would do, and at last they put some calico strips across the top of their hut in a pattern which said they would meet some ship coming up the mouth of the Kuching River and allow the party to come into Kuching and into our camp, so they did. But it took a long time before anybody came. Suga had us up on the top parade ground and gave us a great lecture and said that the Japanese had surrendered, that the Americans had dropped terrible bombs on Hiroshima and Nagasaki, and they had completely devastated both cities, which were flattened and burnt to the ground. A terrible thing to do, he said, which after what they'd been doing to us seemed a bit strange, but I think, in fact, Suga had family in Hiroshima and I think he'd lost most family members, so he understandably was upset about that. He said that things were not as clear as they might appear to us. There was quite a large garrison of Japanese troops in Kuching and that there was dissension amongst their officers over whether they would take any notice of the surrender or would fight on, and Suga said that in this situation we'd be in greatly difficult circumstances. There was nothing we could do about it, of course, but take his word for it.

Eventually, of course, the Japanese didn't take that action. He told us that some Japanese in other parts were retreating to inland areas and setting up their own sort of garrison places, and they would fight it out to the end, and that this could well happen in Kuching, and that we would be eliminated if this happened. So the situation was pretty uncomfortable and we really didn't know what was going to happen. Incidentally, I should say that papers were recovered from the Japanese headquarters detailing a plan they had to eliminate all of us in the Batu Lintang camp, and we escaped by about three days, I believe. If the Japanese hadn't surrendered we'd have all been disposed of. They had horrible plans: they were going to eliminate all the women and children by putting them in the huts and pouring petrol on the place and setting fire to everything and then marching off the able-bodied people into the jungle with heavy loads, and if they dropped they would shoot them – that had happened on other occasions. The people who were not fit to go off on these trips, the death marches they were called, were simply to be shot in camp. So we escaped that and, I gather, it was by about three days. I had some reason to be grateful for the American aircraft which dropped the atom bomb.

Anyway, eventually some Australian troops arrived on the scene, but in the meantime, in order to keep us fed, better fed, the Australians were flying in DC3s with food, and this was wonderful, of course, because they dropped not only food but clothing and boots and hats and medical supplies. We discovered that the Japanese medical officer, Captain Yamamoto I think was his name, had a whole store full of Red Cross medicines which he'd hung on to and hadn't issued. He was certainly one of the nastier members amongst the Japanese for doing that because he could have saved so many lives.

So there we were, in a sort of period of waiting to see what would happen, but eventually the Australians arrived. We were called up to a parade – we'd pulled down most of the wire between the various sections of the camp by this time and we were mingling and greeting each other, people who hadn't seen each other for a long time, in the same camp, were able to get together. I met quite a lot of people, including Agnes Keith and so on, while this was going on. This Australian Brigadier arrived on the scene with a party, and shortly after that General Wootton, who commanded the Australian 9th Division, came into the camp and again we had a big parade up at the top and the Japanese flag was lowered and the Union Jack was raised, and Suga kept out of the way. Of course, he was put into a hut under isolation awaiting trial, but he cut his throat with a table knife and committed suicide, which was the honourable thing then to do. A strange fellow, Suga.

That parade I remember very well, because I was told by the Senior Officer, Webster, that we were going to have a Guard of Honour for General Wootton and that I was to command it, and that seemed a strange thing to me; I was a volunteer, I wasn't a Regular. But he said that we'd got some rifles and that the men from the Other Ranks camp – there were a number of them who were not that sick, who had volunteered to go on this parade – and it was about a platoon strength. So I met these blokes and I didn't think it was such a very good idea – I thought it was a bit much – but I changed my mind afterwards, because we had one practice and, just looking at these blokes, it was obvious that they thought this was a wonderful thing to do and to be able to do. So there we were; we marched up to the Jap headquarters and presented arms to General Wootton, and I think it was a very moving moment for him, so it was for me too.

Well, eventually we were all released in one way or another. I was a bit privileged, in a way, because of a friend of mine who came looking for me, I think arranged things so that I, with Colonel Webster and various chevron majors, were taken out in a Catalina and flown from the Kuching River to Labuan, where the Australians had set up a base of some sort and a field hospital where I spent the night. Then we had a week at an Australian hospital at Halmahera island, where we were subjected to all sorts of tests, de-wormed and so on by the medical personnel, and we were given some regular food on a breakfast, lunch, dinner basis, and I even got a bottle of beer, I think, on one occasion.'

Marjory de Malmanche, having described her escape from Singapore and eventual capture by the Japanese in Sumatra, relates her experiences during her years as a prisoner of the Japanese:

'Then we were all told we were to leave the hospital and were going to a different part of the camp, and that we didn't need transport because it wasn't very far. So we quickly gathered up all we could, because they said everybody's to be out in two hours or something like that, and Dr Lyon said, "Well, some of these patients can't possibly walk," and so they gave us two trips in an ambulance to this place we were going to – we didn't know where it was. Everybody else had to pick up what they could and walk, and our destination was a jail and it was quite a big place and one big tree in it, and when we got there we found that the only place we could have used as a ward was full of old gentlemen. They locked themselves in and we had all our wounded and ill patients, and so we had to lay them all down in the shade under this tree and the Japanese came and evicted the old men. Then, of course, when we went into the ward – what we decided to make into a ward – it was filthy. You've no idea what they'd been doing, using everything as lavatories and things like that, so we all had to set to and clean everything up, which took us almost into the night, but there were beds there and then, after we'd cleaned it all up, we transferred our patients into this place.

There was one great big shed that had been used by the prisoners as a workshop. I suppose about 200 people squeezed in there and then a whole lot more put down their mattresses in a big open shed, and slept there. Then there was a cow shed and this was adapted into quarters for about 20 nuns and a few children they had with them. When we got there too it was awful – the toilets and everything were disgusting and all the pipes and things had been broken in an earthquake. The doctors got on to the Japs and they fairly quickly made a whole lot of outdoor latrines – you know, sort of just concrete with holes in, out in the open – and we were there for about three or four months. Some of the women couldn't stand it any more and the Japanese took them away.

One was a very attractive woman and she could play the piano and sing and do all those sort of things, and they were taken up a mountain to a place where the Japanese General was, and they were taken to this big hall where there was a piano. So she sat down and played the piano and sang and everything like that, and she had quite a good time, and in fact she became his mistress. She was there for some time and eventually he was transferred to somewhere else, but he was very good to her and used to send things to her, but, of course, when she came back to the camp she was most unpopular and pretty well ostracised.

Then one day we were told to get all our things together and walk to the railway station, and then we spent all night in the train travelling, and we reached Fort de Kock high up in the mountains in Sumatra. Beautiful country – it was brilliant moonlight and in the train going it was absolutely lovely to see these native houses. So anyway, we arrived at the station and we were all told to get out of the train and go behind the station to relieve ourselves. I had a kitten with me and the kitten relieved itself too.

Then we were all put into trucks and set off again for our destination, and it was still almost dark, and when we'd gone so far up in the mountains we stopped. It was a straight road, and on one side of the road it was moonlight, with huge fields and a few native houses, and on the other side it was a lot of mountain tops and drops and things like that. Then we saw why they'd stopped, because the sun rose and it was absolutely amazing. On one side it was as though the whole place was on fire, and the other side of the road was calm moonlight – a most amazing sight – and then we set off again. Eventually, about 4 o'clock in the afternoon, we'd had to cross a big river on rafts, all of us, the trucks and everything, and then we arrived at our destination, Bankinang. It was huge – it was all new actually, all great big buildings, all wood, you know.

Well, we found that there were five big buildings and they were all two-storeyed and they were just platforms, an upstairs platform and a downstairs platform. Everybody had a space of 6 feet by 3 and it was all very well for people with a large family because they'd roll up their mattresses by day and had quite a nice space, but for one single person it was a bit grim, that small space. There was earth on the floor and the roofs were made of atap. There were about 500 people in each hut.

Part of one of these huts we took to make into a hospital, and there was a little hut that the Japanese had built, thinking it would be the hospital hut, you see; well, that was stupid because we had so many sick people, and then there was a whole lot of people with dysentery – we had to put those in isolation – so we nurses stayed in the little hut and there was only just room for us. There was a little part of this hut, at the front, where the doctor had her office and saw all her patients, and where the two doctors slept, and all we nurses slept in the rest of the place. We were quite close together and just had room for our mattresses, and sometimes rain water came in. That was our home for two years.

The guards didn't treat us too badly at all; in fact, one of them was very sympathetic towards us. Once in three months a medical official came to see Dr Lyon, who was in charge, and he'd bring an orderly with him, and on one occasion this orderly came into our little hut, our part of the hut, and he had this newspaper parcel. He didn't speak English but he pointed to one of our plates, an enamel plate, and so we gave it to him and he shook a whole lot of shrimps, dried shrimps, into it for us. Then out of his pocket he took his wallet and showed us a photograph of a woman and two little girls, his wife and children, and then he had to go away, sneak back again quickly. So they weren't all nasty.

We had a very high wooden fence, and outside that we had a tiger fence. There was space to walk between the two fences and the guards at night used to walk between them. Sometimes tigers came and we heard them; they don't roar, they make a sort of grunty noise. There was a little dog that lived in the camp and it used to go mad and rush out barking and shrieking.

Then the Japanese got women who would do so to go out and clear the jungle – it had been burnt off all round the huts, but they wanted it all cleared. So these women got a little bit extra food for doing that, and it was lovely to get out of the camp because of the constant noise. It was only silent for about a couple of hours in the middle of the night. So the women cleared all these remains of the trees and pulled out the roots and weren't allowed to bring anything in. Some people brought orchids in, and of course they were thrown away – you couldn't have them – and people used to put a couple of leaves up their panties and things like that to get them in.

Eventually they cleared the whole place, a great big space, and then they had to dig it all up and they planted sweet potatoes or something. Of course, in the night, the wild animals came and took the lot, so the next thing they brought a whole lot of stakes, fencing stakes sort of thing, and all the children were given a stake and they all ran out with these – they looked like a little army with them. They put a fence round and then it was all replanted again and got quite a crop, really, by the time we had to go. I went out once or twice but they didn't expect us really to do much work because we were working in the hospital most of the time, but it was nice to get out away from the constant noise.

Then part of the time we had Malay guards – a lot of Malay women were in the camp, many married to Dutch planters. The Malay guards were all right. I think they did a bit of hobnobbing – some of these women had got to the stage where, especially for cigarettes or anything like that, they'd do anything, a lot of them. You know they had affairs, you might say, with the guards.

We really had no idea about how the war was going. We got an idea when a Japanese went out to speak to a guard out where they were growing those plants and there was a burst of hysterical laughter and the guard told the women they could all go inside now, and from that incident we got to know the war was over. Well, the Officer in Charge then told the camp committee. Then they brought in all sorts of food for us. The first thing that arrived was a big truck with a whole lot of, I don't know what, fish, huge, frozen, but they were unfreezing and then the men were allowed to come from their camp, which wasn't far away. We never saw each other, the men and women, but they, the men, were only a couple miles or so away in an old rubber storehouse. They had to come in in batches because of lack of clothing – the same pair of shorts came on different men. They were set to to cut up these huge fish and things like that, and I got mine in the middle of the night. I don't know what time it was, but to have this lovely fish... And then we had plenty of food.

After about 10 days all we English women were taken back to civilisation more or less, and the Dutch still had to wait there and had quite a bad time, some of them. We were lucky, and I suppose we were about three weeks in Padang, and then a couple of planes came and took us back to Singapore.

I was quite ill. I'd had dysentery for 18 months, untreated, and now I got dengue fever for the third time. With just a few New Zealanders we were in Raffles Hotel, and one day two New Zealand Army Officers came to see me and said, "Would you like to go to New Zealand?" I hadn't been able to contact my husband, you see – the signals went wrong and he didn't get a message from me – so I was really feeling rotten, so when they said, "Would you like to go to New Zealand?" I said, "Yes."

So then very quickly I was on a plane and we had an interesting journey too, stopping at various places in Australia. I was taken back to New Zealand and stayed with my in-laws for about six months. Then I went back to Singapore, but I took a long time to get there because shipping was so upset at that time. I was quite healthy by then. Of course I had to go back as a nursing sister, and then I was re-united with my husband and eventually we returned to New Zealand.'

With the Dutch capitulation on the Island of Java, at the partly completed aerodrome at Tasik Malaja where Pilot Officer Sydney Scales, RNZAF, together with 3-4,000 other men found themselves prisoners of war, all was confusion. The lack of accommodation, the ready access to jungle, and bush still uncleared on the site made it extremely difficult for the Japanese guards even to institute a nominal role. Planes, equipment and petrol dumps, still very accessible on the aerodrome, created a situation where escape to Australia using one of the planes received serious consideration, but for various reasons was decided against. So Syd Scales and his colleagues decided to leave the camp in the same way they had entered it:

'We had our transport, Bedford trucks, still in the camp, so we decided to pinch a Bedford truck, cut the perimeter wire and get out, timing it so that the motorcycle patrol which was going round would be just past us when the wire was cut. We filled the truck with posts and tools that were lying about to support a story we'd made up that we were going down to mend a bridge, down south at a place called Simpang, which we heard had been blown by the Dutch. All this worked – we got away one morning, snipped the wire, drove the truck through and away. Well, we got down to the bridge at Simpang, nobody stopped us, we didn't see a soul on this road, and the bridge was blown, but the natives at that stage had ferried people across on big bamboo rafts they'd made. We drove the truck on to the big raft, went across to the other side and drove further on down the road towards the south coast of Java. Then we ran out of petrol, and there was none to be had, so we decided to hike the rest of the way. We took what food we had and carted it down to the coast to a place called Tjipatoedjah.

There were 13 of us, three squadron leaders, a flight lieutenant, a couple of pilot officers and some "erks", and we saw the headman at this small native village. We had plenty of imprest money and were able to hire an atap hut from the headman of the village, and he told us he'd provide us with chickens and goats and a certain amount of rice, at a price. So this was all arranged and we settled down to try and find a boat, but we had no luck at that – the coast was rather exposed and there were no harbours.

We then decided to try and build a boat with the help of a Dutch planter we had met. He had a sawmill on his property with plenty of timber, Java teak, and he had a whole lot already cut there, which was seasoned, and he said he'd arrange for the timber to be rafted down to where the river came out at Tjipatoedjah on the coast. My CO and I had had some sailing experience and he and I used to go up to the planter's place at night, and over some gins discuss plans for the boat. I remember well an occasion when Squadron Leader Shopee, an old Australian bush pilot, and I went out in a dugout canoe to find a suitable place to lay out a slip and build this boat. I was up in the bow and I reached up my hand to grab a branch to pull the boat in and Shopee yelled out, "Freeze, hold it!" and I froze, and he said, "Take your hand away slowly." I took it away slowly. He said, "You were just about to put your hand around a krait," which is a small colourful, poisonous snake. He said, "If you'd woken that thing up you would have had it."

Then while we were waiting for this timber we had a message from the headman of the village to say the Japanese were coming, coming to pick us up. So we didn't know what to do, quite frankly. A lot of us had malaria and dysentery, and so after a considerable discussion we decided to wait for the Japs and see what happened, because obviously in our state of health we weren't going to get far. There was no use running; there was nowhere to run to.

Well, eventually the Japs came down in a lorry and they were a bit obstreperous, started to push us around a bit, little chaps with long bayonets, rather forbidding. Then with the most marvellous luck in the world, the Jap sergeant, who could speak very good English, he noticed my shirt – it had a New Zealand flash on the shoulder – and he said, "Oh, New Zealand."

I said, "Yes."

He said, "Do you play rugby?"

I said, "Yes, I used to at school."

He said, "I play rugby. Were you in the New Zealand Universities team that toured Japan in 1936?"

I said, "No I wasn't, but I had a friend who was," and we started to talk rugby!

Anyway, that broke the ice and this little sergeant, who had been a graduate of the Tokyo University before he was drummed into the Army, he became quite friendly. He handed cigarettes out all round and his troops took the cue from him and started to produce photographs of their children and so on, and the atmosphere was quite nice, the tension was off.

They took us by lorry to this temporary prison camp at a place called Garoet, and on the way they'd stop every now and again and buy some frozen fruit sticks for us, and they'd give us cigarettes and were very friendly. As soon as we got in there the official Jap guards took over, and from then on the trouble started. We were in Garoet for about three or four weeks, and then we shifted to a more permanent camp in Baundung. We went by train and the carriages were crowded, the windows were shut, and it was terribly hot and stuffy. There were no stops and it took many hours, during which time most of us developed a raging thirst. At Baundung we walked along this road, some hundreds of us, with the local inhabitants jeering at us, but behind them there were a lot of Dutch, European, women waving to us. Anyhow we finished up in this Baundung camp and were able to line up at a fresh water tap, swallowing this lovely cool water.

That first camp, as camps go, was a good one. We stayed there for about a year and the Jap commandant was quite amenable to the inmates doing things for themselves. One of the British senior officers there was the well-known author, Lieutenant Colonel van der Post, who had been, I believe, a member of an embassy staff in Japan before the war. He did a marvellous job of liaison between the Japs and the prisoners, because the Japs respected him because of his seniority and because of his ability to speak good Japanese. Under the aegis of van der Post we established a university in there, because there were men with every ability in the camp. There were university lecturers, artists, plumbers – you name it, there was someone of every trade there – and the commandant allowed us to organise this university. We also had a stage organisation, which was called BTC, which meant British Theatricals Company, and for this we had been given the use of an old gymnasium in this camp which had been a Dutch barracks. We had very talented musicians in the camp – a drummer from Jack Payne's band, a great jazz band in England at the time, whose name was Bernie Weller. There were actors, there were musical experts, composers, and they made up songs and wrote the music, which was copied on typewriters which the Japanese had allowed us to have, and this was all copied and duplicated. They turned on some marvellous shows. At one stage we were making our own duplicating paper and we even had a camp magazine, which was posted up in the barracks so that all the blokes could read it.

That was a good camp, no doubt about that, and the Japs used to take us for physical jerks every morning at 6am Tokyo time, and we'd all have to bow towards Tokyo at the start of the callisthenics, and they had a cheer leader on the stage, all dressed up in gym costume, and he'd show us the exercises he wanted us to do.

This didn't last for very long. Towards the end of '42, early '43, the Japanese were making up working parties to go to the Thailand railway and going overseas to build railways and aerodromes at Baundung and the islands, and that's where all the dreadful atrocities happened, of course. That's when they really started to drive the prisoners. Very little food and lots of brutality. I was lucky insofar as I'd had malaria and dysentery early. The Japanese were only taking fit people on these working parties, so I didn't go.

There was another New Zealander by the name of Bill (Phil) Phillips in the camp who was a bit of a radio whiz, and he'd managed to get hold of an old Philco radio set. He pulled it to bits and used the parts for a little two-valve set which he built into a box and buried it under the tiles of a big stone bench where we used to do the cooking in our cottage. We had a scare one night when Phil had the set out and had it in pieces to find out why it had started malfunctioning when the alarm went out that the Japs were doing an inspection. So the big panic was what to do with all the radio parts, and I had a dose of malaria at the time and I was lying shivering on my bunk, so they decided to put all these – I had a mosquito net round – put all these bits and pieces in my bunk, with me, under the blanket. Now the prison guards didn't know much about malaria – they thought it was a catchable disease. So they came in the door, thumping, banging with their rifles and looked at all the blokes, looked at their bags and everything, and then they pointed to the mosquito net. "What's that, what's that there?" They were told it was a sick man – I had "sakit panos", which means heat sickness. Our blokes turned on the pantomime saying, "Oh very bad, shush, quiet," and they said, "Oh, ah-so, ah-so," and away they went. I was sweating furiously underneath that mosquito net. Yes, I well remember that.

Some months after they'd made up the working parties, we were transferred to Batavia to a camp called Cycle camp. It wasn't too bad, but our big problem at this time was food, and a lot of chaps were suffering from malnutrition. There was very little Jap brutality in that camp, and I think the Japanese at this stage – we were getting to the end of '44 – the Japs were getting as tired with the war as we were.

At one stage towards the end the Japs appealed to the prisoners for anybody with any motor engineering experience to volunteer to go down to Tanjong Priok docks and the old General Motors factory and restore a lot of trucks and transport, which had deteriorated round Batavia in previous years. There would be extra food for this job and, of course, most blokes jumped at it and in no time at all they had hundreds of "motor mechanics".

We spent six weeks down there, and I think in all that time we only got three trucks into going order. The great lark was, you'd get this moveable overhead crane, you'd yank out an engine out of a truck, and something would go wrong with the crane and the whole lot would drop on to the concrete floor and smash up the engine block. There were many other ways of sabotaging parts and equipment, and the Japs, at that stage, had nobody technical around and, given a plausible excuse, they were inclined to accept this and do nothing about it.

Well, we were still in Cycle Camp at the end of the war, and we knew the war was finishing because there were various radios in the camp. Then one day a marine parachuted down, came into the camp, and everybody cheered like hell. He announced officially that the war was over and that we were to stay in our camp in the meantime, and that no action was to be taken against the Japanese, who had promised that they would look after us until such time as everybody was released.

So this made us all very happy. The only trouble was we couldn't celebrate because we didn't have any grog, we didn't have much food to celebrate. But eventually the Japs did us very well – they sent in all sorts of food, clothing and all the stuff they could have sent us before because there was lots of it about. They sent in a whole lot of Red Cross parcels and medical supplies which they had been storing somewhere. In the whole 3½ years I was in prison camp I got six-tenths of a Red Cross parcel, and you were supposed to get one a week. They and the medical supplies which came with them would have saved many lives of POWs if they had been made available earlier.

It was an amazing piece of work the way the New Zealand Air Force organised our repatriation. First thing that happened was that a Flight Lieutenant Edwards of 40 Squadron, I think it was, landed his Dakota at the Jap-controlled airport and demanded transport to the nearest prison camp in which there were New Zealanders. The result was that the Japs had rallied round and next morning we were on our way to Singapore. It was marvellous. We were the first away and I drew a cartoon which we dropped over the camp on our way out and which was brought about because the Americans and Australians were so sure they would be the first out. I spent ten days convalescing and being marvellously looked after, and then I was flown home to New Zealand.'

Lieutenant John Hickley RN has previously described events leading up to his capture by the Japanese, and now recalls his 3½ years as a prisoner of war:

'So now we have got to the stage where I have been picked up by this Japanese destroyer and we, the survivors, were taken to a captured Dutch

Japanese Prisoner of War Reunion:
Marjory de Malmanche and John Hickley in 1991.

hospital ship where we were all housed in various parts of the vessel. Sailors, poor chaps, they had a bit of a rough deal; the officers were put in the beds in the wards, but then conditions there were very miserable. But I suppose we were saved, and I can remember so well the first bit of food there, it was one rice ball, which was better than nothing. Well, I think it was a week in this hospital ship before the powers that be decided what to do with us, and we were taken on board to Makasar, which was the capital of the Celebes.

So having got to Makasar we were marched in what clothes we had, barefoot, to a camp, which was an ex-Dutch barracks. I can't remember how many miles out of the town, but it was pretty unpleasant and this camp was run by a madman, a Japanese gentleman called Yoshida, and I am happy to say that although he was highly efficient, he got his come-uppance after the war when he was shot as a war criminal.

The Japanese always insisted on separating the officers from the men and the troops. Those that were well were formed into working parties to do whatever jobs they had to do in the town. I wouldn't say we had nothing to do; first thing of course was to feed all this mob. We were joined fairly soon by contingents of the Dutch Army, who just marched into the camp in their full order with haversacks full of clothing and food. We had just absolutely damn all, no money, no clothes, nothing, and the situation was getting worse and worse. Fortunately, after the senior officers and specialists had been winkled out and sent to Japan for interrogation, we were left with a magnificent gentleman called Lieutenant Commander George Cooper, who was First Lieutenant of *Exeter*, to hold the can and look after us, and my goodness me, he did well. I've seen him take one or two nasty beatings for us, and after the war he was decorated with the OBE.

A cry went out very soon for more working parties. A working party of sailors went inland to construct an airfield, besides the ordinary working parties in the docks. They generally came back, these working parties came back, with a few little perks and they were all searched of course, but food, food, food was the essential thing. The Dutch, of course, were loaded with guilders, and it was arranged by George Hooper that we would get a loan from the Dutch for x number of guilders so that we could purchase legally food which at those stages was allowed to come in the camp from the local trader. And, in fact, as time went on we weren't doing too badly. The worry at the early stages, certainly with me, was what the hell's going to happen if anybody tries to escape? Because we'd heard stories of people always escaping from POW camps in Germany – and good luck to them – they seemed to take it as a game really.

However, our question was soon answered when I believe it was about four Dutchmen made a break for it, and, of course, being of the right skin colour and speaking the local language, they reckoned they were in pretty good shape to escape. However, these chaps were betrayed and we did not actually witness the decapitation, but they got the chop, full stop and that's the end of that. So it put a bit of a dampener on any thought of escaping, so we all sobered up a bit.

Now there was a working party formed, chiefly of sailors, to go to a place called Pombola, which was a jungle camp where I was sent with about ten officers and a couple of hundred sailors and Royal Marines to reclaim land. The soil was red, which meant that it was bauxite, and this was bad. It was a typical jungle camp – atap sheds, earth floors and one table down the middle – and then that was our accommodation. We had to dig our own latrines, there was one cookhouse, and mosquitoes were rife. We had no medical service or supplies, and the work was pretty hard, from 7 in the morning till 5 at night. Food was awful – rice pap three times a day, no meat – and people started to go sick, and I was fortunate I suppose in that I didn't get malaria. I only got malaria once there, and dysentery was rife. Now, without going into all the gruesome stories, I personally read the burial service for, I think, 16 of our lads who had died, and we buried them in the jungle. It was terrible and this went on until we were down to, I don't know, about 20 people, and so we were thankfully shipped back to Macassar, to our old camp, where we were segregated from the rest of the people. We were not allowed to talk to our mates, so we corresponded by semaphore. So that was a nasty little experience.

Now back in the camp at Macassar we were formed into an officers' draft of about 200 mixed British and Dutch, and were duly sent to Batavia to this huge camp called Cycle Camp. Now, it had its good and bad points. Its good points were that we were meeting new friends, which was a marvellous asset, but food wasn't any better. It was a question of a gathering place for all working drafts to be formed, and sure enough I got picked for all sorts of working drafts. One of them was being sent to a camp which was the old civil jail, and there I spent a few charming months. In the cell was one army officer, one air force officer and one sailor and myself.

It was soon obvious in this side of the camp that the best way to survive was to get a job, and Hickley found his way into the bakery, which wasn't a bad thing because it was there, strange to relate, that we did make our own bread, which was generally colourless or brownish purple, but it was rather like a football. And it had yeast with which to blow up the bread and a little bit of fresh fruit juice. You don't have to be very much of a whiz-kid to put that, yeast and juice, together to make some very good plonk. Be that as it may, this life had its lighter side. The fact that I was picked for the officer in charge of the officers' working party at this jail, it sounds very good, and indeed it had its points of being able to get away from the camp every day. But, on the other hand, I took the can back for quite a lot of the misdemeanours committed by some of these officers.

I was back for a spell at Cycle Camp before being picked for another draft which was going overseas – we thought it would be Japan. And it was a draft of over a thousand of mixed nationalities, and we were stuffed in the hold of a blooming ship. So it was from Batavia up to Singapore, where we were housed in a camp in River Valley Road, which was guarded by Sikhs, gentlemen who had gone over to the Japanese. So this was what you might say just a sort of a break in the trip while the ship in which we were due to sail waited on a convoy to leave Singapore for wherever it was. We supposed Nippon. And this was not good – all down in the hold and conditions awful. The Japanese escort craft were continually dropping depth charges for submarine attack. It was all right for sailors, like myself, who knew what the sound of a depth charge was, but for the unfortunate soldiers it must have been pretty hairy. Now in this draft, we must have left about the end of May, beginning of June, because the guards very soon were all quizzing us about places in France, which we took naturally to mean that the D-Day landings had taken place, which indeed was what happened. This was a marvellous morale booster for us all.

There it was. I won't go into the details of what the conditions under which we lived were like, but they weren't good. And at Formosa we were transferred to another merchant ship, because, I think, the steering of this craft had gone on the blink, as they say. And so we tried our luck in this next ship in the convoy, and the passage continued and we were getting nearer and nearer Japan. The guards started to get very excited going to see home again, of course, and we were just wondering where the hell we were going. But I must say, at this stage, the convoy in which we were sailing at night was darkened, which is against the Todd Rules if you're carrying prisoners of war.

So when our catastrophe happened, it really was unfortunate that the Japanese had not subscribed to the Geneva Conventions. However, you can imagine about 800 or so poor chaps stuffed in the hold – there was the question of how the hell to get out in an emergency. Everybody, of course, wanted to have a billet near the ladders at the bottom of the hold. And in this particular sad night, I was wakened, as we all were, by one almighty crack, and it was a torpedo which had been fired successfully by an American submarine who, not knowing that there were prisoners on board, was perfectly justified in doing this. The ship went down mighty quick, in about a minute, and as the ship went down I was fortunate, to put it mildly, to come to the surface in a sort of an air bubble underneath the hatch and on to the surface. I swam for quite some time in the middle of the night. I started off hanging on to, I think it was, a kapok pillow or something of that nature, and then later on when daylight came I found myself near a large plank of timber which was a bit of the hatch combing, and hung on to that. There was a Dutch doctor at the other end. I can remember in the daylight, on another bit of wood floating past, was a bloody old rat there cleaning his whiskers because the hold was full of rats.

However, I think I was on the surface for about 12 hours when we saw a small escort craft stopped in the distance starting to pick up survivors. And it took a lot of courage, a bold decision, to drop everything and swim for it, which I did. I don't know how many yards it was, but it felt like about half a mile to swim to this craft, which was stopped. Fortunately on board this craft was our Korean guard, Mini, who had been picked up by this ship and was telling the captain, in my language, that these people in the water being picked up belonged to him and we must be saved.

We were then taken into Nagasaki, so we must have been about 40-odd miles out to sea. And we weren't in very good shape when we got to

Nagasaki, and found ourselves in a building which was fairly close to the Mitsubishi shipyards, and this is where the truth came out – that we had been sunk by an American submarine. And, of course, we were all grilled as soon as we arrived. What had we seen? Had we seen a submarine? The answer was no. It turned out that I was the senior British officer to survive and very soon the Japanese commander of the camp hauled me out on a parade and told me to sign a bit of paper to say that I would not escape. I said no. I'd heard of the word duress, and I got a nudge from some of the people on parade – "You can sign it under duress" – which I did. And it was a nasty moment, because having been threatened with death, I realised that they meant what they said.

The death toll from the ship was 600, I think, out of 800, and of course we were in a pretty poor state. Eventually we were kitted up with certain clothes, Japanese uniform, and spent a miserable time there. And the boys were working in the Mitsubishi shipyards, and they were the chaps who really saw what goes on outside. They didn't work very hard, of course. If anybody died, that was when I again had to go with the coffin to the crematorium, and after the coffins had been disposed of, we were given a sort of huge pair of chopsticks to take out half a dozen bones or whatever it was from this tray and stuff it in an urn. The Japanese guards were very peaceful on these occasions and would offer you a cigarette while you were waiting for the cremation to take place.

But it was in this camp in Nagasaki that I got my first Red Cross parcel; we were sunk in July '44 and I suppose it was before Christmas that we were given a Red Cross parcel, a Canadian Red Cross parcel, which we had to share with one other. Joy, joy, joy, and the milk powder – "Klim", I think it was – and we all realised that the need of the sick was greater than for us, so we gave that to the hospital for our sick people, where one or two started to get pneumonia, etc. The guards were unpleasant in a way with the Red Cross parcels, because they stipulated that we had to eat it by a certain time and so on, and we had to hand in the tins when they were empty. There was a Japanese corporal there who ran the store for Red Cross supplies and I noticed that he was wearing very smart boots issued by the Red Cross. But eventually we did get a few Red Cross clothes, which was marvellous, because the winter was very, very cold there. The buildings were made of, I might say, three-ply wood and goodness knows what. We had, believe it or not, seven blankets. It sounds an awful lot, but if the blankets are made of paper it doesn't mean much. And food was getting less and less. Returning to this Red Cross clothing, I received – I think we drew lots – a pair of Red Cross long-johns, and my goodness me they were a Godsend, marvellous.

So, in this particular camp we had to dig our own trenches for air raid shelters. We often saw B29s, which the Japanese called B Nijuku, flying over, and they never dropped anything on us. I was the senior boy there and I had always access to the camp commander's office for one thing and another. Even he wasn't too bad. It was pretty obvious that the tide was turning and I was together with three other fellows and we were picked up one day from this camp and told to get packed. It didn't take too many minutes to do that, and we were on another draft.

It turned out that we were taken to the station, and finished up in a place in the north of the island called Fukuoka. And we jumped on board this craft, another sea voyage, everybody's heart fell, a sea voyage across to Darien in South Korea, but we arrived there safely, in one piece, thanks be to God. And it was by train from there up to Manchuria, Mukden, so we travelled around a bit. And I should have said, that at the time of taking this last sea passage, we'd met up with a lot of the officers who'd been incarcerated in Formosa, and it was marvellous to meet new friends. This camp in Mukden was pretty basic – I think you'd call it that – cold as anything in the winter. But we arrived there in the late summer when it started to get cool, and it now comes to the time when our lives were at stake because it was obvious from the grapevine that the tide had turned in a big way for the Japanese in the Pacific War, and it was later known, after the war of course, that in the event of the Allies landing on the mainland of Japan, all prisoners of war would be liquidated.

And it was one day, I can't remember what actual day of the week it was, when we sighted in this camp some parachutes landing outside the camp several miles away. And this turned out to be American airborne troops who were doing, you might say, a recce, and they were the forerunners of the forces that rescued us. The Japanese had to surrender their arms, and we were made to witness that and we were not allowed out of the camp for 48 hours after this armistice. It was a thrill, and our nerves, my nerves certainly, were on edge wondering which way the cat was going to jump, because we had been issued with extra rations which we thought were for a forced march, which may have been the case. Be that as it may, the Lord was on our side and we were very fortunate in being saved by the atomic bomb, and I repeat that we were very much saved by the atomic bomb, because had the atomic bomb not been used we would not be here.

Two further matters I must mention. The first thing is about disease and sickness. I say here that the main illnesses were malaria, dysentery, beriberi (and these included dengue, which I had), pellagra, and tropical ulcers, which I also had. Quinine was like gold dust, and in one camp we made a witches brew of pawpaw leaves; it tasted ghastly but seemed to work rather well. Malnutrition and vitamin deficiencies contributed largely to other ailments, the smallest scratch became a large ulcer, and I still carry a few marks. And another little bit which I suppose is of interest is that if you had a temperature of 103 degrees Fahrenheit or below you were fit for working parties.

Now, one final piece: I am now reading this from a bit of paper which I wrote years ago. In it I say, 'Imagine in this day and age living for 3½ years without receiving a letter, seeing a newspaper or having wireless news,' yet such was my case. Only in Cycle Camp did I hear authentic news from a most secret wireless concealed in the heel of a modern wooden clog, and the unknown, to me, operator was a very brave man indeed. I was allowed to send a total of four postcards from Java and Japan, which were delivered to my parents in England. They had 18 months living without the knowledge that I'd been torpedoed or reported missing by the Admiralty before they announced that I was a POW. These 3½ dead years certainly had repercussions when we were released, and for me it took years and years to settle down. We knew nothing of the campaigns in the theatres of war, and the pictures of many aspects of the war, concentration camps, etc, which we were shown later on looked awesome, absolutely frightening. Forgive but, for me, never forget. Amen.'

APPENDIX

The contributors

Barber, Robert Hugh was born in 1915 in Hatfield, Hertfordshire, and went to school in Oakham, where he excelled in sports and became Head of his House. He joined the Metropolitan Police and in 1939 was accepted for a short service commission in the Royal Air Force. As a Pilot Officer he took part in the Battle of Britain, was shot down and badly injured. Despite this he continued in the Air Force in demanding non-operational roles. After the war Robert Barber left the Air Force and went into business, and retired in New Zealand. He died in 1998 soon after his tape had been recorded.

Begg, Richard Campbell was born in Wellington, New Zealand in 1924. The family emigrated to South Africa in 1937 and Richard, after matriculating in 1939, worked for a year or so before joining the Royal Navy. He travelled in an ageing troop ship, which took eight weeks en route from Cape Town to Liverpool, arriving in September 1941. After six months at Dartmouth Naval College he went to sea, serving in a variety of ships, first in the Home and then in the East Indies Fleet. After the war Lieutenant Begg resigned his commission, studied medicine and practised in New Zealand as a general practitioner, and then as a specialist in public health.

Bennison, Alan was born in 1918 in Dunedin, New Zealand, and completed his education at the Technical High School in Ashburton, where he entered the Public Works Department. Always keen on aircraft, he applied to join the RNZAF in March 1939, and on the outbreak of war was accepted for training. In April 1940 he left for the United Kingdom, where he was duly promoted to the rank of Sergeant Air-gunner. He saw service in the Battle of Britain and in the Middle East. Back in the United Kingdom he became an Instructor teaching new crews in the use of radar. At the end of the war he returned to New Zealand, where he worked for the Direct Importing Company (DIC) and now lives in retirement in Ashburton. He retired from the RNZAF Reserve with the rank of Flight Lieutenant in 1973.

Blair, Roy Ian was born in 1915, and from an early age lived in Nelson, New Zealand, where he went to school, then worked with the City Council. He joined the Volunteer Army and was commissioned in June 1938. At the outbreak of war he was posted to the Second NZEF in the 27th Machine Gun Battalion and served in Egypt and Palestine, taking part in the battles leading to El Alamein and on to Tunisia. He went on to serve in Italy from Cassino to Faenza, returning to NZ with the rank of Major. He joined the Territorial Army in 1949 and retired in 1960 with the rank of Colonel. After the war he worked as the accountant for the Nelson Hospital Board, eventually becoming Chief Executive Officer to the Board. He was awarded the OBE in 1945 and the ED in 1954.

Brown, Bernard Walter, born in 1917 in Stratford, New Zealand, was educated there and then had a job at the Post Office. He was accepted for a short service commission in the RAF and saw service in the Battle of Britain, during which was shot down and badly wounded. He was then sent to the RAF Training Command School in Rhodesia and later ferried brand new Wellington bombers to North Africa. Bernard then transferred to the British Overseas Airways Corporation (BOAC) and later British European Airways (BEA), spending 25 years in civil aviation before returning to New Zealand, where he bought an orchard in which he and his wife worked until his retirement.

Brown, George Arthur was born in 1911 in Wellington, New Zealand, but spent most of his childhood and school life in Greymouth. In 1937 he worked his passage to Britain hoping to join the Air Force, but missed out, so he returned home and rejoined the Territorials. As a Second Lieutenant in the 20th Infantry Battalion he left New Zealand on 5 January 1940 for the Middle East and served in Greece and Crete, where he was wounded, taken prisoner and his leg had to be amputated. Captain George Brown was eventually repatriated to New Zealand where his leg was re-amputated and he was fitted with an artificial limb. He married and became Managing Secretary to the Hospital Board at Westport, later retiring for health reasons and becoming Secretary to the Christchurch St John Ambulance Association before retiring to Nelson.

Brown, Robert Alfred was born in 1917 at Liverpool and went to school there, leaving at the age of 14. After working in a number of jobs, including going to sea as a steward, he became an insurance agent. In 1940 he enlisted in the Army, trained in signals and eventually, as a Corporal, was put in charge of radio sets at 176 Brigade HQ, 59th Infantry Division. He took part in the invasion of Europe and the fighting in North West Europe. After the war he was stationed in Greece before being demobilised. Robert Brown could not settle and eventually emigrated to New Zealand and got a job building caravans. Later he ran a family store in a seaside town and then went into the motel business. He retired to Nelson and died suddenly in February 2000.

Bryson, William Urquhart, born 1913 in Dunedin, New Zealand, soon moved to Christchurch, where he went to school and then took up a pharmacy apprenticeship. He entered the Navy in January 1941, commenced training in England, and was soon at sea as an Ordinary Seaman seeing service in the Mediterranean. He underwent officer training and was posted to landing craft, in which he took part in the Dieppe Raid and then the D-Day landings. After the war Lieutenant Bryson completed his pharmacy training and worked in that profession in Nelson, where he now lives in retirement.

Burdekin, Alan George was born in 1917 and lived on his father's farm near Reddish outside Manchester, where he went to school. He attended Agricultural College at Rease Heath, then worked on his father's farm at Belper. He joined the RAF Volunteer Reserve in March 1939, training as a wireless operator/air-gunner. He took part in the Battle of Britain, was commissioned and went on to air-sea rescue duties operating from Walrus amphibian aircraft. After the war Alan Burdekin went back to farming but soon emigrated to New Zealand, where he joined the RNZAF Reserve in which he attained the rank of Flight Lieutenant. He is now retired and lives outside Blenheim.

Burton, Gerald Francis was born in 1917 at Wanganui, New Zealand. He was orphaned when he was 12 years old and, after some years in an orphanage, he and his older brother Jack moved to Christchurch where they found employment, and Gerald started studying accountancy. When war broke out they decided to apply to join the Air Force, but, having no secondary school education, were initially turned down for pilot training. However, their interviewers, impressed by their determination and enthusiasm, reversed this decision and they studied hard, hired a private tutor and not only passed the entrance examination, but came top in their group. They trained in New Zealand, achieved their wings and became Sergeant Pilots. Gerald saw service in New Zealand, then in the South Pacific, achieving promotion to Flight Lieutenant before the war ended. After the war Gerald married and eventually developed a manufacturing business in Stratford. He has made several trips to Air Force reunions overseas and at one of them had the well-deserved honour of laying and dedicating two memorial plaques at the Admiral Nimitz Memorial Park in Texas; one was for the six airmen from his No 30 Squadron lost overseas, and the other to his brother Jack, who was killed while covering US marine landings in the Solomon Islands.

Campion, William John was born in 1919 in Liverpool, was educated there and passed the school certificate examination before leaving school at the age of 16 to join the railways. In 1937 he joined the Territorial Army, and served in the Artillery during the war with service in France at the time of the 'Phoney War'. He then took part in the invasion and liberation of Europe, suffering severe injuries when involved in the collection of explosive devices. He spent the rest of his service in Germany. Sergeant John Campion was demobilised in 1946, married and later got a position with the East African Railways and Harbours, living in Tanganyika and then Nairobi. After Independence he emigrated to New Zealand where he worked in Government Service and is now retired in Nelson.

Carson, Allan James was born in 1922 in Dunedin, New Zealand, where he received his education and was a keen athlete. He joined the Air Force in 1942 and went to Canada to train as an observer, but health reasons intervened to preclude this, so he returned to New Zealand, where, in June 1943, he completed an administrative course. This was followed by service in Operations and Intelligence in the South Pacific. Allan Carson was subsequently commissioned as a Pilot Officer. He completed three tours as Squadron Intelligence Officer with 19 Fighter Squadron operating in the Pacific Theatre. After the war be became a Child Welfare Officer in the New Zealand Education Department and served in various districts before retiring in Nelson.

Checketts, John Milne was born in 1912 in Invercargill, New Zealand, and left school to become an engineer in the motor industry. In October 1940 he joined the RNZAF and, as a Pilot Officer, went to Britain in September 1941 and was posted to a Hurricane Training Unit at Sutton Bridge. He saw extensive service in Great Britain and over Europe as a fighter pilot and was involved in operations up to, during and after the invasion. Wing Commander Checketts, DSO, DFC, Polish Cross of Valour and USA Silver Star, continued in various senior positions in Britain and New Zealand. He finally resigned his commission in 1954 and took up aerial top dressing (fertilising rural land from the air). He is now retired in Christchurch and much involved with the Air Force Museum at Wigram. His biography, *The Road to Biggin Hill*, by Vincent Orange, was published in 1987.

Dawick, Kenneth was born in 1916 in Palmerston North, New Zealand, where he went to school. He did an apprenticeship in printing and during this time learned to fly and joined the Air Force Reserve. Soon after the war started he was called up into the RNZAF, trained on largely obsolete aircraft, earned his wings in June 1940, and arrived in Britain in September of that year. He did conversion training into modern aircraft and, as a fighter pilot, had a long period on operations before going to Aden as an

Instructor at the Training School there, and was commissioned as a Pilot Officer. He then went back into active operations in the Western Desert and other parts of the Middle East, being promoted to Flying Officer and then Flight Lieutenant. Towards the end of 1943, after three years of overseas service, he returned to New Zealand. He had a spell as a Training Instructor before transferring to the Reserve in 1945. Kenneth Dawick tried his hand at horticulture before finally joining the nursing staff at a local psychopaedic hospital, and is now retired and lives at Levin.

de Malmanche, Marjory was born in 1909 in Boxmoor, near Watford, Hertfordshire. She did her general nursing training at King Edward Memorial Hospital in Ealing, London, beginning in 1926 when she was 16. She joined the Overseas Nursing Association and worked at a hospital in Shanghai for three years before returning to Singapore, where she married. She then worked at the Sepoy Lines Maternity Hospital at Singapore. On the day the Japanese entered Singapore she was evacuated in a ship that was then bombed and sunk by the Japanese. Her progress to Padang in Sumatra is well covered in her account, as is her final capture by the Japanese and her years in a prison camp. At the end of the war Marjory was repatriated to Singapore and eventually she and her husband went to New Zealand, where she now lives in retirement.

Denby, Arthur Godfrey, born in 1921 in Bingley, West Yorkshire, joined the Navy in 1940 and in 1942 was a signalman in the 'County' Class cruiser HMS *Norfolk*, in which he was involved in a number of Russian convoys. Many years later he was awarded a Medallion from the Russians in recognition of this service. He then served in a fast mine-laying cruiser for a time in the Pacific. However, the war soon ended and, instead of mines, the ship carried vast loads of beer for the use of the ex-prisoners of war scattered around the region. As a result of his service in this area Arthur Denby was able to see the effects of the devastating bombing in Japan and elsewhere at first hand and very soon after the surrender. He returned to England, got his discharge from the Navy and opened up a family grocery business. He and his family later emigrated to Australia and then New Zealand, retiring at Brightwater outside Nelson. Sadly Arthur Denby died suddenly in 1998.

Dickens, Desmond Antony George, born in 1924 in Weston-super-Mare, Somerset, into a family with a long sea-going tradition, was educated at the Merchant Naval College at Pangbourne. He joined the NZ Shipping Company's vessel *Dorset* as an apprentice in August 1941 and had a variety of experiences at sea, including the 'Pedestal' convoy that saved Malta. Captain Dickens achieved command of various ships in the NZ Shipping Company, then became an Elder Brother and later Deputy Master at Trinity House.

Frater, Kenneth Carrol, born in Richmond, New Zealand, in 1919, was educated at Wakefield School, leaving when he was 13. He had a variety of jobs, finally driving a mail freight truck. In November 1939 he enlisted in the NZ Army as a Driver in the Second NZ Supply Column, part of the 5th Brigade, and saw service in Greece and North Africa right up to the final defeat of the Axis forces in Tunisia. Corporal Frater arrived back in New Zealand on furlough in March 1944. When the war ended he married, settled down to family life, was a general storekeeper for ten years, then a farmer for 13 years, and finally worked in agricultural research before retiring. He now lives in Motueka.

Friend, Albert Bernard was born in 1920 in London where he had his schooling, after which he did a course of study leading on to aircraft designing. He was called up in 1940 and applied for pilot training, but his education level was considered insufficient and he became an air-gunner/radio operator. He has given a spirited and perceptive account of service in many postings, in the United Kingdom, Malta, Burma and in the D-Day landings and beyond. He was promoted to the rank of Flying Officer, and had further postings to the Middle East and to Bari in Italy, from where he had some interesting experiences flying into Sofia, Bucharest and South Africa. Albert Friend was demobilised in 1946 and joined BOAC, but was made redundant after 12 years service. He then travelled overland driving a Bedford van through Europe, Iran, eventually arriving in India, where he boarded a ship to travel to New Zealand. His family joined him there. He worked in New Zealand for a number of years and later retired to Wakefield near Nelson.

Gard'ner, John Rushton was born in 1918 in Dunedin, New Zealand. He had his schooling there and later at Nelson College. After a spell in the Public Works Department he was accepted for a short service commission in the RAF and was under training when war broke out. He saw service in the Battle of Britain, then in Europe, which encompassed D-Day and beyond. He was then posted to the Air Ministry, later spent eight months in New Zealand, and returned to a permanent commission with the RAF in 1948. His subsequent postings included a spell with the Americans converting into modern aircraft, and operating with the US Marine Corps in the Korean War. Further promotions and senior postings followed, including staff work at the Joint Command Headquarters in Aden. His final appointment was as British Air Attaché to Brussels. Group Captain Gard'ner retired from the RAF in 1965, returning to New Zealand where he went into orcharding, in which he worked for 11 years before retirement.

Gawith, Alan, born in 1916 at Masterton, New Zealand, lived on a farm and attended a variety of schools and boarding colleges. He started studying for law in 1935, but this failed to appeal, and he applied for and was accepted for a short service commission with the RAF and commenced training in Britain in June 1938. He was engaged in night-fighter operations and daylight shipping convoy protection during the Battle of Britain, then on night 'Intruder' patrols over Europe, for which he was awarded the DFC. Early in 1942 he was on the staff of HQ No 9 Group until late in 1943, when he took a Staff College course. In February 1944 he was attached to the US Ninth Air Defense Command as Senior British Liaison Officer, which involved him in the planning for the invasion in Normandy and some six months service in France, for which he was awarded the US Bronze Star medal. At the end of 1944 he took command of the RAF Station Cleave, in Cornwall. Then, after the war ended, because of family commitments and with mixed feelings, he returned to New Zealand, transferred to the RNZAF Reserve, completed his law degree and entered a busy practice. Alan Gawith lives at Monaco, Nelson.

Gladstone, Arthur Edward was born in 1921 at Alexandra, New Zealand, where he had his early schooling before going to boarding school at Oamaru, which he enjoyed and where he excelled at sport. In 1938 he started work at the Bank of New Zealand and joined the Territorials. In December 1941 he was called up and in January 1943 Private Gladstone, Machine Gun Battalion, arrived in Egypt in time for the final months of the North African Campaign. He then went on to see service in Italy, where he met his wife to be, learned Italian and became Unit Historian with the rank of Sergeant. Arthur Gladstone stayed on in Italy for another year, after which he and his wife arrived back in New Zealand, where he took up accountancy, living first in Alexandra and then moving to Nelson, where he brought up his large family and duly retired.

Green, Robert William was born in 1920 in Chester, England, where he went to school and matriculated. He gained a position with the technical staff of the Roads and Bridges Department of Cheshire County Council. In August 1940 he was enlisted into the Royal Corps of Signals and trained as an electrician. A posting to the 3rd Division followed, where he served with the 7th and 76th Field Regiments of Artillery until demobilisation in 1946. He took part in the fighting in Europe from D-Day to VE Day, then served in Palestine. He was three years a Signalman and three years a Corporal. After demobilisation he went back to his position with Cheshire County Council. He married a New Zealander in 1947, qualified as a Civil Engineer in 1949, and emigrated to New Zealand. He worked for the Ministry of Works and various Catchment Boards, finally becoming Chief

Engineer to the Nelson Catchment Board, where he spent 23 years before retirement.

Greer, Harold John was born in 1922 at Invercargill, New Zealand, and soon moved to Gore where he attended school. After two years at High School he joined the New Zealand Railways. In 1942 he was called up into the Division of Signals and in May 1943 arrived at Maadi Camp in Egypt, where he received further training, then Divisional Signalman Greer, 5th HQ Brigade, set off for Italy where he saw long and arduous service. After the end of the European war Signalman Greer returned to New Zealand to his old job, but found it hard to settle, so he got a job in a butcher's shop. He married and started a family and eventually opened his own business in Riversdale, where he worked for 25 years before retiring to Nelson.

Hannah, Leo Gordon was born in 1913 in Stratford, New Zealand. He soon moved to Napier where he had his schooling. He qualified in medicine at the Otago Medical School in 1937 and was about to commence post-graduate study in London when war broke out and he joined the Royal Army Medical Corps. He saw service in the Western Desert, then in the D-Day operations and beyond. He spent some six months in the Army of Occupation in Germany. After demobilisation Dr Hannah returned to his post-graduate studies, then medical practice in Nelson, New Zealand, where he now lives in retirement.

Hayter, James Chilton Francis was born in 1917 at Timaru, New Zealand. He lived on a remote farm but completed his education at Nelson College, then worked on sheep farms. He obtained his private pilot's licence and, just before the war, joined the RAF on a short service commission. He had varied experience as a bomber pilot in France, then in fighters in Britain, the Middle East and Europe. He was awarded the DFC and Bar and was twice mentioned in despatches. Squadron Leader Hayter returned to New Zealand after the war and went into farming, eventually getting his own farm, which he sold in 1960 to become navigator in a survey ship for close on ten years, operating mainly off South America. Although retired he has, until recently, managed farms from time to time.

Hickley, John, born in 1913 in Walsall, Staffordshire, went to school at Scarborough and entered Dartmouth Naval College as a cadet in 1927. In 1931 he went to sea as a Midshipman, then, in 1935, as a Sub Lieutenant and later as a Lieutenant, he served in destroyers in the Mediterranean and Home Fleets. He was in the destroyer HMS *Foresight* in the action against the French off Dakar, during which his ship was damaged. He became First Lieutenant of HMS *Arrow* engaged in East Coast convoys, then she hit an acoustic mine. He was then appointed First Lieutenant of the destroyer

HMS *Encounter*, in which he saw service in the Mediterranean, but was soon off to the Far East as escort to the battleship HMS *Prince of Wales*. He saw that ship and the battlecruiser HMS *Repulse* being sunk by Japanese bombing, and shortly afterwards his own ship was sunk in the Java Sea and he became a prisoner of war. On his release after the war, Lieutenant Commander Hickley continued in the Navy in various positions until his retirement, after which he worked and lived for a time in the Outer Hebrides. Eventually Commander Hickley and his wife Joan emigrated to New Zealand and are now settled in active retirement there.

Hill, Roger, born in 1910, spent his early years in Brighton, Sussex, and was educated at Pangbourne Merchant Navy College. From there he was accepted for public school entry into the Royal Navy. During his early naval career he served in a number of different classes of ships in various stations, including China and the Mediterranean, where he had some experience of the Spanish Civil War. Eventually, in early 1942, as a Lieutenant Commander, he achieved his own command, a 'Hunt' Class destroyer, HMS *Ledbury*. This was followed by command of the Fleet destroyers HMS *Grenville* and HMS *Jervis*, and he saw service in the Arctic, Channel and Mediterranean, taking part in Russian convoys, the 'Pedestal' convoy to Malta, the landings in Italy and the invasion of Europe, Operation 'Overlord'. Lieutenant Commander Roger Hill, RN DSO DSC, then took the *Jervis* to Belfast where she was paid off and he was sent to command an Air Station, which he did not particularly enjoy. He had not been feeling well, was hospitalised and eventually invalided out of the Service. He continued at sea for a period and then went out to New Zealand, where he worked on the Docks for a while and then taught maritime subjects at Nelson Technical College. He became a member of the Nelson Harbour Board, wrote his book *Destroyer Captain*, and farmed his smallholding outside Nelson. His is now retired and living at Arrowtown in Central Otago.

Hunt, David was born in 1919 in Wolverhampton, Staffordshire, and after school went to Birmingham University to study for his BSc. However, an exciting glider trip persuaded him to apply for a short service commission in the Royal Air Force. He was accepted and during his training the war started. He was a fighter pilot in the Battle of Britain, during which time he was shot down, sustaining severe injuries. After prolonged hospitalisation he continued in the Air Force, calibrating air defences around London, then after D-Day he became Station Adjutant at Aberporth in Wales. David Hunt was demobilised in July 1945 with the rank of Flight Lieutenant. After the war he joined the family business in Wolverhampton and later worked in Southern England, where he studied accountancy. Later he emigrated to New Zealand and is now retired in Nelson.

Jenkinson, George Richard was born in Northern Rhodesia in 1919 and went to school in South Africa for nine years before joining the Customs Department in Northern Rhodesia. When war broke out he travelled up to Nairobi, joined the RAF and started his training there. He then completed his training in Salisbury, was sent to South Africa as a Flying Instructor, then after a couple of years was posted to Britain. There he joined a Pathfinder Squadron flying Mosquito aircraft. Flight Lieutenant George Jenkinson returned to Northern Rhodesia after the war, was awarded a Nuffield Scholarship and studied for a medical degree at the University of Witwatersrand in South Africa, qualifying in 1952. He practised medicine in what is now known as Zambia, eventually retiring to live in England, where he died in 1998.

Jervis, Stanley Godfrey was born in 1912 in Auckland, New Zealand, where he went to school and was then employed in a large pastoral farming company. He became a member of the RNVR in Auckland. Soon after the outbreak of war he was commissioned as a Sub Lieutenant and served in several small ships in the Far East before joining the escort vessel HMS *Syvern* operating from Suda Bay in Crete, where he experienced the German attacks on Greece and Crete. He then served in the battleship HMS *Valiant* in the Mediterranean, and later in HMS *Oribi*, an 'O' Class destroyer, in which he was Second Lieutenant and took part in operations in the Arctic and in the Atlantic. In March 1945 he went out to command a frigate in the British Pacific Fleet but, owing to the Japanese surrender, this command was not taken up. Lieutenant Commander Jervis DSC took his discharge, returned to New Zealand to his wife Peggy and small child and his job at Dalgety's, where he became Executive Manager for Bay of Plenty and Hawkes Bay, and subsequently retired.

Kean, Richard James, born in 1914 in Dunedin, New Zealand, attended 17 different schools but still gained his Proficiency Certificate at the age of 12 when he left school and found a job. He joined the Territorials at the age of 18 as a cavalryman in the Otago Mounted Rifles. Later he transferred to the Artillery. He was one of the New Zealand advance party sent to the Western Desert, served in Greece and Crete, and took part in the battles in the Western Desert leading to the Battle of El Alamein. He was then hospitalised with jaundice and on recovery was posted as an Instructor at base camp before returning to New Zealand. Richard Kean rejoined the NZ Territorial Force in 1948 and retired in 1953 with the rank of Warrant Officer 1. He has worked hard for the Returned Servicemen's Association and now lives in retirement in Wakefield, near Nelson.

Kerr, Donald was born in 1919 in Nelson, New Zealand, completing his schooling at Nelson College before entering the family's jewellery business in 1938. He became a talented gymnast, champion in springboard diving, and joined the Territorials. With the outbreak of war he went through the Officer Cadet Training Unit, was commissioned as a Second Lieutenant and joined the NZ Armoured Corps. He served in Italy with distinction. Captain Donald Kerr MC returned to New Zealand at the end of the war and went back into the family business but continued his military interest by joining the Tank Unit in the Territorials. He took an active interest and participated in community and professional affairs and was a devoted family man. He died on 15 February 1999.

Lander, Harold, born in 1923 in Chesterfield, Derbyshire, went to Chesterfield Grammar School where he did well at sports, was a prefect and was in the Cadet Corps. In 1941, after a year at university, he was called up and eventually went to the Armoured Corps OCTU at Sandhurst. While training in mountain warfare he broke his ankle, was in hospital on D-Day and went back into tanks as a Lieutenant in the King's Own (Lancashire) Regiment, Royal Armoured Corps. He was actively involved in tank warfare advancing across North Western Europe and into Germany, and towards the end of the war received shrapnel wounds necessitating hospital treatment. After the end of the war he was posted to Belsen Barracks, next door to the infamous concentration camp, as Motor Transport Officer. He declined an offer of a permanent commission, was demobilised in 1947, completed his university degree in modern history, and became a teacher. He is now retired and living in Poulton-le-Fylde, Lancashire.

McGowan, Roy Andrew, born in 1917 in Bristol, Somerset, passed his matriculation at Bristol Cotham School and went to sea as a deckhand on a freighter in midwinter; deciding that the sea was not for him, he joined the Royal Air Force Volunteer Reserve in 1937. With war imminent, his employers agreed for him to be released to undertake six months training in early 1939. He was posted to 66 Squadron training in Spitfires with the rank of Sergeant Pilot. In May 1939 he was commissioned as a Pilot Officer and posted to 46 Squadron, flying Hurricanes. The Squadron was sent to Norway after the British had captured Narvik during the German invasion of that country, but was evacuated shortly afterwards. Many men from the Squadron, with their planes, were embarked on the aircraft carrier HMS *Glorious*, but fortunately for Pilot Officer McGowan he travelled in a smaller ship, which made the passage successfully. *Glorious* was attacked by the German battlecruisers *Scharnhorst* and *Gneisenau* on 8 June 1940 and sank with heavy loss of life. Roy McGowan served in the reconstituted Squadron throughout the Battle of Britain, was shot down and badly wounded. After discharge from hospital he was put on non-operational duties, first in New Zealand, then as a Squadron Leader in command of an

Armament Practice Camp in Scotland. He eventually returned to operational flying and took part in the final stages of the war in Italy flying Spitfires. Squadron Leader Roy McGowan was demobilised in 1946, could not settle into his pre-war employment and joined BEA; then in 1954 he was employed as the Regional Director (Asia and Pacific) of the International Air Transport Association based at Singapore. In 1981 he retired and he and his wife went to live in New Zealand.

Mackie, John Bullamore was born in 1910 in Dunedin, New Zealand, where he had his formal education and excelled in sports and shooting. He was awarded degrees, MSc (Hons) in 1933 and BE in Mining in 1936 in absentia. He was engaged in prospecting for gold then tin in the Federated Malay States (now Malaysia) for a year or so, then joined the Colonial Service Mines Department in 1936. He had joined the Federated Malay States Volunteers, and when the Japanese invasion occurred the force was mobilised and Captain Mackie saw service throughout that short campaign and was made a prisoner of war when the British surrendered at Singapore. He spent some years in prisoner of war camps in both Singapore and Borneo. At the end of the war, on his release, John Mackie returned to New Zealand to recuperate, then went back to the Federated Malay States to help in the rehabilitation of the mining industry there. After a year or so he resigned and returned once more to New Zealand, where Professor Mackie became the first head of the new Department of Surveying, which he had been asked to organise, at the University of Otago. In 1949, when Compulsory Military Training was introduced, he joined the Royal NZ Engineers and retired from the NZ Army in 1955 with the rank of Major, having been awarded the ED with Clasp. He was awarded the OBE in 1995 for services to surveying and the community. He retired to Nelson in 1976.

McMurtry, Randal George Cannon was born in 1919 in Kikiwa, a remote farming settlement in New Zealand, went to a tiny school there and became adept at bushcraft and shooting, but soon moved to the family home in Richmond and went to Stoke School and Nelson College. In the family tradition he elected to go into one of the services and, at the end of 1938, worked his passage to Britain and joined the Wiltshire Regiment. He was soon selected for officer training and was commissioned back into the Regiment in early 1940. He saw service in Madagascar in the landings there and throughout India, Iraq, Iran, Syria and the Middle East before taking part in the landings on Sicily and the toe of Italy. He received gunshot wounds in Sicily and Captain McMurtry was taken prisoner in Italy. After the European war ended he was appointed Junior Staff Officer for the Provost Marshal in London, having served out an earlier appointment to the Indian Civil Service that terminated when India was granted independence. He resigned his commission in New Zealand in 1948 and became a farmer. Farming, politics, education and equestrian sports occupied his spare time, and he was awarded a QSM for his involvement with equestrian sports. He is also an author of some renown.

Musters, John Vivian Auchmuty was born in Malta in 1917 into a naval family. He joined the Royal Navy as a Cadet in 1935. From 1939 to 1942, as a Sub-Lieutenant then a Lieutenant, he served in HMS *Renown*, as Captain's Secretary and as the main armament range-spotting officer in *Renown*'s actions against the German fast battlecruisers *Gneisenau* and *Scharnhorst* at the beginning of the Norwegian Campaign and later against Italian forces in the Mediterranean. Later he served in the aircraft carrier HMS *Victorious* operating in the Home, Eastern and British Pacific Fleets and was mentioned in despatches. After the war he held various sea and shore appointments. He was promoted to Commander in 1952, and retired in 1970. He and his wife Ann emigrated to New Zealand in 1990, where they lead an active life in Nelson.

Newth, Keith Lewis was born in 1910 in Wakefield near Nelson, New Zealand, did all his schooling in that area and, when he was old enough, he became a driver, first on trucks and then on buses. When the war broke out he volunteered to join the Army and, as a Corporal of Regimental Signals in the NZ 20th Battalion of Infantry, he saw service in North Africa, Greece and Crete. Back in North Africa he was wounded and taken prisoner by the Germans. Keith Newth was eventually repatriated to New Zealand and later joined Newmans Coach Service, driving buses around the South Island of New Zealand and delighting his tourist passengers with his descriptions of the beautiful countryside. He finally settled into retirement at Nelson.

Prebble, Edward Shard was born in London in 1907 and had his early schooling there. In the First World War he witnessed the bombing of London and saw a Zeppelin being shot down in flames. Moving to Worthing he attended various schools and finally boarded at a public school, where he did well at sports and became Head Prefect. After a spell working in Paris, he was employed as a stock-keeper in a quilt factory in London, and eventually became Factory Manager. He learned to fly, joined the Civil Air Guard then the Home Guard, and once more experienced the bombing of London. Called up at the age of 33 in 1940, he attended OCTU on the Isle of Man and was commissioned in August 1941 into the 8th Dorsets. As a lieutenant he converted into the Royal Artillery as Troop Commander of 101 Anti-Aircraft Unit. The Regiment sailed for North Africa in late 1942, where he saw service in Tunisia, then Italy and Yugoslavia. Lieutenant Colonel Edward Prebble MC then returned to England where his wife was not well, and took his discharge from the Army.

He rejoined his firm as a traveller, but later expanded his role to take in other agencies. He eventually retired in 1970. In 1972 he and his wife emigrated to Nelson, New Zealand.

Prendergast, Brian was born in 1923 in Manchester, England, and lived in Rochdale, where he had his schooling, which was slightly disrupted by his being in the Home Guard with night watches on the moors. He then had a temporary position in the Ministry of Labour prior to joining the Navy in 1941 as an ordinary seaman serving in the Mediterranean, then as a Sub Lieutenant RNVR in the Submarine Service in the Far East. Brian Prendergast was demobilised in Hong Kong with the rank of Lieutenant RNVR and took a job as Second Mate of an ex-tank landing ship (LST), taking relief supplies from Shanghai to North China for UNNRA (United Nations Relief Agency). During one of these trips the Communists fired at the ship, and afterwards, by way of an apology, invited the crew to a banquet. After this Brian Prendergast returned to England and qualified in medicine, practising in Britain then in New Zealand. He lives an active life in retirement in Nelson.

Ramsay, Norman Hugh Donald was born in 1919 in Hull, East Yorkshire, and lived there until the age of 12, then, after a year in London, he went to live with his father in Southampton. At the age of 16 he became an engineering apprentice at Vickers Supermarine. He joined the RAF Volunteer Reserve and when war broke out was called up, qualified as a pilot and was posted to his first Squadron as a Sergeant Pilot, flying Spitfires. He fought in the Battle of Britain after which his Squadron took part in Fishery Protection Patrols. While in this squadron he received his commission. After a spell in Training Command he flew to Malta and took part in the Allied invasion of Sicily. He was awarded a DFC. Back in the United Kingdom he was unwell and was eventually found to have amoebic dysentery. After a prolonged illness and convalescence he was posted back into Spitfire training, teaching such skills as night flying, gunnery, etc. After the war he transferred to the Permanent Force and continued flying fighters until the age of 35. Flight Lieutenant Ramsay DFC retired from the RAF in 1962, went out to New Zealand with his family and worked in Air Traffic Control in Civil Aviation for a short while before leaving to undertake work selling industrial safety equipment. He is now retired and living in Sumner, Christchurch.

Rodgers, Alexander was born in 1917 in Hector on the west coast of New Zealand. He went to a Convent School nearby where he became School Dux. With the outbreak of war he joined the Engineers, had three months training, got married, and in May 1940, as a Sapper in the NZ 7th Field Company, sailed with the NZ Second Echelon, which was diverted to

Britain and eventually arrived in Suez. He fought in Greece and in Crete, where he was wounded and taken prisoner. On his release after the war ended he returned to New Zealand where he rejoined his wife and family. He then moved to take up a position in Motueka where he still lives and is a Patron of the Returned Services Association. He has been awarded the Gold Badge and National Life Membership of the New Zealand Ex-Prisoners of War Association for meritorious service.

Rooke, Christopher Charles Kirshaw was born in Maymyo, Burma, in 1921 and went to school in England when he was nine years old. He enlisted in the Army, went through OCTU and was commissioned and served in the 1st Battalion, Royal West Kent Regiment. He volunteered for an attachment to the Indian Army and joined the Frontier Force Rifles in 1942. He transferred to the Chindits and was in the second Chindit Operation in Burma in 1944, during which he was wounded. Captain Christopher Rooke spent a period in India in hospital and convalescing, then returned to the United Kingdom where his recuperation continued. He then worked for a period in Army Welfare before being demobilised in February 1947. He went out to South Africa where he took his BA, married and started his teaching career. In 1957 the family, which now included three children, emigrated to New Zealand, where he taught at Nelson and Waimea Colleges until he retired.

Scales, Sydney Ernest was born in Ashburton, New Zealand, in 1916, where he did his primary schooling, then went to Timaru Boys High School. Here his artistic ability was recognised and encouraged. He got a job as a journalist cadet with the *Timau Herald* and started to draw part-time. As a small boy he had had a flight in an aeroplane and was greatly enamoured, so much so that he joined the Civil Reserve of Air Pilots in 1937 and, after the declaration of war, joined the RNZAF and trained as a pilot. He gained his wings, was promoted to Sergeant Pilot and served in South East Asia, where he was commissioned, finally achieving the rank of Flight Lieutenant. After the war he studied art and, with a rehabilitation grant, he enrolled at the Central School of Art in London; all this time he was developing his skills as a cartoonist, many of them depicting life as a prisoner of war. Then, for the next 30 years, he worked as cartoonist for the *Otago Daily Times* in Dunedin, becoming one of the foremost cartoonists of his day. He married, had three children, has been retired for close on 19 years and lives in Motueka.

Scott, William Lindsay McDonald was born in Fiji in 1924, where his father was a District Commissioner. When he was four years old the family moved back to England, living in Dartford, then in Woking. He matriculated at Guildford Grammar School and went to Cambridge

University, where he joined the University Air Squadron. He joined the RAF and received his pilot training in Canada. He was posted to the Far East in No 203 Squadron flying Liberators on anti-shipping operations in the Bay of Bengal. He remained in the RAF, retiring as a Group Captain in 1978. During that time he took part in air operations in Aden, Vietnam and Borneo, and commanded St Andrews University Air Squadron, No 39 Squadron in Malta and RAF Wyton in Huntingdon. His last appointment was as Head of Air Intelligence in Germany. He and his wife moved to New Zealand in 1988 and live in Nelson.

Seeney, William Lewis was born in London in 1910 and lived in Ealing, where he went to school and college, excelling in both soccer and cricket. When he was 16 he became an apprentice printer. He was in the Artillery in the Territorial Army and when war broke out was one of the first to be sent to France. Back in Britain after the 'Phoney War', Lance Bombardier Seeney was sent to a Coastal Defence Battery in the Orkney Islands, after which he went through an OCTU. Lieutenant Seeney was then posted to South East Asia where he saw service in Burma. Captain Seeney eventually arrived home in England, saw his infant daughter for the first time and settled back into his work in the printing industry. Later he emigrated to New Zealand, worked in Dunedin and eventually retired to Motueka.

Smith, Bruce McKay was born in 1919 in Christchurch, New Zealand, where he went to school until he was 16, after which he studied agriculture at Lincoln College. At the outbreak of war he volunteered for the Army and was drafted into the Artillery. He saw service in North Africa, Greece and Cretek, then Italy. Sergeant Smith eventually returned to New Zealand, went back to his studies at Lincoln College and was awarded his Diploma in Agriculture in 1946. He then farmed on various properties, married and later drew a farm on a land ballot where he and his wife brought up their large family. They now live in retirement near Motueka outside Nelson.

Teague, Charles James was born in 1919 in Middleton, North Yorkshire, and was educated at Pickering. After leaving school at the age of 14 he became an apprentice mechanic at a garage, then he was called up into the RAOC. After training at Aldershot he joined the Ulster Rifles as a Private (mechanic). He saw service in Britain, then in Europe in 'Operation Overlord'. Sergeant Teague was demobilised soon after the war ended. He went back to his old job at Scarborough, then moved to Scotland, where he was married. He lived with his wife and family in Bermuda for a number of years before returning to Scotland, where he retired. Charles Teague and his wife emigrated to New Zealand about nine years ago.

Teague, Trevor Raymond was born in 1923 in Christchurch, New Zealand, and had his schooling and matriculated there. He became interested in flying and attended the Air Training Corps. He was called up and joined the RNZAF, trained in New Zealand, was awarded his wings in 1942, and left for Britain in 1943, where he did further training flying Wellingtons, Stirlings then Lancasters. Trevor Teague was based at Mildenhall and was flying his fourth bombing mission in a Lancaster over France when his plane was shot down. He landed safely by parachute and spent eight days attempting to get to the Spanish border when he was captured by the Germans and was made a prisoner of war. At the end of the war Flying Officer Trevor Teague was flown back to England to find that he had been awarded his commission the day prior to being shot down. He returned to New Zealand, married in 1947, and progressed in his position in the Department of Justice, eventually to become the Registrar of the Supreme Court in Nelson, and is now retired.

Thompson, Rex Montgomery Crowther was born in 1915 in Hastings, New Zealand, and was educated at a number of schools. When he left school he drove for a passenger transport company and in 1938 bought his own company operating from Collingwood in the South Island. He served as a Driver in the NZ Army Service Corps in North Africa, Greece and Crete, where he was captured by the Germans and spent the rest of the war as a prisoner of war in Germany and Poland. After his release Rex Thompson was discharged from the Army in October 1945 and went back to his transport business in Collingwood. He now lives in retirement in Nelson.

Thornton, Leonard Whitmore was born in 1916 in Christchurch, New Zealand, and early on in life decided on the Army as a career. He trained at the Military College, Duntroon, in Australia, and graduated in 1937, when he was awarded the King's Medal as the most outstanding graduate of the year. He was commissioned in the NZ Artillery and served in North Africa, Greece and Italy. He commanded the NZ Army from 1960 to 1965 and was then appointed Head of the NZ Defence Force until 1971. From 1972 until 1974 he was NZ Ambassador to Vietnam and Cambodia. Subsequently he served on several prestigious committees. Leonard Thornton was awarded the OBE in 1945, the CBE in 1957 and made a KCB in 1967. Lieutenant General Sir Leonard Thornton was a keen military historian and enjoyed music and painting, at which he excelled. He died on 10 June 1999.

Urwin, Ralph (Reginald) was born in 1925 in South Shields, County Durham. Leaving school he became an apprentice surveyor in coal mines, a reserved occupation, but despite that he tried to join the Navy; he failed, so signed on in the Merchant Marine in 1941. He served as a seaman in ships in the Atlantic, on the East Coast of Britain and in the Arctic, where his ship was sunk by a U-boat. He was rescued and became a prisoner of war in Germany. After his release Reginald Urwin spent a little more time at sea, but soon decided to go out to New Zealand, where he attended a Polytechnic College for a while, then took an engineering position in Wellington. He married in 1948 and later went to live and work in Karamea on the west coast of the South Island. As the children grew older he and his wife moved into Nelson. Reginald died on 23 March 1999.

Walker, James Ian Bradley was born in 1920 in New Plymouth, New Zealand, where his parents were dairy farmers. They moved to Auckland in 1927. Due to the depression Ian left school at the age of 13 and joined the workforce to help the family budget. In January 1940 he joined the RNZAF. He was seconded to the RAF, arriving in Britain in May 1940. Here he qualified as an air-gunner with the rank of Sergeant and flew in Blenheims, then Beaufighters, in the Battle of Britain. Transferring to bombers, he was tail gunner in a Wellington that crashed in Belgium. He was severely injured and spent the next two years as a prisoner of war, which is all vividly described in this book. On his release Warrant Officer Walker took his discharge and returned to New Zealand, where he worked in the furniture industry until retirement in 1983. He is married with two daughters, leads a very active and happy retirement, holding, as he does, a strong (non-sectarian) Christian belief.

Index